LESSONS from the NEW COLD WAR

ABOUT THE EDITOR

Hal Brands is the Henry A. Kissinger Distinguished Professor of Global Affairs at the Johns Hopkins School of Advanced International Studies, a senior fellow at the American Enterprise Institute, and a columnist for *Bloomberg Opinion*. He is the author of many books, including *The Eurasian Century: Hot Wars, Cold Wars, and the Making of the Modern World* (2025); *Danger Zone: The Coming Conflict with China*, with Michael Beckley (2022); and *The Twilight Struggle: What the Cold War Teaches Us About Great-Power Rivalry Today* (2022). He is the editor of *War in Ukraine: Conflict, Strategy, and the Return of a Fractured World* (2024); *The New Makers of Modern Strategy: From the Ancient World to the Digital Age* (2023); and *COVID-19 and World Order: The Future of Conflict, Competition, and Cooperation*, with Francis J. Gavin (2020). He has been a special assistant to the secretary of defense, a member of the secretary of state's Foreign Affairs Policy Board, and a member of the US-China Economic and Security Review Commission.

LESSONS

FROM THE

NEW COLD WAR

AMERICA CONFRONTS
THE CHINA CHALLENGE

EDITED BY

Hal Brands

Johns Hopkins University Press

Baltimore

© 2025 Johns Hopkins University Press
All rights reserved. Published 2025
Printed in the United States of America on acid-free paper
9 8 7 6 5 4 3 2 1

Johns Hopkins University Press
2715 North Charles Street
Baltimore, Maryland 21218
www.press.jhu.edu

Library of Congress Cataloging-in-Publication Data is available.

A catalog record for this book is available from the British Library.

Library of Congress Control Number 2025019086

ISBN 978-1-4214-5344-6 (paperback)
ISBN 978-1-4214-5345-3 (ebook)
ISBN 978-1-4214-5346-0 (ebook o)

*Special discounts are available for bulk purchases of this book. For more
information, please contact Special Sales at specialsales@jh.edu.*

EU GPSR Authorized Representative
LOGOS EUROPE, 9 rue Nicolas Poussin, 17000, La Rochelle, France
E-mail: Contact@logoseurope.eu

Contents

LESSONS from the NEW COLD WAR

Introduction

Lessons from the New Cold War

Hal Brands

Of all the crises, conflicts, and uncertainties of our moment, it is the rivalry between America and China—the New Cold War—that will most fundamentally shape the present age.[1] That contest is a battle, in the shadowy space between war and peace, between the world's greatest powers. Its outcome will shape the international system, and the fate of humanity, for many years to come. In the best case, this struggle is likely to be long, tense, and littered with nasty perils. In the worst case, it could cause history's most cataclysmic military showdown. Successfully waging, and winning, that competition will be the defining strategic challenge of our time.

Beijing knows this: For decades, it has been striving to displace America as the preeminent power in Asia and, ultimately, the world. As Xi Jinping himself has argued, China is "building a socialism that is superior to capitalism" and charging into a "future where we will win the initiative and have the dominant position."[2] In the most recent decade, the United States has begun to meet that growing threat. Two presidents, from different political parties, have identified China as the foremost danger to America's security, prosperity, and global influence. America's

Hal Brands is the Henry A. Kissinger Distinguished Professor of Global Affairs at the Johns Hopkins School of Advanced International Studies, a senior fellow at the American Enterprise Institute, and a columnist for *Bloomberg Opinion*. His most recent book is *The Eurasian Century: Hot Wars, Cold Wars, and the Making of the Modern World* (2025).

military, its economy, and parts of its government have already been remade by the demands of competition with Beijing; over time, that rivalry could come to suffuse so many aspects of our lives. In a polarized, bitterly divided country, anti-China measures are among the few things that still command bipartisan support.[3]

But are those measures effective? Is America winning the New Cold War? It can be hard enough to tell who is winning a hot war, amid the chaos and carnage of combat. It is harder still in cold wars, where success is often incremental and victories may be measured in hidden intelligence coups, subtle shifts in diplomatic loyalties, or influence over key supply chains, rather than territory won on the battlefield. Yet assessing progress is crucial to knowing whether America has the right strategy. Winning this contest requires learning its lessons so far.

This was the goal of a conference I hosted at the Johns Hopkins School of Advanced International Studies (SAIS) in April 2025.[4] There are few better places for such a gathering. Johns Hopkins has had a campus in China since the 1980s: It has experienced the ups and downs of the relationship firsthand. The current dean of SAIS, James Steinberg, is one of America's most respected China hands. A group of experts who attended the conference probed key aspects of the rivalry, from the tech war to the battle for military supremacy in the Western Pacific, and assessed its overall trajectory. The timing for this exercise was propitious, given that it has been roughly a decade since America declared cold war against China—and given that this contest could last decades more.

The findings, in the chapters that follow, are complex and varied. The authors engage in all the debate one would expect on weighty, contentious issues. What follows is my own effort to distill a few key conclusions on the course, consequences, and potential outcome of the New Cold War.

First, the New Cold War started before you probably think it did. That rivalry has been a centerpiece of US foreign policy since 2017, when Donald Trump accused China of trying to "shape a world antithetical to U.S. values and interests."[5] Yet its origins go a long way back.

The US-China rivalry is the latest installment of a millennia-long series of clashes between established and emerging powers—between those who make the global rules and those who mean to revise them. It is, similarly, part of a recurring fight over whether liberal or illiberal states will run the world.

In this sense, there's nothing new about the New Cold War. Yet that struggle is also deeply rooted in the strategic ambitions of China and its ruling elites.

When Xi promises the "great rejuvenation of the Chinese nation," he's simply saying that China—once the mightiest of empires—must reclaim its rightful place atop the world.[6] Since the Chinese Communist Party (CCP) seized power in 1949, its leaders have anticipated the day when China would vault past the United States. As one participant remarked during the conference, "Mao Zedong didn't starve 30 million people to death during the Great Leap Forward just to become the top steel producer in Asia." The CCP's long-term vision was always global in scope.[7] Even when the United States and China were tacit allies against the Soviet Union during the first Cold War, or when Washington was helping Beijing grow and prosper in the 1990s, Chinese leaders believed that America—the reigning, liberal hegemon—was bent on suppressing and containing a rising, illiberal challenger. One cold war might have ended, Deng Xiaoping remarked in 1989, but another had already begun.[8]

Since then, Beijing has been gathering the strengths needed to prevail in that rivalry: The military buildup that is now transforming Asia's strategic landscape dates back to the early 1990s. And America itself has been competing for longer than many observers appreciate.

After the US-Soviet Cold War ended, America sought to engage and enrich an emerging China, not least in hopes that it would also enrich itself. Yet Washington also maintained strong alliances, and lots of air and naval power, in the Pacific to keep Beijing from reordering that region. Aspects of this effort to harden the region against Chinese revision—such as America's ardent, enduring courtship of India—date back a generation or more.[9] Even the development of thriving trade and investment ties had subtler, more geopolitically subversive motives: Engagement was meant to tame a rising China, by binding it to a US-led international system, and perhaps transform it, by empowering liberalizing forces within. When CCP officials say that America has long sought to shape and constrain China, they aren't wholly wrong.[10]

What changed, as the 2010s unfolded, was that a clash that was once guarded and ambiguous—a sort of silent struggle between rivals that insisted, in public, that they saw each other as partners—entered a newer, starker phase. Economic engagement was hardly mellowing a China that was becoming more autocratic and aggressive, especially once Xi took the helm in 2012. Engagement, indeed, had created a monster—a China that was now rich, capable, and confident enough to destabilize the American-led order in Asia and beyond. China's growing strength was activating America's strategic anxieties. The result was the more intense, dangerous competition now underway.

Second, the New Cold War has killed globalization—so winning that struggle requires shifting from "one world" to two. The US-China rivalry is, fundamentally, an economic and technological rivalry. Economic power is the foundation of all other forms of power. The countries that dominate the key technologies of an era usually dominate that era, as well.[11] For years, Americans hoped economic integration—the pursuit of a single, seamlessly integrated global system—would open a path to peace. Now, as geopolitical tensions surge, interdependence is a vector for vulnerability.

China is trying to insulate its economy from foreign pressure while seizing control of key chokepoints and supply chains. It uses the sheer scale of its market, its manufacturing base, and its predatory trade practices to bend other countries to its will. The United States has fought back with tariffs, technological and financial curbs, and other tools of economic warfare. Under Joe Biden, America also launched a new era of industrial strategy featuring investments in semiconductors, electric vehicles, and other underpinnings of modern economic strength.[12]

That tech and trade competition is a fight for the economic high ground in the 21st century. It is equally a fight to shape the alignments of other states. China's multi-continent Belt and Road Initiative and various follow-on projects have used lending, infrastructure, and other inducements to lure countries into Beijing's orbit.[13] Huawei's bid to build the world's 5G telecommunications networks is also meant to hard-wire Chinese influence into nations around the globe.

For years, the resulting fears and frictions have been fragmenting the world economy. Even before the mega-shock of Trump's second-term tariffs on China, the borderless globalization of the post–Cold War era had become a casualty of the New Cold War. Yet thriving in this ugly new era will take more than just breaking up with Beijing.

Yes, America and its friends must build higher walls around China, so they can limit its access to Western markets, money, and technology—and decrease their dependence on a strategic foe. Yet Washington must also *deepen* integration with friendly countries, if it is to achieve resilience without autarky and generate the collective scale needed to compete with a country that has made itself the world's factory floor. The alternative—indiscriminate, omnidirectional protectionism—

will only backfire by breaking the coalitions, and crushing the prosperity, needed to keep the democratic community ahead and China behind.[14]

"One world" is no longer possible. Reconciling ourselves to "two worlds" is the only way to win the New Cold War.

Thus, a third theme: The US-China rivalry is about coalition-making and coalition-breaking, and the outcome is too much in doubt. Three times in the 20th century, America beat down aspiring Eurasian hegemons with help from big, geographically diverse groups of friends.[15] Today, every aspect of US strategy toward China—from securing supply chains to patrolling the South China Sea—will be easier if Washington has powerful partners on its side. Yet rallying that coalition is challenging, this time around, because China can use both seductive carrots, such as legitimate trade and strategic corruption of elites, and punishing sticks, in the form of military and economic pressure, to pull those relationships apart.

For most of the last decade, America was winning that contest—mostly because Beijing kept shooting itself in the foot. China's bullying of neighbors built a vast arc of Asian enmity, running from India to Japan. Its COVID-era wolf warriorism and backing for Russia's invasion of Ukraine alienated countries on multiple continents. The United States began rallying the advanced democracies against Chinese coercion. It started building partnerships to thwart China's bid for mastery in 5G telecommunications, semiconductors, and other key technologies. A web of diplomatic and military relationships—the Quad, the Squad, AUKUS, and many others—was creating a nascent Indo-Pacific security network.[16] China seemed to have stumbled into a time-honored trap. Its autocratic ambition and aggression were driving potential victims together—and pushing them closer to the super-power across the seas.

But "nascent" is the crucial word, because the counter-China coalition is shot through with gaps and ambiguities. There are overlapping alliances but no true collective defense pact—nothing like NATO—in the Indo-Pacific. That threatens to make rallying a concerted response to Chinese aggression a geopolitical pickup game. Key countries remain parochial in their pushback against China: India welcomes American help along its Himalayan frontier but might not lift a finger if Beijing assaults Taiwan. Defense spending, up and down the Western Pacific, is inadequate; democratic trade, financial, and technological dependencies on China remain all too real. Not least, Trump began his second term by trying to line up the allies against China, while simultaneously pursuing policies—punishing protectionism, threatening to take territory from some of those same countries—that seemed likely to bolster Beijing by ripping America's coalition apart.[17]

Meanwhile, a rival coalition is forming. Beijing isn't all-in on its ties to Russia, North Korea, and Iran, that rogues' gallery of revisionists. But it sees those ties, especially to Russia, as a means of insulating itself from US sanctions, accessing high-end military technology, and ensuring that the Eurasian giants can fight "back to back" against their foes.[18] US officials have even warned that Moscow might aid China in a conflict against America in the Western Pacific, perhaps as revenge for Washington's proxy war against Russia in Ukraine.[19]

A cohesive, global alliance of democracies could still outclass a league of Eurasian autocracies. But there's danger in the way that coalition politics are shifting on both sides.

Allies matter in a cold war, but also in a hot war: The privilege of waging the former is the reward for deterring the latter. A fourth lesson, alas, is that the chances of hot war are rising, and America isn't nearly ready for the challenge.

The root cause of that problem is the transformation of the Western Pacific military balance. A generation ago, the People's Liberation Army was still an antiquated, land-focused force. A Chinese invasion of Taiwan would have been a "million-man swim." Today, the PLA is a formidable, high-tech military. China possesses the world's largest missile inventory and navy. Its rapid-fire nuclear buildup will soon give it better options for deterring or coercing the United States. China's forces regularly conduct complex, menacing exercises all around Taiwan; its factories pump out ships and ammunition at wartime rates. A buildup that has been going for decades is reaching its ominous crescendo. "Today the intelligence couldn't be clearer," Secretary of the Air Force Frank Kendall warned in 2023. "China is preparing for a war and specifically for a war with the United States."[20]

Some analysts think that war could happen this decade; others believe the PLA won't be ready to take Taiwan or tangle with America until the 2030s. What no serious analyst disputes is that the trends are running in the wrong direction.

The Pentagon has gained access to bases in the Philippines and other locations in recent years, but it is struggling to develop the operational concepts—the ways of war—needed to beat back a Chinese onslaught. For every promising idea—such as the Replicator Initiative, meant to use drones and other cheap capabilities to turn the Western Pacific into an impassible "hellscape"—there are two or three causes for pessimism.[21]

Stockpiles of laser-guided bombs and long-range missiles are inadequate even for a short war. The defense industrial base is far too decrepit to sustain the US military in a long war. America has the world's best navy, but it can't quickly replace ships lost in combat: That's the very weakness that doomed Japan in World War II.[22] Nor is the United States ready for the economic dimensions of hot war: As Hugo Bromley and Eyck Freeman point out, it lacks well-developed contingency plans for punishing large-scale Chinese aggression.[23]

"Asia First" advocates hope stricter prioritization can bring strategic salvation. By shifting resources from the Army to the Air Force and the Navy, and from Europe and the Middle East to the Western Pacific, they claim, the United States can find the resources, and the focus, needed to deter a bellicose Beijing. The hitch, unfortunately, is that America's present defense budget probably isn't sufficient to beat China even if the Pentagon simply stops operating in other theaters. And if Washington abandons Europe and the Middle East, it could lose the leverage—and allies—it needs to contain China in peacetime or war.[24]

What's more, strategy can't ignore political realities, and the hard truth is that US policymakers have *never* been able to focus exclusively on Asia in recent years. Just as Trump's team was reportedly finalizing a China-focused defense strategy in early 2025, it was surging aircraft carriers, strategic bombers, and missile defenses to the Middle East.[25] Prioritization is important, but global threats are unabating. The United States will surely need more resources in the Pacific. It probably can't find them just by skimping elsewhere.

The price of failure could be astronomical. If America can't defend the Western Pacific, a demoralized Taiwan might simply capitulate to China. Or perhaps an opening window of opportunity will tempt Beijing to reorder the region by force. The result might be a Sino-American conflict that brings on global depression by breaking key trade routes and supply chains—and one that, by pitting nuclear-armed great powers against one another, brings risks of apocalyptic escalation. The greatest, most existential danger of our era is that Cold War II will turn into World War III.

Of course, great-power rivalries aren't all about crises and war plans. They involve patient, persistent efforts to gather intelligence, win the information war, and build the soft power that bolsters other forms of global influence. America won the first Cold War because it did well enough—never perfectly—at these subtler aspects of competition.[26] Today, it is struggling.

For years, the United States found it hard to mobilize resources to compete with Chinese infrastructure projects in the developing world, not least because it can't just tell private-sector firms to prioritize the public interest. Its information-war capabilities shriveled after the first Cold War; its institutions are often sluggish and clumsy in waging the propaganda fight. According to published reports, its intelligence agencies are still recovering from the demolition of their human-source networks in China.[27] The United States was, slowly, rebuilding competitive muscle in these and other areas. Now it seems to be slashing to the bone.

Since January 2025, Trump has disestablished the US Agency for International Development, jeopardizing key foreign aid projects.[28] The National Endowment for Democracy has been starved of the funds it uses to support civil society groups that monitor and contest the creeping expansion of Chinese influence from Eastern Europe to Southeast Asia.[29] The shuttering of Radio Free Asia and the Global Engagement Center certainly won't make the US more competitive in the quest for information supremacy.[30] America also needs to be careful lest it lose the values game.

China isn't exactly a juggernaut in this area. Its presence in the Global South is pervasive but often pernicious, in that it entrenches corruption, environmental degradation, and autocracy. The abrasive, arrogant diplomacy of the COVID era was a warning about just how imperious an ascendant China will be. As detailed empirical work by Larry Diamond and Frances Hisgen of the Hoover Institution makes clear, Beijing isn't selling global populations on a world under Chinese leadership.[31] But America is bleeding legitimacy right now.

It needn't be this way: Global polling shows that America's democratic values give it an advantage over autocratic rivals.[32] But the increasingly polarized, dysfunctional nature of American politics is eating into that advantage. So is the fact that the United States is presently governed by an administration that engages in flagrantly illiberal behavior at home and shows little interest in promoting or defending democracy abroad. Those characteristics threaten to compound a global democratic recession that plays to an autocratic China's advantages. A fifth lesson, then, is that hard power alone won't win the New Cold War.

Perhaps there are possibilities between winning and losing: Almost since the moment America acknowledged the New Cold War was underway, its leaders and intellectuals have been looking for an off-ramp. The first Trump administration chased a trade deal that was supposed to transform the relationship, before it collapsed under the weight of a made-in-China pandemic. The Biden team then sought, unsuccessfully, to win Beijing's cooperation on climate change even as it competed on technology and security issues. Trump then hammered China with tariffs early in his second term, while also talking about his desire for a big, beautiful deal with Xi. Outside analysts, and some government officials, have periodically proposed purchasing Sino-American peace by trading Taiwan or the South China Sea away.[33] They might as well save their energy: A sixth lesson is that there is no grand bargain to be had.

Fights to define the global order, between antagonists with sharply conflicting ideologies and interests, rarely end in handshakes and half-measures. Sometimes, they culminate violently, as happened with the world wars. When they end peacefully, as the first Cold War did, it's typically because one side wins and the other side accepts that it is has lost.[34] There's little reason to think the US-China rivalry will go differently, because that relationship is fundamentally, and ever more obviously, zero-sum.

China can't have what it wants—a sphere of influence in the Asia-Pacific region and, eventually, a perch of global primacy—without eclipsing or wrecking American power. America can't maintain the positions of strength it has built, and defended, over decades without denying China the greatness and glory Xi seeks. Likewise, an illiberal world that feels perfectly safe for the autocrats who run China will be one that seems increasingly uncomfortable for democracy in America and other countries around the globe.

Perhaps the United States could purchase a temporary respite if it abandoned Taiwan or blessed Chinese dominance of the Western Pacific: Trump and some of the neo-isolationists around him have occasionally speculated about such a deal. But why would that deal hold as China's power, confidence, and contempt for a retreating America grew?[35] Indeed, the real danger in desperately seeking a grand bargain is that it will undercut American strengths—and allied cohesion—that are needed to keep Beijing contained.

That's not to say that dialogue is worthless, much less that war is inevitable. Diplomacy can be useful, over time, in negotiating tactical pauses or identifying common interests. During the original Cold War, Washington and Moscow worked together to limit nuclear proliferation; they periodically agreed to moderate the hostility of their rivalry. Dialogue can also reduce risks of miscalculation and provide insights into how the other side sees the world. But whatever its twists and turns, this struggle is likely to persist until there is a winner. The sooner Americans accept that, the more likely they'll come out on top.

This conference occurred in the wake of Liberation Day—two days after Trump sent global markets into free fall by announcing the highest US tariffs since the Great Depression. (Just a few days—and heaps of economic damage—later, he declared that he was pausing those tariffs on the rest of the world while further raising them on China.) The head-spinning events of Trump's second term reveal a final lesson: The trajectory of an epic, system-shaping contest hinges on the choices of individuals and on the profound changes, in American policy and politics, underway.

Personality counts on both sides, of course. The Sino-American rivalry is rooted in geopolitics and ideology, but it is also inseparable from the actions of Xi Jinping. Xi put Chinese statecraft into a new gear of aggressiveness; he has been far more willing to court international censure and American enmity than his immediate predecessors were. Xi deemphasized the pedal-to-the-metal economic growth of an earlier era in favor of ideological indoctrination and neo-totalitarianism. His personal impact on his country, and on the Sino-American contest, is rivaled only by Donald Trump.

Trump was, in many ways, the first of the new cold warriors. He campaigned for president, in 2016, on the claim that China was raping America.[36] His first administration began assembling the policies—on everything from trade to Western Pacific security—meant to rebuild American advantage. Yet Trump's first term also left a legacy of embittered allies, incompetent or downright illiberal behavior, and questions about America's commitment to a healthy global order. His second term has seen even greater extremes.

During his first months in office, Trump rained economic hammer blows on Beijing, promised a trillion-dollar defense budget, and pushed the Pentagon to prioritize Taiwan and the Western Pacific. But he also touted, predictably, his friendship with Xi Jinping: "One of the smartest people in the world."[37] He waged economic and rhetorical campaigns against US allies and demanded territorial concessions from fellow democracies. He aggressively pushed the limits of executive power and turned the state's coercive capabilities against his political foes.

No one, including Trump, can say exactly where this is heading—or, more profoundly, what sort of nation Trump's America will become. But it has all created the possibility that the US-China rivalry might devolve into a slugging match between two aggressive, revisionist powers trying to tear down the liberal order, a fight in which much of the world might lose no matter which side won.[38] And it reminds us that the contours, and perhaps the outcome, of this rivalry will depend crucially on whether Donald Trump chooses to responsibly prosecute the New

Cold War he declared nearly a decade ago—or sets about destroying the very things an American president should be trying to defend.

NOTES

1. Some of the ideas in this essay were originally developed in a shorter piece published in April 2025. See Hal Brands, "The US Is Already Losing the New Cold War to China," *Bloomberg Opinion*, April 26, 2025.

2. Daniel Tobin, "How Xi Jinping's 'New Era' Should Have Ended U.S. Debate on Beijing's Ambitions," CSIS, May 8, 2020, https://www.csis.org/analysis/how-xi-jinpings -new-era-should-have-ended-us-debate-beijings-ambitions.

3. Craig Kafura, "Americans Feel More Threat from China Now than in Past Three Decades," Chicago Council on Global Affairs, November 12, 2023, https://globalaffairs.org /research/public-opinion-survey/americans-feel-more-threat-china-now-past-three-decades.

4. That conference was sponsored by the America and the World Consortium, a project involving Johns Hopkins SAIS, Duke University, the University of Texas, and the University of Florida.

5. The White House, *2017 National Security Strategy of the United States of America*, December 2017, p. 25, https://trumpwhitehouse.archives.gov/wp-content/uploads/2017 /12/NSS-Final-12-18-2017-0905.pdf.

6. Elizabeth Economy, introduction to *The Third Revolution: XI Jinping and the New Chinese State* (Oxford University Press, 2019).

7. Tobin, "How Xi Jinping's 'New Era.'"

8. Rush Doshi, *The Long Game: China's Grand Strategy to Displace American Order* (Oxford University Press, 2021), 47.

9. See Ashley Tellis's contribution to this volume.

10. Hal Brands, "Democracy vs Authoritarianism: How Ideology Shapes Great-Power Conflict," *Survival* 60, no. 5 (2018): 61–114.

11. The point is made at greater length in my book *The Danger Zone*. Hal Brands and Michael Beckley, *Danger Zone: The Coming Conflict with China* (W. W. Norton, 2002).

12. See the chapters by Liza Tobin and Chris Miller, respectively.

13. The chapter by Audrye Wong addresses this issue in detail.

14. Kurt M. Campbell and Rush Doshi, "Underestimating China: Why America Needs a New Strategy of Allied Scale to Offset Beijing's Enduring Advantages," *Foreign Affairs*, April 10, 2025. https://www.foreignaffairs.com/china/underestimating-china.

15. Hal Brands, *The Eurasian Century: Hot Wars, Cold Wars, and the Making of the Modern World* (W. W. Norton, 2025).

16. See Michael Green's contribution to this volume.

17. These are among the subjects discussed in Rana Mitter's essay in this book.

18. Hal Brands, "The Battle for Eurasia," *Foreign Policy*, November 8, 2023, https://foreignpolicy.com/2023/06/04/russia-china-us-geopolitics-eurasia-strategy/.

19. Daniel Flatley, "US Spies See China, Russia Militaries Working Closer on Taiwan." *Bloomberg*, May 2, 2024, https://www.bloomberg.com/news/articles/2024-05 -02/us-spies-see-china-russia-militaries-working-closer-on-taiwan.

20. Seth G. Jones, "China Is Ready for War," *Foreign Affairs*, October 2, 2024, https://www.foreignaffairs.com/china/china-ready-war-america-is-not-seth-jones. See also the chapter by Francis Gavin on the nuclear issue.

21. Josh Rogin, "The U.S. Military Plans a 'Hellscape' to Deter China from Attacking Taiwan." *The Washington Post*, June 10, 2024, https://www.washingtonpost.com /opinions/2024/06/10/taiwan-china-hellscape-military-plan/. The shortfalls of US operational concepts are among the challenges discussed in Michael Mazarr's chapter.

22. Seth G. Jones, *Empty Bins in a Wartime Environment: The Challenge to the U.S. Defense Industrial Base* (Rowman & Littlefield, 2023); Stephen Biddle and Eric Labs, "Does America Face a 'Ship Gap' with China?," *Foreign Affairs*, March 19, 2025, https://www .foreignaffairs.com/united-states/does-america-face-ship-gap-china.

23. See the chapter by Bromley and Freyman in this volume.

24. Kori Schake makes these points in her essay for this volume; see also Hal Brands, "Putting 'Asia First' Could Cost America the World," *Bloomberg*, August 25, 2024, https://www.bloomberg.com/opinion/features/2024-08-25/putting-asia-first-could -cost-america-the-world.

25. Alex Horton and Hannah Natanson, "Secret Pentagon Memo on China, Homeland Has Heritage Fingerprints," *The Washington Post*, March 29, 2025, https:// www.washingtonpost.com/national-security/2025/03/29/secret-pentagon-memo -hegseth-heritage-foundation-china/.

26. Hal Brands, *The Twilight Struggle: What the Cold War Teaches Us About Great- Power Rivalry Today* (Yale University Press, 2022).

27. Mark Mazzetti, Michael S. Schmidt, Matt Apuzzo, and Adam Goldman, "Killing C.I.A. Informants, China Crippled U.S. Spying Operations," *The New York Times*, May 20, 2017, https://www.nytimes.com/2017/05/20/world/asia/china-cia-spies -espionage.html.

28. Gerald Imray, "Trump's Permanent USAID Cuts Slam Humanitarian Programs Worldwide: 'We Are Being Pushed off a Cliff,'" *AP News*, February 27, 2025, https:// apnews.com/article/trump-usaid-aid-cut-doge-musk-dbaf0e89d72938caabee8251f7 dfb4a7.

29. Joshua Kurlantzick, "Trump's Cuts to Democracy Promotion like the NED Already Hit Asian Organizations Hard," Council on Foreign Relations, March 3, 2025, https://www.cfr.org/blog/trumps-cuts-democracy-promotion-ned-already-hit-asian -organizations-hard.

30. "Radio Free Asia Says It Will Fully Shut Down by End of April Without Court Intervention," *Reuters*, March 31, 2025, https://www.reuters.com/sustainability/boards -policy-regulation/radio-free-asia-says-it-will-fully-shut-down-by-end-april-without-court -2025-03-29/.

31. See the chapter by Diamond and Hisgen.

32. Sharon Seah, Joanne Lin, Melinda Martinus, Kristina Fong, Pham Thi Phuong Thao, and Indira Zahra Aridat, "The State of Southeast Asia: 2025 Survey Report," ISEAS Yusof Ishak Institute, April 3, 2025, https://www.iseas.edu.sg/centres/asean-studies-centre /state-of-southeast-asia-survey/the-state-of-southeast-asia-2025-survey-report/.

33. Charles L. Glaser, "A U.S.-China Grand Bargain? The Hard Choice Between Military Competition and Accommodation," *International Security* 39, no. 4 (2015): 49–90; Andrew Byers and J. Tedford Tyler, "Can the US and China Forge a Cold Peace?," *Survival* 66, no. 6 (2024): 67–86.

34. Michael Beckley, "Delusions of Détente," *Foreign Affairs*, August 22, 2023, https://www.foreignaffairs.com/united-states/china-delusions-detente-rivals.

35. Hal Brands, "The US Is Losing the Contest to Divide the World," *Bloomberg*, March 31, 2025, https://www.bloomberg.com/opinion/features/2025-03-31/us-is-losing-the-contest-to-divide-the-world-to-russia-china.

36. Jeremy Diamond, "Trump: 'We Can't Continue to Allow China to Rape Our Country,'" *CNN*, May 2, 2016, https://www.cnn.com/2016/05/01/politics/donald-trump-china-rape/index.html.

37. "Trump Tariffs Live Updates: Trump's 'Explosive' Global Tariffs Set to Take Force—Including a 104% Rate on China," *BBC News*, April 8, 2025, https://www.bbc.com/news/live/cp8vyy35g3mt; Paul McLeary, Joe Gould, and Connor O'Brien, "Trump, Hegseth Promise Record $1 Trillion Pentagon Budget," *Politico*, April 7, 2025, https://www.politico.com/news/2025/04/07/hegseth-trump-1-trillion-defense-budget-00007147.

38. This possibility is among the subjects explored by Rana Mitter, Jude Blanchette, and Michael Beckley in their contributions to this volume.

PART I / Trade, Technology, and Economics

Chapter One

America First vs. China's Brute Force Economics

Liza Tobin

In his first term, President Donald Trump upended decades of American foreign policy when he set in motion a shift from engagement to strategic competition with the People's Republic of China (PRC). Eight years later, the unprecedented nature of the China challenge has become axiomatic across the federal government and is increasingly recognized by states, corporations, and international partners. The economic and techno-industrial elements of the challenge, unparalleled in both scope and scale, are the most confounding to policymakers. Yet they are precisely what America and other democratic market economies must master to prevail in systemic rivalry with the PRC.

Early in his second term, President Trump's approach to China appears ambiguous, indicating a potential shift from the confrontational stance that defined his first administration. In the first weeks after returning to office, the president noticeably downplayed the China challenge in his rhetoric, mentioning it infrequently but respectfully, keeping the door open to a deal with General Secretary Xi Jinping while pursuing more immediate wins elsewhere: reasserting US dominance in the Western Hemisphere, championing the Department of Government Efficiency, imposing tariffs, combating fentanyl, and angling to be both dealmaker

Liza Tobin served as China director on the National Security Council staff, where she led the development of multiple US strategies and policies related to China.

She is grateful to Addis Goldman for his invaluable editorial assistance and substantive contributions throughout the drafting process.

and peacemaker in Ukraine. While some of these issues are related to China, Trump's early priorities raised questions about his attitude toward the bilateral relationship. Soon after declaring a trade war on the entire world on April 2, Trump appeared to stumble into an "isolate China" strategy, granting a 90-day tariff reprieve to most of the world while raising tariffs higher on China.[1] Even while escalating trade decoupling with Xi Jinping, Trump repeatedly said that a deal was possible.[2]

Regardless of how the administration ultimately approaches China policy, Beijing continues to aggressively pursue its strategic objectives. Xi has intensified pressure on Taiwan, testing allied resolve in the Indo-Pacific, and has doubled down on an industrial strategy that risks inflicting a "China Shock 2.0" on advanced economies. Attempting to maintain a friendly holding pattern with China, if that is Trump's intention, is unrealistic over the long term. The Chinese Communist Party (CCP) possesses agency and will inevitably reassert itself as a vexing issue on Trump's agenda, whether because the deal he hopes for with Xi fails to materialize or disappoints, or because Beijing's provocations compel him to pivot to a harder stance.

Trump would not be the first US president to pursue an illusory grand bargain with Beijing and overestimate his ability to manage the tenor and direction of bilateral relations. Before an assessment of the challenge confronting the second Trump administration—a challenge magnified since Trump's interregnum, owing to China's emergence as a technological superpower—it is worth tracing how America's recognition of the China threat has evolved across administrations. Despite significant progress in understanding Beijing's capabilities and strategic ambitions over the years, Washington's response to the CCP's economic and technological offensive remains fragmented and incomplete.

The Engagement Illusion and China's Brute Force Economics

On the eve of the PRC's accession to the World Trade Organization (WTO) in 2001, President Bill Clinton claimed that China's economic integration into the global economic system would "move China in the right direction . . . and advance our own economic interests."[3] The president was not alone in this sentiment. Buoyed by optimistic visions of unfettered globalization and the "end of history," the policy of engagement garnered enthusiastic support on both sides of the aisle throughout the 1990s and into the new millennium. For roughly two decades after the end of the Cold War, it seemed that trade and economics could be extricated from national security.

Today those visions lie in ruins. China's integration into the global economy enabled it to become America's most daunting economic competitor. At every turn, the CCP has sought absolute rather than comparative economic advantage in key sectors and made a mockery of the idea of a "level playing field." Especially since the rise of Xi in 2012, Beijing has systematically exploited the system it was expected to uphold by embracing a distinct mode of economic statecraft that I refer to as "brute force economics." From preferential lending, forced technology transfer, and market access restrictions, to massive subsidies, currency manipulation, theft of intellectual property, and the use of non-tariff barriers, I use this analytic frame to capture "the aggressive, evolving, and often opaque web of policies and tactics" that the regime uses to increase comprehensive national power at other nations' expense.[4]

The PRC's approach is distinguished from garden-variety mercantilism by its force, scale, and ruthlessness. Unlike in pluralistic systems, the CCP—a Marxist-Leninist regime—can bring the full weight of its party-state apparatus and private sector to bear on strategic economic priorities, unconstrained by the need to navigate congressional approvals, independent courts, or public debate. The sheer size of China's internal market, meanwhile, provides unique scale advantages to Chinese corporations, which benefit from staggering levels of state support.[5] Finally, the CCP's ruthlessness is available for all to judge, from coercing neighboring countries like Japan, the Philippines, and Australia to conducting whole-of-nation industrial espionage campaigns against rivals including the United States.[6]

China's economic ascent stems from both legitimate innovation and systematic rule-breaking. Beijing has methodically built its technological capabilities through disciplined planning, large-scale investments in physical and human capital, and a constantly adjusting mix of carrots and sticks, resulting in a formidable production and innovation ecosystem. Americans tend to respect a worthy rival yet struggle when confronting an adversary whose success combines genuine ingenuity with deliberate exploitation of international norms. Over the last decade, advanced democracies have progressed through the stages of grief, reluctantly abandoning the comforting notion that "making the pie bigger" through free trade with an autocracy was feasible.

Beijing always had a very different goal in mind. This has become obvious under Xi, who explicitly seeks to increase the world's dependence on China while reducing China's dependence on the world. In effect, China's approach to economic statecraft amounts to a permanent trade war. The CCP's brute force playbook is designed to turn China into a high-tech manufacturing superpower with veto power over critical global supply chains. China is already responsible for over 30% of global manufacturing output, surpassing the combined output of the other four largest economies (US, Germany, Japan, and India). But China is not just producing textiles, toys, and televisions like it was when it entered the WTO. Over the past few decades, Chinese firms have moved rapidly up the value-added chain, capturing dominant market share across a range of advanced, dual-use industries that matter for economic competitiveness and national security.[7]

China's techno-industrial power is daunting. The PRC has roughly 230 times the shipbuilding capacity of the United States,[8] and it accounts for 80% of the global commercial drone market.[9] China produces over 80% of the world's lithium-ion batteries,[10] while its share in all the manufacturing stages of solar panels exceeds 80%.[11] Since 2017, China's electric vehicle (EV) exports have surged 13,300% to $42 billion in 2023; in that year, China accounted for nearly 70% of global EV production.[12] China is the world's largest producer of active pharmaceutical ingredients,[13] and it accounted for over 30% of global legacy chip production in 2023 (lower-end semiconductors that power everything from military systems to dishwashers).[14] To make matters worse, the PRC controls up to 70% of rare earth minerals production and 90% of their processing, positioning itself as *the* indispensable supplier of key material inputs with applications across every sector of the global economy.[15]

China's advanced industrial might—the sheer scale of its high-tech manufacturing capacity—is its key asymmetric advantage over the United States. In fact, this is how Beijing views the issue. Recent Chinese policy guidance suggests that manufacturing is "the main battlefield" in strategic competition with the United States.[16] In recent years, Xi has doubled down on advanced industrial sectors—so-called "new forces of production" (新质生产力) such as EVs—as the key drivers of Chinese economic growth into the future.[17]

This is especially critical, as AI and robotic automation fundamentally transform the nature of industrial production, providing the PRC with new and rapidly evolving sources of competitive advantage in the race to lead the fourth industrial revolution.

In the 2010s, it was a common refrain that "China can't innovate," that it merely steals and copies.[18] This assumption has been thoroughly debunked. It is precisely the PRC's strategic focus on developing industrial capacity that has enabled it to innovate across a wide range of advanced technology sectors. Contrary to popular belief, advanced manufacturing is one of the highest forms of knowledge work. It is no longer the low-skill, low-cost activity it was once assumed to be. It is where design, engineering, and innovation meet the physical world. Manufacturing is not just about producing goods—it's about creating and constantly improving the complex systems that enable production at scale. Manufacturing integrates multiple domains of expertise: materials science, advanced computing, robotics, supply chain management, and workforce training. It is the embodiment of applied problem-solving and does not simply involve an "army of millions and millions of human beings screwing in tiny screws to make iPhones."[19]

Industrial production has wide-ranging spillover benefits and is intimately linked to innovation, but these ideas were lost on American policymakers during the heyday of globalization. Control over production processes shapes the trajectory of technological development, determines which innovations can scale, and dictates who gains access to critical capabilities. China's manufacturing prowess has created powerful innovation feedback loops, providing the CCP with a platform to accelerate technological development across diverse domains and industries.

China's manufacturing-led innovation model has enabled it to establish leadership positions in emerging industries that matter for the future. China has emerged as a formidable competitor in genomics, biotechnology, and pharmaceuticals. In AI, it has cultivated indigenous competitors to American giants like OpenAI, embracing open source as an advantage. In robotics, Chinese firms have made tremendous progress, boasting globally competitive capabilities and the largest install base of industrial robots in the world. Meanwhile, the PRC is rapidly expanding its nuclear energy fleet, with 30 reactors under construction compared to few new builds in the United States. As AI accelerates innovation and converges with other emerging domains, additional sectors will become contested, adding further complexity to the United States' capacity to manage strategic technology competition.

It is well documented that the CCP uses China's industrial dominance for coercion and retaliation, but its toolkit has evolved significantly since Trump's first term.[20] We should expect Beijing to increasingly use tariffs and other "provocations" by the Trump administration as a pretext to implement long-standing plans to eliminate US competitors and replace them with domestic alternatives. When Trump imposed a second round of fentanyl tariffs on China in early 2025, for example, Beijing banned imports of US firm Illumina's gene sequencers, creating a market opportunity for MGI—a domestic competitor the CCP had cultivated for years.[21] Similar retaliation that targets firms in sectors where China has long wanted to reduce foreign market share anyway, like film, pharma, and semiconductors, should be expected.

From Open Arms to Raised Shields: America's Long Journey to China Reality

How did we get here? The George W. Bush administration welcomed China with open arms, granting it most-favored-nation status and facilitating its entry into the WTO. But just five years later, in 2006, when Beijing issued its Medium- and Long-Term Plan for Science and Technology Development, which called for China to "leapfrog in priority fields," including telecommunications, rare earth minerals, biotechnology, and many others, the Bush administration should have begun to realize that Beijing's goals were different from Washington's. Although the "pivot to Asia" of Barack Obama's administration in 2011 reflected a recognition that a more comprehensive approach to China was needed, President Obama pulled punches to secure Beijing's participation in the Paris Agreement, an international treaty on climate, and failed to fundamentally alter the terms of trade or the geoeconomic balance of power in America's favor.

The first Trump administration did more to shift the Overton window on China policy than any of its predecessors since the Nixon administration, establishing the new normal of bluntly confronting China's predatory trade and economic practices. President Trump most notably used tariffs, and to a lesser degree export controls and other tools, to target predatory trade practices and constrain Chinese technology giants like Huawei. During his first term, two opposing factions—dealmakers and decouplers—jockeyed for influence inside his administration. In January 2020, dealmakers achieved the Phase One trade deal—which ended up being largely a flop after China failed to fulfill its purchase agreements or make meaningful structural reforms.[22] Decouplers seized the reins decisively only by the spring of 2020, after Trump blamed China for the COVID-19 pandemic, which he believed cost him the election, and ordered decoupling from China. The administration's most active period of counter-China policies ensued for the last 10 months of Trump's term.

When President Joe Biden entered the White House in 2021, his advisors largely agreed with the Trump administration's assessment of the China challenge, maintained and even increased his tariffs, and tried to create a coherent framework for the use of policy tools like export controls. Export controls on advanced AI chips and related technologies enacted by the Biden administration in October 2022 demonstrated prescience—implemented as they were nearly two months before ChatGPT's public release dramatically showcased AI's transformative potential to the world.[23] Though the regulations later required several rounds of updates to close loopholes, they struck at a critical vulnerability by targeting the specialized semiconductors and manufacturing equipment that form the foundation of AI development—highlighting the Biden administration's determination to maintain America's technological edge in this strategic domain.

Biden's China strategy distinguished itself from Trump's by adding a strong emphasis on domestic industrial policy, achieving landmark legislation with the CHIPS and Science Act, the Infrastructure Investment and Jobs Act, and the Inflation Reduction Act, along with more public emphasis on coordination with allies, especially in Europe. The Trump administration had also expanded coordination with allies and partners on China policies, but these efforts were publicly drowned out by Trump's harsh rhetoric about allies, particularly in Europe.

By the end of Biden's term, attempts to keep restrictions within a "small yard, high fence" were increasingly strained. China's rapid progress in dual-use technologies like quantum computing, biotechnology, and aerospace made it difficult to contain decoupling to a limited set of dual-use sectors. The administration faced mounting pressure to widen restrictions as China achieved breakthroughs that narrowed technological gaps faster than anticipated, causing the "small yard" to expand. Just five days before Biden left office, his administration broke new ground by announcing export controls on certain biotechnology equipment because of concerns related to AI and data science.[24]

The China Challenge in 2025

There are two competing schools of thought on the scale of the China challenge. Some depict China as an unstoppable juggernaut and imply that competing for broad-spectrum techno-economic preeminence is ultimately futile. Others believe that the Chinese economy is in irreversible decline and that it is only a matter of time before the PRC either collapses like the Soviet Union or faces an inwardly turning future of demographic decline. Undeniably, the Chinese economy faces numerous acute challenges, from local government debt crises and a real estate market in the doldrums to a persistent lack of domestic consumption.[25] Externally, an expanding group of trade partners have woken up to the realities of China's brute force playbook and are putting up barriers to Chinese exports.

China's economic problems, however, should not be viewed as a sign that it presents less of a threat to US economic security interests, at least in the next few years. In theory, slower growth means fewer resources for Beijing to plow into its military and techno-industrial programs. But in practice, these resource constraints could take years to manifest in a downsized challenge for Washington.

Even at very low rates of annual growth, China's economy is already very large, and its outlays for technological development, although substantial in gross terms, account for a modest percentage of its GDP.[26]

China presents a more complex techno-economic challenge in 2025 than it did when Trump last left office. Despite strategic groundwork laid by both the Trump and Biden administrations, China has intensified its brute force economic practices and accelerated efforts to rewire global supply chains to its advantage—often adapting to and circumventing US restrictions. While China is unlikely to displace America's sheer economic size or the dollar's reserve currency status soon if ever, its technological capabilities have advanced considerably. The second Trump administration must now contend with this paradoxical China: more technologically capable and globally ambitious, yet simultaneously facing serious internal economic headwinds. The PRC is a complex adversary that will demand competitive strategies more sophisticated than those of Trump's first term.

The Dilemma of Trump 2.0: Dealmaker or Decoupler?

President Trump's second term comes at a pivotal juncture in the US-China rivalry. His April 2025 tariffs hikes on China, on top of earlier fentanyl levies, represented the most significant trade decoupling move since China joined the WTO. Yet it remains unclear whether Trump will translate this disruptive shift into a sustainable strategy or allow dealmaking instincts to override economic security imperatives and squander America's narrowing window to counter China's brute force strategy.

American industry's unpreparedness for sudden decoupling—with deeply entangled supply chains for pharmaceuticals, semiconductors, and critical minerals—guarantees tariff policy turbulence as Trump's trade team seeks to design and implement a strategy that balances multiple objectives. The true strategic direction will emerge over months and years, not days or weeks. A key question is whether Trump recognizes that a substantive economic deal with China is even less likely now than in January 2020, when the Phase One agreement was signed. Since then, not only has China's trade surplus grown,[27] but the CCP has intensified efforts to insulate its economy from the US, prioritizing export-driven growth and technological self-reliance while suppressing the structural reforms American trade negotiators have long sought.

Will Trump's second term be dominated by decoupling or dealmaking? For evidence of the former, we can look at his team and their policy preferences. Trump has assembled the most hardline-on-China economic and national security group of advisors in decades, installing China hawks in leadership and key staff positions at the National Security Council, the Treasury Department, the Department of Commerce, the Department of State, the Office of the US Trade Representative, and elsewhere.

Early signals from his team indicate a clear intent to accelerate economic decoupling with China. On day one, the White House issued the America First Trade Policy memo, followed a month later by the America First Investment Policy memo. While global in scope, both memos focus extensively on China. The trade memo launched reviews of the full range of China's brute force economic practices, from tech transfer and intellectual property theft to trade circumvention—an oblique reference to China's use of Mexico as a conduit to evade US tariffs. The investment memo initiates a process to financially decouple the United States and China by increasing restrictions on two-way investment while facilitating increased investment flows with friends. But the memo appears to be a product of bottom-up staff initiative rather than top-down guidance from the president. Five days after signing the memo, Trump contradicted it (probably inadvertently), saying, "We want them to invest in the United States. That's good. That's a lot of money coming in. And we'll invest in China."[28] Trump's instincts appear hawkish on trade but dovish on investment, and it remains unclear if policymakers in Washington and Beijing will prioritize accelerated financial decoupling during Trump's second term.

Despite headlines suggesting Trump will sound the death knell for American alliances,[29] members of his team are working quietly behind the scenes to strengthen China-related coordination with key allies, just as they did in his first administration. Evidence can be found in joint statements with allies early in the Trump administration that emphasize opposition to China's rapid nuclear buildup, aggression in the East and South China Seas, support for the Russian war machine, and harmful industrial overcapacity, as well as American expressions of support for Taiwan.[30] Here again, it remains to be seen whether Trump's non-isolationist advisors can channel his disruptive tendencies toward a recalibration of alliances that is both more sustainable and addresses American voters' concerns about bearing disproportionate costs—or whether Trump will override them and push further than in his first term toward alliance rupture.

As far as Trump the dealmaker goes, the president did not make China a front-burner issue in the early months of his second term, maintaining a notably cordial demeanor toward Xi. "I like President Xi very much . . . we've always had a good relationship," he said in February.[31] Trump has signaled interest in a deal that could include issues such as transferring partial ownership of TikTok to an American buyer (while allowing Beijing to control the app's algorithm), tariff concessions, and perhaps Chinese direct investment in the United States.

Are we seeing a replay of the early days of Trump 1.0, when his Palm Beach summit with Xi in April 2017 produced a "100 day plan" to boost trade and cooperation,[32] only to collapse four months later when Trump—frustrated by China's inaction—launched a Section 301 investigation that led to tariffs?[33] There is reason to suspect that the Trump administration is not waiting for sequential failure but is running both "good cop" and "bad cop" tactics simultaneously. Yet uncertainty remains. Another possibility is that Trump's fundamental views on China have evolved since his first term, owing to a realization that China is now a more formidable rival than it was in 2017. Like many American politicians before him, Trump's instincts may tell him to coexist with, rather than constrain, China—an appealing but ultimately unsustainable approach that will cede America's strategic position over time.

Trump himself thus emerges as the second biggest X factor in his own China strategy. The first is Xi Jinping. The superficial calm in early 2025 is unsustainable, and the logic of strategic rivalry will inevitably reassert itself. The structural and ideological forces driving competition are too powerful, and the CCP's commitment to technological self-reliance is too entrenched. The question isn't whether this facade will crack, but when and how dramatically it shatters, and whether the United States and its allies will be positioned for success when it does.

Outlook

Positioning the United States to prevail in the techno-economic competition with the PRC requires getting three things right. First, the United States needs a stronger *pushback* toolkit to protect its technological advantages and insulate its domestic market and firms from PRC brute force economics. Second, the United States must continue to *promote* US domestic competitiveness, with policies that cement American leadership in AI and rebuild advanced industrial capacity in critical technology sectors. Third and finally is *pooling* market demand with other democratic market economies,[34] so that democracies together can form a large enough counterweight to China's brute force economics, providing their firms with sufficient access to addressable markets as their access to China's market is increasingly cut off by forces in Beijing and Washington.

1. Pushback

To prevail in techno-economic competition with China, the United States must defend its existing advantages while actively countering Beijing's efforts to leap-frog ahead in critical sectors. This requires strategic and aggressive use of the full toolkit at Washington's disposal—from tariffs and export controls to sanctions, investment screening, import restrictions, and cybersecurity and research security guardrails—and the creation of new tools and authorities to stay ahead as threats evolve.

In the second Trump administration, success will hinge on how sharply its policies focus on China as a unique strategic threat, rather than treating it as just another trade competitor. One signal will be how Trump's tariff strategy evolves: whether it ends up targeting China with precision or continues to spread tariffs equally across multiple trade partners, risking recession, inflation, and diluted focus. A related test will be how the administration uses tariffs with countries like Mexico—either as an end in itself or as leverage to close loopholes that China exploits to bypass US trade barriers.

Equally important is how the administration approaches technology decoupling. A key indicator will be the strategic use—or neglect—of underappreciated tools like the Department of Commerce's Information and Communications Technology and Services (ICTS) authority, created by Trump in 2019 to restrict commercial transactions involving foreign adversaries across a wide array of internet-connected technologies. After years of dormancy, the Biden administration revived ICTS in 2024 to target Chinese and Russian "connected vehicles"—AI-enabled mobile data centers posing risks of surveillance and sabotage. The resulting rule, which entered into force in March 2025, effectively bans Chinese-made or -controlled vehicles in the United States.[35] Whether Trump rolls back, maintains, or expands these restrictions to other technologies will speak volumes about his administration's decoupling intentions.

More broadly, the Trump team's ability to match the speed and complexity of technological innovation will determine the effectiveness of its protection strategy. Past policy templates—like semiconductor export controls—won't translate neatly to other sectors such as biotechnology, pharmaceuticals, robotics, and open source AI, where US chokepoints are, in many cases, absent or harder to pinpoint. These domains require fit-for-purpose guardrails. This in turn requires forming strategic public-private partnerships and leveraging the technologies themselves—such as deploying AI systems to improve the monitoring and enforcement of export controls. China's swift AI advances, exemplified by models released by companies like DeepSeek, will test whether the administration has a coherent plan and the political will to implement it.

2. Promote

In recent years, the United States has launched a generational effort to re-build its industrial base, particularly in high-tech and manufacturing-intensive sectors. The Biden administration's large-scale federal investments aimed at revitalizing semiconductor manufacturing, modernizing infrastructure, and advancing clean energy technologies. This marked a decisive turn toward a more active, government-led industrial policy. Core focus areas have included artificial intelligence, quantum computing, and biotechnology, supported by regional tech hubs, public-private partnerships, and workforce development initiatives, designed to reduce dependence on geopolitical rivals and respond to vulnerabilities exposed by the COVID-19 pandemic.

With Trump's return to the White House, the future of modern American industrial strategy is uncertain. While Trump has promised a "resurgence" of American manufacturing, his approach differs markedly from his predecessor's. Rather than direct federal investment, the Trump administration emphasizes tariffs, tax cuts, deregulation, and energy expansion as primary tools for reindustrialization. As Vice President J. D. Vance said in March 2025 at a Michigan plastics plant, "We are going to be guided by a very simple principle: Build in this country, we cut your taxes, we reduce your regulation, we reduce your energy costs."[36] Trump has frequently explained his tariff agenda by emphasizing, "There are no tariffs if you manufacture or build your product in the United States."[37] He has criticized subsidy-heavy programs like CHIPS, particularly its support for foreign firms such TSMC, which he blames for "stealing" America's chip industry. Instead, Trump has used tariff threats to pressure companies to expand US production.

As of early 2025, while his sweeping tariff agenda has created significant business uncertainty, it has also arguably catalyzed substantial domestic investments—including TSMC's announcement of an additional $100 billion for semiconductor manufacturing and research and development in Arizona (supplementing its previous $65 billion commitment, already the largest foreign direct investment in US history) and drugmakers' announcements of major new investments in US plants.[38] Whether Trump's policy mix will deliver an American manufacturing renaissance or engineer an extended period of economic uncertainty and recession is a key question.

3. POOL

The United States now confronts a fundamental inflection point in global trade policy. After decades of liberalization that politicians on both sides of the aisle now blame for a loss of American manufacturing jobs, policymakers are reassessing core assumptions. Systemic rivalry with China and the emergence of transformative technologies like AI necessitate a different approach. The times demand a transition from universal liberalization toward a tiered system that applies different rules and expectations to real market economies versus adversarial non-market economies. Such restructuring would recognize both domestic economic realities and changing geopolitical imperatives, potentially creating more resilient supply chains while addressing long-standing concerns about fairness in global commerce.

The Biden administration understood the strategic imperative to rally allies around a coordinated response to China's predatory economic model. But its efforts to do so, like the Indo-Pacific Economic Framework, lacked teeth. Sensitivity to domestic labor concerns prevented the Biden administration from offering meaningful carrots—increased access to America's massive domestic market—to persuade partners to align with US objectives. (To be fair, America's market was already one of the most accessible in the world.)[39] At the same time, diplomatic restraint kept the Biden administration from using sticks to change partners' behavior, such as threats to withdraw market access.

In late 2024, US Trade Representative Catherine Tai, after visiting all 50 American states, concluded that "Americans feel that there's something wrong with the system" and captured the administration's sentiments about trade:

> For many years, USTR focused almost exclusively on the export opportunities that we could create through free trade. But those policies failed to recognize that . . . [o]ur superpower is our consumption power. . . . [C]ountries . . . want access to our market. But in focusing so much on exports, we neglected to give enough consideration to imports, and the consequences of those imports on our workers and businesses. . . . [W]e are seeing a growing consensus that we need to reimagine the rules of globalization . . . We can . . . chart a course in which we shape trade rules so that they deliver better results for working people—here, and abroad.[40]

Trump shares Tai's ambition of delivering "better results for working people," but his early weeks in office made it clear that he intends to drive a much more forceful reset than his predecessor—deploying aggressive tariffs and demands for greater burden-sharing to radically reshape America's relationships with its trade partners. His US trade representative, Jamieson Greer, brings a deep familiarity with China's brute force economics and has called for strategic decoupling from China. Greer's priors suggest a vision for replacing universal free trade with a dual-track system separating "non-market economies" like China's from market economies. For China, this means replacing WTO rules with a system of "managed trade" using tariffs, quotas, and investment restrictions and even revoking China's Permanent Normal Trade Relations status.[41]

It remains unclear whether Greer and like-minded officials can harness Trump's disruptive tariff agenda productively. The rejection of outdated trade assumptions could break ground for a new system to emerge that creates meaningful separation between China and real market economies. On the other hand, it could also trigger economic chaos that alienates allies and undermines faith in the US government and market. In congressional testimony in 2024, Greer acknowledged that such a fundamental shift would entail both costs and benefits and would ultimately be a question of political will: "If a President is not committed to fundamentally changing the U.S. trade relationship with China, no amount of existing or new tools will make a difference."[42]

A defining test for Trump's China strategy will be whether he moves beyond unilateral reshoring to embrace friendshoring—leveraging allies and partners in sectors where American self-sufficiency is impractical. Shipbuilding, a sector Trump has promised to rebuild, exemplifies this challenge: Trump's domestic manufacturing focus will inevitably confront the reality that cooperation with Japan and South Korea—the only significant alternatives to Chinese dominance—is essential. The United States, the European Union, Japan, and the United Kingdom together account for around 56% of global consumption—more than quadruple China's 13%.[43] This ratio becomes even more favorable when South Korea, India, Australia, Canada, Mexico, and others are included. Pooling market demand with other market economies is thus essential for a successful counter-China strategy, but it is unclear if the Trump administration will embrace such a strategy.

There are other internal contradictions in Trump's economic agenda that further complicate his administration's approach to the China challenge. His enthusiasm for Chinese automakers establishing US plants, expressed on the campaign trail, exists awkwardly alongside the ICTS regulations restricting Chinese vehicles.

These tensions highlight the fundamental choice facing the second Trump administration: Will it develop a coherent strategy that distinguishes between economic competitors and strategic adversaries, aligning economics with security through durable partnerships? If successful, Trump has the opportunity to build a high-bar trade architecture that safeguards American interests and unites democratic market economies against China's brute force economics. The future of global trade depends on whether his administration can achieve this alignment or drifts into a world of fractured supply chains, rising costs, and strategic uncertainty.

NOTES

1. Matt Pottinger and Liza Tobin, "China and America Aren't Just in a Trade War. It's a Fight for the Twenty-First Century," *The Free Press*, April 9, 2025, https://www .thefp.com/p/china-america-fight-for-supremacy-xi-jinping-trump.

2. Greg Norman, "Trump 'Optimistic' China Will Make Tariff Deal, White House Says," *Fox Business*, April 11, 2025, https://www.foxbusiness.com/politics/trump -optimistic-china-make-tariff-deal-white-house-says.

3. "Full Text of Clinton's Speech on China Trade Bill," *The New York Times*, March 9, 2000, archived at https://archive.nytimes.com/www.nytimes.com/library/world/asia /030900clinton-china-text.html.

4. Liza Tobin, "China's Brute Force Economics: Waking Up from the Dream of a Level Playing Field," *Texas National Security Review* 6, no. 1 (Winter 2022/2023): 81–98, https://tnsr.org/2022/12/chinas-brute-force-economics-waking-up-from-the-dream-of-a -level-playing-field/.

5. More than 99% of listed firms in China received direct government subsidies in 2022. See Frank Bickenbach et al., *Foul Play? On the Scale and Scope of Industrial Subsidies in China*, Kiel Institute for the World Economy, April 2024, https://www.ifw -kiel.de/publications/foul-play-on-the-scale-and-scope-of-industrial-subsidies-in-china -32738/. In 2022, Beijing's $248 billion in industrial policy spending dwarfed comparable US and European efforts. See Gerard DiPippo, Ilaria Mazzocco, and Scott Kennedy, *Red Ink Estimating Chinese Industrial Policy Spending in Comparative Perspective*, Center for Strategic and International Studies, May 23, 2022, https://www.csis.org /analysis/red-ink-estimating-chinese-industrial-policy-spending-comparative -perspective.

6. Tobin, "China's Brute Force Economics."

7. Robert D. Atkinson, *China Is Rapidly Becoming a Leading Innovator in Advanced Industries*, Information Technology and Innovation Foundation, September 16, 2024, https://itif.org/publications/2024/09/16/china-is-rapidly-becoming-a-leading-innovator -in-advanced-industries/.

8. Matthew P. Funaiole, "The Threat of China's Shipbuilding Empire," Center for Strategic and International Studies, May 10, 2024, https://www.csis.org/analysis/threat -chinas-shipbuilding-empire.

9. Zeyi Yang, "Why China's Dominance in Commercial Drones Has Become a Global Security Matter," *MIT Technology Review*, June 26, 2024, https://www.technologyreview.com/2024/06/26/1094249/china-commercial-drone-dji-security/.

10. William Allen Reinsch et al., *Friendshoring the Lithium-Ion Battery Supply Chain: Battery Cell Manufacturing*, Center for Strategic and International Studies, June 6, 2024, https://www.csis.org/analysis/friendshoring-lithium-ion-battery-supply-chain-battery-cell-manufacturing.

11. Yasmina Abdelilah et al., *Special Report on Solar PV Global Supply Chains*, International Energy Agency, July 2022, https://www.iea.org/reports/solar-pv-global-supply-chains.

12. Zhou Weihuan and Henry Gao, "Major Economies Are Taking Aim at China's EV Industry. Here's What to Know," World Economic Forum, September 16, 2024, https://www.weforum.org/stories/2024/09/major-economies-are-taking-aim-at-china-s-ev-industry-here-s-what-to-know/.

13. Brian J. Miller and Vrushab Gowda, "Combating China's Quest to Dominate American Pharmaceutical Markets," American Enterprise Institute, August 27, 2024, https://www.aei.org/op-eds/combating-chinas-quest-to-dominate-american-pharmaceutical-markets/.

14. Reva Goujon et al., *Thin Ice: US Pathways to Regulating China-Sourced Legacy Chips*, Rhodium Group, May 13, 2024, https://rhg.com/research/thin-ice-us-pathways-to-regulating-china-sourced-legacy-chips/.

15. Philip Andrews-Speed and Anders Hove, *China's Rare Earths Dominance and Policy Responses*, Oxford Institute for Energy Studies, June 2023, https://www.oxfordenergy.org/publications/chinas-rare-earths-dominance-and-policy-responses/.

16. *Implementation Opinions of Seven Ministries Including the Ministry of Industry and Information Technology on Promoting the Innovative Development of Future Industries* (translated from Chinese), Center for Security and Emerging Technology, February 12, 2024, https://cset.georgetown.edu/publication/future-industry-implementation-opinions/.

17. Arthur Kroeber, "Unleashing 'New Quality Productive Forces': China's Strategy for Technology-Led Growth," Brookings Institution, January 30, 2024, https://www.brookings.edu/articles/unleashing-new-quality-productive-forces-chinas-strategy-for-technology-led-growth/.

18. Regina M. Abrami, William C. Kirby, and F. Warren McFarlan, "Why China Can't Innovate," *Harvard Business Review*, March 2014, https://hbr.org/2014/03/why-china-cant-innovate.

19. Secretary of Commerce Howard Lutnick used this phrase to describe the return of manufacturing jobs to the United States. See https://www.theverge.com/news/644320/us-commerce-secretary-howard-lutnick-says-well-be-making-iphones-in-the-us.

20. See, for example, testimony of Victor Cha, Jamil Jaffer, and others at a hearing of the Committee on Rules, "Examining China's Coercive Economic Tactics," May 10, 2023, https://www.congress.gov/118/meeting/house/115789/documents/HHRG-118-RU00-20230510-SD118.pdf; Aya Adachi, Alexander Brown, and Max J. Zenglein, "Fasten Your Seatbelts: How to Manage China's Economic Coercion," MERICS, August 25, 2022, https://merics.org/en/report/fasten-your-seatbelts-how-manage-chinas-economic-coercion.

21. Andrew Silver, "China Bans Imports of Illumina's Gene Sequencers Right After Trump Tariff Action," *Reuters*, March 4, 2025. Beijing probably had Illumina in its crosshairs already after the US Congress considered legislation (the Biosecure Act), which did not pass, that would have restricted Chinese biotech giants like BGI and MGI in the US market.

22. Steve Goldstein, "China Bought None of the $200 Billion It Promised from the U.S. Under 'Phase 1' Trade Deal, Study Reveals," *MarketWatch*, February 10, 2022, https://www.marketwatch.com/story/china-bought-none-of-the-200-billion-it-promised -from-the-u-s-in-phase-one-trade-deal-study-reveals-11644505449.

23. Bureau of Industry and Security, "Export Controls on Semiconductor Manufacturing Items," Interim Final Rule, *Federal Register*, October 7, 2022; OpenAI, "Introducing ChatGPT," November 30, 2022, https://openai.com/index/chatgpt/.

24. David Shepardson, "US Imposing New Export Controls on Biotech Equipment over China Concerns," *Reuters*, January 15, 2025, https://www.reuters.com/technology /us-imposing-new-export-controls-biotechnology-equipment-2025-01-15/.

25. Daniel H. Rosen and Logan Wright, "China's Economic Collision Course," *Foreign Affairs*, March 27, 2024, https://www.foreignaffairs.com/china/chinas-economic -collision-course.

26. Liza Tobin, "Is US Security Dependent on Limiting China's Economic Growth?," Brookings Institution, October 3, 2023, https://www.brookings.edu/articles/is-us -security-dependent-on-limiting-chinas-economic-growth/.

27. Keith Bradsher, "China's Trade Surplus Reaches a Record of Nearly $1 Trillion," *The New York Times*, June 12, 2025, https://www.nytimes.com/2025/01/12/business /china-trade-surplus.html.

28. The White House, Remarks by President Trump Before Cabinet Meeting, February 26, 2025.

29. See, for example, Marc Champion, "The Transatlantic Alliance as We've Known It Is Dead," *Bloomberg*, February 17, 2025, and Andrew Roth, "How JD Vance emerged as the chief saboteur in the transatlantic alliance," *The Guardian*, March 1, 2025, https://www.theguardian.com/us-news/2025/feb/28/jd-vance-volodymyr-zelenskyy.

30. See Department of State, "Statement of the G7 Foreign Ministers' Meeting in Charlevoix," March 14, 2025; The White House, "United States—Japan Joint Leaders' Statement," February 7, 2025.

31. The White House, "Remarks by President Trump at the World Economic Forum," January 23, 2025, https://www.whitehouse.gov/remarks/2025/01/remarks-by -president-trump-at-the-world-economic-forum/.

32. David Nakamura and Emily Rauhala, "U.S. and China End Summit with 100-Day Plan to Boost Trade and Cooperation," *The Washington Post*, April 7, 2017.

33. Office of the United States Trade Representative, "USTR Announces Initiation of Section 301 Investigation of China," August 18, 2017, https://ustr.gov/about-us/policy -offices/press-office/press-releases/2017/august/ustr-announces-initiation-section.

34. Liza Tobin and Robert D. Atkinson, "The Missing Piece in America's Strategy for Techno-Economic Rivalry with China," *Lawfare*, October 3, 2023. See also Special Competitive Studies Project, *Economy: Panel Interim Panel Report*, November 2022, https://www.scsp.ai/wp-content/uploads/2022/11/Economy-Panel-IPR-FINAL-Version.pdf.

35. Liza Tobin, "Europe Should Emulate Biden's Restrictions on Chinese Smart Cars," Council on Foreign Relations, *Asia Unbound* (blog), October 22, 2024, https://www.cfr.org/blog/europe-should-emulate-bidens-restrictions-chinese-smart-cars.

36. Jacob Adams, "Vance Vows Accountability for Offshoring Jobs," *The Daily Caller*, March 2025.

37. Aislinn Murphy, "President Trump Looks to Bring Manufacturing Back to US with Tariffs," *Fox Business*, February 18, 2025.

38. Meagan Parrish, "Pharma's US Manufacturing Moment: Where Companies Are Making the Biggest Moves," *PharmaVoice*, April 11, 2025, https://www.pharmavoice.com/news/pharma-manufacturing-tariff-trump-lilly-novartis-novo-amgen-jnj/745092/.

39. Before Trump's second term, the United States had some of the lowest tariffs in the world. Hanna Dougal and Marium Ali, "Where Are the Highest, Lowest Tariffs? Trump's Reciprocal Tariffs Explained," *Al Jazeera*, April 2, 2025, https://www.aljazeera.com/news/2025/4/2/where-are-the-highest-lowest-tariffs-trumps-reciprocal-tariffs-explained.

40. Katherine Tai, "Reflections on USTR's Visit to the 50 States," Office of the United States Trade Representative (blog), December 2024, https://ustr.gov/about-us/policy-offices/press-office/blogs-and-op-eds/2024/reflections-ustrs-visit-50-states.

41. Jamieson Greer, Testimony Before the U.S.-China Economic and Security Review Commission, May 23, 2024, https://www.uscc.gov/sites/default/files/2024-05/Jamieson_Greer_Testimony.pdf.

42. Greer, Testimony.

43. Pottinger and Tobin, "China and America Aren't Just in a Trade War."

Chapter Two

Assessing the US-China Chip Competition

Chris Miller

"**M**odern wars are fought with semiconductors," Senator Ben Sasse declared in May 2020.[1] At the time, most Americans thought only rarely about chips. Few knew what chips did or how they were made. Yet by 2020, semiconductors were beginning to play a central role in American statecraft, as the US government came to realize their importance—and to understand China's ambitions in the industry. When, in 2021 and 2022, the pandemic disrupted semiconductor supply chains and caused manufacturing delays for autos, medical devices, and agricultural equipment, the scope of a modern economy's reliance on chips became clearer. And as the 2022 launch of ChatGPT set off a boom of investment in artificial intelligence, the role of chips in catalyzing technological progress took center stage.

Semiconductors, political leaders in the US and China have come to realize, are key inputs shaping the balance of power. The world's most valuable tech companies cannot operate without them. Advanced manufacturing capabilities—from defense to medical devices—require many types of high-end chips to function. And advances in artificial intelligence have hinged on the development of ever-more-powerful processors.

Chris Miller is a professor at the Fletcher School at Tufts University and is a nonresident senior fellow at the American Enterprise Institute. He has an MA and PhD in history from Yale University and a BA in history from Harvard University. His latest book is *Chip War: The Fight for the World's Most Critical Technology*.

In Beijing and in Washington, therefore, chips are a major focus of US technology policy—and of competition. In the US, Presidents Donald Trump and Joe Biden both imposed tariffs on their import from China. Congress passed more than $50 billion of subsidies via the CHIPS and Science Act to revitalize the US chip manufacturing industry. The US has imposed sweeping restrictions on the transfer of chips and chipmaking tools to China, pushing other countries like Japan, the Netherlands, Taiwan, and Korea to do the same. And Beijing has responded by continuing to pour money into its chip industry, driving toward self-sufficiency in the only large-scale manufacturing industry where China still relies primarily on imports to satisfy its demand.

Over the past decade the US government has set chips at the center of its technology policy—and set tech at the center of competition with China. Semiconductor policy has been complicated by an effort to achieve multiple contradictory policy aims. The US government first realized the power it wielded over the world's chip industry by using restrictions as a punitive tool against ZTE, a Chinese telecom firm, for violating sanctions on Iran. Second, the US began imposing tariffs on chips from China, as semiconductors became intertwined with broader US-China trade disputes. Third, the US started restricting the transfer of chips and chipmaking tools to China with the aim of slowing China's technological advances. Fourth, the US has begun to limit use of Chinese-made chips in US systems over fears of Chinese espionage or sabotage. Finally, in preparation for potential Chinese escalatory measures in the Taiwan Strait, the US has tried to reduce its dependence on Taiwan's chipmakers. These tactics are all reasonable, but they are at times contradictory. The struggle to turn these competition tactics into a coherent strategy has been a challenge for US policymakers.

The US and its allies started the chip war with significant technological and economic advantages that their policies aimed to maintain. Yet China has chipped away at this gap and, in some places, has completely closed it. Companies from the US and allied countries have generally been unwilling partners in the government's chip efforts, preferring the pre–chip war status quo, even at the cost of long-term losses of market share and technological advantages to Chinese competitors. At times, Western firms have passively or even actively undermined US policy, by turning a blind eye to Chinese smuggling of prohibited technologies or by tweaking products to avoid US restrictions.

The US government's effort to limit the impact on industry by imposing policies that were more "scalpel" than "hammer" has left open gaps that Western and Chinese firms have exploited more rapidly than the government could close them.

The glacial pace of government action has compounded its disadvantages versus fast-moving firms. This misalignment between firms and government has enabled China to make substantial progress in closing the technological gap. Nevertheless, in comparison to a counterfactual scenario in which the US government had continued ignoring the chip industry, the US is in a stronger position and China is worse off. In that sense, both China's chip war and the US chip war launched in response have both been partial successes.

China's Chip War

For the United States, the chip war began in the first Trump administration, when—as detailed below—the US government first realized the power it had over the chip industry, as well as the centrality of semiconductors to modern manufacturing and AI. For China, the chip war started several years earlier. "Call forth the assault," Xi Jinping had declared to a conference of senior Chinese technology and political leaders in 2016, as he urged industry to shake China's reliance on imported semiconductors. Beijing had realized the existing structure of the chip industry—in which the high-value steps in the chipmaking process were dominated by the US, Europe, Japan, Korea, and Taiwan—was not in its economic interest. What's more, the fact that China spent as much money each year importing chips as it spent importing oil presented a security vulnerability as well as an economic risk. To address this concern, China has pursued three broad lines of effort: building production capacity, seeking technology leadership in design and manufacturing, and acquiring supply chain self-sufficiency.

1. Build Production Capacity

In 2014, China established a National Integrated Circuit Industry Investment fund to promote its chip industry. Provincial and local governments quickly followed with their own funds, and other state-linked investors also reoriented toward the chip industry. As early as 2014, in other words, China had passed its own version of the CHIPS Act. Since then, China's share of global chip production has shot upward, driven largely, though not exclusively, by lower-tech chips, where China could produce at quality levels that were generally comparable to leading foreign firms.

For these more commoditized low-end chips, Chinese firms could win market share by pricing aggressively, thus taking advantage of state-subsidized capital costs and corporate governance structures that prioritized market share over profitability. Since the Chinese government began prioritizing the chip industry in

2014, its production capacity has soared, mitigating some of its reliance on imported chips. China has coupled this production increase with formal and informal pressure on Chinese firms to reduce purchases of foreign-made chips. For example, Chairman Xi on national television was seen asking one manufacturer whether the chips in its products were produced locally.[2] China has set quantitative targets for the auto industry to source chips locally.

2. Build Technology Leadership

China coupled this production capacity buildout with an effort to acquire more cutting-edge capabilities, which were controlled by foreign firms. The subsidies that enabled the production capacity buildout also facilitated expensive research and development, with little need to worry about immediate profitability. It also enabled the hiring of foreigners and Chinese citizens who had worked at foreign chip firms. China's SMIC, for example, has hired large numbers of Taiwanese employees, including former executives from TSMC. China coupled this with an active regime of technology transfer requirements on foreign firms if they wanted to build local facilities or retain access to the Chinese market. And Chinese firms, with state support, began trying to buy leading Western chip firms outright, succeeding in some transactions before investment screening agencies like America's Committee on Foreign Investment in the United States began blocking nearly every deal involving China and chips.

3. Supply Chain Independence

China's third aim, which was prioritized less at first but has become more important over time, has been to build a self-sufficient chip supply chain. Given that almost all the key steps in the chipmaking process were dominated by non-Chinese firms—from the silicon wafers and other materials to the chip design software and the manufacturing tools—this was a particular challenge. China's early rounds of subsidies focused more on chip manufacturing than on replicating other steps in the supply chain, which were more technically and economically challenging. However, as the US has weaponized China's supply chain dependencies, China has poured money into developing its own electronic design automation software and into trying to build out domestic chipmaking tools, especially for the tools where it still lags the cutting edge.

China's policies, in other words, launched the chip war, aiming to take market share from Taiwan, Korea, and the US—and to reduce Beijing's technological vulnerabilities. The US was provoked to respond because continued Chinese investment and localization—and thus loss of US market share and diminution of US technological leadership—seemed both highly likely and deeply risky.

Aims of US Chip War Policies

The US responded to China's chip war with a series of moves designed to slow China's technological advances, limit its market share growth, and mitigate the cybersecurity and economic security risks of increased reliance of US manufacturers on Chinese components. These tactics each developed over time—from the first Trump administration through the Biden administration—and appear likely to be broadly continued by the current administration.

On their own, each of these moves has been logical and coherent, but as detailed below, they were also at times contradictory. For example, efforts to cut China off from advanced technology ran counter to efforts to maintain US market share, because US firms found they couldn't continue to supply major customers like Huawei. Similarly, tactics that might help one segment of the chip supply chain might hurt another. For example, cutting off sales of advanced chipmaking equipment to China helped hold back Chinese firms like SMIC, which aspired to manufacturing cutting-edge chips. This has helped to solidify the near-monopoly of TSMC, the world's leading chipmaker, but it has come at the expense of the Western manufacturers of chipmaking tools, which face up-and-coming Chinese competitors stepping into a market that they are prohibited from servicing. These contradictory dynamics have undermined the efficacy of the overall US strategy.

1. Chip Restrictions as Punitive Tool

The US government first came to understand the significance of semiconductors—and the shape of the semiconductor supply chain—when punitive measures against Chinese tech and telecom firms ZTE and Huawei illustrated their dependence on US semiconductor technology. In March 2016, after ZTE was found to have violated US sanctions on Iran, the Commerce Department threatened to ban it from buying technology from the United States.[3] Eventually a deal was struck between the US and ZTE after the Chinese firm paid a fine and admitted to selling chips, servers, and routers to North Korea.[4] Yet, a year later, it violated this agreement, sparking Commerce Secretary Wilbur Ross in 2018 to implement a ban on ZTE purchasing US components or software for seven years.[5]

This move illustrated the extraordinary dependence of a Chinese tech firm on American components. After the ban was put in place, it emerged that ZTE sourced around a quarter of its components from American firms. For years, economists had spoken abstractly about complex supply chains, especially in the electronics sector. But ZTE's international dependence illustrated this starkly. Media reports suggested that sanctions "threatened to drive the company out of business."[6] One of its key dependencies was on US-origin chips.[7]

Eventually the US cut another deal with ZTE, and the ban was lifted.[8] However, the implications of Chinese firms' dependence on US chips began to reverberate through the US government. ZTE wasn't the only firm that was dependent. So, too, was Huawei, which the US government eyed warily given its complex ties to the Chinese state and its global expansion in telecom networks. In May 2019, the US government added Huawei to a previously obscure Commerce Department authority called the Entity List, which restricted US companies' ability to transact with it.[9] Over the subsequent months the Commerce Department would further tighten this rule.

Finally, in August 2020, the US radically ramped up the power of the Entity List by adding the "Foreign Direct Product Rule," which restricted Huawei from buying chips made with US technology without a license.[10]

Since the ZTE affair, the US government learned something that Chinese leaders had long realized: Almost every chip in the world is made with US technology, including machines and software. This was especially true for the world's leading chipmaker, Taiwan's TSMC, which in 2020 counted Huawei as its second-largest customer.[11] China's leadership had been pushing to domesticate the country's own semiconductor supply chain precisely for this reason. And as the US government ramped up efforts to punish and slow Chinese telecom firms' global expansion, semiconductors emerged as the primary tool.

The impact on Huawei was significant, even though the US quickly issued licenses to allow US and foreign firms to continue selling certain products to the company.[12] Although the company's finances are opaque, it's clear the US measures had a substantial impact. Huawei was forced to divest its smartphone business and reported a dramatic decline in revenue in 2021.[13]

The Huawei saga illustrated the contradictory dynamics undergirding chip policy. US firms were provided licenses to sell chips to Huawei that were deemed not to contradict US security interest. For many of these companies, Huawei was a primary customer, so the impact on their revenue—and, in the longer run, their market and technological leadership—would be impacted by an inability to sell. However, the fact that the US restrictions on Huawei were immediately followed by the issue of licenses substantially reduced the impact on Huawei. It was given space to retool its supply chains and, according to its CEO, found ways to replace over 13,000 components with domestic equivalents. The company still relies on foreign supply for certain capabilities like memory chips and advanced fabrication (which, as discussed below, it has used shell companies to procure from Taiwan's TSMC). Yet it continues to play a major role in China's technological advances—and today is more self-sufficient than it has ever been.

2. Chips and US Trade Policy

The Foreign Direct Product Rule emerged as Washington grasped the importance of semiconductors—and the fact that key chokepoints in their production are all controlled by the US or close partners. China, by contrast, had realized this at least a half decade earlier. In 2014, Xi Jinping first declared semiconductors a "core technology" and established the National Integrated Circuit Industry Investment Fund, which set aside $23 billion to bolster China's chip industry.[14] Provincial and local governments piled in with large funds of their own.

In 2019, a study by the Organisation for Economic Co-operation and Development (OECD) found that, though many governments subsidized their chip industries, China's subsidies were uniquely large and generous. It noted how various "investment vehicles [. . .] have profoundly reshaped China's semiconductor industry, combining to give the state a stronger influence over domestic companies."[15] It also highlighted how the Chinese government was taking direct and indirect equity stakes in chip firms—a much more direct form of subsidy than the cheap loans or tax credits for research and development that other governments used. SMIC, the leading Chinese chipmaker and a would-be competitor to Taiwan's TSMC, saw state ownership increase from 15% in 2004 to over 45% in 2018. "Government provision of equity finance to the semiconductor industry appears to be largely a Chinese phenomenon, and one that has intensified in recent times," the OECD concluded.[16]

Reports like these put semiconductors at the center of US-China trade disputes over China's non-market industrial policy practices. In March 2018, the Office of the US Trade Representative issued a Section 301 report investigating Chinese tech transfer requirements and intellectual property issues.[17] Shortly thereafter, the Trump administration began imposing tariffs on imports from China, including semiconductors.[18]

Although Trump declared a truce in the trade war in December 2018, and the two sides signed a "Phase One" deal in early 2020, the issue of semiconductor trade persisted, even with the change of administration.[19] The Biden administration kept the broad-based tariffs Trump had imposed and pursued new tariffs in specific, strategic sectors. Semiconductors were near the top of the list of critical sectors. In December 2023, the House of Representatives Select Committee on China called on the Commerce Department to impose tariffs on foundational semiconductors from China.[20] The Commerce Department in September 2024 increased the tariff rate on Chinese chips to 50%, doubling the prior rate.[21] Finally, in December 2024, the Commerce Department launched a new Section 301 investigation into China's chip industry, setting the stage for potential future tariff increases or other trade measures.[22]

3. Restricting China's Chip Technology

After the US government realized that the entire world relied on American inputs to make chips, policymakers concluded that preventing China from playing a bigger role in the chip supply chain was not simply an economic interest but a strategic imperative. In 2018, after Chinese firm Fujian Jinhua was deemed to have stolen trade secrets from Micron—which, alongside two Korean firms, was one of only three major producers of critical DRAM (dynamic random access memory) chips—the US government used the Huawei playbook against it.[23] The firm was banned from buying US chipmaking tools and equipment—and unlike Huawei, it did not receive licenses to continue buying any critical inputs. Its production immediately ground to a halt.[24]

Around the same time, US officials began quietly pushing the Dutch government to halt sales of an advanced EUV (extreme ultraviolet) lithography tool to SMIC, the leading manufacturer of processor chips in China.[25] EUV lithography tools are critical for advanced chipmaking; their production is controlled by a single firm, the Netherlands' ASML, which in turn relies on the US for critical inputs, manufacturing, and software. In 2019, it was reported that SMIC's order for an EUV tool—which would have been the first shipped to China—had been delayed.[26] It later emerged that the Dutch decision was partly due to US pressure. Later in 2020, the US restricted exports of US equipment to SMIC, aiming to limit its ability to produce more advanced chips.[27]

When Biden took office, his administration ramped up these restrictions. In October 2022, it imposed new restrictions on the transfer of chipmaking tools to China, banning certain tools from the entire country and other tools from being shipped to certain firms or facilities.[28] The Dutch and Japanese, who also produce high-end chipmaking tools, soon announced their own restrictions, which roughly corresponded to US rules, though with additional loopholes.[29] Though advanced chipmaking tools were restricted, tools used for making less advanced chips continued to be legal to sell to China. The many types of tools that are used in making both more and less advanced chips were subjected to complex controls, allowing their installation in certain facilities but not others.

The Biden administration also imposed new controls on the sale of advanced GPU (graphics processing unit) chips, which are used for artificial intelligence, to China. The US had previously imposed controls on the sale of supercomputing technology to adversaries, but these supercomputer controls were lax and had little impact. The new GPU controls threatened to be far more restrictive because they banned sale of certain chips not only to specific Chinese firms or supercomputers but to the entire country. Because almost all of these GPU chips were designed by US firms (especially Nvidia) and produced by US partners (mostly TSMC in Taiwan), the US had substantial ability—at least in theory—to restrict China's access to computing power needed for artificial intelligence.

4. Chips and Cybersecurity

China's subsidies for its own chip industry were partly aimed at mastering the most cutting-edge chips for AI and advanced computing. However, much of the money China spent went toward building capacity to manufacture mainstream semiconductors used in consumer electronics or industrial applications. The scope of China's investment was vast, implying significant increases in Chinese firms' market share in these segments.

The prospect of becoming more reliant on Chinese chips—for cars, construction equipment, industrial facilities, or other infrastructure—was a matter of deep concern within the US government. Washington had already taken aggressive action to limit Huawei's expansion in telecom equipment in the US and around the world, on the fear that Huawei could use its position either for espionage or simply to shut down telecommunication during a crisis. Secretary of State Mike Pompeo had gone as far as to threaten to cut intelligence sharing with Germany unless it limited Huawei.[30]

Relying on Chinese-made chips, some security experts believed, presented similar challenges. Electronic systems became more complex every year—and as more devices were networked together and made remotely operable, the cybersecurity risks grew. In the past, US chips had been discovered to have included design errors that undermined encryption, for example. The US government worried that Chinese-designed chips might have deliberate backdoors. Alternatively, power management chips—widespread across electronic systems—might be manipulated so that they caused a power surge that disabled an entire device.

National security officials didn't only perceive significant risk in using Chinese chips in sensitive defense or intelligence applications—they also worried that the proliferation of Chinese chips across Western civilian supply chains could present new opportunities for espionage or sabotage.

In 2022, Congress passed a provision called 5949, which prohibited federal agencies from buying chips produced by Chinese firms SMIC, YMTC, and CXMT.[31] This provision was explicitly about government procurement but implicitly intended as a signal to private firms that these Chinese companies were considered unreliable suppliers and that future regulation might impact the ability of firms to procure their chips, too.

The Biden administration also launched investigations into connected capabilities in several specific sectors that highlighted the risks of Chinese electronics and software. After a long investigation, it imposed restrictions on the use of Chinese software and components in connected vehicle systems, over concerns about espionage and remote access capabilities.[32] Similarly, in 2024, a congressional investigation reported that Chinese shipping cranes were discovered to have unexpected modems that allowed remote access—which, if used, could paralyze US ports.[33] This report did not explicitly call out the use of Chinese chips, but it highlighted the risks of reliance on Chinese electronics. Given that an expanding market share for Chinese chipmakers would almost certainly be correlated with market share expansion for Chinese systems designers, policymakers saw these two risks as intertwined.

5. Chip Policy as Insurance Policy

The final aim of US policy was to build resilience, in case—as many officials thought increasingly plausible—China might disrupt Taiwan's ability to export chips via a quarantine, blockade, or outright attack. The pandemic illustrated how dependent nearly every US industry was on semiconductors. Taiwan, meanwhile, was the world's most critical producer of chips, both for ultra-advanced nodes and for many mainstream semiconductors. In the early 2020s, studies found that a loss of access to Taiwan would cause almost inconceivable disruptions to US manufacturing operations and several trillion dollars of economic damage.

The Pentagon had unique concerns about its own supply chains and ability to procure chips amid a crisis. It held a series of consultations with industry about mitigating this problem—and found that it was difficult and costly to solve.[34] The Trump administration and Congress concluded that part of the solution was to bolster chipmaking in the United States. However, for most companies, there was a significant cost differential between US and Taiwanese production, so the industry wouldn't invest more on its own.[35]

In 2022, Congress passed the CHIPS Act, aiming to provide tax credits and subsidies to chipmakers that built new plants in the United States. The legislation catalyzed a series of major investments, including from medium-size US players like Texas Instruments and GlobalFoundries, as well as from foreign behemoths like TSMC and Samsung. TSMC announced initial plans for a 65-billion-dollar investment in Arizona across three plants, which was the largest foreign investment in US history. Samsung announced a dramatic expansion of its footprint in Texas. And Intel—a once-leading US chipmaker that had fallen on hard times—announced an aggressive expansion plan across four different US states.

At the aggregate level, the CHIPS Act catalyzed a surge of investment. Yet not every project was a success. Intel was forced to cut back its capital expenditures as its business model failed to produce better results. Samsung was widely reported to have struggled to attract customers for its new facilities. Many of the medium-sized players had much better results. So, too, did TSMC. Despite having significant issues with permitting and acquiring the right workforce, TSMC has a plant operational in Arizona with quality comparable to that in Taiwan, though with higher costs. In 2025, it followed this with an additional $100 billion in promised investment, doubling down on its US manufacturing operations.

Assessing the China-US Chip War

Has China's chip war worked? As noted above, China's chip war had three main lines of effort: building production capacity, achieving cutting-edge capabilities, and acquiring supply chain independence.

When it comes to chip design, Huawei's HiSilicon arm demonstrated in the late 2010s that it could design high-end application processors for smartphones, one of the most complex types of chips. Now Huawei is trying to expand use in China of its GPU, though it still appears to lag behind market-leader Nvidia. China has yet to produce a high-end central processing unit—used in data centers or laptops—that has won significant market share outside China. And for many other specific types of chips, China still relies on imports. Nevertheless, China has made itself one of the world's leaders in chip design, behind only the US and Taiwan.

For chip manufacturing, however, China still lacks cutting-edge capabilities at scale. In 2024, it emerged that Huawei was using shell companies to produce chips at TSMC—an embarrassing failure of US export controls but also evidence of the significant limitations of China's own chipmaking capabilities. The most advanced chip plants in China, moreover, are still full of imported tools and chemicals—evidence that China hasn't achieved supply chain independence, either.

China is still also heavily reliant on importing semiconductors for its manufacturing base. True, it has built a vast quantity of new chipmaking capacity. It is expected to open 26 new fabrication plants (fabs) during the half decade from 2022 to 2026, versus 19 from Taiwan.[36] Yet in dollar terms, China imports over twice as many chips as it did in 2014, when Chairman Xi declared this a priority. Even though China's own chip manufacturing base has expanded dramatically, China generally produces simpler, cheaper chips. The high-end chips that smartphones, data centers, and personal computers require are still largely imported.

Has America's Chip War Worked?

America's chip war has had five main tactics: punishing individual Chinese firms, especially Huawei; countering Chinese subsidies; restraining China's technological advances; addressing cybersecurity concerns; and insuring itself against an attack on Taiwan.

The restrictions on Huawei have been at best only partially successful. The firm's expansion in Western telecom markets was certainly slowed, but the company was able to innovate around many of the barriers the US imposed. It remains a technological juggernaut and is more closely tied to the Chinese state than ever before. It is also more deeply tied to China's chip industry, including to SMIC, China's leading chip manufacturer, which is now manufacturing GPUs for Huawei.

Countering China's subsidies has also been a challenge. The US has imposed tariffs on chips imported from China, but many of the Chinese chips in US supply chains are assembled into devices in third countries and, thus, are not tariffed. Meanwhile, as noted above, China's tremendous capacity expansion continues apace. It has played a role in discouraging US firms from investing and has driven Wall Street to advocate that US manufacturers of mainstream semiconductors reduce their own capital expenditure—exactly the result one would expect from heavily subsidized Chinese competition. The US has thus far failed to mobilize a response.

The increasing use of Chinese chips in Western supply chains has made efforts to address cybersecurity concerns posed by Chinese chips more difficult. The more Chinese chips, the greater the cybersecurity attack surface. Certain priority industries, including port cranes and autos, have faced specific regulatory efforts. Yet barring further policy change, US manufacturing supply chains look likely to become more, not less, reliant on Chinese-made chips. A December 2024 survey by the US Commerce Department found that 44% of companies included in the survey "were unable to determine whether their products contained any chips manufactured by PRC-based foundries," while 38% reported their products had some Chinese chips.[37] Only 17% of respondents were able to report definitively that their products included no Chinese chips. Moreover, the report found that "most products used in U.S. Government and defense industrial base supply chains likely contain at least one PRC-origin chip."[38]

Have China's technological advances been contained? It seems highly likely that SMIC, China's leading chipmaker, would be producing more advanced chips at greater scale if it had been allowed to buy cutting-edge chipmaking tools. Instead, it is now struggling—and currently failing—to ramp up capacity to meet all of Huawei's cutting-edge demand. This has kept China's access to GPU chips somewhat limited, slowing to some degree its ability to develop and deploy big AI systems.

However, it must also be noted that the chip controls have been highly leaky. TSMC was discovered to have been producing for a Huawei-controlled shell company, which allowed Huawei to access two million AI chips that it could not have produced domestically.[39] Singapore, Malaysia, and other countries in Southeast Asia are widely believed to be smuggling hubs for GPU chips into China.[40] The smuggling of chips has undermined the aim of controls: reducing China's access to computing power at the scale AI requires.

Finally, US efforts to build insurance against a Chinese disruption of Taiwan's chip industry have also been limited in their impact. The CHIPS Act undoubtedly catalyzed an investment boom in the chip industry. Yet TSMC's market position has, if anything, consolidated. The fact that the company has a small but growing footprint in Arizona does provide some diversification. For now, though, the company produces almost all the world's AI chips, as well as critical processors for Apple's iPhones and other key US products. Therefore, for the foreseeable future, US technology firms will remain highly dependent on supply from Taiwan. So, too, will China. And Taiwan will continue to hope that its centrality to the world's chip industry deters China from forcibly changing the status quo.

It is comparatively straightforward to analyze the impact of any one of these tactics. When it comes to a strategy—bringing these tactics together, prioritizing some goals over others—the US has found itself torn between competing goals. The debate hasn't primarily been partisan. Most of these tactics have been embraced to different degrees across administrations, with disagreements occurring less along traditional partisan lines and more around business interests and perceptions of China. The CHIPS Act, for example, was passed by Congress with bipartisan support, though President Trump has disparaged it. Legislation to empower the Committee on Foreign Investment in the United States and congressional pressure to tighten export controls have also come from both parties.

One area of disagreement is about the costs that policymakers are willing to impose on US firms and the US economy by limiting their access to the Chinese market or by forcing changes to their supply chains. A second disagreement is over the willingness to anger China, with some officials across both the Biden and Trump administrations preferring more conciliatory approaches to technology policy, and either preventing or delaying action. A third debate is over the extent to which allies should be coerced to align their policies with those of the United States.

The persistence of these debates reflects a tension thus far unresolved in US technology strategy toward China. How much disruption—to supply chains, to markets, to companies, to other US diplomatic goals—are we willing to tolerate in pursuit of technological advantage? Certainly more than US leaders would have accepted a decade ago. Yet rapid changes still bring costs as well as potential competitive benefits. In many ways the US tech sector—and thus America as a whole—has benefited immensely from the status quo, which makes it hard to change. Silicon Valley's own view has shifted in recent years, but the idea that competition with China should be an organizing principle is still a minority view, coexisting alongside an alternative view that technology should be widely shared.

As a result, after a decade of chip competition, the largest market for many US chip firms is China, and the largest supplier of many key categories of chips to China is US firms. Both countries have chosen to let technology competition coexist uncomfortably alongside interconnected supply chains. The tariffs and counter-tariffs that Trump and Xi levied in spring 2025 may change this, but given that most of the chips the two countries exchange transit via third countries, and are thus not impacted by bilateral tariffs, this impact is unclear. For now, neither side has perceived the potential competitive benefits of a more abrupt change as outweighing the economic costs of such a disruption. Zero-sum technology competition has had to persist alongside economic relationships that powerful groups in both countries still perceive as positive-sum—a complicated context that explains much of the occasional incoherence of both America's and China's chip war strategies.

NOTES

1. Brooke Singman, "GOP Senator Calls to 'Strangle' Huawei in Wake of New Sanctions," *Fox News*, May 15, 2020, https://www.foxnews.com/politics/gop-senator -calls-to-strangle-huawei-in-wake-of-new-sanctions.

2. Coco Feng, "'Are Your Chips Made Locally?' Xi Jinping Prods Construction Vehicle Maker About Semiconductors amid Self-Sufficiency Push," *South China Morning Post*, March 9, 2023, https://www.scmp.com/tech/policy/article/3212932/are-your-chips -made-locally-xi-prods-construction-vehicle-maker-about-semiconductors-amid-self.

3. Paul Mozur, "U.S. Restricts Sales to ZTE, Saying It Breached Sanctions," *New York Times*, March 7, 2016, https://www.nytimes.com/2016/03/08/technology/us -restricts-sales-to-zte-saying-it-breached-sanctions.html.

4. Paul Mozur and Cecilia Kang, "U.S. Fines ZTE of China $1.19 Billion for Breaching Sanctions," *New York Times*, March 7, 2017, https://www.nytimes.com/2017 /03/07/technology/zte-china-fine.html.

5. Steve Stecklow, Karen Freifeld, and Sijia Jiang, "U.S. Ban on Sales to China's ZTE Opens Fresh Front as Tensions Escalate," *Reuters*, https://www.reuters.com/article/world /us-ban-on-sales-to-chinas-zte-opens-fresh-front-as-tensions-escalate-idUSKBN1HN1OX/.

6. Claire Ballentine, "U.S. Lifts Ban That Kept ZTE from Doing Business with American Suppliers," *New York Times*, July 13, 2018, https://www.nytimes.com/2018/07 /13/business/zte-ban-trump.html.

7. Stecklow, Freifeld, and Jiang, "U.S. Ban on Sales to China's ZTE."

8. Ballentine, "U.S. Lifts Ban."

9. David Shepardson and Karen Freifeld, "China's Huawei, 70 Affiliates Placed on U.S. Trade Blacklist," *Reuters*, May 16, 2019, https://www.reuters.com/article/business /chinas-huawei-70-affiliates-placed-on-us-trade-blacklist-idUSKCN1SL2W4/.

10. US Department of Commerce, "Commerce Department Further Restricts Huawei Access to U.S. Technology and Adds Another 38 Affiliates to the Entity List," press release, August 17, 2020, https://2017-2021.commerce.gov/news/press-releases/2020 /08/commerce-department-further-restricts-huawei-access-us-technology-and.html.

11. Cheng Ting-Fang and Lauly Li, "TSMC Halts New Huawei Orders After US Tightens Restrictions," *Nikkei Asia*, May 18, 2020, https://asia.nikkei.com/Spotlight /Huawei-crackdown/TSMC-halts-new-Huawei-orders-after-US-tightens-restrictions.

12. US Department of Commerce, "Huawei Temporary General License Extension Frequently Asked Questions (FAQs)," May 18, 2020, https://www.bis.doc.gov/index.php /documents/pdfs/2446-huawei-entity-list-temporary-general-license-extension-faqs/file; "Huawei Braces for a Steep Drop in Overseas Smartphone Sales," *Bloomberg*, June 16, 2019, https://www.bloomberg.com/news/articles/2019-06-16/huawei-braces-for-a-steep -drop-in-overseas-smartphone-sales.

13. Dan Strumpf, "Huawei Sells Off Honor Phone Business as U.S. Sanctions Bite," *Wall Street Journal*, November 17, 2020, https://www.wsj.com/articles/huawei-sells-off -honor-phone-business-as-u-s-sanctions-bite-11605609850; Dan Strumpf, "U.S. Restrictions Push Huawei's Revenue Down by Nearly a Third," *Wall Street Journal*, December 31, 2021, https://www.wsj.com/articles/u-s-restrictions-push-huaweis-revenue -down-by-nearly-a-third-11640934969.

14. OECD, "Measuring Distortions in International Markets: The Semiconductor Value Chain," OECD Trade Policy Papers No. 234, December 12, 2019, http://dx.doi.org /10.1787/8fe4491d-en.

15. OECD, "Measuring Distortions in International Markets," 51.

16. OECD, "Measuring Distortions in International Markets," 70.

17. Office of the United States Trade Representative, *Findings of the Investigation into China's Acts, Policies, and Practices Related to Technology Transfer, Intellectual Property, and Innovation Under Section 301 of the Trade Act of 1974*, March 22, 2018, https://ustr.gov /sites/default/files/Section%20301%20FINAL.PDF.

18. Ana Swanson, "White House Unveils Tariffs on 1,300 Chinese Products," *New York Times*, April 3, 2018, https://www.nytimes.com/2018/04/03/us/politics/white-house -chinese-imports-tariffs.html.

19. Keith Bradsher and Alan Rappeport, "U.S.-China Trade Truce Gives Both Sides Political Breathing Room," *New York Times*, December 2, 2018, https://www.nytimes .com/2018/12/02/business/trade-truce-china-us.html; Lucy Bayly, "U.S. and China Sign Phase One of Trade Deal After Almost Two Years of Sparring," *NBC News*, January 15, 2020, https://www.nbcnews.com/business/economy/u-s-china-sign-phase-one-trade -deal-after-almost-n1116201.

20. Select Committee on the Strategic Competition Between the United States and the Chinese Communist Party, "Reset, Prevent, Build: A Strategy to Win America's Economic Competition with the Chinese Communist Party," US House of Representatives, December 12, 2023, https://selectcommitteeontheccp.house.gov/media/policy-recommendations /reset-prevent-build-strategy-win-americas-economic-competition-chinese.

21. Mackenzie Hawkins and Jenny Leonard, "US to Gather Intelligence on Chinese Chipmakers as Biden Mulls Tariffs," *Bloomberg*, December 21, 2023, https://www .bloomberg.com/news/articles/2023-12-21/us-to-gather-intelligence-on-chinese-chipmakers -as-biden-mulls-tariffs; David Lawder, "US Locks in Steep China Tariff Hikes, Some Industries Warn of Disruptions," *Reuters*, September 13, 2024, https://www.reuters.com /business/us-locks-steep-china-tariff-hikes-many-start-sept-27-2024-09-13/.

22. Office of the United States Trade Representative, "USTR Initiates Section 301 Investigation on China's Acts, Policies, and Practices Related to Targeting of the Semiconductor Industry for Dominance," press release, December 23, 2024, https:// ustr.gov/about-us/policy-offices/press-office/press-releases/2024/december/ustr -initiates-section-301-investigation-chinas-acts-policies-and-practices-related -targeting.

23. Alan Rappeport, "U.S. to Block Sales to Chinese Tech Company over Security Concerns," *New York Times*, October 29, 2018, https://www.nytimes.com/2018/10/29/us /politics/fujian-jinhua-china-sales.html.

24. Kathrin Hille, "Trade War Forces Chinese Chipmaker Fujian Jinhua to Halt Output," *Financial Times*, January 28, 2019, https://www.ft.com/content/87b5580c-22bf -11e9-8ce6-5db4543da632.

25. Alexandra Alper, Toby Sterling, and Stephen Nellis, "Trump Administration Pressed Dutch Hard to Cancel China Chip Equipment Sale Sources," *Reuters*, January 6, 2020, https://www.reuters.com/article/world/uk/trump-administration-pressed-dutch -hard-to-cancel-china-chip-equipment-sale-so-idUSKBN1Z50H4/.

26. Cheng Ting-Fang and Lauly Li, "Exclusive: ASML Chip Tool Delivery to China Delayed amid US Ire," *Nikkei Asia*, November 6, 2019, https://asia.nikkei.com/Economy /Trade-war/Exclusive-ASML-chip-tool-delivery-to-China-delayed-amid-US-ire.

27. Ana Swanson and Raymond Zhong, "U.S. Places Restrictions on China's Leading Chip Maker," *New York Times*, September 26, 2020, https://www.nytimes.com /2020/09/26/technology/trump-china-smic-blacklist.html.

28. Ana Swanson, "Biden Administration Clamps Down on China's Access to Chip Technology," *New York Times*, October 7, 2022, https://www.nytimes.com/2022/10/07 /business/economy/biden-chip-technology.html.

29. Jenny Leonard and Cagan Koc, "Biden Nears Win as Japan, Dutch Back China Chip Controls," *Bloomberg*, January 27, 2023, https://www.bloomberg.com/news/articles /2023-01-27/japan-netherlands-to-join-us-in-chip-export-controls-on-china.

30. David Brunnstrom, "Pompeo Tells Germany: Use Huawei and Lose Access to Our Data," *Reuters*, May 31, 2019, https://www.reuters.com/article/world/pompeo-tells -germany-use-huawei-and-lose-access-to-our-data-idUSKCN1T10HE/.

31. National Defense Authorization Act for Fiscal Year 2023, 117th Congress, Pub. L No. 117-263, Sec. 5949, December 23, 2022.

32. David Shepardson, "Biden Proposes Banning Chinese Vehicles, 'Connected Car' Technology from US Roads," *Reuters*, September 23, 2024, https://www.reuters.com /business/autos-transportation/biden-proposes-banning-chinese-vehicles-us-roads-with -software-crackdown-2024-09-23/.

33. Dustin Volz, "Chinese Cargo Cranes at U.S. Ports Pose Espionage Risk, Probe Finds," *Wall Street Journal*, September 12, 2024, https://www.wsj.com/politics/national -security/chinese-cargo-cranes-at-u-s-ports-pose-espionage-risk-probe-finds-1bc4b75b.

34. Don Clark, "Pentagon, with an Eye on China, Pushes for Help from American Tech," *New York Times*, October 25, 2019, https://www.nytimes.com/2019/10/25 /technology/pentagon-taiwan-tsmc-chipmaker.html.

35. Asa Fitch, Kate O'Keefe, and Bob Davis, "Trump and Chip Makers Including Intel Seek Semiconductor Self-Sufficiency," *Wall Street Journal*, May 11, 2020, https:// www.wsj.com/articles/trump-and-chip-makers-including-intel-seek-semiconductor-self -sufficiency-11589103002.

36. Stephen Ezell, *How Innovative Is China in Semiconductors?*, Information Technology & Innovation Foundation, August 19, 2024, https://itif.org/publications/2024/08/19 /how-innovative-is-china-in-semiconductors/.

37. Bureau of Industry and Security, Department of Commerce, "Public Report on the Use of Mature-Node Semiconductors,", January 2024, p. 1, https://www.bis.gov /media/documents/public-report-use-mature-node-semiconductors-december-2024.pdf.

38. Bureau of Industry and Security, "Public Report," 3.

39. Gregory C. Allen, "DeepSeek, Huawei, Export Controls, and the Future of the U.S.-China AI Race," Center for Strategic and International Studies, March 7, 2025, https://www.csis.org/analysis/deepseek-huawei-export-controls-and-future-us-china-ai -race.

40. Kristina Partsinevelos, "Nvidia's Unofficial Exports to China Face Scrutiny After Arrest of Silicon Smugglers in Singapore," *CNBC*, March 3, 2025, https://www.cnbc.com /2025/03/03/nvidia-unofficial-exports-to-china-face-scrutiny-after-singapore-arrests.html.

Chapter Three

China's Economic Statecraft and the US Response

Audrye Wong

Economic interdependence has facilitated China's use of economic statecraft— the manipulation of trade or investment ties for political purposes. Globalization and China's integration in the world economy certainly brought about many material benefits and enabled more rapid growth for many countries, China included; at the same time, increasing strategic concerns and great-power competition have sharpened the policy dilemmas of managing China's geoeconomic heft alongside continued economic openness. This chapter focuses on Beijing's use of positive inducements, analyzing the choices and effectiveness of such tools, before turning to assess the scope and impacts of US policy responses.

While China's economic statecraft has altered the strategic calculations for many countries and could have far-reaching implications for the trajectory of great-power competition, Chinese influence is not a foregone conclusion. Beijing has encountered considerable pushback and often shot itself in the foot. At the same time, the diffuse benefits of economic interdependence—that often arise quite naturally—remain a powerful draw that requires Washington to offer concrete alternative or complementary economic opportunities. US-led investment initiatives have ramped up in recent years, providing a promising multilateral basis to

Audrye Wong is an assistant professor of political science and international relations at the University of Southern California and a Jeane Kirkpatrick Fellow at the American Enterprise Institute. Her research focuses on China's economic statecraft, information operations, and foreign influence activities.

change the economic statecraft landscape, but the ability of the US to stay in the game effectively in the long term may well be constrained by recent changes in internal political leadership.

The Landscape of Beijing's Geoeconomic Initiatives

Economic statecraft has long been an important component of China's foreign policy. During the Cold War, the Chinese government distributed foreign aid to undermine support for the Soviet Union and the United States. Today, scholars within China regard the country's economic diplomacy as having transitioned into a new phase. Beijing has adopted a more proactive role in pushing its own economic initiatives, particularly as economic and security interests have become more intertwined. In particular, China's relative success after the 2008–2009 financial crisis sparked a major shift in Beijing's approach, leading it to become more ambitious and confident in its economic statecraft. Arguably, Beijing's new initiatives represent an underlying dissatisfaction with existing US-led regional frameworks and highlight a desire among Chinese elites to take on a greater regional leadership role.

Under President Xi Jinping, these trends have accelerated in the form of more concrete initiatives and the development of a more aggressive form of economic statecraft. China's "going out" strategy of encouraging outward investment by Chinese firms was repackaged into the sweeping Belt and Road Initiative (BRI, formerly One Belt One Road), which is now part of the Chinese Communist Party constitution and is seen as Xi's signature foreign policy initiative. As such, the BRI constitutes a substantive and significant part of Beijing's desire to reform the international order into one conducive to its interests.[1] While stemming from the "March West" strategy—originally articulated by influential Peking University scholar Wang Jisi,[2] who advocated for China to focus its foreign policy engagement on Central Asia and the Middle East and to minimize zero-sum tensions with the United States in East Asia—the BRI has now expanded into a far-reaching, if tenuously defined, global initiative that is provoking further geopolitical concerns. With local Chinese governments and Chinese companies (state-owned and private) eager to jump on the bandwagon for political benefits and profit-seeking motives, the BRI quickly ballooned to encompass a seemingly limitless variety of projects across multiple continents.

Scholarly estimates of the scale of overseas Chinese investment vary considerably, depending on the methodology used. The AidData project at the College of William and Mary puts the figure of Chinese official development financing, including official aid and unofficial financing flows, at US$680 billion from 2014 to 2021. The China Overseas Development Finance database, run by Boston University's Global Development Policy Center, which employs a stricter definition of financing by state policy banks, recorded US$277.8 billion of commitments in the same time period. China's Ministry of Commerce reports BRI investments totaling US$126.14 billion from 2014 to 2021 and US$212.6 billion from 2014 to 2024, although official government statistics are likely suspect; while these figures show a continuous increase each year (even during the COVID-19 pandemic), most independent scholarly analyses have found dips in overseas Chinese investment and financing in recent years. The American Enterprise Institute's China Global Investment Tracker, run by Derek Scissors, calculates the total value of overseas construction and investment projects (beyond the BRI and beyond just developing countries) to be US$1.7 trillion between 2014 and 2024.

Evolution and Recalibration of the Belt and Road Initiative

The BRI has gone through various rounds of rebranding, due to a combination of political pushback and economic headwinds. As will be discussed in the following section, Beijing's "subversive carrot" tactics, including extensive corruption and other violations of the rule of law, have encountered public backlash in many places, leading to growing skepticism toward the BRI and related projects. But its enshrinement in the Chinese constitution and its implications for Xi's foreign policy legacy suggest that the BRI is here to stay.

In 2017, Beijing responded to criticism by seeking to curb corruption and "irrational" overseas BRI investments[3] and by increasing monitoring and regulatory efforts to crack down on illegal activities.[4] During the 2018 summit of the Forum on China-Africa Cooperation, Xi emphasized cooperation on vital infrastructure as opposed to "vanity projects."[5] At the second Belt and Road Forum in April 2019, Chinese leaders went beyond the usual bland rhetoric of "win-win" by emphasizing mantras of quality infrastructure, zero corruption, high transparency, and clean governance.[6] An analysis of BRI policy documents by one Chinese scholar noted a greater focus on broader development issues and sensitivity to global public opinion in 2023, as compared to more economically oriented language in 2015 statements.[7]

In addition to rhetorical shifts, the Chinese government implemented institutional changes. In 2018, it established the China International Development Cooperation Agency (CIDCA) to better coordinate foreign aid. This agency is directly supervised by the State Council and reports to the foreign minister. A 2021 directive clarified that CIDCA and the Ministry of Foreign Affairs should make long-term strategic plans for aid allocations, while the Ministry of Commerce, which had traditionally been the most influential agency involved in foreign aid and had typically emphasized economic goals, was relegated to a primarily implementing role.[8]

Environmental, social, and governance (ESG) considerations also became more prominent in Chinese financing decisions, including at the two major policy banks and the State Administration of Foreign Exchange. An AidData study found that environmental and governance risk safeguards had increased considerably in Chinese overseas infrastructure financing contracts post-2017, although the de facto implementation of risk mitigation continues to lag behind.[9] The same study argued that Beijing's efforts to de-risk overseas projects, including ESG and debt repayment risks, underscore its continued ambition underlying the BRI.

The trendy tagline is now "small yet beautiful" (*xiaoermei*)—prioritizing smaller-scale and more economically viable projects in digital and green infrastructure, such as data centers, rather than the previous emphasis on massive transportation and power projects. Additionally, the landscape of Chinese financiers has become more diverse: While the two major policy banks, China Development Bank and China Eximbank, are tightening their purse strings, other actors such as state-owned enterprises, private companies, provincial banks, and Chinese venture capital firms are becoming more active.[10]

Beijing has also taken pains to emphasize multilateral cooperation and the non-zero-sum nature of its geoeconomic initiatives. Indeed, studies suggest that working with other countries and multilateral institutions could help China's goal of reducing debt repayment risks.[11] At the 2023 BRI Forum, Foreign Minister Wang Yi of the People's Republic of China (PRC) told reporters that the BRI was an open platform that could be aligned with other connectivity initiatives such as the EU's Global Gateway.[12] He again emphasized that China was "willing to synergize high-quality Belt and Road cooperation" at the 2025 Munich Security Conference.[13] On the other hand, Wang described the US-led Partnership for Global Infrastructure and Investment as positive "competition" to accelerate development in the Global South, while criticizing attempts at zero-sum politicization.[14]

GLOBAL DEVELOPMENT INITIATIVE

China is also doubling down on another grand economic diplomacy effort—the Global Development Initiative (GDI), first announced by President Xi Jinping at the 2021 UN General Assembly and framed as a call to achieve the UN's

Sustainable Development Goals and the 2030 Agenda. While it remains a broad and sweeping vision, Beijing has actively touted the GDI in bilateral and multilateral venues over the past year. The GDI has ostensibly garnered international support, as seen by the launch of a 55-nation strong Group of Friends of GDI at the UN and in its appearance on the agenda of the Davos World Economic Forum. In June 2022, Xi chaired a "High-Level Dialogue on Global Development" with leaders of 18 countries, ranging from Malaysia and Cambodia to the BRICS nations (Brazil, Russia, India, China, and South Africa). Xi also promoted the GDI alongside a parallel Global Security Initiative (GSI) during a whirlwind series of overseas diplomatic visits in fall 2022, including at the Shanghai Cooperation Organization summit, the G20 summit, and the inaugural China–Arab States summit. In September 2022, the Foreign Ministry released a list of 50 first-pool GDI projects, largely centered on poverty reduction, pandemic response, and food security.[15]

Compared to the BRI's initial launch, China has taken pains to emphasize its role through the GDI as a positive-sum global player providing debt relief, grants, public goods, and capacity-building to address development inequities, as well as working compatibly rather than competitively with existing regional and multilateral development frameworks. Additionally, Beijing has portrayed these initiatives as contrasting with supposed US preoccupation with great-power competition and Washington's economic and political containment of China. The parallel framing of the GDI and GSI (and the subsequent addition of a Global Civilization Initiative) can be seen as Beijing's attempt to stake out a global vision spanning the economic, security, and political domains. As the PRC foreign minister put it at the 2025 Munich Security Conference, these three initiatives aim to address a perceived "deficit" in development, security, and governance.[16] This rhetoric again positions China as an alternative to the purportedly interventionist and destabilizing stance of the United States.

Subversion Alongside Seduction: How Effective Are China's Economic Inducements?

From the BRI to the GDI, the lure of the Chinese market and the financing and growth opportunities offered by Chinese investments—all enabled by the impressive growth of the Chinese economy over the last few decades—have entrenched widespread perceptions of China as an indispensable economic partner. Many assume that Beijing has easily leveraged its economic clout to buy acquiescence to its political interests. But the track record is mixed. China has met with some successes but also many failures in its attempts at influencing the policy choices of other countries. The strong gravitational pull of the Chinese economy does not necessarily mean that others are altering their political orbits. In this section, I introduce a framework to evaluate China's economic inducement strategies and their political impacts.

SUBVERSIVE CARROTS

My research shows how the effectiveness of inducements depends on both China's approach—subversive versus legitimate—and the strength of domestic political institutions in recipient countries.[17] China often provides economic inducements in illicit and opaque ways that circumvent political processes and institutions—what I call "subversive carrots." Chinese companies have offered bribes and kickbacks, sometimes with the tacit approval of Chinese officials, to elites in countries receiving investment or aid projects. At other times, Chinese companies have bypassed the process of competitive bidding and regulatory approval to secure a contract, often at inflated costs, generating extra profits for both Chinese actors and local elites. In many ways, this approach reflects China's domestic political economy, where businesses depend on political connections, corruption is widespread, and few regulations govern foreign investment and foreign aid.

Subversive carrot tactics have allowed China to make inroads in places where leaders can act with relative impunity, but they have backfired in countries where leaders face accountability mechanisms. Cambodia is a classic case of subversive carrot success in a low-accountability system, where Chinese largesse through murky aid and investment projects has bought Cambodian advocacy for Beijing's expansionist positions on the South China Sea disputes. At a 2012 meeting of ASEAN (the Association of Southeast Asian Nations), Cambodia wielded its position as chair to block discussions of these disputes, leading to an unprecedented failure to issue a joint statement. The Cambodian foreign minister cut off delegates who tried to raise the issue and stormed out of the room when they proposed a watered-down statement. A Filipino delegate at the meeting recounted to me how the PRC vice foreign minister was "given a platform to lecture us on Scarborough Shoal" while the Filipinos were denied the chance to voice their concerns. Government officials I interviewed in the region described Cambodia's behavior at the summit as the result of a "straight-up monetary deal" in which Beijing paid off the Cambodian government in exchange for its support. In the months before the meeting, senior Chinese leaders visited Phnom

Penh, offering additional grants and loans for infrastructure and development projects worth hundreds of millions of dollars. Since this incident, ASEAN has become increasingly divided and incapable of dealing with these territorial disputes.

While seemingly an easy and cheap approach, subversive carrots also spark public dissatisfaction and elite contestation, with Beijing and Chinese-financed projects often getting entangled in political scandals and campaign rhetoric. In the Philippines, corrupt telecommunications and rail projects in the 2000s led to public backlash and a Senate investigation. In Malaysia, a major corruption scandal implicating Chinese-financed investments and involving the incumbent prime minister led to a resounding electoral defeat, marking the first opposition victory in the country's history. The succeeding administration quickly suspended a number of Chinese projects and renegotiated plans for a major railway.

On a strategic level, the negative spillover effects on Beijing's global image (along with heightened use of coercion) has undermined China's attempts to position itself as a great power that ostensibly promotes win-win cooperation and preaches noninterference in internal affairs. In a global survey of developing country elites, researchers found that leaders appreciated the economic potential of BRI investments but maintained concerns over the lack of transparency, low quality, limited local capacity-building, and heightened corruption. In general, compared to the United States and many other countries of the Organisation for Economic Cooperation and Development (OECD), China was seen as having similar levels of raw influence but of a less positive ilk.[18] On the other hand, continued democratic backsliding globally could provide more opportunities for Beijing to use subversive carrots to greater effect, potentially creating a cycle where illicit economic influence further entrenches the hold of authoritarians.

Legitimate Seduction

In other cases, building up pro-China constituencies through legitimate inducements has successfully created contestation over how to manage issues with Beijing. This approach is rooted in a broader logic of economic interdependence: China seeks to cultivate foreign stakeholders that have an interest in good relations. Beijing promotes trade and investment in the hope that groups that benefit from economic exchange with China will lobby their own governments to seek cooperative relations with the country. Convinced by these elites of the importance of the Chinese economy, political leaders will work to minimize any disagreements with Beijing.

In present-day Germany, we see the political influence of business groups invested in continued economic ties with China alongside internal divisions among politicians and key ministries on national strategy toward China. Berlin has traditionally chosen an approach that prioritized economics and the principle of *Wandel durch Handel*, or "change through trade." In 2019, Germany exported almost US$118 billion of goods to China, which represented over half the value of all EU exports to the country. Additionally, access to the Chinese market has been a big draw for major German companies. Germany's blue-chip industrial behemoths, such as Volkswagen, Siemens, and chemical manufacturer BASF, were among the first Western firms to invest in China in the 1980s. Automakers, including BMW, Daimler, and Volkswagen, have major production facilities located in China, with a third or more of their profits generated there.

By many accounts, German industry has been very influential in Berlin's policymaking toward China. As chancellor from 2005 to 2021, Angela Merkel made a dozen trips to China, often consulting with major German firms beforehand and bringing high-level business delegations with her to Beijing. In 2013, after German automakers lobbied to avoid confronting China over trade practices, Berlin successfully stopped the EU from imposing duties on Chinese solar panel imports. In 2020, Merkel led the push to conclude the EU's investment deal with China, despite requests from the incoming administration of Joseph R. Biden to hold off and coordinate on policy.

Her successor, Olaf Scholz, was the first G7 leader since the pandemic to visit China in November 2022, accompanied by a sizable business delegation. Before his trip, Scholz went against the advice of his ministers and the EU to agree to Chinese investment in Hamburg, the country's largest seaport. During his second trip to Beijing in April 2024, the chancellor remained reluctant to speak out publicly about Taiwan or human rights issues such as Tibet or Xinjiang. Reports suggest that German businesses urged his team to downplay concerns over Chinese overcapacity and focus on maintaining German access to the Chinese market. Additionally, Scholz requested to delay impending arrests of German citizens over spying for China and asked the European Commission to delay announcing a case on discriminatory Chinese procurement practices in medical devices. Also, Berlin had previously denied a request by Taiwan's then vice president–elect to travel as a private citizen through Germany (whereas she was allowed into other European countries such as Belgium and Poland).

The gap between Germany and the rest of Europe has been evident over the EU's 2024 anti-subsidy investigation into Chinese electric vehicles (EVs). Berlin's position is driven by a strong fear of Beijing imposing retaliatory tariffs against German automakers, as admitted frankly by the German economy minister. The German chancellor described the EU's move as "protectionist," while the CEO of Mercedes-Benz urged Brussels to do the opposite—to lower rather than raise tariffs on Chinese EVs in order to ensure a "level playing field" and build "economic win-win situations"—language that not only parroted Beijing's win-win narrative but was also ironic given analyses of Chinese government subsidies leading to overcapacity and artificially cheap EVs.

Evaluating the Lure of Inducements

Beijing's economic statecraft has been most effective at achieving short-term transactional goals, such as vetoing a multilateral statement, as with Cambodia in ASEAN. Hungary, Serbia, and Greece have on various occasions vetoed EU statements. In general, China's economic statecraft has operated more by preference multiplication—empowering groups with overlapping preferences to advocate for more cooperative ties with China. Persuading actors to change their policy preferences has been more difficult for Beijing. Legitimate inducements that operate by the law, bring economic benefits to the public, and engage a broad range of stakeholders are more likely to shift attitudes. My interviews with elites in Malaysia found that despite previous pushback against corruption-tainted Chinese projects, an established record of other economically beneficial Chinese investments has entrenched national and local politicians' views of China's economic importance along with their desire to minimize confrontation over issues such as the South China Sea and Xinjiang.

Beijing appears best able to achieve influence through the diffuse latency of economic interdependence. China as a crucial economic partner remains a compelling narrative for many countries, often conditioning the attitudes and decisions of many political leaders. Perhaps the deepest economic influence comes paradoxically when Beijing may not have set out to achieve an explicit political goal but can subsequently leverage such influence during moments of critical decision-making.

On the flip side, Beijing's growing use of economic coercion has also made countries more fearful of becoming too reliant on China. The Chinese government's refusal to restructure bad debts could negatively affect China's image in the Global South and certainly its claims to be a benevolent provider of development where it is needed most. How Beijing responds to these issues will shape its reputation and how enticing its economy will remain.

Driving Wedges: Inducements as a Disruptor

Economic inducements can help a rising challenger such as China gain strategic influence without inciting immediate counterbalancing or censure, unlike the overt use of military force. While subversive carrots can peel off targeted elites, legitimate seduction done right promises broader benefits to recipient countries as well, making it harder to turn down the lure of China's economic statecraft (rooted also in its large market size, cost advantages, and innovative technologies). By altering the perceived costs and benefits for individual countries, inducements can create divisions and undermine multilateral coordination on responding to Beijing's actions.

While a fundamental political realignment toward Beijing remains unlikely, economic statecraft has been able to drive wedges within countries as well as between different countries, thus inhibiting effective China-skeptic coalitions—particularly useful for a rising power seeking to reduce opposition to its interests as well as inhibit alignment with US interests. While Washington by and large sees Beijing as a geopolitical rival threatening US dominance and leadership, many developing countries prefer to view China through the lens of trade, investment, and development. By making even starker the trade-offs of concrete economic benefits versus relatively abstract shifts in the security order, economic inducements further accentuate these differing priorities. In Asia, while seeking continued US presence in the region, many countries view China as the inevitable economic center of gravity and have publicly articulated that they do not want to have to choose between the two great powers. Even traditional US allies and partners such as South Korea remain eager for closer economic ties with China, which has in turn shaped their willingness to openly criticize China or be seen as siding with Washington.

One major lesson that Beijing has drawn from Russia's 2022 invasion of Ukraine is the challenge that the United States faces in creating and sustaining a global coalition to counterbalance Chinese influence. If most governments outside of a small group of like-minded allies and partners have preferred not to publicly criticize and isolate Moscow—a relative pariah in the international system—for its unprovoked use of military force, things will likely be even harder when it comes to censuring a country that is a much more central and integrated player in the global economy.

Ultimately, Beijing's economic statecraft will make it harder for Washington to marshal a united and sustainable coalition against China. Even if Beijing has a spotty record of effectively using inducements, it has been sufficient to sow divisions and create roadblocks to multilateral coordination. While it may not be easy for China to stake out its own geopolitical claims, at the very least it is able to undermine US efforts to counter Beijing's presence and influence.

Responding to Beijing: Policy Initiatives by the United States and Its Partners

While matching the scale of Chinese overseas investment and development financing remains challenging, the United States has slowly ramped up its efforts to compete and counter Beijing's dominance. One of Washington's first important actions was to modernize its development financing institutions. The bipartisan BUILD Act passed by Congress in October 2018 created a new US development agency, the US International Development Finance Corporation (DFC), replacing the outdated Overseas Private Investment Corporation (OPIC).

The new DFC has an expanded set of tools at its disposal, including authority to make equity investments beyond just loans, provide technical assistance, and take on riskier capital arrangements; it also has greater flexibility to work with non-US investors and a higher spending cap of $60 billion compared to OPIC's $29 billion.[19] Unlike China's state-led approach, the DFC would continue to emphasize the importance of mobilizing private capital to support sustainable development alongside US foreign policy goals. Reportedly, the first Donald Trump administration had planned simply to eliminate OPIC, but skilled advocacy by senior officials was able to highlight its importance in countering Beijing's influence and promoting Trump's America First agenda.[20]

In 2019, the United States, Japan, and Australia announced the Blue Dot Network (BDN), established to provide certification for infrastructure projects that meet high standards of sustainability, transparency, and developmental impact. This subsequently became a multilateral initiative through the OECD that was officially launched in April 2024.[21] The goal is similarly to provide private investors with greater confidence in markets that may be seen as traditionally riskier, thus stimulating greater financial flows and investment into developing economies. As of March 2025, three certified projects (in Brazil, Turkey, and Palau) were listed on the BDN website.[22] Analysts have noted that the governments of developing countries need to be incentivized to jump through additional hoops of certification, for instance through tangible advantages in lending rates or loan terms.[23]

In 2021, the G7 announced the Build Back Better World (B3W) initiative, aiming to "leverage the private sector for US$40 trillion in quality infrastructure investment by 2035," under the four pillars of health care, gender equality and equity, climate and environment, and digital technology.[24] The B3W was relaunched the following year as the Partnership for Global Infrastructure and Investment (PGI), adding new pillars of energy security and digital connectivity. Then-president Biden announced that the United States would mobilize US$200 billion of investment through grants, federal financing, and the private sector, with an overall goal from G7 countries and the private sector of US$600 billion over the next five years.[25]

Compared to B3W, PGI has demonstrated a greater emphasis on "hard" infrastructure projects, such as solar power and clean energy as well as telecommunications and undersea cables.[26] Announcements by the Biden administration during subsequent G7 summits highlighted US$30 billion mobilized by the US in 2023 and US$60 billion in 2024, although the additional $30 billion in 2024 appears to be largely broad capital commitments from private investors (such as BlackRock, KKR, and Microsoft).[27] A preliminary manual tally of US and partner commitments until 2024, based on public announcements, gives a total figure of US$94 billion in concrete projects, not including technical assistance.

Under the PGI, Washington has also prioritized the establishment of economic corridors designed to spur broader commercial partnerships and local economic development. A flagship project is the Lobito Corridor, centered on a rail line linking Angola's Lobito Port to the Democratic Republic of the Congo (DRC) and landlocked Zambia, along with additional investments in those and neighboring countries in solar power, data centers, telecommunications and internet connectivity, agribusiness, and critical minerals mining and processing. Perhaps the largest symbol of US efforts to counter Chinese presence in Africa—Beijing has been involved in the nearby TAZARA railway project and is dominant in cobalt mining in the DRC—the Lobito Corridor aims to boost trade and facilitate export access to global markets for these mineral-rich economies. During his trip to Angola in December 2024, then-president Biden pledged another US$600 million to the project, for a total US investment of US$4 billion. Additional commitments from partner countries and African banks bring the total value to US$6 billion.

In April 2024, the United States, Japan, and the Philippines also announced the Luzon Economic Corridor, with three initial projects: a US$868-million Subic-Clark railway connecting special economic zones in the two cities (former sites of US naval and air bases), a $174-million facilities expansion at Clark International Airport, and a $152-million Clark National Food Hub to boost the local agricultural sector. The Luzon Corridor is significant because it represents the PGI's first major foray into Southeast Asia.[28] European and Arab governments have also signed under the PGI banner a memorandum of understanding for an India–Middle East–Europe Economic Corridor, although details remain scarce and progress has been slowed by ongoing conflicts in the region.[29]

Another multilateral initiative of note is the Minerals Security Partnership (MSP), launched in June 2022 with the goal of accelerating the development of diverse critical-minerals supply chains, including the coordination of development finance institutions and export credit agencies of partner governments. While the Biden administration emphasized the significance of clean-energy industry as well as adherence to ESG sustainability standards, the second Trump administration has removed such references and reemphasized mining investments.[30] As of September 2024, the MSP claimed 32 projects in progress across a range of critical minerals, largely in upstream extraction and midstream processing.[31] Seven projects were identified as reaching key milestones, including a copper exploration project in Zambia, germanium processing in the DRC, graphite mining in Tanzania, and other projects in Canada, the United States, and Australia.

Taking Stock and Looking Ahead

A common criticism from the developing world has been that Washington attempts to pressure countries not to accept Chinese investment and financing due to great-power rivalry, while failing to demonstrate sustained political commitment or concrete alternatives to fill the infrastructure gap and support economic development. The PGI certainly represents the most tangible and large-scale effort to get the United States and its partners into the game.

As many of these projects are still in relatively early stages—and infrastructure projects tend to have a long time horizon—it is currently difficult to assess the full impact of the PGI and related initiatives. While some of this private sector investment might have occurred anyway, the PGI (and MSP) umbrella sends a strong political signal of Western commitment and potentially has a catalytic effect on spurring more private capital flows.

The arrival of the second Trump administration since January 2025 could disrupt this recent positive momentum. Trump's focus on tariffs as a punitive measure will distract political focus from investments as an important way to win global goodwill and promote global development alongside US foreign policy interests—and to counter China. The effort by the Department of Government Efficiency, led by Elon Musk, to slash government spending will certainly affect the ability of the US to marshal resources for foreign investment and aid, particularly given the recent axing of agencies such as USAID, which has played an important role in providing technical assistance and implementing feasibility assessments for PGI-related projects.

The new administration has so far tacitly supported PGI, including joint statements with Japan and India on high-quality infrastructure partnerships. In April 2025, the acting US ambassador to Angola led a publicity tour of the Lobito Corridor to signal continued US commitment.[32] At the same time, the Trump administration appears to be focused on minerals access, while other projects involving food security, telecommunications, and broader economic development (including those funded by USAID) have already been or are likely to be diminished.

The DFC continues to have bipartisan support to reauthorize its mandate, increase its lending cap, and improve institutional functions.[33] But Trump advisors have floated ideas of turning it into a sovereign wealth fund, while an executive order in March 2025 called on the DFC to fund domestic investments into minerals production, which goes against its existing mission.[34] (A previous authorization by Trump to make domestic investments during the COVID-19 pandemic had ended in scandal.) Trump's nominee for DFC head has stated that he wants "pro-market" investments that bring returns for Americans, and he expressed interest in infrastructure and mining projects in Greenland, which the president wants to control.[35]

Given the administration's strong skepticism toward climate change and renewable energy, previously stated commitments to financing clean energy could all be up in the air or dependent on follow-through from other actors such as the European Union; in general, private companies are already starting to scale back their sustainability commitments, and under Trump, Washington has withdrawn from multilateral initiatives such as the Just Energy Transition Partnership, designed to help developing countries transition away from fossil fuel use. This would only give more legitimacy to China's claims of global leadership in clean energy and its touting of green BRI projects. It would also be a missed opportunity for the United States, which is seen by many developing country leaders as the preferred partner over China for ESG sectors.[36]

Additionally, Trump's proclivity for attacking traditional allies and partners will likely make it harder to coordinate complex large-scale investment projects that have often included multiple governments and private investors. Multilateralism has been a key defining feature of PGI projects; for instance, the Lobito Corridor involves not just the United States but also the European Union, recipient country governments, and multilateral financing institutions such as the Africa Finance

Corporation and the African Development Bank. While Trump may be persuaded on the need to compete with China, his administration is likely to adopt a more transactional and bilateral basis for investment decisions and critical minerals access.

Washington also faces two broader challenges. First, the central role of public-private partnerships, with government-led financing as a catalyst for private sector activity, can be an attractive alternative model but makes it harder to be a peer competitor with Chinese financing and investment that is often state-led (although that is changing). This also makes it harder to overcome structural market challenges, such as displacing Beijing's dominance in the critical minerals sector, where Chinese overproduction has led to falling prices of minerals such as graphite. Even with DFC financing and other sources of support, private companies are finding it challenging to operate in mining and processing.[37]

Second, the United States and its partners need to pair investment projects with on-the-ground public diplomacy and credit claiming. Beijing has been particularly adept at seizing the narrative upper hand that China is the indispensable number one economic partner (even if that is not true) and at sending ambassadors and government officials with much public fanfare to project launches (Chinese officials also often pen accompanying opinion pieces in local papers). This has entrenched widespread public and elite perceptions of the importance (or inevitability) of continued Chinese economic presence.

Even though China's record of economic statecraft has been rocky, and many countries no longer look at China through rose-tinted glasses, the lure of the Chinese market and Chinese financing remains, especially when there are not many alternatives available. Interestingly, the two countries could be converging in terms of approaches: Beijing is rebranding itself as a high-quality investor in line with international standards, while Washington has been venturing more into hard infrastructure. Concrete US commitment to development financing as well as infrastructure and investment projects, which are still very much in demand in the Global South, will give Washington greater political legitimacy (and benefit recipient countries) while limiting Beijing's ability to divide and conquer on issues that it cares about.

NOTES

1. Avery Goldstein, "China's Grand Strategy Under Xi Jinping: Reassurance, Reform, and Resistance," *International Security* 45, no. 1 (2020): 164–201.

2. Yun Sun, "March West: China's Response to the U.S. Rebalancing," Brookings *Up Front* blog, January 31, 2013, https://www.brookings.edu/blog/up-front/2013/01/31 /march-west-chinas-response-to-the-u-s-rebalancing.

3. "China to Curb 'Irrational' Overseas Investment by Domestic Firms in 'Belt and Road' Projects," *Reuters*, August 18, 2017, https://www.reuters.com/article/business /china-to-curb-irrational-overseas-belt-and-road-investment-state-planner -idUSKCN1AY1UE/.

4. "China to Set Up System to Monitor Its Firms Overseas," *Reuters*, November 28, 2017, https://www.reuters.com/article/business/china-to-set-up-system-to-monitor-its -firms-overseas-idUSKBN1DS0YI/.

5. "China-Africa Summit: Xi Denies Money Being Spent on Vanity Projects," *BBC*, September 3, 2018, https://www.bbc.co.uk/news/world-africa-45394668.

6. Jane Perlez, "China Retools Vast Global Building Push Criticized as Bloated and Predatory," *New York Times*, April 25, 2019, https://www.nytimes.com/2019/04/25 /business/china-belt-and-road-infrastructure.html.

7. Kunling Zhang, "A Policy Analysis of the Belt and Road Initiative," in *China: Regaining Growth Momentum After the Pandemic*, ed. Ligang Song and Yixiao Zhou (ANU Press, 2024).

8. Jingdong Yuan, Fei Su, and Xuwan Ouyang, "China's Evolving Approach to Foreign Aid," Stockholm International Peace Research Institute, May 2022, https://doi .org/10.55163/WTNJ4163.

9. Bradley C. Parks, Ammar A. Malik, Brooke Escobar, et al., *Belt and Road Reboot: Beijing's Bid to De-Risk Its Global Infrastructure Initiative*, AidData, College of William and Mary, November 6, 2023, https://www.aiddata.org/publications/belt-and-road-reboot.

10. Abdou Rahim Lema, "From a 'Project of the Century' to 'Small Is Beautiful': The Changing Face of the BRI in Africa," Munk School of Global Affairs & Public Policy, July 4, 2023, https://munkschool.utoronto.ca/belt-road/research/project-century-small -beautiful-changing-face-bri-africa.

11. Parks, Malik, Escobar, et al., *Belt and Road Reboot*.

12. Ministry of Foreign Affairs, The People's Republic of China, "Wang Yi: China Is Willing to Align the Belt and Road Initiative, an Open Platform, with Other Connectivity Initiatives," October 19, 2023, https://www.fmprc.gov.cn/eng./xw/zyxw/202405 /t20240530_11332366.html.

13. Zichen Wang, "Wang Yi at Munich Security Conference," *Pekingnology*, February 15, 2025, https://www.pekingnology.com/p/wang-yi-at-munich-security-conference.

14. Ministry of Foreign Affairs, "Wang Yi."

15. Ministry of Foreign Affairs, The People's Republic of China, "List of First-Batch Projects of GDI Project Pool," https://www.mfa.gov.cn/eng/zy/gb/202405/P020220921624707087888.pdf.

16. Wang, "Wang Yi at Munich Security Conference."

17. Audrye Wong, *Subversion and Seduction: China's Economic Statecraft* (Oxford University Press, forthcoming); Audrye Wong, "How Not to Win Allies and Influence Geopolitics: China's Self-Defeating Economic Statecraft," *Foreign Affairs*, May/June 2021.

18. Samantha Custer, Ana Horigoshi, and Kelsey Marshall, *BRI from the Ground Up: Leaders from 129 Countries Evaluate a Decade of Beijing's Signature Initiative*, AidData,

College of William and Mary, March 2014, https://www.aiddata.org/publications/bri
-from-the-ground-up.

19. Daniel F. Runde and Romina Bandura, "The BUILD Act Has Passed: What's
Next?," Critical Questions column, Center for Strategic and International Studies,
October 12, 2018, https://www.csis.org/analysis/build-act-has-passed-whats-next.

20. Mercy A. Kuo, "The US International Development Finance Corporation and
China Insights from Riva Levinson," *The Diplomat*, October 25, 2018, https://thediplomat
.com/2018/10/the-us-international-development-finance-corporation-and-china/.

21. See Department of State, "Blue Dot Network," https://www.state.gov/blue-dot
-network/.

22. Blue Dot Network, https://www.bluedot-network.org/projects.

23. Matthew P. Goodman, Daniel F. Runde, and Jonathan E. Hillman, "Connecting
the Blue Dots," Center for Strategic and International Studies, February 26, 2020,
https://reconasia.csis.org/connecting-blue-dots/.

24. Conor M. Savoy and Shannon McKeown, "Opportunities for Increased Multilateral Engagement with B3W," Center for Strategic and International Studies, May 6, 2022,
https://www.csis.org/analysis/opportunities-increased-multilateral-engagement-b3w.

25. The American Presidency Project, "FACT SHEET: President Biden and G7
Leaders Formally Launch the Partnership for Global Infrastructure and Investment,"
June 26, 2022, https://www.presidency.ucsb.edu/documents/fact-sheet-president-biden
-and-g7-leaders-formally-launch-the-partnership-for-global.

26. See The White House, "ADDITIONAL PGII PROJECTS," June 2022, https://
bidenwhitehouse.archives.gov/wp-content/uploads/2022/06/Other-PGII-projects.pdf.

27. See The White House, "FACT SHEET: Partnership for Global Infrastructure and
Investment at the G7 Summit," May 20, 2023, https://bidenwhitehouse.archives.gov
/briefing-room/statements-releases/2023/05/20/fact-sheet-partnership-for-global
-infrastructure-and-investment-at-the-g7-summit/; The American Presidency Project,
"FACT SHEET: Partnership for Global Infrastructure and Investment at the G7
Summit," June 13, 2024, https://www.presidency.ucsb.edu/documents/fact-sheet
-partnership-for-global-infrastructure-and-investment-the-g7-summit-0.

28. Kevin Chen, "The Luzon Economic Corridor: A Badly-Needed Win for the US in
Southeast Asia?," *The Diplomat*, May 20, 2024, https://thediplomat.com/2024/05/the
-luzon-economic-corridor-a-badly-needed-win-for-the-us-in-southeast-asia/.

29. Abdul Moiz Khan, "The India-Middle East-Europe Economic Corridor (IMEC):
Too Little, Too Late?," Carnegie Endowment for International Peace, December 12,
2023, https://carnegieendowment.org/sada/2023/12/the-india-middle-east-europe
-economic-corridor-imec-too-little-too-late?lang=en.

30. US Department of State, "Minerals Security Partnership," accessed April 11,
2025, https://2021-2025.state.gov/minerals-security-partnership/.

31. US Department of State, "Joint Statement of the Minerals Security Partnership
Principals' Meeting 2024," September 27, 2024, https://2021-2025.state.gov/joint
-statement-of-the-minerals-security-partnership-principals-meeting-2024/.

32. Jon Eligon, "Angola Rail Line Offers Clues to Trump's Africa Policy," *New York
Times*, April 2, 2025, https://www.nytimes.com/2025/04/02/world/africa/trump-angola
-lobito-corridor.html.

33. Committee on Foreign Affairs, "East Asia & Pacific Subcommittee Chairwoman Young Kim Delivers Opening Statement at Hearing on Reauthorizing the U.S. Development Finance Corporation," March 11, 2025, https://foreignaffairs.house.gov/press-release/east-asia-pacific-subcommittee-chairwoman-young-kim-delivers-opening-statement-at-hearing-on-reauthorizing-the-u-s-development-finance-corporation/; William Hennigan, "Reauthorizing DFC: A Primer for Policymakers," Council on Foreign Relations, March 31, 2025, https://www.cfr.org/article/reauthorizing-dfc-primer-policymakers.

34. Adva Saldinger, "Scoop: Elon Musk's DOGE Takes Aim at Millennium Challenge Corporation," *Devex*, March 25, 2025, https://www.devex.com/news/devex-invested-us-dfc-could-face-radically-different-future-under-trump-109711.

35. Matthew Goldstein and Maureen Farrell, "Benjamin Black Weighs Shift in U.S. AID's Funding. A Billionaire's Son Has Some Ideas," *New York Times*, March 2, 2025, https://www.nytimes.com/2025/02/26/business/usaid-dfc-ben-black.html.

36. Custer, Horigoshi, and Marshall, *BRI from the Ground Up*.

37. See Jon Emont, "Why the U.S. Keeps Losing to China in the Battle over Critical Minerals," *Wall Street Journal*, March 10, 2025, https://www.wsj.com/business/china-us-critical-minerals-fight-50b5cbda.

Chapter Four

The Missing Pillar

Economic Contingency Planning in an Era of US-China Competition

Hugo Bromley and Eyck Freymann

In December 2023, the House Select Committee on Strategic Competition with the Chinese Communist Party released its first full report on the US-China economic relationship. Its most alarming finding came from a tabletop exercise simulating a Taiwan crisis.[1] The exercise showed that a sudden break in US-China economic ties would impose huge costs on the US economy.[2] The report's conclusion was blunt: "The United States lacks a contingency plan for the economic and financial impacts of conflict with the PRC." Worse, "no office in the U.S. Government bears primary responsibility for assessing the costs to the U.S. and global economy of a conflict with the PRC nor for doing contingency planning for how the United States and its allies would respond economically."

This oversight threatens the entire US strategy in the Indo-Pacific. American policymakers have always known that the PRC harbored ambitions to overturn the regional order established after the end of the Chinese civil war in 1949. The policy of engagement was premised on the idea that economic interdependence could moderate PRC ambitions and even turn China into a responsible actor. But

Hugo Bromley is a research associate at the Centre for Geopolitics at the University of Cambridge and an affiliated research associate at Robinson College, Cambridge. He is a historian of British manufacturing and global economic statecraft in the early modern and modern periods. Dr. Bromley received his PhD from the University of Cambridge in 2022.

Eyck Freymann is a Hoover Fellow at the Hoover Institution, Stanford University, and a nonresident research fellow at the China Maritime Studies Institute at the US Naval War College.

there is now broad agreement that this strategy failed. The new US strategy is to outcompete China in trade, tech, and defense, and to "decouple," "de-risk," or "strategically decouple" in key sectors. Indeed, China is pursuing its own strategy of economic self-reliance—even as it prepares its military for what might be an imminent crisis. In a cooperative era, trade ties were stabilizing. In a competitive one, they may be destabilizing.

Our argument here is that an economic contingency plan is essential to deterrence, not that there can be any such thing as an economic deterrent that functions by itself. We do not know what precise combination of factors will shape President Xi Jinping's decisions over Taiwan. If we are not prepared to commit militarily to support the island, threats of economic punishment may well fail to act as a sufficient deterrent. The United States should also consider how its political signaling would evolve during any crisis. But if the United States has no plan for how to respond economically to an invasion, blockade, or quarantine of Taiwan, then its broader deterrence strategy will seem hollow.

Instead of building realistic contingency plans for a rupture, the United States is increasingly hanging deterrence on threats of extreme economic punishment, particularly financial sanctions that weaponize the position of the dollar in the global financial system to limit the target country's access to the global economy. Recent reports from the Center for Strategic and International Studies, the Council on Foreign Relations, the Center for New American Security, the Rhodium Group, and the Atlantic Council argue that sanctions will help deter a blockade or quarantine of Taiwan. One suggests using Russia-style sanctions as a "baseline."[3] The House Select Committee report similarly calls for "severe diplomatic and economic costs" if Beijing moves against Taiwan.[4] The bipartisan STAND with Taiwan Act would also trigger broad sanctions on China's financial system if Beijing used force. Some proposals even link sanctions to a naval blockade of the Malacca Strait.[5] All these plans would compound the challenge for US interests in a crisis. Because sanctions depend on the dollar system, using sanctions to cut off China's trade with third countries would put the US role at the center of global finance at risk. As Emily Kilcrease has warned, "there are no winners in this game."[6]

The decision taken by the Trump administration to launch into a trade war with the PRC in April 2025 does not solve this dilemma, though it fundamentally alters it. At the time of writing, we do not know how the dispute will end. Donald Trump has already been forced to revise his strategy multiple times, including by giving "temporary" exemptions to electronics imports from China. If Trump eventually reaches an agreement with the PRC and lifts some or all of the new tariffs, the challenge of what to do with the bilateral economic relationship in the event of a Taiwan crisis will remain. Furthermore, the willingness of the administration to endure pain for the sake of strategic competition will be in doubt. Even if Trump decides to continue with prohibitive tariffs, key US allies, especially Japan, will continue to trade extensively with the PRC. Any Chinese interference with Taiwan's economic autonomy would cause an economic shock, regardless of the scale of bilateral trade. If we have learned nothing else from recent events, it is that attempts to radically alter the pattern of global trade cause market panic.

Why, then, has America allowed itself to remain so unprepared for a crisis that might be imminent? With the death of engagement, not only has economic interdependence become a potential liability, but key tools of US economic statecraft have been blunted. The broader problem is that sanctions were designed for a world of engagement. Since the late 1990s, sanctions have been most effective against terrorist organizations and weak states like Iraq, Iran, and North Korea—and when passed through the UN Security Council with China's acquiescence. Since Russia's 2014 invasion of Ukraine, we have been living in a different world. Since 2022, despite the full-scale invasion of Ukraine, the United States and European Union have hesitated to sanction Russia's primary function in the global economy: supplying oil and gas. Meanwhile, Russia and China have been building a new financial system that allows them to trade without dollars.[7]

Ukraine exposed flaws in the idea of "weaponized interdependence"; a Taiwan crisis would destroy it. The US probably could not weaponize the global economy against the world's top source of industrial output before April 2024. Subsequent events have only thrown this further into doubt. China has real weaknesses—rising debt and unemployment, stagnant demand, and a shrinking population. These factors may make a Taiwan crisis more likely. But they do not change China's role in global supply chains. Proponents of sanctions-led approaches and immediate decoupling alike have increasingly had to acknowledge these facts.

This chapter explores the history of sanctions and offers a new approach. It builds on our earlier report, *On Day One: An Economic Contingency Plan for a Taiwan Crisis*. We start with the US approach to sanctions and Taiwan before the current era of intense US-China competition. We then track the shift to a policy of "derisking" and tech controls under Trump and Joe Biden. Finally, we propose a new model for economic contingency planning. The US should spend less time talking about extreme ways it might try to punish China economically, and more time planning how to protect the global economy in a moment of crisis while defending its other vital interests, including helping allies decouple from China.

Sanctions: A Policy of Engagement

En route to Beijing in February 2009, Secretary of State Hillary Clinton told reporters how the Obama team planned to deal with China. "Successive administrations and Chinese governments have been poised back and forth on [human rights and Taiwan], and we have to continue to press them," she said. "But our pressing on those issues can't interfere with the global economic crisis, the global climate change crisis, and the security crisis."[8] As Jeffrey Bader of the National Security Council explained, it was a "classic Washington gaffe"—a hard truth spoken out loud.[9]

The comment marked a shift from Clinton's earlier views. In 1995, as First Lady, she had condemned the Chinese Communist Party for human rights abuses at a conference in Beijing. Her husband criticized George H. W. Bush for responding weakly to the Tiananmen Square massacre and had supported sanctioning China in response.[10] But over time, the Clinton team reversed course and ultimately embraced a policy of political and economic engagement with China. The George W. Bush administration continued the policy, partly because the September 11 attacks made it impossible to focus on East Asia, and partly because both parties came to believe that pulling back from trade with China would be too costly. Believing that commerce would gradually pull China in the direction of liberalization, Bush and Treasury Secretary Hank Paulson put economic dialogue first. Security talks led by Deputy Secretary of State Robert Zoellick were a secondary track.

When Barack Obama assumed the presidency in 2009, he was determined not to repeat what he saw as Clinton's mistake: making bold statements on values, then walking them back. In *The Audacity of Hope*, Obama argued that China was mainly an economic, not a military challenge.[11] His administration pushed for deeper engagement, drawing China into talks on climate and nuclear issues. These were areas more and more tied to sanctions. The economic and security tracks were merged into a single dialogue.

Such engagement was possible because the Taiwan Strait was calm. Jiang Zemin had taken a tough stance during the 1995–1996 crisis, but his successor, Hu Jintao, was weaker and more restrained. Under Bush, the destabilizing force in cross-Strait relations was Taiwanese President Chen Shui-bian. To deter Chen from unilaterally pursuing "Taiwan independence," Washington and Beijing made strong coordinated statements in support of the status quo.[12] Meanwhile, Beijing was pursuing its own strategy of economic interdependence with Taiwan. As cross-Strait trade boomed, Ma Ying-jeou was elected president of Taiwan and pursued diplomatic rapprochement. Taiwanese firms like Foxconn became essential middlemen as US multinationals dove head-first into the mainland market. The only potential threat came during the 2012 Taiwanese presidential campaign, when Ma faced Tsai Ing-wen, who came from the same party as Chen. The Obama team decided to step in. During the campaign, they remarked that Tsai "left us with distinct doubts about whether she is both willing and able to continue the stability in cross-Strait relations the region has enjoyed in recent years."[13] The remarks contributed to Ma's reelection.

After the global financial crisis, the United States was too distracted to confront China systematically on its flagrant violations of its World Trade Organization commitments. The Obama administration did slow the engagement process, ending the Doha Round. But it saw the bilateral economic relationship as too important to risk. When Obama raised China's currency and trade practices in 2009, top officials like Lawrence H. Summers and Timothy Geithner advised against retaliation. They agreed that China's actions were harmful but argued that the impact on the US economy was "in fact quite small."[14] Instead, the Obama team focused on bringing China into climate talks and getting at least quiet support on North Korea and Iran.

For Obama, sanctions were about global cooperation through multilateral institutions, including by working with China. A united world, acting through the United Nations, would regulate access to the global economy to enforce common rules, particularly on nuclear nonproliferation. Sanctions on North Korea were already in place. The challenge was compliance, and China voted for UN Resolution 1718, which tightened enforcement.[15] Iran was a tougher case. In 1996, Congress had passed the Iran and Libya Sanctions Act, which introduced the concept of secondary financial sanctions, but it failed due to pushback from Brussels. In the 2000s, Treasury official Stuart Levey began using financial tools unilaterally. He targeted Iran's access to global banks. The Obama team started with diplomacy, then shifted toward a multilateral approach. China's support was key to that plan.

The Obama economic playbook against Iran took shape in two phases. First, the United States pushed for UN sanctions like those used on North Korea. China blocked much of this but agreed to language that let the United States target Iran's banks. Congress thought this was too weak and passed new laws hitting Iran's oil sales and central bank. China complained but quietly cut its oil imports, citing economic security.[16] In the second step, the United States let Iran keep exporting oil but blocked access to the funds. This move—again with quiet support from

China—helped bring Iran to the table.[17] The campaign ended with the 2015 nuclear deal, the Joint Comprehensive Plan of Action.

After 2012, US cooperation with China visibly began to break down. Chinese foreign policy had started becoming more assertive after the financial crisis, and the trend continued under Xi. The first major flashpoint was not Taiwan but the South China Sea. As part of the "pivot to Asia," Obama sought closer ties with ASEAN (the Association of Southeast Asian Nations), hoping to strengthen a regional order that could manage China's rise. His idea was to move away from a Cold War "hub-and-spoke" model toward regional economic integration through the Trans-Pacific Partnership. Since Washington was committed to closer relationships with ASEAN, it couldn't simply ignore China's illegal militarization of the South China Sea. But neither did it dare to confront China over the matter.

Obama saw China's moves as destabilizing for the region but not something that should threaten the bilateral economic relationship. In a 2014 speech at West Point, Obama said, "China's economic rise and military reach worries its neighbors." But he framed "regional aggression that goes unchecked—whether in southern Ukraine or the South China Sea" as a global concern, not a threat to the United States itself. As with Ukraine, the Obama team believed that military action—or even indirect involvement—would be a mistake.[18]

Meanwhile, Vladimir Putin was proving in Crimea that sanctions do not necessarily deter great powers from regional aggression. Russia is a permanent member of the UN Security Council, so any truly multilateral sanctions were out of reach. Instead, the Obama administration applied "scalpel-like" sanctions that sought to impose asymmetric pain on Moscow without disrupting global energy markets.[19] At first, they faced strong resistance from European allies—especially Germany. Only after Russian proxies shot down Malaysia Airlines Flight 17 did the United States and the European Union expand sanctions. Even then, they barely touched Russia's financial system.[20] China offered no help on these first Russia sanctions, and the Obama administration made no real effort to bring it into the process. Unsurprisingly, the sanctions failed to change Russia's behavior. Meanwhile, Russia and China deepened their economic ties and strategic alignment.

From "Decoupling" to "De-Risking" and Back Again

By the time the first Trump administration openly embraced "strategic competition" with China in 2017, it should already have been clear that coercing China through economic threats alone would be difficult. In retrospect, this was the time to begin to push a coordinated, interagency US economic statecraft agenda.

Instead, the agencies in charge were given only skeleton crews and scarce ana-lytical resources. Yet the failure ultimately lies at the strategic level: a lack of clarity on the *purpose* of US economic statecraft against China, coupled with a lack of strategic imagination about the need for scenario planning.

From the outset, the first Trump administration pursued multiple objectives si-multaneously. On the one hand, they sought to redress the wildly unbalanced trade relationship. They argued—correctly—that China's financial repression, sub-sidies, currency manipulation, mass IP theft—and, after 2008, exploding debt—were unfair and illegal. The US Trade Representative and the Commerce Depart-ment began to implement more robust economic statecraft policies, with limited support from Treasury and Congress. On the other hand, the national security community saw China's potential domination of emerging technology as the key issue. Worry about Xi's "Made in China 2025" strategy began under Obama.[21] The fear was that China might weaponize technology to suppress dissent at home and spread authoritarianism abroad. Under Trump, several agencies began to work to-gether to challenge China's 5G ambitions. As the 2017 *National Security Strategy* put it, China's malign economic policies now threatened US values and national secu-rity, not just US jobs. Together these two critiques—Trump's and the technocrats'—added up to a searing indictment of engagement. The *National Security Strategy* claimed that the promise of engagement "for the most part, turned out to be false."[22]

The obvious conclusion was that the United States needed to unwind economic interdependence. However, Trump's economic agenda was initially different: to *reshape* interdependence to be more favorable to US interests. By the end of Trump's term, the administration's rhetoric had become as confused as the pol-icy. "'Decoupling' is an interesting word," Trump said in 2020, after the Phase One trade deal had put tariffs on hold. "Whether it's decoupling or putting in massive tariffs like I've been doing already, we will end our reliance on China, because we can't rely on China."[23] But what "reliance" meant was never defined. Some Trump advisers outside of the economic departments floated the idea of cutting trade to zero. But no serious plan was proposed to make that happen.[24]

Meanwhile, Trump's "maximum pressure" policies against Iran and North Korea gave the US false hope that unilateral US sanctions had real coercive power. Early in his term, Trump got China to tighten sanctions on North Korea by threat-ening secondary sanctions against noncompliant Chinese banks.[25] After he withdrew from the Joint Comprehensive Plan of Action, he sanctioned individual Chinese firms caught dealing with Iran, and China pulled back.[26] But Europe's response was revealing. The UK, France, and Germany created INSTEX, a new system to help firms trade with Iran without using dollars.[27] INSTEX failed, largely because Iran was not a large enough market to justify the risk. However, it illustrated the risk that overuse of sanctions could push even close US allies off the dollar system. China redoubled its efforts to expand the Cross-Border Interbank Payment System (CIPS), which it deemed, fundamentally, a sanctions-busting tool.[28]

The arrival of the Biden administration shifted US policy from "decoupling" to "de-risking." Biden paused most Trump-era trade policies but did not roll them back. Meanwhile, his administration sped up efforts to secure an edge in high-end technologies. Industrial policy and export controls became the main tools. To stimulate allied cooperation, the Biden administration began to threaten economic retaliation against allies that failed to comply with US economic statecraft against China. The consummate example was the Foreign Direct Product Rule, which Biden used to encourage Japan, South Korea, the Netherlands, and others to cut support for China's semiconductor supply chain. These policies caused friction with allies but showed that there was now a bipartisan consensus in favor of unilateral action to secure US technological dominance.

The Biden team succeeded in two key goals. It limited China's access to advanced semiconductors and production equipment, and it spurred massive investment in US manufacturing.[29] At the same time, this strategy required close cooperation with the Taiwanese chip giant, TSMC. This cut directly against the policy of cross-Strait economic engagement that the Chinese Communist Party and the Kuomintang had pursued since the early 2000s. Indeed, limiting Taiwan's economic interdependence with China now seemed to be a US strategic interest, too.

The Biden administration's rejection of full decoupling implicitly acknowledged that the US and Chinese economies would remain tightly linked—at least unless China's aggression forced a sudden rupture. But China was becoming more aggressive: accelerating military modernization and intensifying gray-zone activity in the South China Sea and around Taiwan. In 2023, then–CIA Director Bill Burns said Xi Jinping had told the People's Liberation Army to be ready to take Taiwan by 2027. Later that year, in a meeting with President Biden, Xi reportedly explained the conditions under which China might use force to achieve "reunification."[30]

As US attention refocused on Taiwan, it also became clear that China could potentially undermine the island's autonomy without launching a full invasion. A total blockade—or even a partial "quarantine"—could fatally undermine its economic autonomy, and ultimately its political future.[31]

With resupply operations risky and the threat of nuclear escalation always present, the old impulse returned: reach for sanctions. Think-tank reports advocated developing a range of potential sanctions packages. They argued that sanctions would badly harm both sides but harm China relatively more. Some analysts suggested that in the worst-case scenarios, Washington might force unwilling (European) allies to go along.[32] Implicitly, the argument was that even if Washington were unlikely to execute such extreme threats, simply stating the threats would support deterrence. Sanctions had transformed from a tool that required China's cooperation to a threat of economic mutually assured destruction.

The reach for sanctions misunderstood the challenge America would face in many Taiwan scenarios. In the quarantine scenario, China could claim sovereign control over some or all of Taiwan's trade. It could demand that vessels entering or leaving Taiwan clear customs at a mainland port but allow compliant vessels through. In such a scenario, the burden of economic escalation would fall on the United States.[33] Responding to such actions with sanctions on China could trigger a financial crisis, devastating the US economy. If the only US contingency plan is a threat of economic mutually assured destruction, Washington is setting up to deter itself.

The Biden administration's sanctions-led response to Russia's full-scale invasion of Ukraine ensured that future sanctions on China would be even more costly and risky. In late 2021, Biden explicitly made sanctions the main form of deterrence by ruling out direct military intervention. After this failed, the G7 imposed historic sanctions, but it once again let Russian oil and gas keep flowing. Russia's financial stability wobbled through March 2022, but the central bank quickly stabilized the situation.[34]

China took this opportunity to lay the rhetorical and practical groundwork for a future Taiwan crisis. Its diplomats cast Western sanctions and tariffs as signs of US overreach. Its bankers promoted CIPS around the world as an alternative to SWIFT, with considerable success. In the first half of 2023, China's offshore currency (CNH) was used to settle 75% of Russia's trade with the PRC and 25% of its transactions with other countries, according to Russia's Ministry of Economic Development.[35] China cast these efforts as a principled defense of globalization against a declining, revisionist, and protectionist United States. As Xi and Putin's famous pre-invasion joint statement put it, the 21st century would be shaped by "multipolarity, economic globalization, the advent of information society, cultural diversity, and transformation of the global governance architecture."[36]

Building the Economic Pillar

Since taking office in January 2025, Donald Trump has added to the confusion over his economic objectives that began at the end of his first term. At the time of writing, the "reciprocal" tariff regime proposed in April 2025 has been "paused" in general and substantially modified in the case of China. It is still unclear whether the aim is full decoupling or an attempt to force a total reset of the PRC's model of political economy. If it is the latter, it is almost certain to fail. Xi has made manufacturing dominance central to his political narrative, and being perceived as forced into an economic rebalancing that he has clearly been unwilling to adopt for the last five years would be a major threat to regime stability. The US options are complete retreat, a face-saving deal that accepts a modified version of the status quo, or attempting to turn tariffs aimed at maximizing pressure on Beijing into a sustainable program of decoupling. If we end with either of the former options, this crisis will have achieved little except to demonstrate our unpreparedness for a sudden rupture with China. The lesson Beijing will take from this is clear.

If America is committed to pursuing strategic competition with China, it must build its coalition through incentives rather than coercion. The logic of strategic competition is antithetical to autarky or the creation of quasi-imperial "spheres of influence" through force, which deny the importance of leadership over any form of global system. If that is truly the Trump administration's objective, it can abandon not only Taiwan but the entire "competition" framing. But if America is *not* pursuing autarky, it needs to build and sustain a coalition aimed at countering China. It also needs to create an incentive structure that gives third countries that wish to be neutral a reason to at least comply with US export controls and rules-of-origin requirements. The biggest tool the United States has to achieve this remains access to its market. The United States, Japan, the United Kingdom, Australia, and Canada together make up 36% of global GDP. In any non-autarkic future, most of the $1 trillion a year of imports that come from China today will have to be substituted from elsewhere. This is a powerful incentive, but it is credible only if it can be done in a politically and economically sustainable way.

In this new era of competition, America still needs an economic contingency plan for a Taiwan crisis. US-China trade cannot be brought to a halt overnight. The tariffs have already been modified and are likely to be modified further. Furthermore, a world without engagement is a world in which financial sanctions cannot function. If the United States is seeking to reorder the entire global trading system, using sanctions against China would represent a fundamental threat to the position of the dollar. The chances of European cooperation, let alone that of other third states, are slim to none.

The United States, moreover, still needs a plan to help its allies reduce their vulnerability to China if Beijing shows itself willing to use military force to reshape its near abroad. The Indo-Pacific is not Europe. It has no NATO-style alliance structure and no equivalent to the European Common Market to prevent a general turn away from trade. US partners in the region are far more economically dependent on China, and vulnerable to China's economic coercion, than European countries were to Russia in 2022. If China shows that it can coerce its neighbors into submission without paying any real costs, the United States will be unable to sustain the regional order in the Western Pacific—or win strategic competition. But unless the United States shows those countries a pathway to decoupling from China, they will struggle to support America in any crisis.

Using unilateral actions to force allies and partners to partially decouple from China, even if they proved effective, is a pathway *into* a crisis, not out of one. Export controls have already pushed Taiwan further from economic ties with the mainland. The more China and Taiwan have distinct technological systems, the harder it is for the Chinese Communist Party to sustain the narrative of inevitable "reunification." The less China benefits relative to the United States from Taiwan's semiconductor manufacturing base, the less China has to lose if Taiwan's chip supply is destroyed or cut off. To prevent this outcome, robust military deterrence is necessary but not sufficient. America needs an economic contingency plan that would secure its relevant interests in the crisis. Sustaining a US-led international trading system, based on the dollar, would be one of those interests, as would helping allies sustainably break their dependence on Chinese production. Crucially, any contingency plan must represent an affirmative vision for the future of the international trading system.

Congress and the US interagency apparatus must design a contingency plan that matches these interests. If the interagency is unable to do so, then as in previous periods in US history, from the Taiwan Relations Act to the Plaza Accord, Congress must lead. If sanctions can no longer serve as the main tool of US economic statecraft, the focus inevitably shifts to trade policy. In a crisis, America would have to use these tools in close coordination with allies. It would need to take account of market forces to ensure that it is not fighting the gravity of capital markets. Given the scale of US government action in such a crisis, Congress will need to play a much bigger role than it does today in routine trade matters. A central interagency coordinating body will need to be established. It should be vested with sufficient authority, resources, and scalable governance structure that it can spring into action in a fast-moving crisis.

We propose a model of "avalanche decoupling" as an alternative economic contingency plan for a crisis. If China crosses US red lines, Congress should commit to canceling permanent normal trade relations and work with core US allies to create a ratcheting discriminatory tariff or quota, starting at current levels and rising by a predictable amount each month. The speed of the ratchet could be customized by sector to prioritize decoupling in critical goods first. This phased approach would give firms time to shift and rebuild supply chains. It would reduce the inflationary shock. It would also allow the market to guide the process of reshoring, rather than attempting to direct it from Washington through command-and-control.

In any event, shifting US economic strategy from sanctions to trade policy will require tackling new challenges, particularly transshipment, as well as a broader program of financial aid to support the global economy through any transition. When one country faces trade limits, firms relabel goods and route them through third parties. This happened under Biden and is likely to accelerate under Trump. A blunt and harsh policy toward third countries would only lead to further evasion, destabilizing global supply chains and ultimately threatening the capacity of the United States to monitor its own overseas trade at all. A better approach would link trade enforcement with a plan to invest in global stability. This could include a dollar-based program to support emerging markets and new institutions—open to allies and neutrals—to make trade more transparent and help move supply chains. In essence, America and its allies must plan to establish an Economic Security Cooperation Board. In time, strategic decoupling could give developing countries a chance to draw in new manufacturing at China's expense. But that shift will take time, funding, and—above all—trust that trade rules are fair and consistent. Institutions designed for transparency could also support collective responses to Chinese coercion. If China strikes back with economic retaliation, it will face the same challenges as the United States: evasion, rerouting, and poor enforcement reach.

If the costs of decoupling were not clear before April 2025, they are now in plain sight. The worst effects of a rupture with China do not come from short-term supply shocks. They come from long-term inflation, job losses, and damage to the global trade system the United States itself built. Without a coherent, developed plan to give certainty to markets and reassurance to allies, any rupture risks the collapse of the entire global economy.

When we wrote *On Day One*, we were clear that what we were proposing was a contingency plan for a crisis, not a desirable strategy. By acting so aggressively against China, however, the Trump administration has put American credibility on the line. If the Trump administration fails to get a "deal" it can accept but is determined to pursue this path, there is a strong case for implementing some version of avalanche decoupling now—accepting that allied coordination will be hard to find. This carries enormous risks. It also means that any US economic deterrent will be much weaker. But if the United States is serious about defending Taiwan, it would still need a contingency plan that sustains some form of global trading system and provides key allies with a pathway toward reducing their dependence on the Chinese market. The Trump administration has fired a starting gun on the restructuring of the global trading system away from the last vestiges of cooperation and toward systemic competition. It may yet try to abort the race. But events are fast moving beyond its control. While it is too soon to say precisely what the implications for Taiwan are, the chaos may well make a crisis more likely. If so, the United States needs to prepare—and quickly.

NOTES

1. Select Committee on the Strategic Competition Between the United States and the Chinese Communist Party, *Reset, Prevent, Build: A Strategy to Win America's Economic Competition with the Chinese Communist Party*, December 12, 2023, https:// selectcommitteeontheccp.house.gov/sites/evo-subsites/selectcommitteeontheccp.house .gov/files/evo-media-document/reset-prevent-build-scc-report.pdf.

2. Select Committee on the Strategic Competition, *Reset, Prevent, Build*, 18.

3. Susan M. Gordon, Michael G. Mullen, and David Sacks, *U.S.-Taiwan Relations in a New Era: Responding to a More Assertive China*, Council on Foreign Relations, 2023, 82. See also Jude Blanchette and Gerard DiPippo, *"Reunification" with Taiwan Through Force Would Be a Pyrrhic Victory for China*, Center for Strategic and International Studies, 2022, https://www.csis.org/analysis/reunification-taiwan-through -force-would-be-pyrrhic-victory-china; Robert D. Blackwill and Philip Zelikow, *The United States, China, and Taiwan: A Strategy to Prevent War*, Council on Foreign Relations, 2021, 35–37.

4. Select Committee on the Strategic Competition, *Reset, Prevent, Build*.

5. Fiona S. Cunningham, "The Maritime Rung on the Escalation Ladder: Naval Blockades in a U.S.-China Conflict," *Security Studies* 29, no. 4 (2020): 730–768, https://doi.org/10.1080/09636412.2020.1811462.

6. Emily Kilcrease, "America's China Strategy Has a Credibility Problem," *Foreign Affairs*, May 7, 2024, https://www.foreignaffairs.com/united-states/americas-china -strategy-has-credibility-problem.

7. Eyck Freymann and Calvin Heng, "The Logic of Partial RMB Internationalization: PRC Perspectives on 'Financial War,'" *The China Quarterly*, February 20, 2025, 1–16, https://doi.org/10.1017/S0305741025000037.

8. "Clinton: Chinese Human Rights Can't Interfere with Other Crises," *CNN*, February 22, 2009.

9. Jeffrey Bader, *Obama and China's Rise: An Insider's Account of America's Asia Strategy* (Brookings Institution Press, 2012), 33.

10. Jim Mann, "Many 1989 U.S. Sanctions on China Eased or Ended," *Los Angeles Times*, June 30, 1991, https://www.latimes.com/archives/la-xpm-1991-06-30-mn-2555 -story.html.

11. Barack Obama, *The Audacity of Hope: Thoughts on Reclaiming the American Dream* (Canongate, 2008), 271–324.

12. Shirley A. Kan, *China/Taiwan: Evolution of the "One China" Policy—Key Statements from Washington, Beijing, and Taipei*, Congressional Research Service, July 9, 2007, 23, 72–82, https://sgp.fas.org/crs/row/RL30341.pdf.

13. Kathrin Hille, "US Concerned About Taiwan Candidate," *Financial Times*, September 15, 2011, https://www.ft.com/content/f926fd14-df93-11e0-845a-00144 feabdc0.

14. Bader, *Obama and China's Rise*, 139.

15. Edward Fishman, *Chokepoints: American Power in the Age of Economic Warfare* (Portfolio, 2025), 45.

16. Fishman, *Chokepoints*, 56–57.

17. Fishman, *Chokepoints*.

18. Barack Obama, "Remarks by the President at the United States Military Academy Commencement Ceremony," May 28, 2014, https://obamawhitehouse.archives .gov/the-press-office/2014/05/28/remarks-president-united-states-military-academy -commencement-ceremony.

19. Fishman, *Chokepoints*, 160, 205–206.

20. Fishman, *Chokepoints*, 205–206.

21. Fishman, *Chokepoints*, 237.

22. The White House, *2017 National Security Strategy of the United States of America*, December 2017, 1–68, https://trumpwhitehouse.archives.gov/wp-content/uploads/2017 /12/NSS-Final-12-18-2017-0905.pdf.

23. Jeff Mason, "Trump Again Raises Idea of Decoupling Economy from China," *Reuters*, September 7, 2020, https://www.reuters.com/article/idUSKBN25Z08T.

24. Fishman, *Chokepoints*, 304.

25. Inhan Kim, "Trump Power: Maximum Pressure and China's Sanctions Enforcement Against North Korea," *Pacific Review* 33, no. 1 (2019): 96–124, https://doi.org/10 .1080/09512748.2018.1549589.

26. Dan Katz, "Despite Sanctions, China Is Still Doing (Some) Business with Iran," *Atlantic Council* (blog), July 15, 2019, https://www.atlanticcouncil.org/blogs/iransource /despite-sanctions-china-is-still-doing-some-business-with-iran/.

27. Marie Aftalion, "INSTEX, a Game Changer?," Report of the European Union (EU) Non-Proliferation and Disarmament Consortium, 2019.

28. Gao Xingwei 高惺惟, "Zhongmei maoyi mocaxia renminbi guojihua zhanlüe yanjiu 中美贸易摩擦下人民币国际化战略研究" [Research on the RMB internationalization strategy under the Sino-US trade friction], *Jingji xuejia* 5 (2019): 66.

29. Gregory C. Allen, *Understanding the Biden Administration's Updated Export Controls*, Center for Strategic and International Studies, October 18, 2023, https://www.csis.org/analysis/understanding-biden-administrations-updated-export-controls; Christina DeConcini, Jennifer Rennicks and Shannon Wood, *Inflation Reduction Act Anniversary: How the Law Is Reviving U.S. Manufacturing*, World Resources Institute, August 16, 2023, https://www.wri.org/insights/inflation-reduction-act-anniversary-manufacturing-resurgence.

30. Matt Pottinger, *The Boiling Moat: Urgent Steps to Defend Taiwan* (Hoover Institution Press, 2024), 5.

31. Blackwill and Zelikow, *The United States, China, and Taiwan*, 35–37.

32. See Blanchette and DiPippo, *"Reunification" with Taiwan Through Force*.

33. Blackwill and Zelikow, *The United States, China, and Taiwan*, 35–37.

34. "In an Effort to Choke Russian Economy, New Sanctions Target Russia's Central Bank," *NPR*, February 28, 2022, https://www.npr.org/2022/02/28/1083580974/in-an-effort-to-choke-russian-economy-new-sanctions-target-russias-central-bank?t=1646164495488.

35. "Russia Is Using China's Yuan to Settle 25% of Its Trade with the Rest of the World, Report Says," *Yahoo Finance*, September 28, 2023, https://ca.finance.yahoo.com/news.

36. Government of the Russian Federation, "Joint Statement of the Russian Federation and the People's Republic of China on the International Relations Entering a New Era and the Global Sustainable Development," February 4, 2022, http://www.en.kremlin.ru/supplement/5770.

PART II / Allies, Partners, and
the Struggle for Asia

Chapter Five

Allies, Partners, and Strategic Competition with China

Michael J. Green

Despite the mythology sometimes attached to George Washington's admonition to avoid "entangling alliances," the United States has repeatedly prevailed in strategic competition against hegemonic rivals through the effective employment of what theorists call "external balancing."[1] This pattern began when the colonies defeated Britain through alliance with France and Spain in the American Revolution. In the 19th and 20th centuries, balance-of-power strategies secured America's position in the Pacific; John Quincy Adams forestalled Russian and British expansionism in the Pacific Northwest by playing those two imperial powers against each other; Theodore Roosevelt intervened in the Russo-Japanese War to ensure the those rivals were left "leaning together like exhausted prize fighters" with neither dominant; Douglas MacArthur's campaign in the Pacific Southwest was in reality a coalition victory; and the network of postwar bilateral alliances established in San Francisco in 1951 helped win the Cold War and continues to underpin regional stability and the United States' forward military presence today.[2] Like Blanche DuBois in *A Streetcar*

Michael J. Green is a professor and the chief executive officer at the United States Studies Centre at the University of Sydney. He previously served as special assistant to the president and senior director for Asia on the National Security Council staff and holds positions at Georgetown University and the Center for Strategic and International Studies.

The author would like to thank USSC research associate Kester Abbot for research support on this chapter.

Named Desire, American power in Asia has always depended on the kindness of strangers.

Anxiously Embracing Security Interdependence

None of this is to suggest that the United States has displayed consistency toward allies and partners, of course. Ever attentive to their own Thucydidean dilemma of avoiding either entrapment in unwanted American conflicts or abandonment by America in the face of external threats, US allies in Asia have endured repeated bouts of uncertainty and anxiety about the direction of American policy. To cite just a few examples: At the beginning of the Cold War, the United States denied Australia the joint command-and-basing infrastructure Canberra wanted as assurance of US commitment; in 1969 Richard Nixon sparked debates about nuclear armament in South Korea with his Guam Doctrine pledge to withdraw US ground troops from the region; Jimmy Carter was stopped from unilaterally withdrawing troops from the Korean Peninsula only by Japanese diplomatic intervention and discovery of new enemy divisions north of the demilitarized zone; major protests erupted in Australia and South Korea over their countries' involvement in the Iraq War; and the Obama administration's flirtation in 2013 with Xi Jinping's proposal for a Sino-US condominium under a "New Model of Great Power Relations" sent abandonment chills through Tokyo.[3]

What is remarkable in retrospect is that US alliances in the Indo-Pacific have gone from strength to strength despite these periodic bouts of anxiety and disruption. The only case of dealignment from within the region was New Zealand's decision to deny the US Navy access in the mid-1980s, which resulted in suspension of military cooperation under ANZUS—and that happened in large part because New Zealand was considered not strategically consequential enough to garner support in Washington (as Henry Kissinger quipped at the time, "New Zealand is a strategic dagger aimed at the heart of Antarctica").[4] More commonly, the United States and its Asian allies have repeatedly been able to make the political and military adjustments necessary to recalibrate for changes in domestic politics, bilateral relations, or external threats. As a result, US alliances with Japan, South Korea, Australia, or the Philippines look completely different today than they did a generation ago, and a robust new strategic partnership has emerged with India (since 2013, US security cooperation has also been gradually restored with New Zealand). All of these adjustments were accompanied by friction and sometimes precipitated by political crises—but the external threat environment gave few better options.

This is worth remembering now that President Donald Trump is turbocharging anxieties among many US allies and partners in the Indo-Pacific with criticism of NATO, an unnerving affinity for our allies' major adversaries, and the use of tariffs and economic protectionism as a tool of statecraft against adversaries and allies alike.

Yet if the growing threat from China puts a solid floor under US alliances, it also means that there is greater pressure on those alliances and partnerships to deliver strategic effects. And in that context, disruption from Washington is profoundly unhelpful. American alliances are becoming more integrated and interdependent. With the expansion of China's military threat envelope and the erosion of American air and naval primacy in the Western Pacific, the United States is now far more dependent on Asian allies to contribute sovereign deterrence capabilities and dispersed options for US forward access, basing, and overflight. In a world of diminished relative manufacturing capabilities, the United States also relies more on leveraging the technological and natural resource advantages of our allies and partners—semiconductor technology in South Korea, Japan, and Taiwan; critical minerals in Australia; or Japan and South Korea's long-standing expertise in shipbuilding.[5]

Greater entanglement with allies is therefore exactly what the United States has been doing over four administrations. Moreover, the US government and Congress have become particularly generous about transferring military capabilities to frontline allies and partners, most prominently with the provision of nuclear-powered attack submarines to Australia under AUKUS; sales of Tomahawk and other strike weapons to Japan; or defense technology sharing agreements with India—all of which would have been unthinkable absent the rapidly rising People's Liberation Army (PLA) military threat. While the Trump administration has signaled a retreat from past commitments to NATO, there is no indication that the administration intends to decouple from key allies in Asia in a similar way.

On their end, US allies have generally embraced increased security interdependence with the United States and accepted the risks of entrapment that would imply. From Japanese Prime Minister Shinzo Abe's change in the interpretation of Article 9 of the Japanese Constitution to permit "collective self-defense" operations with the United States, to the US-Australia force posture initiatives, or enhanced US military access and training in Northern Luzon in the Philippines—allies are choosing to shed alibis that were standard protections against entrapment for decades. To be clear, this trend reflects greater fear of China than it does growing confidence in the United States. To give one example, polls in Japan show

90% support for alliance with the United States (with similar numbers in South Korea), but only 25% expressing confidence that they can count on the United States to "do the right thing regarding world affairs."[6] Even under Presidents Barack Obama or Joe Biden, those expressing confidence that the United States would do the right thing in international affairs stood well below the overall level of support for the alliance. Security interdependence may be unavoidable, but it exacerbates the entrapment-versus-abandonment dilemma.

That said, there is no indication that allies or security partners in Asia are de-aligning from the United States even with the current round of intensified abandonment fears—a marked contrast to the discourse in Europe. Any reassurance about the solidity of alliances, however, should be tempered by the reality that strategic competition with China leaves much less margin for error compared with the Russian threat to Western Europe. The integration of alliances and partnerships in Asia is very much a work in progress. Even without formal de-alignment, increased disruption and friction from Washington could interrupt security integration in ways that shift strategic momentum back to Beijing.

The purpose of this chapter is not to assess the threat to alliance integration from America's current political dynamics, but rather to explain what is at stake: first by capturing the structural factors that have led to greater security integration and interdependence; second by highlighting the policy, operational, and geographic gaps that are emerging even with more integration with allies; and finally by anticipating scenarios for alignment strategies going forward, including the possibilities of either greater collective security or Chinese wedge strategies.

Converging Views on the China Threat

China's assault on the sovereignty and security of maritime states in the Indo-Pacific has been unrelenting for over a decade.

It began with the weaponization of economic interdependence in 2010, when Beijing embargoed critical mineral exports to Japan in response to the Japan Coast Guard's arrest of a drunk Chinese paramilitary fishing boat captain who had rammed one of their cutters in the standoff over the Senkaku Islands. In 2012 China blocked fruit imports from the Philippines in pursuit of claims over waters that had been administered by Manila for centuries. South Korea was hit with billions of dollars of damage in 2016 when Beijing embargoed the Lotte Corporation over the planned deployment of US Theater High Altitude Air Defense (THAAD) systems to South Korea. And in 2017 Australia was hit with billions of dollars in nontransparent import bans on barley, beef, wine, cotton and other exports in response to Australian criticism of China's nontransparency on the origins of COVID-19. Numerous other economies—especially Taiwan— have been similarly embargoed in the same period.[7]

Military intimidation by the PLA and paramilitary forces has intensified at an even faster pace. In 2012 Beijing established a new normal around Japan with regular Coast Guard incursions into the contiguous area around the Senkakus backed by PLA Navy surface combatants over the horizon, often in parallel with PLAN exercises on the Pacific Ocean side of Japan or joint operations with Russia in the north.[8] Beijing began constructing artificial islands in 2014, defied President Obama's warnings in 2015, and now has four military airbases in the South China Sea, each larger than Dulles Airport and capable of overwhelming any air force in Southeast Asia and challenging US passage through one of the world's busiest shipping lanes.[9]

In 2020 the PLA ambushed Indian troops in the secluded Galwan Valley of the Himalayas, killing two dozen Indian soldiers, including medics who had been treating injured PLA personnel. That same year the PLA Air Force began crossing the unofficial median line in the Taiwan Strait with daily flights, including the largest incursion ever in March 2025 with fifty fighters and bombers operating around Taiwan.[10] PLA combined arms exercises in late 2024 and early 2025 simulated blockade and invasion near Taiwan's east and west coasts with the deployment of 125 aircraft and more than two dozen PLA surface combatants flanked by China Coast Guard cutters—all now part of the normalization of China's operational tempo around the self-governed island. The list of Chinese military coercion against US allies and partners could fill this entire chapter, but even a short list would be incomplete without also including the China Coast Guard's ramming of Philippine Coast Guard vessels in 2024 and the PLA's unannounced naval exercises between Australia and New Zealand in February 2025, which forced civilian airlines to divert from waters that had not seen hostile forces intrude even in World War II.[11] According to one US Department of Defense report to Congress, the PLA conducted more than 180 coercive and risky air intercepts against US aircraft from fall 2021 to fall 2023 alone, surpassing the combined total for the previous decade. When including incidents with US allies and partners in the region, this number rises to around three hundred cases.[12]

Public opinion of China has unsurprisingly tanked in all these countries, with views of the importance of the United States rising to unprecedented levels.[13] Governments and publics have also taken a more positive view of their neighbors, setting aside historical grievances in the face of larger challenges from China.

Former imperial oppressor Japan is now the most trusted country in Asia (except in China and South Korea); only 6% of Australians polled say they would oppose moving to a formal security treaty with Japan.[14] South Korea and Japan have set aside deeply painful historical issues to focus on a trilateral agenda of security cooperation with the United States through the August 2023 Camp David Principles, though that progress is now under question because of political turmoil in Seoul. India, which had been holding Australia at arm's length after Canberra withdrew from the Quad in 2008, has embraced security and diplomatic cooperation with Australia after the Galwan Valley clash.

Experts within defense and intelligence circles across these countries have also begun noting something that has yet to fully hit the public discourse. While China's aggression appears to the media as a direct intimidation tactic or signal to each of the governments affected, the PLA's expanded operations also indicate unmistakable preparation of a theater-wide campaign plan in the event of conflict in the Taiwan Strait, the East China Sea, or the Philippines Sea. In 2023 the PLA began exercising between Guam and the First Island Chain with the deployment of the Shandong carrier battle group and PLA rocket forces practicing the employment of "carrier-killer" long-range missiles that would be used to hit US Navy combatants operating from Guam and Hawaii.[15] The PLA surface action group (and probably submarine) that circumnavigated Australia in February 2025 included an 055-class DDG armed with 1,000-kilometer surface-to-surface missiles capable of hitting all Australian military installations it passed—installations that are critical to the US dispersed presence in the region and virtually undefended by integrated air and missile defense. Shortly before that exercise, the PLA conducted an 11,000-kilometer missile test into the South Pacific with the range to hit US bases in Guam or forward-posture locations in Australia. In the same time period, the PLA fired ten anti-ship missiles into the Yellow Sea to the west of South Korea. Meanwhile, Chinese surveillance vessels have been mapping the undersea topography in key areas to aid with submarine hunting and cutting of cables in the event of conflict.[16] For allies and partners this means—as Leon Trotsky reportedly said—"you may not be interested in war, but war is interested in you."

Finally, the China military threat has been illuminated for Asian allies by the war in Ukraine. In polls by Japan's cabinet office after the war began, the number of citizens who expressed interest in defense rose to 78.2%, and those who said Japan was in danger of also being similarly attacked rose to 86.2%, with similar reactions in South Korea and especially Taiwan.[17] The leaders of Japan, South

Korea, Australia, and New Zealand attended the inaugural NATO–Indo-Pacific Four (IP-4) summit established after the Russian invasion of Ukraine.[18] Not only do key US allies in Asia see the possibilities of similar assaults on their security by China; they understand the growing alignment of Beijing and Moscow and the need for similar collective action by Euro-Atlantic and Indo-Pacific allies.

Creating "Asian NATOs"

Beijing has criticized the growing integration of US alliances in response to this threat as the creation of "Asian NATOs."[19] Indeed, preventing the amalgamation of America's bilateral alliances (the hub and spokes) into a collective security organization comparable to NATO was a top priority for Chinese foreign policy strategy for the first two decades of the post–Cold War period. With each instance of Chinese coercion, however, the integration and networking of alliances have only deepened. Early moves in the post–Cold War era included the establishment of the US–Japan–South Korea TCOG (Trilateral Coordination and Oversight Group) in 1999; the US-Japan-Australia Trilateral Security Dialogue in 2001; the US-Japan-Australia-India Quad—first in 2005 in response to the Indian Ocean tsunami and then revived as a foreign ministerial by the Trump administration in 2018 and a leaders' summit by the Biden administration in 2021; the Australia-US-UK AUKUS agreement in 2021 to collaborate on the production and delivery of nuclear-powered attack submarines to Australia (Pillar 1) and development of advanced technologies (Pillar 2); and the US-Japan-Australia-Philippines "Squad" in 2024.[20]

None of these minilaterals were explicitly aimed at countering China, even if it was well understood across the region that uncertainty about China was the single most important motivating factor for the participants (though uncertainty about the United States' staying power was a factor as well). Indeed, governments in the region went out of their way to explain that groupings like the Quad were designed to help the region rather than counter any one country. As Chinese coercive military and economic pressure has intensified, however, the pretense that minilateralism is about public goods or diplomatic cooperation has given way to more obvious steps at military readiness, capacity building, and joint planning.

The US-Japan alliance forms the core of many of the minilateral security arrangements taking shape. The stage was set in 2015 by former Prime Minister Shinzo Abe's decision to push for legislation reforming Japan's national security policies and reinterpreting Article 9 of the Constitution to allow for "collective self-defense"—or the use of force in concert with allies and partners when the prime minister judges "Japan's national survival" is at stake.[21] For Abe, the reinforcement of US capabilities and the networking with other security partnerships in the region and beyond became more important than the traditional postwar Japanese priority given to having Article 9 as an alibi to avoid entrapment in military conflicts in Taiwan, South Korea, or Southeast Asia.

The US-Japan-Australia trilateral security relationship (lacking a formal acronym but increasingly referred to as "AJUS") has subsequently developed the most operationally relevant pattern of minilateral integration. The Trilateral Defense Ministers Meeting in Darwin, Australia, in November 2024 was their fourteenth such meeting and used language comparable to that in NATO or the US-Japan Security Treaties by pledging "trilateral policy coordination and to consult each other on regional security issues and contingencies."[22] Australia is now a core member of US-Japan annual defense exercises such as KEEN EDGE, and Japan is the largest third party in US-Australia exercises such as TALISMAN SABRE, with Australia as a core training area for Japan's new Amphibious Rapid Deployment Brigade. Intelligence coordination is being enhanced through Australian secondments to the US-Japan Bilateral Information Analysis Cell and Japan's Joint Operations Command.[23] Japan has also been invited to explore participation in Pillar 2 of AUKUS with a focus on autonomous vehicles.[24]

The US-India strategic relationship, historically plagued by Indian adherence to nonalignment and occasional American disdain for India's strategic importance compared with that of China, is now also achieving levels of cooperation that would cause true Nehruvian nonalignment gurus to blush. Prior to 2008, US-India defense trade was relatively limited, involving modest US sales of naval helicopters and counterbattery radars. In the 2016 annual National Defense Authorization Act, the United States designated India as a major defense partner, and defense sales have increased dramatically since—from less than US$1 billion in 2008 to US$20 billion by 2024.[25] India has also become the leading military partner of the United States, conducting more military exercises and personnel exchanges with the United States than with any other country, and India's hesitation on maritime security cooperation through the Quad is also receding.[26] India's hesitation on explicitly emphasizing maritime security in the Quad has also faded.[27] None of this means that India would engage in a contingency on Taiwan, but broader Indian geopolitical alignment and sovereign capabilities in the Indian Ocean indirectly make the Taiwan conundrum less difficult for Washington, Tokyo, or Canberra.

The US–Japan–South Korea trilateral defense relationship was launched in a formal way in 1998 with assistant secretary–level talks, but that framework has fallen victim to almost cyclical spells of history-infused nationalist confrontation between Seoul and Tokyo. President Biden put things back on track in August 2023 with the Camp David Principles, and within a year the three countries were conducting dozens of joint exercises and activating real-time DPRK missile-warning data sharing.[28] But political fluidity in Seoul and President Trump's dim view of the US military presence on the peninsula suggest that continued progress is not guaranteed.

The US-Philippines security relationship is equally prone to domestic political eruptions, most recently with the America-skeptical presidency of Rodrigo Duterte. Under President Ferdinand Marcos Jr., however, Manila has tightened security relations with the United States as well as with Japan and Australia through the "Squad." After Marcos's initial attempts to resolve Chinese pressure on the Philippines around features such as Second Thomas Shoal were rebuffed by Beijing, Manila agreed in April 2023 on the expansion of the US-Philippines Enhanced Defense Cooperation Agreement (EDCA) to include four new sites.[29] The Philippine Constitution still bans foreign bases, but the ability of US and allied forces to rapidly reinforce critical littoral areas in Northern Luzon sends a strong deterrent signal to China on behalf of Manila while affording access to approaches the PLA might use against Taiwan or Japan.

Taken as a whole (and this section does not include multiple engagements with other militaries from Mongolia to Thailand), the networking of security cooperation from Japan through the First Island Chain to the Philippines and then to Australia and India creates potential strategic depth for US forces, complicates the PLA's freedom of maneuver, and presents future opportunities for horizontal escalation and counterblockade against Chinese sea-lanes. The problem is that officials cannot discuss those eventualities in polite company. And that is just the beginning of the complications with the new Asian NATOs.

Mind the Gaps

The only thing worse than fighting alongside allies is fighting without them, Winston Churchill reportedly quipped. While there is no overt evidence of dealignment by the core allies and partners noted above, further integration faces multiple complications—complications that adversaries can exploit.

First, all US allies and partners in the Indo-Pacific have significantly higher levels of trade dependence on China than does the United States (36% of exports for Australia, 24% for South Korea, and 19% for Japan compared with only 7% for the United States in 2024).[30] Those numbers are tempered by the fact that overall foreign direct investment flows for major US allies are overwhelmingly trans-Pacific rather than with China (a better indication of economic interdependence).[31] Nevertheless, US allies tend to avoid any hint of decoupling or regime change in their official discourse, preferring as even Japan's hawkish ruling Liberal Democratic Party's National Security Commission put it in April 2022, to return to a "productive relationship" with Beijing.[32]

Second, while key allies and partners are increasing readiness, munitions, strike capability, and infrastructure to host dispersed US forces, most still face significant shortfalls. Australia's 2025 budget increased defense spending by only US$628.9 million despite the government's 2023 Defence Strategic Review arguing that the country faced its most serious security environment since World War II.[33] Japan has committed to increasing defense spending to 2% of GDP, but the depreciation of the yen and a heavy reliance on US systems mean that Japan's purchasing power is not increasing as expected. Meanwhile, Xi Jinping promised a 7.2% increase in defense spending in March 2025.[34] Americans are very supportive of alliances, but a majority also want allies to spend more on defense.[35] That pressure will likely increase.

Because of its focus on the North Korean threat and hesitancy about engaging on Taiwan contingencies, South Korea is in a particularly vulnerable position on burden-sharing despite spending more than Japan or Australia as a percentage of GDP (at 2.8% in 2024).[36] The reality is that the US–South Korea alliance brings enormous benefits in terms of the overall balance of power and competition in technology, shipbuilding, and diplomacy, backed by South Koreans' growing alarm at Chinese aggression. Leadership in Seoul and Washington, however, sometimes loses sight of those advantages.

Third, the United States risks losing the competitive advantage offered by the growing convergence of Euro-Atlantic and Indo-Pacific alliances, manifest in the new NATO defense concept, the IP-4, and a host of NATO initiatives with US allies in Asia. Close allies in Asia were shaken by the incoming Trump administration's treatment of President Volodymyr Zelensky and European allies, but even more problematic would be a calculus by Beijing that Europe and America can now be separated in any contingency involving Taiwan. NATO countries are not likely to make significant military contributions to a contingency in Taiwan or the Senkakus, but Europe could impose crippling economic and diplomatic costs on Beijing if China used force against a US ally in Asia.[37] Ultimately, Europe's future is with the United States and its allies (EU foreign direct investment in China is less than $200 billion but over $4 trillion in the United States, even if one discounts shared democratic values). European defection to China will not happen, but Washington risks losing the deterrent effect on China of transatlantic solidarity.

Fourth, while the United States and allies are focusing on integration and hard power, Beijing is preparing to outflank those allies in South Asia, Southeast Asia, and the Pacific islands. PRC aims are clear: to monopolize digital and physical infrastructure in the region and to establish dual-use military bases in places like Sri Lanka or the Solomon Islands that can threaten US approaches to the First Island.[38] And the toolkit is well understood, involving elite capture (bribery), Belt and Road digital and physical infrastructure financing, military intimidation, and aggressive disinformation campaigns. Surveys in Southeast Asia suggest that elites see China as more influential strategically than the United States but not by much, with overwhelmingly positive views of Japan, Australia, South Korea, and the EU.[39] A coordinated strategy could blunt Chinese strategic and operational ambitions in Southeast Asia and the Pacific—but not if the United States is fighting with Europe, tariffing US allies, and withdrawing US funding for democracy support, development assistance, and countering disinformation.[40]

Finally, US trade policy—once seen as the handmaiden of US security policy—has gone from retreat (most notably with the end of American involvement with the trans-Pacific Partnership) to volatile protectionist tariff actions against close US allies. The US-Japan alliance weathered trade friction in the 1980s successfully, and trade disputes in themselves have rarely caused strategic dealignment. But social license for US alliances will be degraded by capricious trade policies that look to like-minded allies like extortion. Even if that does not lead to dealignment, it will render more difficult the political decision-making needed to implement greater integration of alliances in the region.[41]

Scenarios: An Asian NATO or Wedged Apart?

Despite these gaps, trend lines still point to continued integration of US alliances and partnerships in the Indo-Pacific. While a real Asian NATO characterized by collective security commitments is not likely in the near term, increasingly federated defense capabilities across alliances and partnerships are.[42] There are no indications that Beijing will waver from its theater-wide campaign plan or close alignment with Russia and support for North Korea, which will only fuel closer integration among the maritime democracies. Meanwhile new technologies such as AI-enhanced command-and-control arrangements could make it possible to create virtual collective security by creating common operating pictures that allow nations to plug and play while retaining sovereign control of decision-making.[43]

The Trump national security team's continued focus on Asia could inoculate defense relationships against the kind of damage being done to transatlantic relations. However, as one senior Australian national security official put it to the author in March 2025, "we can take nothing for granted with respect to social license for the alliance."

Of course, the other side gets a vote. Beijing's wedge strategies have to date been unsuccessful with key allies and partners but could have greater effect if traditional US economic and soft power tools are squandered. United Front activities, elite capture, Belt and Road investments, and disinformation could all lead local officials to block US access, basing, and overflight arrangements. Greater influence over key ASEAN states could reinvigorate initiatives like SEANWFZ (the Southeast Asian Nuclear Weapons Free Zone) that might be applied unilaterally to block US Navy access. (Beijing was successful in initially convincing Southeast Asian governments that AUKUS was a violation of the nonproliferation treaty.)[44] Trade friction with the United States could prompt future governments in Australia or even Japan to admit China to the Comprehensive and Progressive Trans-Pacific Partnership, which would have a devastating effect on American prestige and leadership on economic rulemaking in the region.

These wedge strategies are not succeeding yet. Allies and partners remain America's trump card in Asia. Coercion and collusion by China and Russia have supercharged their importance. The greatest danger is that Washington might inadvertently pull the plug.

NOTES

1. Michael Beckley, "The Myth of Entangling Alliances," *War on the Rocks*, June 9, 2025, https://warontherocks.com/2015/06/the-myth-of-entangling-alliances/. One of the most influential works on balancing is Kenneth N. Waltz's *Theory of International Politics* (McGraw-Hill, 1979).

2. See Michael J. Green, *By More than Providence: Grand Strategy and American Power in the Asia Pacific Since 1783* (Columbia University Press, 2017), 27–31, 54–55, 97–98; Peter J. Dean, *MacArthur's Coalition: US and Australian Military Operations in the Southwest Pacific Area, 1942–1945* (University Press of Kansas, 2018).

3. Green, *By More than Providence*, 336–345, 377–381, 539.

4. Helen Clark, "Towards a New Synthesis in New Zealand Foreign Affairs and Defence Policies: Opportunities Offered by the 1986 Defence Review," *Australasian Journal of American Studies* 5, no. 1 (1986): 41–49.

5. Japan and South Korea combined have a 40% global market share of the shipbuilding industry compared with a less than 1% US share; see "Only Asia Can Help America

Counter China's Shipbuilding Prowess," *The Economist,* February 20, 2025, https://www
.economist.com/asia/2025/02/20/only-asia-can-help-america-counter-chinas-shipbuilding
-prowess.

6. Jakub Wozniak, "Japan Polling Data Shows Record Levels of Support for JSDF and
US Alliance," *Overt Defense,* March 14, 2023, https://www.overtdefense.com/2023/03/14
/japanese-polling-data-shows-record-levels-of-support-for-jsdf-and-us-alliance/; Karl
Friedhoff, *While Positive Toward US Alliance, South Koreans Want to Counter Trump's
Demands on Host-Nation Support,* Chicago Council on Global Affairs, December 2019,
https://globalaffairs.org/sites/default/files/2020-11/191214_korean_attitudes_on_host
_nation_support_final_.pdf; "Confidence in Donald Trump," Pew Research Center,
June 11, 2024, https://www.pewresearch.org/global/2024/06/11/confidence-in-donald
-trump/.

7. Renato Cruz De Castro, "Facing Up to China's Realpolitik Approach in the South
China Sea Dispute: The Case of the 2012 Scarborough Shoal Stand-Off and Its Aftermath," *Journal of Asian Security and International Affairs* 3, no. 2 (2016): 157–182;
Darren J. Lim and Victor Ferguson, "Chinese Economic Coercion During the THAAD
Dispute," *Asan Forum,* December 28, 2019, https://theasanforum.org/chinese-economic
-coercion-during-the-thaad- dispute/. For a regularly updated overview of maritime
security issues in Asia, see "Asia Maritime Transparency Initiative," Center for Strategic
and International Studies, accessed March 27, 2025, https://amti.csis.org/.

8. Mark A. Green, "China and Russia: Quietly Going Steady," *Wilson Center* (blog),
October 29, 2024, https://www.wilsoncenter.org/blog-post/china-and-russia-quietly
-going-steady.

9. For details, see "Asia Maritime Transparency Initiative."

10. "China Sends More Than 50 War Planes Near Taiwan as 'Punishment' to
Separatism," *ABC News,* March 18, 2025, https://www.abc.net.au/news/2025-03-18
/china-says-military-exercise-near-taiwan-is-punishment/105064156.

11. William Yang, "China Flexes Military Muscle in Indo-Pacific, Testing US and
Allies," *Voice of America,* February 27, 2025, https://www.voanews.com/a/china-flexes
-military-muscle-in-indo-pacific-testing-us-and-allies/7990197.html.

12. US Department of Defense, "Military and Security Developments Involving the
People's Republic of China," news release, October 29, 2023, www.defense.gov/News
/Releases/Release/Article/3561549/dod-releases-2023-report-on-military-and-security
-developments-involving-the-pe/.

13. See Ryan Neelam, *Relations in the Indo-Pacific,* Lowy Institute Poll 2024 Report,
June 3, 2024, https://poll.lowyinstitute.org/report/2024/relations-in-the-indo-pacific/;
Cabinet Office, *Public Opinion Survey on the Self-Defense Forces and Defense Issues (Novem-
ber 2022 Survey),* Government of Japan, March 2023, https://survey.gov-online.go.jp/r04
/r04-bouei/gairyaku.pdf; Wozniak, "Japan Polling Data"; Laura Silver, Christine Huang,
Laura Clancy, and Andrew Prozorovsky, *Views of China and Xi Jinping,* Pew Research
Center, July 9, 2024, https://www.pewresearch.org/global/2024/07/09/views-of-china-and
-xi-jinping/; Laura Silver, Kat Devlin, and Christine Huang, *Unfavorable Views of China
Reach Historic Highs in Many Countries,* Pew Research Center, October 6, 2020, https://
www.pewresearch.org/global/2020/10/06/unfavorable-views-of-china-reach-historic-highs
-in-many-countries/; Friedhoff, *While Positive Toward US Alliance; Views of the U.S,* Pew

Research Center, June 11, 2024, https://www.pewresearch.org/global/2024/06/11/views-of
-the-u-s/; *U.S. Image Generally Favorable Around the World, but Mixed in Some Countries,* Pew
Research Center, January 8, 2020, https://www.pewresearch.org/global/2020/01/08/u-s
-image-generally-favorable-around-the-world-but-mixed-in-some-countries/.

14. See Jared Mondschein and Victoria Cooper, *US Midterms 2022: The Stakes for
Australia and the Alliance,* United States Studies Centre at the University of Sydney,
October 26, 2022, https://www.ussc.edu.au/us-midterms-2022-the-stakes-for-australia
-and-the-alliance.

15. John Dotson, *The PRC Sends a Message to the International Community with Its
December 2024 Naval Exercise,* Global Taiwan Institute, January 8, 2025, https://
globaltaiwan.org/2025/01/the-prc-sends-a-message-to-the-international-community/.

16. Mercedes Page, "China's Shadow Fleet Threatens Indo-Pacific Communications," *The Strategist,* March 25, 2025, https://www.aspistrategist.org.au/chinas-shadow
-fleet-threatens-indo-pacific-communications/.

17. "自衛隊に関心「ある」が78.2%、過去最高に 内閣府世論調査," (Jieitai ni kanshin
'aru' ga 78.2% kakosaiko-ni naikakufu cho-sa) [78.2% "interested" in the Self-Defence
Forces, a record high, according to a Cabinet Office poll], *Mainich Shimbun,* March 7,
2023, https://mainichi.jp/articles/20230307/k00/00m/010/128000c.

18. Gorana Grgic, "How NATO and Its Indo-Pacific Partners Can Work Together in
an Era of Strategic Competition," *Atlantic Council* (blog), August 7, 2024, https://www
.atlanticcouncil.org/blogs/new-atlanticist/how-nato-and-its-indo-pacific-partners-can
-work-together-in-an-era-of-strategic-competition/.

19. Demetri Sevastopulo and Kathrin Hille, "China Accuses US of Seeking
'Asia-Pacific NATO'," *Financial Times,* May 31, 2024, https://www.ft.com/content
/b889d33c-7745-48b7-b847-64f2b3003409.

20. James P. Rubin, "U.S.-R.O.K.-Japan Trilateral Meetings," US Department of
State, November 9, 1999, https://1997-2001.state.gov/briefings/statements/1999/ps991109
.html; Thomas Wilkins, *US-Japan-Australia Trilateralism Takes Off!,* Sasakawa Peace
Foundation, January 21, 2025, https://www.spf.org/iina/en/articles/thomas_09.html;
Dominique Fraser, *The Quad: A Backgrounder,* Asia Society Policy Institute, May 16, 2023,
https://asiasociety.org/policy-institute/quad-backgrounder; Tom Corben, Ashley Town-
hend, and Susannah Patton, *What Is the AUKUS Partnership?,* United States Studies Centre
at the University of Sydney, September 16, 2021, https://www.ussc.edu.au/explainer-what
-is-the-aukus-partnership; Richard Javad Heydarian, "Move Over, Quad; The New Squad
Has Landed," *Asia Times,* May 7, 2024, https://asiatimes.com/2024/05/move-over-quad
-the-new-squad-has-landed/.

21. For details, see Michael J. Green, *Line of Advantage: Japan's Grand Strategy in the
Era of Abe Shinzo* (Columbia University Press, 2022).

22. Richard Marles, Gen Nakatani, and Lloyd Austin III, "Australia-Japan-United
States Trilateral Defence Ministers' Meeting November 2024 Joint Statement,"
Australian Department of Defence, November 17, 2024, https://www.minister.defence
.gov.au/statements/2024-11-17/australia-japan-united-states-trilateral-defence-ministers
-meeting-november-2024-joint-statement.

23. Marles, Nakatani, and Austin, "Australia-Japan-United States Trilateral Defence
Ministers' Meeting"; C. Todd Lopez, "U.S. Intends to Reconstitute U.S. Forces Japan as

Joint Forces Headquarters," US Department of Defense, July 28, 2024, https://www
.defense.gov/News/News-Stories/Article/Article/3852213/us-intends-to-reconstitute-us
-forces-japan-as-joint-forces-headquarters/.

24. See Marles, Nakatani, and Austin, "Australia-Japan-United States Trilateral
Defence Ministers' Meeting."

25. Marles, Nakatani, and Austin, "Australia-Japan-United States Trilateral Defence
Ministers' Meeting; "USIBC Prepares Executive Defense Mission to DefExpo 2020,"
USIBC press release, US-India Business Council, January 29, 2020, https://www.usibc
.com/press-release/usibc-prepares-executive-defense-mission-to-defexpo-2020/.

26. Abhinandan Mishra, "India Becomes the US' Top Military Exercise Partner,"
Sunday Guardian, September 22, 2024, https://sundayguardianlive.com/top-five/india
-becomes-the-us-top-military-exercise-partner; Office of the Spokesperson, "Joint
Statement by the Quad Foreign Ministers," US Department of State, January 21, 2025,
https://www.state.gov/joint-statement-by-the-quad-foreign-ministers/.

27. "Joint Statement by the Quad Foreign Ministers."

28. Victor Cha, *The Legacy of Camp David: The United States, South Korea, and Japan
to Establish a Trilateral Secretariat*, Center for Strategic and International Studies,
September 25, 2024, https://www.csis.org/analysis/legacy-camp-david-united-states
-south-korea-and-japan-establish-trilateral-secretariat; "United States-Japan-Republic of
Korea Trilateral Ministerial Joint Press Statement," US Department of State, December 19, 2023, https://www.defense.gov/News/Releases/Release/Article/3621235/united
-states-japan-republic-of-korea-trilateral-ministerial-joint-press-statem/.

29. "Philippines, U.S. Announce Locations of Four New EDCA Sites," US Department of Defense, April 3, 2023, https://www.defense.gov/News/Releases/Release/article
/3349257/philippines-us-announce-locations-of-four-new-edca-sites/.

30. "United States Exports by Country," *Trading Economics*, 2025, https://
tradingeconomics.com/united-states/exports-by-country.

31. See "U.S. Remains World's Top Destination for Foreign Direct Investment for
12th Consecutive Year," US Department of Commerce, April 4, 2024, https://www
.commerce.gov/news/; "Foreign Direct Investment (FDI) Pledges and Inflows to South
Korea in 2024, by Country," *Statista*, February 2025, https://www.statista.com/statistics
/1478253/south-korea-fdi-inflows-by-country/; "Statistics on Who Invests in Australia,"
Australian Department of Foreign Affairs and Trade, 2024, https://www.dfat.gov.au
/trade/trade-and-investment-data-information-and-publications/foreign-investment
-statistics/statistics-on-who-invests-in-australia; "FDI Inflows into India Cross
$1 trillion, Establishes Country as Key Investment Destination," *The Hindu*, December 8,
2024, https://www.thehindu.com/business/Economy/fdi-inflows-into-india-cross-1
-trillion-establishes-country-as-key-investment-destination/article68962301.ece.

32. Quoted in Michael J. Green, "The Real China Hands," *Foreign Affairs*, November 1, 2022, https://www.foreignaffairs.com/united-states/real-china-hands-what-us-can
-learn-from-asian-allies.

33. Kirsty Needham, "Australia to Speed Up $1 Billion in Defence Spending in
Budget, Says Defence Minister," *Reuters*, March 24, 2025, https://www.reuters.com
/world/asia-pacific/australia-speed-up-1-billion-defence-spending-budget-says-defence
-minister-2025-03-24/; *National Defence: Defence Strategic Review 2023*, Australian

Department of Defence, 2023, https://www.defence.gov.au/about/reviews-inquiries
/defence-strategic-review.

34. Christopher Bodeen, "China Will Increase Its Defense Budget 7.2% This Year,"
AP News, March 5, 2025, https://apnews.com/article/china-defense-budget-taiwan
-4ac7cbdc7d5b889732cd55916ff7eb36.

35. See Jared Mondschein and Victoria Cooper, "US Midterms 2022: The Stakes for
Australia and the Alliance," United States Studies Centre at the University of Sydney,
October 26, 2022, https://www.ussc.edu.au/us-midterms-2022-the-stakes-for-australia
-and-the-alliance.

36. Kim Hyun-bin, "Korea's Defense Spending Tanks 11th Globally," *Korea Times,*
January 13, 2025, https://www.koreatimes.co.kr/.

37. Agathe Demarais, "China Should Worry About Europe If It Attacks Taiwan,"
Foreign Policy, September 19, 2024, https://foreignpolicy.com/2024/09/19/china-taiwan
-war-eu-europe-economic-sanctions/.

38. See for example, Peter Connolly, "Grand Strategy: Inside China's Statecraft in
Melanesia," *Australian Foreign Affairs* 17 (February 2023), https://www.australianforeign
affairs.com/articles/extract/2023/06/grand-strategy.

39. ISEAS, *The State of Southeast Asia 2025,* April 2025.

40. "A U.S. Retreat in the War of Ideas," *Wall Street Journal,* March 19, 2025,
https://www.wsj.com/opinion/radio-free-asia-radio-liberty-donald-trump-elon-musk
-ronald-reagan-902c8c37.

41. See, for example, Cameron Stewart, "'Disrupter' Turnbull Questions Worth of
AUKUS, Challenges US Alliance in Light of Trump Presidency, *The Australian,*
March 28, 2025, https://www.theaustralian.com.au/commentary/disrupter-turnbull
-questions-worth-of-aukus-challenges-us-alliance-in-light-of-trump-presidency/news
-story/cfab9ab68fea2dbb820717922436c7b9.

42. Michael J. Green, Zack Cooper, and Kathleen H. Hicks, *Federated Defense in
Asia,* Center for Strategic and International Studies, December 11, 2014, https://www
.csis.org/analysis/federated-defense-asia.

43. See Aspen Strategy Group, *Intelligent Defense: Navigating National Security in the
Age of AI,* The Aspen Institute, October 16, 2024, https://www.aspeninstitute.org
/publications/intelligent-defense/.

44. Andrew Tillett, "China Rallies Opposition to Australia's Nuclear Submarine
Plan," *Australian Financial Review,* July 21, 2022, https://www.afr.com/politics/federal
/china-rallies-opposition-to-australia-s-nuclear-submarine-plan-20220721-p5b3gq.

Chapter Six

Great Expectations

India amid US-China Competition

Ashley J. Tellis

Since the beginning of this century, the United States has courted no other country as ardently as India. This engagement is remarkable because prior bilateral ties had often been frosty, even antipathetic. Consequently, Washington's overtures toward New Delhi—which have included unprecedented reversals in major US policies, hyperbolic characterizations of their association, and promises of advanced technology otherwise reserved for allies—have frequently raised eyebrows among those attempting to make sense of the new US enthusiasm for India.

On the face of it, this eagerness should not be surprising: Washington's evolving rivalry with Beijing makes New Delhi a natural partner. After all, India is a large country; it is a rising power in its own right; it is adjacent to China; and it has its own conflicts with Beijing, which makes it an attractive confederate consistent with Kautilya's oft-quoted maxim, "The enemy of my enemy is my friend."

That the United States has sought India's cooperation in its competition with China is, therefore, understandable. It explains why Washington has overlooked India's recent illiberalism; its indifference to a US alliance; the Sino-Indian convergence on many global issues; the frequent Indian opposition to the United States in multilateral institutions; and India's ties with Russia. Moreover, although

Ashley J. Tellis is the Tata Chair for Strategic Affairs and a senior fellow at the Carnegie Endowment for International Peace.

The author is deeply grateful to Hal Brands, Kenneth I. Juster, Dan Markey, and Arthur C. Tellis for their most helpful comments on this chapter.

India is still significantly weaker than China, Washington's assiduous wooing of New Delhi confirms that US policymakers nonetheless have great expectations of India, viewing it as pivotal to constraining China in Asia and globally.

India, for its part, has been happy to respond to US overtures, but on its own terms. Although rarely echoing the florid descriptions of the partnership proffered by American officials, India has welcomed US actions insofar as they help to expand its own power. Building up its national capabilities comprehensively is a core Indian interest and enables New Delhi to balance Beijing better than any international partnership, including that with Washington. Consequently, even when seeking US largesse, India has adamantly protected its "strategic autonomy"; the United States is the most valuable, but only one, of many partners.

Equally important, India has also sought to avoid malignant confrontations with China—otherwise the singular challenge that propels US-India cooperation—on the astute calculation that "even with neighbors with whom there are serious issues, there should be hope that the price of a pragmatic settlement will be less than the costs of a difficult relationship."[1] New Delhi's response to American courtship has thus been remarkably subtle even as Washington's enchantment with India for restraining China has grown by leaps and bounds.

This survey examines India's contributions toward advancing US interests in the ongoing rivalry with China. To that end, it reviews how successive US administrations have engaged India over the past quarter century, considering both India's responses and the other relationships impacting US-India ties. The analysis suggests that, despite dramatic improvements in US-India relations, Washington's ambitions regarding India vis-à-vis China—where international order, security collaboration, and economic intercourse are concerned—still await full realization. The differences in US and Indian national goals, New Delhi's abiding desire to remain non-allied, and India's significant frailties ensure that an alliance-like relationship in all but name still lies beyond reach.

The US Engagement of India vis-à-vis China

The transformation of US-India relations after the Cold War began substantively with George W. Bush. Through the dramatic decision to reverse long-standing US nonproliferation policy and offer India an epochal "nuclear deal," Bush sought to correct past estrangements and construct "a new . . . strategic partnership in the 21st century, not just on nuclear cooperation but on every area of national endeavor."[2]

Although some in his administration championed this agreement eyeing Indian cooperation in the anticipated competition with China, Bush himself betrayed no such interest. Rather, enamored of India's liberal democracy and its new economic success, he imagined its "potential to become one of the great democratic powers of the twenty-first century"[3] and a sturdy US partner on diverse global issues.

Although Bush reengaged Pakistan to India's chagrin during his Global War on Terrorism (GWOT), this campaign opened doors to closer ties with New Delhi. Yet US-India relations avoided any manifest fixation with China because both US-China and China-India relations remained largely on an even keel during the Bush years. The concerns about growing Chinese power, however, were just below the surface in India and in important parts of the US government. But the overall US strategy toward China focused on keeping Beijing supportive of the GWOT and productively enmeshed with the United States and its Asian neighbors. Consequently, aiding India's rise to create the "objective constraints that limit the misuse of Chinese power,"[4] while simultaneously reinforcing Beijing's incentives for positive cooperation, came to define the Bush administration's approach to India.

This strategy did not require any sacrifices of New Delhi, although it was hoped that India would support US endeavors whenever possible. On the issues of terrorism, counterproliferation, and the International Criminal Court, for example, New Delhi backed US positions because they dovetailed with Indian interests. But on other matters, such as the Iraq war, limiting cooperation with Iran, or supporting US aims in the World Trade Organization, India's response varied from tepid to oppositional. All the same, these were halcyon years for India. Washington was exceedingly generous toward New Delhi and, apart from seeking an Indian Army division for stabilization operations in Iraq, asked little in return. This liberality was viewed as strengthening a country that generally supported the US-dominated world order. Despite India's own ambitions, both prime ministers during the Bush era, Atal Bihari Vajpayee and Manmohan Singh, acquiesced to American unipolarity because it bolstered Indian power while functionally restraining China.

Barack Obama succeeded Bush when the United States was reeling from the global financial crisis and the enervating wars in Afghanistan and Iraq. The transformed relationship with India was an exceptional success, but, given both wider US troubles and his own pragmatism, Obama sought stable ties with Beijing because he believed that the US-China relationship "will shape the 21st century, which makes it as important as any bilateral relationship in the world."[5] Obama consequently pursued Chinese cooperation, emphasizing low politics, and became the first US president to visit China during the first year in office. Although this trip was not entirely successful, it nonetheless unnerved India because tightening Sino-American relations usually do. This effort came on the heels of many early administration faux pas involving India, including talk about mediating in Jammu and Kashmir.

Although by now China under Hu Jintao was becoming more confident globally—presuming waning US hegemony because of the financial crisis— Obama did not view Beijing as a dangerous threat to US interests during his first term, nor did he conceive of India as a critical restraint on rising Chinese power. Rather, he emphasized India's importance as a US partner on global issues because of its economic success and democratic credentials. Desirous of this becoming "a defining partnership of the century ahead,"[6] Obama continued Bush's legacy of strengthening bilateral ties by dramatically endorsing India for permanent membership in the UN Security Council and key nonproliferation regimes; seeking improved economic relations and resolving disagreements about global trade; and intensifying defense cooperation as the "linchpin"[7] of expanded regional partnerships in support of a declared pivot to Asia.

Enhanced US-India defense cooperation took off after Obama's reelection, which coincided with Xi Jinping's ascendency in Beijing and China's increasing assertiveness. Beyond the previous engagement activities, it now centered on defense industrial collaboration aimed at improving India's military technology on the promise that India would eventually become a "net security provider"[8] in the Indian Ocean region (IOR). This desire would finally produce the contrived designation of India as a "major defense partner"[9] of the United States. Given its perennial concerns about China, India welcomed these initiatives. Its new prime minister, Narendra Modi, had attempted to engage Xi Jinping by striking reciprocal visits after his 2014 election, but the absence of breakthroughs facilitated increased US-India defense ties. Washington's suspicions of Beijing deepened during Obama's second term when Xi demanded peer status with the United States by reiterating claims for "a new type of great power relationship,"[10] while militarizing reefs in the South China Sea and insinuating sweeping Chinese rights over the area.

Given these challenges, Obama sought to provide reassurance by increasing US diplomatic engagement with Southeast Asia, pursuing new trade agreements such as the Trans-Pacific Partnership, and initiating freedom-of-navigation operations, but he did not seek to position India as an instrument for checking China in Southeast Asia or elsewhere. In part, this was because Washington recognized that

New Delhi would resist any such role, not having the capabilities to do so anyway. The IOR, however, was another story. India had important equities here and the capabilities to make a difference. The new Chinese presence in these waters since 2009 had already increased Indian anxieties, and while the United States could not cede responsibility for the basin's security to India, it nonetheless viewed Indian support here as valuable. Consequently, the administration began developing a IOR strategy for the first time in decades and the "Joint Strategic Vision for the Asia-Pacific and Indian Ocean Region" negotiated with India envisaged New Delhi providing important public goods with US support.[11]

By the end of Obama's presidency, India was viewed as an important security partner, especially in the IOR. There were still significant disagreements on bilateral and multilateral trade, Afghanistan, and Iran. Russia had by now also become troublesome in Europe, but it was viewed in Washington as a declining power and, hence, New Delhi's ties with Moscow were not yet a serious hindrance. US and Indian ties with China, however, were marked by growing disquiet, although both were reasonably managed. This enabled Obama to persist with engaging both Beijing and New Delhi but, in an important evolution of Bush's policy of largely building Indian power vis-à-vis China, Washington now sought active, even if still low-key, Indian contributions toward strengthening peace and prosperity in the Indo-Pacific. The Obama years thus presaged the eventual US hard balancing of China even though the administration itself neither pursued such a policy nor sought to inveigle India into it.

Both elements would change dramatically with Donald Trump's arrival as president in 2016. Trump entered office determined to punish China because he believed its trade practices generated unfair deficits that led to America's deindustrialization. Although Trump's views on trade—and his opposition to China—were often idiosyncratic, his administration contained many traditional Republicans who viewed China both as an economic threat and as a dangerous peer competitor intent on displacing the United States as the global hegemon. This aspect of US attitudes proved appealing to India, which had by now suffered several unpleasant Chinese incursions along its border. The Doklam Crisis of 2017, when Chinese troops sought to build a road in Bhutan's territory, threatening India, strengthened Indian perceptions of Chinese bullying, and New Delhi's resolute stand against Beijing was welcomed by the Trump administration, which presumed that India would demonstrate strong solidarity with its own anti-China campaign.

India, however, had other ideas. In an arresting turn, Modi dramatically intensified his outreach to Xi even as US-China relations progressively frayed, engaging in two high-profile summits at Wuhan and Mamallapuram in 2018 and 2019, respectively. During the first encounter, he privately made bold overtures intended to resolve the outstanding Sino-Indian disputes conclusively. This heightened diplomacy with Beijing, reflecting canny realpolitik, was deemed opportune because China might accommodate India precisely when it was under growing pressure from the United States. Unfortunately for Modi, Xi—apparently judging that Chinese strength permitted resisting both New Delhi and Washington successfully—gave little ground, but the twin summits proved that whenever possible India would seek to avoid exacerbating tensions with China while simultaneously averting deleterious entanglement in the larger US-China rivalry.

Consequently, New Delhi regularly demurred when Trump officials sought to elevate the Quad—an ad hoc grouping of the United States, Japan, Australia and India—through high-level meetings for fear of offending China. These reservations faded as Chinese belligerence toward India intensified. The May 2020 Sino-Indian border clashes, which produced the first loss of life on both sides in decades, markedly changed India's attitude. Perceiving an opportunity to bind India more deeply in its competition with Beijing, Washington responded wholeheartedly to New Delhi's requests for military equipment, real-time intelligence, and diplomatic support.

The national security cohort within the Trump administration had always perceived India as an important instrument in confronting China, as reflected in the "US Strategic Framework for the Indo-Pacific."[12] The administration went further than its predecessors in increasing India's eligibility for advanced US technology and even rechristened the storied US Pacific Command the Indo-Pacific Command in recognition of the IOR's (and India's) growing significance. But in another example of New Delhi's strategic adroitness amid Washington's courting, India—despite its newfound enthusiasm for the Quad—refused to support the administration's desire to securitize this grouping by institutionalizing new military arrangements against Beijing. Instead, India, with grudging US acceptance, transformed the Quad into a diplomatic instrument for mobilizing against Chinese threats, increasing regional public goods, and building local capacities for undertaking constabulary missions.

Although bilateral US-India military cooperation increased significantly during the Trump years and India echoed the administration's criticisms of China's violations of the rules-based "free and open Indo-Pacific,"[13] this posture obscured New Delhi's affinities to Beijing's position on the United Nations Convention on the Law of the Sea (UNCLOS). India also parried the US quest for coalitional solutions to the Chinese military threat, and it avoided developing any collaborative defense mechanisms against future Chinese aggression. Despite the deepening strategic partnership with Washington, New Delhi remained obdurately nonaligned. Its ties with Moscow steadfastly endured and its procurement of advanced Russian weapons persisted despite running afoul of US law. But its disappointment notwithstanding, the Trump administration, eyeing India's significance vis-à-vis China, never applied sanctions against India.

If Trump turned out to be an unexpected president in 2016, his successor Joseph R. Biden turned out to be an unexpected China hawk. The COVID-19 pandemic had pushed US-China relations to their nadir in the last year of Trump's presidency, becoming the dénouement to the aggressive trade war unleased by the United States. Although belittling China as a rival while he was a presidential candidate, Biden persisted with Trump's treatment of China as an adversary, bringing new energy and discipline to this effort. In short order, Biden dispensed with his initial support of democracy internationally in favor of renewing US alliances and partnerships against China (and Russia). He preserved Trump's tariffs, instituted industrial policy in the United States, and expanded export controls against Beijing, aiming to preserve US advantages in high technology and the sunrise sectors of the global economy. Strategic competition with China thus unexpectedly became a defining motif of Biden's presidency, but, unlike Trump, he sought to cement various international partnerships aimed at limiting Chinese power.

The US engagement with India, accordingly, scaled new heights. The Modi government's treatment of minorities was downplayed, and Modi himself was enthusiastically received by Biden in the White House in 2023. India's relations with China were already in tatters because of the May 2020 border crisis: New Delhi had frozen Chinese investments, limited the use of its technology applications, and refused to do business as usual until Beijing had restored the territorial status quo ante. This meltdown in Sino-Indian relations was a godsend to Washington, which sought to clutch India more closely in its own intensifying rivalry with China.

The American embrace of India consequently became more fervent, and Biden, echoing a late-Trump locution, described the relationship with tongue-twisting hyperbole as the "US-India Comprehensive Global and Strategic Partnership."[14] To actualize the rhetoric, the administration intensified defense cooperation—to include expanded military exercises, new arms sales and military technology transfers, and extensive intelligence sharing—while inaugurating new partnerships in critical and emerging technology and expanding earlier initiatives on defense innovation. The administration also sought to weave India into its efforts at "friendshoring," encouraging businesses present in China to consider India as an alternative investment destination. Most conspicuously, the administration accentuated the QUAD as the preeminent Asian forum for mobilizing pressure against Beijing, though this grouping was somewhat eclipsed by the later AUKUS (Australia-United Kingdom-United States) and "Squad" (comprising the United States, Australia, Japan, and the Philippines) initiatives that promised military benefits to US deterrence efforts against China.

India, for its part, responded enthusiastically to Biden's overtures. These comported perfectly with India's desire to increase its own national capabilities and, given the parlous state of Sino-Indian relations, Washington's effusive attention to India, especially through the QUAD, gave it the leverage to nudge China into reconsidering its obstreperousness toward New Delhi. This strategy paid off when the two countries agreed to resolve their border crisis in October 2024, an outcome fostered in part by the uncertainties associated with Trump's possible return to the White House. In any event, even as India's gusto for the QUAD increased, its desire to prevent the group from becoming the fountainhead of US military pushback against China had not diminished, though it privately expressed openness to exploring some common military activities.

India's determination to preserve—nay, even expand—its ties with US adversaries, such as Russia, however, did not flag. US-India relations became scratchy during Biden's final months because Modi's visit to Moscow roughly coincided with NATO's 75th anniversary celebrations, a reminder that India's purchases of Russian oil and arms helped prolong the murderous war in Ukraine. That India preserved the White House's support, despite uneasiness in other parts of the US government about Indian policies on trade, human rights, Bangladesh and the attempted assassination of American citizens, spoke volumes for how much Washington valued New Delhi in the ongoing competition with China. In fact, not since the Bush administration had India so many enthusiasts championing its cause in high places.

The history of the last twenty-five years illustrates how the United States has cultivated India in search of a partnership that could contribute toward successfully balancing China—with the evolution of their relations deeply tied to their respective deteriorating ties with Beijing. No other country has been comparably courted by Washington, and American rhetoric has often conveyed the impression that the United States needs India more than India needs the United States to constrain Chinese power.

The Bush administration's original vision centered on assisting India's rise so that a multipolar Asia could produce a "moderating effect on PRC [People's Republic of China] behavior."[15] That idea was attractive when US-China relations were relatively stable but, in any case, it has not yet been realized. And it may never be given the huge disparity in Sino-Indian power, which if it ever closes, will take decades.

In the interim, as US-China competition has intensified, an alternative aim unsurprisingly has gained ground: soliciting India's collaboration in limiting China's assertiveness. Despite offering significant blandishments, however, Indian cooperation, from a US perspective, has still not yielded full fruit because New Delhi's ambitions and capabilities differ considerably from Washington's in the three areas that matter most to the United States: preserving global primacy, promoting cooperative defense, and protecting economic vitality.

The Spaces in Our Togetherness

Washington's goal of preserving US global primacy is intimately linked to the international distribution of power. Since 1945, and even during the high tide of bipolarity, the United States has towered above all others where "comprehensive national power" is concerned. A risen China threatens that preeminence in unprecedented ways. Consequently, US grand strategy externally has focused on balancing Beijing by, inter alia, strengthening rival powers such as Japan and India, encouraging Southeast Asian solidarity, and bolstering more distant allies such as Australia, the United Kingdom, and France, while encouraging varied forms of strategic cooperation among them all. This strategy aims to weave a continental net around China, thus protecting American unipolarity at the global apex by fostering regional multipolarity within Asia.

China, obviously, has different ambitions. Given its multifaceted success, it aspires to build a unipolar system in Asia that subordinates its regional competitors to first achieve bipolarity with the United States before eventually replacing it as *the* global hegemon. India, for its part, has goals that differ from those of both the United States and China. It seeks, initially, a multipolar Asia where India and China are equals surrounded by other peers. But, in contrast to both Washington and Beijing, New Delhi ultimately desires multipolarity at the global level as well with neither the United States nor China singularly, or in concert or opposition, remaining dominant.

India today is far from realizing these goals. A strong US-India partnership is therefore essential in the interim: Washington can aid the growth of Indian power to enable Asian multipolarity, with New Delhi hoping that it can thereby achieve its global ambitions inexorably. US-Indian interests, thus, converge regionally—

both seek a China balanced by others in Asia—but they diverge globally, where India desires multiple great powers, whereas both Washington and Beijing prefer to rule the roost alone.

Therefore, even as India seeks US assistance for its ascendency, it protects its relationships with other key states, such as Russia. Despite its current weakness, Russia is viewed as an important actor to "balance China while constraining Pakistan,"[16] and supporting its viability aids the evolution toward continental and global multipolarity. Beyond nostalgia, ingrained habit, or functional dependence, India's efforts to protect these ties are in fact animated by a larger vision that is suspicious of concentrated power in international politics because it prevents weaker states such as India from exploiting the cleavages that would otherwise persist.

For just these reasons, India actively participates in various groupings like the BRICS and the Shanghai Cooperation Organization—which include both US rivals and its own—while vigorously championing the Global South as well. Although limiting Chinese influence in these fora is a significant consideration for New Delhi, expanding India's sway in an egalitarian international system is just as important.

Given India's interest in multipolarity at both the regional and global levels, New Delhi has acted unilaterally and bilaterally with the United States and other partners, and through the QUAD, to economically and militarily assist countries in the Indo-Pacific while also aiding the production of shared goods that increase India's influence and position it as an alternative to China. Unfortunately, for India and the United States, these investments have not succeeded in meaningfully constraining the growth of Chinese power or diminishing its influence in Asia or globally.

All the same, US-Indian interests durably converge on balancing China at the regional level. But their divergence at the global level, which has been more of a nuisance than an insurmountable obstacle thus far, could become corrosive if domestic developments in each country drove them in divergent directions, or if India's differences with the United States about global order intensified, or if Indian power rapidly expanded in ways that threaten US primacy or interests.

Even if these challenges are averted, significant differences lie beneath the surface. They account, at the Indian end, for the reluctance to collaborate with Washington on mutually supporting security arrangements and the desire to avoid climactic confrontations with Beijing—the latter partly because of India's frailties but, equally, because of its judgment that China's bid for global influence cannot be defeated irrevocably even by the United States, thus leaving it as a significant power in any future multipolar order. At the US end, the gap in Washington and New Delhi's goals implies that the United States—despite professed claims to the contrary—will likely remain unwilling to share its most advanced civilian and military technologies as well as its exquisite intelligence with India as it does with those allies who bolster American hegemony out of both political conviction and strategic necessity.

The bottom line, therefore, is that India and the United States will cooperate vis-à-vis China as circumstances demand, but this effort will not naturally extend to buttressing American hegemony, thus making the US-India partnership selective when it comes to the high politics of global order.

These constraints are reflected in defense collaboration. Although the last two-odd decades have witnessed big improvements, India's discomfort with an exclusive embrace of the United States has eliminated the possibility of collective defense, where an attack on one is treated as aggression against both. But New Delhi's relentless desire to preserve its freedoms of association and action has also limited the potential for cooperative defense understood as negotiated commitments about shared responsibilities for preventing wars, responding to crises, and countering aggression.

Consequently, the United States and India might offer mutual assistance during a clash with China, but such a felicitous outcome would materialize only amid a conflict. And if it did, it is more likely—thanks to the asymmetries of power—to involve US assistance toward India than the reverse. As a result, neither Washington nor New Delhi can exploit any preplanned support to deter Chinese aggressiveness to begin with. Even if reciprocal assistance were to emerge during a conflict, most significant combined operations would ordinarily lie beyond reach because India's military forces are not integrated with their US counterparts in ways that would be necessary to prosecute any high-end combat operations against China.

In principle, India could assist the United States in wartime by allowing US forces to use its physical facilities, supporting assets, or material stocks to prosecute their missions against China. Or Indian forces could independently conduct operations against China to aid US forces either in the IOR or in more distant theaters such as the South or East China Seas. (The notion that India could pressure China along the Himalayas to tie down Chinese military forces during a Sino-American war does not merit serious consideration because other than possibly manpower advantages, India is outclassed in firepower, intelligence, sustainment, and command and control.) Or India could simply limit its cooperation to diplomatic and economic pressure against China.

Whether New Delhi actively confronts Beijing in these ways will depend on the prevailing state of Sino-Indian political and economic relations, the Sino-Indian military balance, and India's perception of the stakes and possible outcomes of the war for its interests. Although India's decisions cannot be reliably predicted a priori, its traditional preference for avoiding conflicts involving third parties—whether friends or adversaries—suggests that it would be unlikely to physically interject itself in any Sino-American struggle short of a direct Chinese attack on India simultaneously, even though it would obviously desire a US victory given its own competition with Beijing.

Beyond political and perhaps economic solidarity with Washington, New Delhi might contribute tacit military support for US combat operations if it can avoid injurious Chinese retaliation in the process. Given India's geography, worldview, and material deficiencies, it is unreasonable to expect more. But it implies that India's contributions toward assisting the United States in what would be its most dangerous wartime predicament are likely to be modest. India already supports US efforts to build regional resilience against China, and it collaborates in peacetime through constabulary and intelligence activities. But combined operations in war will remain elusive for a long time to come.

If aiding the United States in preserving its global primacy and strengthening cooperative defense are constrained, India does better—but still not as well as it could—in sustaining US economic vitality.

US global primacy derives in the first instance from its formidable military capabilities, which enable commanding the commons, protecting allies, and upholding the international order that serves its interests. Maintaining these coercive instruments, in turn, depends on a strong economy marked by superior innovation. The ability to constantly generate new products and processes faster than others across expanding markets worldwide permits the United States to enjoy superior economic returns that improve welfare at home while underwriting the puissant military that bestows influence abroad.

Developing advanced technology faster than one's rivals thus increases US prosperity and power and, hence, it is no surprise that US-China competition—like every iteration before it—involves a struggle to dominate the cycles of innovation.

India contributes to the success of the US innovation system through its labor force in US corporations, the growth engine of the US economy. These contributions occur in two ways: through its skilled professionals working in the United

States on temporary visas, and increasingly—and more importantly—through the 1,200 (and growing) US global capability centers in India that employ approximately 1.3 million Indian citizens in support of their corporate parents' commercial activities worldwide.

The conspicuous Indian presence in Silicon Valley and in American boardrooms further testifies to the value of Indian nationals and émigrés in advantaging the US technology base in the competition with China, corroborating the "growing suggestive evidence that immigrants play a key role in US innovation."[17] India's foreign direct investment in the United States, now totaling around $60 billion, is an additional, albeit modest, contributor to American competitiveness.

The Indian impact on US innovation is therefore notable and remains a bright spot when India's contributions to US interests are assessed. But it is, more dismally, accompanied by the Indian government's neo-mercantilist attitude to international trade, which prevents US business from enjoying easy access to the Indian market in ways that would increase its profitability and, by extension, enlarge US economic power even while producing welfare gains for Indian citizens. Admittedly, the United States itself, despite pioneering the international trading system, has become destructively protectionist in recent years. But the American economy, which is the world's largest, is still remarkably open, thus making its recent trade distortions (prior to Trump's return to office) arguably a modest blemish.

In contrast, Narendra Modi's India pursued industrial policy long before the United States followed suit and, additionally, piled on tariffs and duties to protect India's inefficient economy against foreign competition. The results have been deleterious to India itself, but they have also prevented New Delhi and Washington from expanding bilateral economic growth to their advantage vis-à-vis China. They have also limited India's ability to deepen its trading links with Pacific Asia, thus failing to undercut China's economic dominance even in proximate regions such as Southeast Asia. One widely regarded survey has actually placed India last in political and strategic influence and next to last in economic influence in the ASEAN community.[18]

The failure to expand external openness has had a further consequence: frustrating the US strategy of stimulating "friendshoring," that is, encouraging Western (and particularly US) companies to shift investments away from threatening rivals like China toward well-disposed countries such as India. Washington's effort to mitigate excessive dependence on Chinese manufacturing is gaining traction as reshoring to the United States increases, but the push toward friendshoring appears to have disproportionately benefited Mexico, Vietnam, Singapore, and Taiwan more than India. This outcome is owed largely to India's inhospitable business environment and its market access constraints. India's continuing high dependence on Chinese inputs and intermediate goods does not help either. Although there have been a few conspicuous successes of diversifying foreign investments in India—stimulated largely by deliberate Indian political and economic incentives interacting with corporate efforts at risk mitigation—the larger openness to international trade is still elusive, which implies that the Indian contribution to enhancing US economic vitality (and its own) falls short of what it should be.

On balance, therefore, when India's contributions to advancing US interests in the competition with China across three metrics are examined—preserving global primacy, promoting cooperative defense, and protecting economic vitality—the successes attained do not yet reflect the grandiloquent characterizations of the strategic partnership.

Conclusion: An India Betwixt Weakness and Hesitation

The transformation of US-India relations has been an extraordinary achievement of US foreign policy in the 21st century. Above all, it has positioned India broadly alongside the United States in the competition with China. New Delhi's problems with Beijing would have inevitably brought it closer to Washington, but the bold decisions of successive US presidents starting with George W. Bush helped to erode—but not eliminate—the encrusted Indian suspicions of the United States. Thus, they opened the door to a new relationship that promises benefits for American interests.

The extraordinary breadth of current bilateral engagements illustrates how important this partnership is to Washington and New Delhi. Yet they have not dramatically expanded US and Indian national capabilities so far, and, to the degree that they make a difference, they have benefited India more than the United States. By itself, this outcome is not unnatural: It merely reflects the power asymmetry between the two countries. What is problematic, however, is that deepening US-India ties, while producing common benefits such as expanding minilateral solidarity, rising but still incomplete defense cooperation, and incipiently increasing regional resiliency, have not checkmated the accumulation or the exercise of Chinese power in the Indo-Pacific or globally.

Realizing this objective requires more than coruscating diplomacy. Where India is concerned, it demands fundamental transformations that "depend substantially on its own choices"[19] domestically because only improvements in the material balance of power and the intensified political commitment to use those fruits in solidarity with the United States and its Asian allies will permit the successful balancing of China. To wit, India must first sustain higher trend growth rates than before for an extended period. Further, it must increase its economic openness and integrate deeply into the wider Indo-Pacific trading system both to accelerate its own growth and to provide other states with an alternative to China. Finally, it must build up its military capabilities for missions beyond subcontinental defense, while committing to combined operations outside of the UN flag with foreign partners, especially the United States.

Even if India successfully completes these renovations, however, it will be unable to checkmate China over the next twenty years—the era of maximum danger after which Chinese economic power could stagnate—because of Beijing's enormous current lead and its astonishing technological proficiency. This implies that balancing China effectively will remain primarily a US responsibility with meaningful assistance emerging mostly from Japan, the European allies, and Australia in that order rather than India.

But, on this score, New Delhi's weaknesses are not the only impediment. Its hesitations about embracing the United States even vis-à-vis China are just as significant. India's desire to become a global power, its fierce foreign policy independence, and its drive to foster multipolarity in Asia and beyond inhibit the tightest collaboration possible with Washington. India's legitimate fear of Chinese capabilities, thanks to both disparity and proximity, only reinforces its reluctance to consistently bandwagon with the United States. India, consequently, walks a tightrope, seeking to offset China with as much US assistance as it can obtain without getting snarled in any US-China enmity or collusion that makes it collateral damage.

This choice of a middle path, however rational for New Delhi, nevertheless leaves Washington with diminished incentives to aid India as expansively as each might like. Although both countries have done better than before on this count, there are still thresholds that the United States is unlikely to cross. With Trump's return to the presidency, US policy could go in either direction: a willingness to sell technologies that were previously withheld simply because it is remunerative or to limit access because of heightened US techno-nationalism, all while demanding more of India as the price of American partnership. How the US-India relationship evolves will also depend greatly on the evolution of US-China competition itself. Although the structural imperatives that sustain Sino-American rivalry are real, Trump's eccentricities are striking enough to push it in wildly different directions—including toward a simulacrum of rapprochement that would funda-mentally unsettle New Delhi. His "Liberation Day" tariff decisions have already demonstrated a stunning inability to distinguish between friends and foes, let alone those in between. In such circumstances, the extant Indian hesitations about the United States will not only prove to be justified but will also intensify.

The gap that persists in US-India ties—even when at their best—confirms that it derives from structural and not merely volitional constraints on both sides. While this partnership will probably be more valuable to the United States in peace than in war, the challenge facing both nations is how to sustain its intensification despite falling short of their greatest expectations. Because US-China competition is likely to be long-lived, bolstering the US-India strategic partnership, its infirmi-ties notwithstanding, remains in Washington's continuing interest.

NOTES

1. S. Jaishankar, *The India Way: Strategies for an Uncertain World* (HarperCollins India, 2020), 27.

2. Condoleezza Rice, "Remarks at the Signing of the U.S.-India Civilian Nuclear Cooperation Agreement," Washington, DC, October 10, 2008, https://2001-2009.state .gov/secretary/rm/2008/10/110916.htm.

3. "IV: Work with others to Defuse Regional Conflicts," *National Security Strategy of the United States of America*, September 2002, https://georgewbush-whitehouse.archives .gov/nsc/nss/2002/nss4.html.

4. Ashley J. Tellis, *Opportunities Unbound: Sustaining the Transformation in U.S.-Indian Relations*, Carnegie Endowment for International Peace, 2013, 11, https:// carnegieendowment.org/research/2013/01/opportunities-unbound-sustaining-the -transformation-in-us-indian-relations?lang=en.

5. Barack Obama, "Remarks by the President at the US/China Strategic and Economic Dialogue," Washington, DC, July 27, 2009, https://obamawhitehouse.archives.gov/the -press-office/remarks-president-uschina-strategic-and-economic-dialogue.

6. Barack Obama, "Remarks by the President to the Joint Session of the Indian Parliament in New Delhi, India," Washington, DC, November 8, 2010, https:// obamawhitehouse.archives.gov/the-press-office/2010/11/08/remarks-president-joint -session-indian-parliament-new-delhi-india.

7. Leon Panetta, "Partners in the 21st Century," Institute for Defense Studies and Analyses, New Delhi, India, June 6, 2012, https://www.globalsecurity.org/military// /library/news/2012/06/mil-120606-dod02.htm.

8. Robert M. Gates, "Transcript: Keynote Address by the Secretary of Defense at the Shangri-La Dialogue in Singapore," DVIDS, May 30, 2009, https://www.dvidshub .net/news/34339/gates-delivers-keynote-address-open-asia-security-conference.

9. The White House, "Joint Statement: The United States and India: Enduring Global Partners in the 21st Century," June 7, 2016, https://obamawhitehouse.archives

.gov/the-press-office/2016/06/07/joint-statement-united-states-and-india-enduring
-global-partners-21st.

10. The history of this locution is described in Bonnie Glaser and Jake Douglas, "The Ascent and Demise of 'New Type of Great Power Relations' Between the US and China," *CSCAP Regional Security Outlook 2016* (2015): 28–30, https://www.cscap.org /uploads/docs/CRSO/CSCAPCRSO2016.pdf.

11. The White House, "Joint Statement: U.S.-India Joint Strategic Vision for the Asia-Pacific and Indian Ocean Region," January 25, 2015, https://obamawhitehouse .archives.gov/the-press-office/2015/01/25/us-india-joint-strategic-vision-asia-pacific-and -indian-ocean-region.

12. "U.S. Strategic Framework for the Indo-Pacific," January 5, 2021, https:// trumpwhitehouse.archives.gov/wp-content/uploads/2021/01/IPS-Final-Declass.pdf.

13. US Department of State, "A Free and Open Indo-Pacific," November 4, 2019, https://www.state.gov/wp-content/uploads/2019/11/Free-and-Open-Indo-Pacific -4Nov2019.pdf.

14. The White House, "Joint Statement from the United States and India," June 22, 2023, https://bidenwhitehouse.archives.gov/briefing-room/statements-releases/2023/06 /22/joint-statement-from-the-united-states-and-india/.

15. James Shinn, ed., *Weaving the Net: Conditional Engagement with China*, Council on Foreign Relations, 1996, 4.

16. Ashley J. Tellis, *"What Is in Our Interest": India and the Ukraine War*, Carnegie Endowment for International Peace, April 25, 2022, https://carnegieendowment.org /research/2022/04/what-is-in-our-interest-india-and-the-ukraine-war?lang=en.

17. Shai Bernstein et al., *The Contribution of High-Skilled Immigrants to Innovation in the United States*, NBER Working Paper 30797, December 2022, p. 2, http://www.nber .org/papers/w30797.

18. S. Seah et al., "The State of Southeast Asia: 2024 Survey Report," ISEAS—Yusof Ishak Institute, 2024, 34–37, https://www.iseas.edu.sg/wp-content/uploads/2024/03 /The-State-of-SEA-2024.pdf.

19. Ashley J. Tellis, *India as a New Global Power*, Carnegie Endowment for International Peace, 2005, 50, https://carnegieendowment.org/research/2005/07/india-as-a -new-global-power-an-action-agenda-for-the-united-states?lang=en.

Chapter Seven

Understanding the Evolving Defense Competition with China

Michael Mazarr

The 2022 National Security Strategy argued that the United States confronted a "decisive decade"—a period that would decide emerging great power rivalries, most especially between the United States and China. We are now three years into that decade, and the US-China rivalry has become both more intense and more fluid. It is an appropriate time to ask how the United States is doing. Looking back at the last decade, how have the major elements of the military rivalry between the United States and China evolved? Where has the United States done well, where has it done poorly, and where do trends appear to be heading?

One way to approach this issue would be to make a system-by-system comparison of US and Chinese military capabilities over the last ten years, but military capabilities alone only tell us so much about a defense competition. Another approach would be to assess the operational capacity of the two sides. In the US-China case, for example, the People's Liberation Army (PLA) suffers from a powerful set of operational limitations, ranging from the lack of a readiness focus to poor command culture.[1] The PLA has aired many of these flaws in recent years, developing terms like "The Five Incapables" to catalogue its own weaknesses.[2]

Michael Mazarr is a senior political scientist at the RAND Corporation. He has worked on issues of US defense strategy for three decades, with experience on Capitol Hill, in other research institutions, the US National War College, the US Navy Reserve, and the Office of the Chairman of the Joint Chiefs of Staff.

The challenge of assessing relative progress over the last decade is complicated by the fact that military power is meaningful only when evaluated in terms of specific competing goals, interests, and possible conflict scenarios. In the US-China context, the obvious example is a Taiwan contingency. The United States is perfectly able to defend nearly all its vital interests against Chinese aggression—but a Taiwan campaign is so uniquely challenging that it casts a skewed light on the overall military situation.

In this chapter, I assess the US-China military balance through three alternative lenses. First, I catalog the basic security interests and objectives of both sides, as a way of establishing a baseline against which to measure successes and failures in defense policy. I then examine trends in the balance involving the leading large-scale military scenarios—Taiwan and the South China Sea. Finally I make an argument for five essential components of effective defense policy in the 21st century and evaluate relative progress in each.

Taken together, these perspectives suggest that, for the United States, the last decade has been mostly a story of losing ground in the military balance surrounding the major contingencies, and only modest progress or outright stagnation on the functional indices of national security capability. Nonetheless, especially if the United States can accelerate progress on a few of those indices, the overall security balance between the United States and China is headed for a form of equilibrium. Each of these two great powers is accumulating the defense capacity to defend its most vital interests against the other—with a single possible exception: the hugely uncertain Taiwan contingency.

The Security Objectives of Both Sides

Evaluating trend lines in relative national security capabilities requires some sense of national interests and ambitions. A United States uninterested in defending Taiwan, South Korea, or Israel would not need the military it has today. China's national security muscle would stack up very differently against a mission set limited to capturing Taiwan than it would against an ambition to invade and conquer much of Asia. To establish the context for the comparison that follows, I will first catalog each side's most important interests and objectives and then briefly suggest what those things imply for the trajectory of national security capabilities over the last decade.

A set of US interests and objectives can be compiled from recent National Security Strategies and a broader literature on US national security objectives. The most essential US goals comprise five categories: protection of the homeland (in both physical and digital or informational terms); preventing aggression against the United States, its territories, and its treaty allies; preventing the domination of critical regions by a hostile power; preserving and promoting the requirements for national prosperity; and, most recently, preventing Chinese establishment of a Sino-centric world order that would fatally constrain US sovereign autonomy.[3]

For the last several decades, as a means to these ends more than as an end in itself, the United States has sought a more encompassing objective—a degree of predominance in economic, military, and political terms that establishes it at the top of the global power hierarchy. Yet it has become increasingly evident that this objective is unsustainable. Just what degree of predominance America needs as an essential component of its security strategy is no longer clear, which makes setting objectives—in domains such as technology competition or the contest for influence in the South China Sea—very challenging. One area on which the issue of overextension theoretically plays out is over the US intention to defend Taiwan, an issue I discuss below.

When considering Chinese national security interests and objectives, it is useful to think in terms of three tiers.[4] At the foundation, Beijing seeks to safeguard the stability of the regime and the protection of the homeland. These goals imply preserving the rule of the Chinese Communist Party (CCP), preventing domestic instability, and guarding the security of mainland China from digital, informational, or physical attacks. A second tier involves the most deeply held international goals and ambitions—realizing territorial claims especially in core interests (Taiwan and possibly the South China Sea) and, at some broad level, achieving parity with (and for some but not all observers, clear supremacy over) the United States in leadership of the international system. China's territorial goals, most notably regarding Taiwan, have produced one of its centerpiece military efforts: To develop a counter-intervention capability to prevent the United States from interfering in local fights, including the development of anti-access / area denial (A2AD) capabilities.

The third tier contains the most ambitious—but also ill-defined—interests and objectives of Chinese security strategy. These include the desire to see a future world that is fundamentally Sino-centric in more explicit ways, including economic influence, digital networks, and military power. A related objective is to force US military and even economic power out of the region. Like the US impulse for predominance, however, the goals associated with this wider program are ambiguous and do not mandate specific vital interests. Importantly, the last decade has seen no fundamental changes in these tiers of Chinese interests or goals—only greater assertiveness in attempting to attain them.

Both the United States and China have a set of vital or even existential interests connected to domestic safety, security, and prosperity. Each hopes to achieve more expansive objectives in terms of regional and global influence. But the United States and China have surprisingly few interests or goals that are at once irreconcilable and vital enough to fight for. Over the last decade, neither has developed a capacity to threaten the other side's most vital interests without risking unacceptable damage to itself—whether in economic, digital, or military terms.

China surely covets contested territories, notably Taiwan and the South and East China Seas. The question is whether Chinese leaders are willing to go to war to pursue those goals. While there are circumstances that would compel (or powerfully tempt) Beijing to take aggressive military action, that would endanger China's long-term economic goals, risk alienating the region and world, have immense military costs, and could even threaten the rule of the CCP. China has become adept at gray-zone warfare as an alternative to major conflict, and its history and strategic mindsets are built around patient, long-term efforts to gain advantage. While statements from Xi Jinping and others have been blunter about the goals of unification, the last decade has not seen clear evidence of a radical shift in China's willingness to risk war.

This interpretation of US and Chinese goals has significant implications for how we view the trends of the last decade. China has been catching up in many areas and even taking a lead in several. But there is strong evidence that Beijing hopes—and continues to plan—to achieve its objectives short of war. Beyond Taiwan, the trends of the last decade do not begin to approach a level that would allow China to generate hegemony over the Indo-Pacific region. The character of China's ambitions and risk tolerance suggest that the United States and its core regional allies should be able to create a lasting equilibrium in the regional security equation.

Leading Contingencies: Taiwan and the South China Sea

Relative national security capabilities, and their trajectory over time, can best be understood in terms of specific potential uses or conflicts. In the US-China context, despite the intensity and global reach of their rivalry, only two potential contingencies appear plausible in the coming decade. In both cases, the US relative military position has deteriorated over the last decade, but the strategic significance of this is unclear.

In terms of the Taiwan scenario, China has spent years pursuing specific military capabilities with a laser focus: to deny the United States the possibility of effective intervention in a contingency close to China's coast. These include larger inventories of long-range missiles as well as significantly improved intelligence, surveying, and reconnaissance capabilities, expanded amphibious capabilities, and stronger maritime components of an integrated air and missile defense system.[5] China's recurring exercises around Taiwan have also complicated the US task of gaining strategic warning of a potential blockade or invasion.

Meanwhile, the last decade has seen little in the way of dramatic US posture improvements in the region. Tangible changes in US regional combat power have been slow to materialize: additional Enhanced Defense Cooperation Agreement (EDCA) sites in the Philippines, some rotational small unit deployments of army and marine forces, modest enhancements to US forces in Hawaii, and other steps have not created major new combat power that could be brought to bear in a Taiwan conflict.[6] Important priorities, such as hardening US air bases in the region and creating a logistical foundation capable of supporting wartime efforts, remain at best partially addressed. In some cases, the balance tipped toward China: One recent study suggested that, over roughly the last decade, China added substantially more airfields and hardened aircraft shelters than the United States.[7]

The much called-for shift in US operational approaches to large numbers of more numerous, inexpensive precision weapons of all kinds—unmanned aerial and naval systems, long-range strike missiles, coastal defense anti-ship missiles, smart mines, anti-aircraft systems and more—remains largely conceptual.[8] The Replicator Initiative at the Department of Defense is reportedly on the verge of beginning significant production runs of cheap, attritable drones, but these must be integrated into the force along with operational concepts to guide their use.

Another lost opportunity in the last decade stems from Taiwan's reluctance to spend more, or more effectively, on defense. Only in the last year has Taiwan pledged to spend up to 3% of gross domestic product on defense—but those plans may continue to be hampered by disagreements in the legislature. Beyond increased budgets, Taiwan needs to spend on the right things and address defense budget inefficiencies as well as creating a highly trained, combat-ready reserve able to be called up quickly in the event of war.

China's objective capacity to launch a successful invasion of Taiwan has clearly advanced over the last decade. And yet it remains difficult to judge how a Taiwan contingency would play out. After years of unclassified assessments and war games suggesting that the United States would lose, the US military has invested in new capabilities and force posture initiatives designed to improve its chances (such as expanded production of long-range strike missiles, as I note below). Outside the classified realm, it is impossible to definitively assess that process. No one can know for sure how well the PLA would fight or how hard the Taiwanese military and people would resist. Only two things can be said with some certainty: Over the last decade, China has made significant strides in further complicating any US operation to defend Taiwan; but such a campaign, whether a blockade or full invasion, remains a perilous gamble.

The story is similar in the South China Sea. Military trends in this region have been decidedly negative from US standpoint: China has continued to militarize several land features, it has built more air and maritime power projection capabilities, and much of the same immense missile force that threatens US bases in a Taiwan conflict could be brought to bear in this region.[9] In the meantime, while the US Navy could contest Chinese control in the case of war, few US forces regularly deploy in or near the South China Sea.

Yet this is a far tougher scenario for China. It is almost 300 miles from China's Hainan Island to the Paracel Islands, and over 700 miles to the Spratleys. Projecting power over that distance is a very different prospect from an attack on Taiwan. China's militarized islands are vulnerable to air and missile strikes. Once a war was underway, the United States could surge forces into the region more easily than in a Taiwan contingency. A direct attack on the Philippines would bring the United States into the war, and likely others as well: Large-scale Chinese aggression in this critical waterway would engage the interests of Australia and Japan as well as other claimants to South China Sea territories.

For these and other scenarios, the role of space in military operations has become critical. Trends over the last decade in this domain are complex. China has significantly enhanced its counterspace capabilities—but it has also come to rely more on space for its own military operations, perhaps creating a reason to refrain from attacks.[10] The United States has enhanced its own space capabilities as well, though presumably many of these steps remain classified. Overall, the last decade has left the US space architecture more objectively vulnerable even as unclassified RAND research suggests that China's risk tolerance for aggressive space operations is growing.[11]

In sum, the last decade has seen a decided shift toward Chinese advantage in the military aspects of both contingencies. However, the political and strategic risks of large-scale Chinese aggression remain immense, and China continues to have profound incentives to pursue its objectives short of war. In both cases, sustaining a political bargain on these contested issues remains at least as important to keeping the peace as the military balance.

One issue in this connection that rarely gets seriously debated in Washington, apart from whether the United States *can* defend Taiwan, is whether it *should* do so. A dominant conventional wisdom holds that Chinese possession of the island would dramatically shift the military balance in the region and cause countries throughout the region to doubt US credibility and potentially seek alternative alignments. There are potential responses to those concerns, yet there is little appetite for a serious public debate about them.

Requirements for Defense Policy Success in the 21st Century

I now turn to a more broad-based, functional assessment of how US and Chinese defense and security issues have evolved. I suggest five broad qualities that are likely, together, to determine the outcome of the security competition, and I make an assessment about the trends over the last decade in each.

NETWORKED POWER—ALLIANCES AND ALIGNMENTS

The first critical component of national power and security is a country's international alignments. States, especially great powers, have always sought favorable alignments of power: other great powers allied to them or in more informal partnerships, regional and global networks of influence that protect them. For a globally integrated great power such as the United States, providing for security demands an especially significant degree of concern for the freedom from hostile control of key regions. Alliances and networks play critical roles in realizing those objectives.

In terms of formal and informal security alliances and alignments relevant to the Indo-Pacific, the last decade has been a strong one for the United States. The US-Japan alliance is as vibrant as any point in recent decades. The United States joined with Australia and the United Kingdom in the AUKUS initiative, whose centerpiece submarine force may be decades away but which has already begun spurring other military cooperation. US-Philippine defense cooperation has advanced, as has US strategic engagement with India. Just as important, the United States has encouraged a deepening process of multilateral security cooperation among its allies and friends in the region. Meanwhile, over the last decade China has acquired no new formal allies and has seen regional alignments of power shift against it in response to Chinese aggressiveness. Through its support of Russia's invasion of Ukraine, it has alienated Europe.

The area of networked power—a country's position in global trade, financial, technology, and supply chain networks—tells a different story. While its Belt and

Road Initiative investments have slowed in recent years, China has gained a significant, leading, or dominant position in many sources of networked power.[12] It is the world's leading trading state and the dominant trading partner of most regional countries. It is acquiring significant influence in regional digital networks and actively seeks political and social influence in other countries. Meanwhile, many components of the US-led postwar order are in disarray.

Yet the goal for a great power is not merely to expand alliances indefinitely, or to achieve total control over global networks. Alliances and networks have costs, too. Married to sometimes excessive concerns about credibility, they can fuel strategic overreach and potentially drag great powers into needless wars. We can also measure US progress over the last decade, therefore, in terms of restraining excesses in national security commitments and developing greater burden sharing from friends and allies. On this score the United States arguably made little progress. US defense planners have repeatedly tried to decisively reduce US commitments in the Middle East without much success. The United States failed to develop any kind of transatlantic bargain with Russia that would have moderated defense requirements. It abandoned nuclear deals with North Korea and China.

In terms of formal alliances, then, the United States remains in a very strong position, and China has little prospect of shifting that balance—though concerns remain about the massive overhang of US global commitments. But measured by broader networked power and the less formalized alignments that come with it, China has made substantial inroads. This broader trend in informal alignments could have significant national security implications—for example, in the US ability to rally a world consensus against aggression over Taiwan. Then, too, while the United States is in a much stronger position in terms of formal alliances, it is also vastly more dependent on allied permissions and contributions than China for any significant contingency in the region. Should China be able to coerce or persuade key allies to deny US operating rights during a conflict, the US strength could turn into a vulnerability.

Institutional Innovativeness

A second broad way of understanding the evolution of relative national security positions is to consider the innovative capacity of each side's national security institutions. Over the long term, the innovative drive of a defense establishment will be one of the most important determinants of relative power. This is especially true in an era of transformative technological advances, when great powers have the potential to seize commanding advantages in such areas as artificial intelligence, quantum computing, and biotechnology.

It is difficult to render a precise verdict on relative trends in military innovation over the last decade. The evidence does, however, support two conclusions. US defense innovation remains powerfully hamstrung by bureaucratic and political barriers. Meanwhile, China, while its truly breakthrough innovations may be relatively limited, has been pushing ahead rapidly in many established technology areas to catch up to the United States.

The United States has instituted many experimental offices and initiatives aiming to spur innovation across the national security establishment.[13] The basic defense bureaucracy, however, remains brutally slow-moving, inefficient, ossified, and demoralizing. Part of the way to measure innovative capacity is not merely in developing new ideas but in producing and implementing them—and US defense institutions have spent the last decade working mightily to field relatively small numbers of new capabilities. Examples include unmanned systems, most of which remain in experimental status, and hypersonic weapons, of which the United States has but a tiny handful. Recent defense policy initiatives mean that the *coming* decade is likely to see more progress, but as of now that remains largely theoretical.

In terms of bureaucratic constraints on innovation, China's PLA and the Chinese government have certainly aired powerful self-criticisms of their ability to innovate. Yet the Chinese government is emphasizing, and investing in, scientific and technological innovation in general, through such initiatives as the Made in China 2025 program and its Military-Civilian Fusion program.[14] China enjoys second-mover advantages in many areas of defense technology, allowing it to steal, copy, and improve upon existing systems and capabilities—a form of in-progress innovation that has allowed it to close significant gaps with the United States and even gain a technology lead in some domains such as long-range fires and drones and unmanned systems.

The verdict on the last decade in terms of innovation must be a daunting one for the United States. Its defense institutions remain largely mired in bureaucratic quicksand, with an impressive but very limited set of innovation offices and initiatives. Meanwhile, China—though its own institutions may be equally slow-moving and resistant to bold new capabilities—has been innovating in catch-up mode, developing large numbers of new systems across many areas. Michael Griffin, former Defense Department Under Secretary for Research and Engineering, has summarized the current state of relative innovation by saying that the United

States requires over 16 years to get from idea to fielded operational capability, a path China can travel in less than half the time.[15]

PROCUREMENT AGILITY AND REBALANCE OF THE FORCE TO ASYMMETRIC TOOLS

Apart from innovating at the frontiers of technology, great powers engaged in security competitions must also build enough high-quality weapons and other military equipment. If one side in a strategic rivalry can produce and deploy weapon systems far more quickly, if its weapons are cheaper, more reliable and more effective, this will accumulate to a major long-term advantage.

In these terms, China has gained significant advantage over the United States during the last decade. The United States has made meaningful progress in a few areas—notably ramping up production of long-range strike missiles such as the Joint Air-to-Surface Standoff Missile (JASSM), notably its Extended Range version, past 700 per year with a near-term goal of 1,100 per year.[16] More broadly though, the US defense production system continues to suffer from two serious challenges: It is drowning in policies, procedures, regulations, and laws that make defense procurement a painfully slow, ineffective, and overly costly process; and it is far too small. Because of these problems, the US defense industrial base (DIB) has repeatedly failed to bring new systems into the force in cost-effective and timely ways and has suffered through a string of high-profile acquisition failures over the last decade-plus. Seth Jones and Alexander Palmer at the Center for Strategic and International Studies published a major analysis in 2024 on relative US and Chinese defense industrial capabilities.[17] The basic message was clear: China is surging to outpace the United States in many areas, and the US DIB remains slow, inefficient, and not adaptive enough.

William Greenwalt and Dan Patt found that US defense industrial processes have become exceptionally slow—but also that China has a different approach, pursuing an ongoing process of incremental, experimental advances across many variants of any systems.[18] Even when operating at peak effectiveness, moreover, the US DIB suffers from another problem: Its capacity has shrunk to dangerously low levels. If there were a war, and if the US Joint Force suffered significant losses, it would take between 10 and 20 years to replace many categories of major combat systems.[19]

Meanwhile, China has spent the last decade building a vast manufacturing capability, both directly in its defense industrial base and in areas of dual-use products with military applications. A leading example is shipbuilding, an area in which China now owns a massive advantage. In critical domains, especially maritime assets, China now has the capacity to reconstitute during and after a major conflict to a vastly greater degree than the United States.

China's defense industry does have challenges. China depends on US and allied suppliers for critical materials and components. China has significant defense industrial workforce challenges.[20] Open-source analysis based on anecdotal evidence suggests that the Chinese defense industry is highly bureaucratized, fragmented, and inefficient in important ways and continues to be hampered by corruption.[21] It lags in some key areas, such as jet engine design and production, and continues to depend on Russian technology in some domains.[22]

Nonetheless, in terms of defense procurement and related issues, such as the size and capacity of defense industrial bases and the ability to produce multiple types of new systems, the last decade has clearly belonged to China. The United States has made minimal progress in dealing with its long-standing procurement issues. Its defense industrial base remains small and dominated by a few prime manufacturers. Despite these trends, however, the United States remains competitive in the production of major combat systems, and their quality is still generally believed to be higher than Chinese counterparts. Except in selected areas such as shipbuilding and drones, a determined US effort to reform its defense production capabilities could likely produce a lasting overall equilibrium in terms of region-wide security rivalries.

DIGITAL SOVEREIGNTY: CYBER AND AI COMPETENCE

Leading economies and defense establishments are becoming increasingly dependent on digital networks and advanced computing. Protecting such networks will increasingly be a sine qua non of national security, both for the purpose of homeland defense but also to safeguard the foundation for power projection. Leading powers now employ sophisticated cyber operations to understand, take positions in, and at times disrupt or damage these networks.

During the last ten years, China has placed operations in the virtual realm at the center of its military and national security concepts. Its "Three Warfares" doctrine suggests that military and political advantage can be gained from campaigns in the domains of public opinion, psychological warfare, and legal warfare. The Chinese concept of "system destruction warfare"[23] identifies the informational systems underlying military operations as the center of gravity of future success and calls for plans to cripple an enemy's core military and wider social systems in war. Chinese theorists developed notions of "informatized" and "intelligentized" warfare, both referring to the central role of informational, digital, and artificial intelligence elements of future warfare.

China has not only developed impressive capabilities for prevailing in the digital domain, therefore; it has integrated these approaches deeply into its concepts of warfare. It acquired immense capabilities and demonstrated growing sophistication in cyber and information operations.[24] It has demonstrated repeated success in gaining access to a vast array of critical infrastructure and information networks.

Assessing US cyber capabilities is made difficult by the fact that very little is known in the unclassified world about US offensive cyber abilities. Nor is there much open-source information available about Chinese cyber vulnerabilities, though one would have to presume that China's systemic challenges—for example, with older operating systems in place in many parts of the nation's infrastructure—are likely on a par with the United States if not worse. In terms of cyber defense, the Department of Defense and other elements of the US government have made significant efforts over the last decade to protect government networks and to catalyze improved cybersecurity throughout the civilian sector. The general consensus appears to be, however, that while important progress has been made, significant and continuing vulnerabilities exist especially in civilian critical infrastructure.

Reviewing these broad trends, the best open-source judgment would be that the United States has lost significant ground in the relative position in digital sovereignty. This judgment is conditional; it could be that the United States has developed potent cyber tools over the last decade that remain highly classified. But there is little question that US digital sovereignty appears to be much more at risk than it was a decade ago. The United States is also disproportionately vulnerable in this domain because of its requirement to project forces from great distance in ways subject to disruption through cyberattack.

Bold and Creative Operational Concepts and Force Design

The fifth and final functional issue is operational concepts—how each side proposes to fight a war to achieve their objectives in general and in key contingencies. Such concepts may be the deciding factor in victory or defeat. Any effort to evaluate US and Chinese operational concepts will suffer from the obvious challenge that leading ideas on each side are kept secret. But there is enough open-source evidence about the basic approaches of each side to make some broad judgments.

On the US side, the last decade has seen the stirrings of some good new ideas, but too little joint integration, actual implementation, and transformation. Within the services, interesting ideas have been germinating but remain incomplete as comprehensive concepts of warfare. These include Multi-Domain Operations (MDO), the Air Force's Agile Combat Employment (ACE), the Navy's Distributed Maritime Operations (DMO), and more. At the joint level, the Joint Warfighting Concept has been in development for some years but remains classified. In support of evolving concepts, the services have been experimenting with new force designs and demonstrating evolving operational capabilities. These include the Army's Security Force Assistance Brigades (SFABs) and Multi-Domain Task Forces (MDTFs), its recent "transforming in contact" experiments with unit types, the Air Force's One Force Design initiative, and the Navy's Force Design 2045. The US Marine Corps has undertaken some of the boldest operational concept and transformation programs with its Force Design 2030 plan, which reoriented the service away from its dominant focus on amphibious operations. All the services are experimenting with these concepts in exercises and wargames.

This is an impressive record of anticipatory foresight, experimentation, operational concept development, and service change initiatives. Yet it is not clear that any of these initiatives seem ready to establish the foundation for war-winning capabilities any time soon. Many of the concepts focus on some form of distributed operation with a fundamentally reactive purpose—to deal with the threat of Chinese joint firepower strike campaigns. Interservice collaboration on concepts remains incomplete at best. Services continue to figure out exactly how some approaches, such as MDO and ACE, will work in practice and have not put in place the logistical or force structure capabilities necessary to support them.

On the Chinese side, the last decade has seen significant innovations in publicly reported operational concepts.[25] China in a sense started in the position of the United States in the Cold War—with a very specific operational problem to solve, that being US intervention in contingencies on China's periphery. Its new concepts, from System Destruction Warfare to "intelligentized" war, and its force construction in support of those ideas have established a compelling approach to their specific military problem. Notwithstanding these advances, China confronts very serious challenges in large-scale power projection, even for a Taiwan campaign.

The last decade, therefore, has seen China settle onto clear ideas for how it intends to fight, concepts that have created serious operational challenges for the United States. The US military has responded with concepts and forces and approaches trying to deal with those new challenges. The full details on implementation, and even the elements of those concepts, remain classified. But strong open-source evidence suggests that the US military is only partway to any compelling way of fighting—supported by the systems and force designs that would be required—in the Indo-Pacific.

The Overall Picture

A primary theme of this analysis has been that institutional and structural factors lay the groundwork for sustained national security capabilities, power, and influence. If that is true, then the last decade has been a major lost opportunity for the United States. Over the last decade, apart from witnessing the publication of many commissions and blue-ribbon reports on the challenges catalogued above, the United States has made only halting progress in improving innovation, reforming procurement, or making notable progress in digital sovereignty or fully functioning operational concepts. Nor has it generated dramatically greater burden sharing on the part of allies or partners or freed itself from other military commitments.

Yet China's standing in these areas surely has problems too. One challenge is that we are unlikely to know—certainly at the unclassified level but even classified—how well the PLA is doing in some of these areas of longer-term, more structural competition. As of today, most open-source analysis concludes that Chinese political and military leaders, keenly aware of their own shortcomings, remain uncertain of the potential for victory in major war.[26] In some sense, the fact that China has closed the gap with the United States is hardly surprising. China is a rising, somewhat revisionist power devoting increasing resources to national security capabilities. It benefits from catch-up advantages in copying existing technologies and approaches. China also has the advantage that it is for the time being optimizing its military for a small number of missions, whereas the United States sustains an immense global posture.

This comparison hints at the complexity of any judgment about relative trajectories over the last decade. China has clearly made gains in complicating the most demanding US missions focused on China's periphery. But in other ways, the competition is approaching something of a stalemate. Neither side can seriously threaten the other's homeland—with cyber, conventional, or nuclear weapons—without the prospect of proportional retaliation. Neither has any motive to do so, outside the context of a major war over other issues. Developments over the last ten years have not altered any of these fundamental truths, and they are likely to remain locked into the security relationship going forward.

China has clearly made progress on its central goal of preventing the United States from contesting Chinese application of force in its own neighborhood. But that risk is qualified in three important ways. First, the United States has the potential to reverse the trend, at least to a degree, by clearing out obstacles to major investments in and deployments of new technologies, catalyzing large-scale production of existing precision weapons, and demanding that Taiwan provide more capabilities for its own defense.

Second, in terms of contingencies beyond Taiwan, for China to undertake large-scale aggression against Japan or the Philippines, would require it to project power over much greater distances, against a more powerful coalition, and in ways that would unveil a militaristic appetite far beyond the narrower historical claims around Taiwan. The changes in relative military capability over the last decade have not fundamentally altered the prospects for the United States to lead a counter-hegemonic coalition to forestall Chinese adventurism beyond Taiwan.

Third, the emerging military context is creating an increasingly perilous environment for military aggression of any kind. Some observers have long suggested that the United States and its allies should respond to Chinese counter-intervention and A2AD capabilities with a "Blue A2AD" approach—efforts to confront China with large inventories of smart weapons, long-range strike systems, air defenses, offensive cyber options, and other tools to threaten Chinese power projection with massive costs.[27] US allies are increasingly investing in the systems needed for such concepts, such as Japan's counterstrike capabilities, the Philippines' new focus on anti-ship missiles, and Australia's plans to acquire various types of strike and anti-ship missiles. A region in which large-scale, long-range power projection is increasingly ruled out would deeply complicate any Chinese efforts to militarily coerce the region and help achieve the core US objective of preventing Chinese military hegemony.

It may therefore make sense to assess the last decade in relative national security capabilities on two very separate metrics: one for the Taiwan scenario, and one for all other military missions and national security concerns. The former trend will be difficult for the United States to counteract unless Taiwan takes much more decisive action on its own defense. The latter trajectory, however, can be stabilized in a way that protects US national interests, including the security of its allies in the region. The United States can aspire to a stable security equilibrium in which vital US interests are protected even as China gains peer or near-peer capabilities across a wide range of defense and national security domains. The gap will continue to close, however, and the United States needs a clear sense of what a stable outcome looks like on the way to 2035 and beyond.

In setting the context for success in such terms, the agenda for the United States remains as it was a decade ago. It is long past time to radically overhaul Department of Defense procurement policies and risk appetite for the pursuit of new systems. It is time to embrace more incremental and experimental forms of innovation. It is time to get serious about deeper interoperability with key allies (provided larger geopolitics dynamics allow it). The United States can ensure that China never gains the ability to impose its military terms throughout Asia and turn back the clock at least a bit on the feasibility of armed aggression against Taiwan. But it must, finally, get serious about building a more dynamic, innovative, continually adaptive defense establishment.

NOTES

1. Timothy R. Heath, *The Chinese Military's Doubtful Combat Readiness*, RAND Corporation, 2025, https://www.rand.org/pubs/perspectives/PEA830-1.html.

2. Dennis J. Blasko, "The Chinese Military Speaks to Itself, Revealing Doubts," *War on the Rocks*, February 18, 2019, https://warontherocks.com/2019/02/the-chinese -military-speaks-to-itself-revealing-doubts/.

3. Michael Mazarr, Bryan Frederick, and Yvonne K. Crane, *Understanding a New Era of Strategic Competition*, RAND Corporation, 2022, 7, https://www.rand.org/pubs /research_reports/RRA290-4.html.

4. Andrew Scobell et al., *China's Grand Strategy: Trends, Trajectories, and Long-Term Competition*, RAND Corporation, 2020, https://www.rand.org/content/dam/rand/pubs /research_reports/RR2700/RR2798/RAND_RR2798.pdf.

5. Audrey Decker, "Chinese Satellites Are Breaking The US 'Monopoly' On Long-Range Targeting," *Defense One*, May 2, 2024, https://www.defenseone.com /threats/.

6. For a recent summary, see Rupert Schulenberg, "Reinforcement and Re-distribution: Evolving US Posture in the Indo-Pacific," IISS, Military Balance Blog, March 27, 2025, https://www.iiss.org/online-analysis/.

7. Thomas H. Shugart III and Timothy A. Walton, *Concrete Sky: Air Base Hardening in the Western Pacific*, Hudson Institute, January 2025, https://www.hudson.org/.

8. See, for example, the "hedge force" proposed by Bryan Clark and Dan Patt, *Hedging Bets: Rethinking Force Design for a Post-Dominance Era*, Hudson Institute, February 2024, https://www.hudson.org/.

9. J. Michael Dahm, "Beyond 'Conventional Wisdom': Evaluating the PLA's South China Sea Bases in Operational Context," *War on the Rocks*, March 17, 2020, https:// warontherocks.com/2020/03/beyond-conventional-wisdom-evaluating-the-plas-south -china-sea-bases-in-operational-context/.

10. Jonas Vidhammer Berge and Henrick Stalhane Hiim, "Killing Them Softly: China's Counterspace Developments and Force Posture In Space," *Journal of Strategic Studies* 47, nos. 6–7 (2024): 940–963, https://doi.org/10.1080/01402390.2024.2388658.

11. Howard Wang, Gregory Graff, and Alexis Dale-Huang, *China's Growing Risk Tolerance in Space: People's Liberation Army Perspectives and Escalation Dynamics*, RAND Corporation, 2024, https://www.rand.org/pubs/research_reports/RRA2313-2.html.

12. One of the leading efforts to assess shifting network power is the Lowy Institute Asia Power Index. See the 2024 version at https://power.lowyinstitute.org/countries/china/.

13. I cataloged some of these in Michael Mazarr, *Defending Without Dominance: Accelerating the Transition to a New U.S. Defense Strategy*, RAND Corporation, 2023, https://www.rand.org/pubs/perspectives/PEA2555-1.html.

14. Department of Defense, *Military and Security Developments Involving the People's Republic of China 2024*, Annual Report to Congress, 2024, 27, https://www.defense.gov/.

15. Katrina Manson, "Robot-Soldiers, Stealth Jets and Drone Armies: The Future of War," *Financial Times*, November 16, 2018, https://www.ft.com/content/442de9aa-e7a0-11e8-8a85-04b8afea6ea3.

16. John A. Tirpak, "Lockheed Gets $3.5 Billion for JASSM/LRASM Missiles as It Eyes 'Extreme Range' Variant," *Air and Space Forces,* September 30, 2024, https://www.airandspaceforces.com/lockheed-jassm-lrasm-missiles-contract-extreme-range/.

17. Seth G. Jones and Alexander Palmer, *Rebuilding the Arsenal of Democracy: The U.S. and Chinese Defense Industrial Bases in an Era of Great Power Competition*, Center for Strategic and International Studies, March 2024.

18. William Greenwalt and Dan Patt, *Competing in Time: Ensuring Capability Advantage and Mission Success Through Adaptable Resource Allocation*, Hudson Institute, February 2021, 36, https://www.aei.org/wp-content/uploads/2021/02/Greenwalt_Competing-in-Time.pdf.

19. Mark F. Cancian, *Industrial Mobilization: Assessing Surge Capabilities, Wartime Risk, and System Brittleness*, Center for Strategic and International Studies, December 2020, 38, https://www.csis.org/analysis/industrial-mobilization-assessing-surge-capabilities-wartime-risk-and-system-brittleness.

20. Cortney Weinbaum et al., *Assessing Systemic Strengths and Vulnerabilities of China's Defense Industrial Base*, RAND Corporation, 2022, https://www.rand.org/pubs/research_reports/RRA930-1.html.

21. Tai Ming Cheung and Thomas G. Mahnken, *The Decisive Decade: United States-China Competition in Defense Innovation and Defense Industrial Policy on and Beyond the 2020s*, Center for Strategic and Budgetary Assessments, 2023, 23–26, https://csbaonline.org/research/publications/.

22. "How Developed Is China's Arms Industry?" CSIS *ChinaPower*, n.d., at https://chinapower.csis.org/arms-companies/.

23. Jeffrey Engstrom, *Systems Confrontation and System Destruction Warfare: How the Chinese People's Liberation Army Seeks to Wage Modern Warfare*, RAND Corporation, 2018, https://www.rand.org/pubs/research_reports/RR1708.html.

24. "Chinese Hacking Is Becoming Bigger, Better and Stealthier," *The Economist*, March 25, 2025, https://www.economist.com/china/2025/03/25/chinese-hackers-are

-getting-bigger-better-and-stealthier. See also U.S. China Economic and Security Review Commission, "China's Cyber Capabilities: Warfare, Espionage, and Implications for the United States," 2022, at https://www.uscc.gov/sites/default/files/2022-11/Chapter_3_Section_2--Chinas_Cyber_Capabilities.pdf

25. Edmund J. Burke, Kristen Gunness, Cortez A. Cooper III, and Mark Cozad, *People's Liberation Army Operational Concepts*, RAND Corporation, 2020, https://www.rand.org/pubs/research_reports/RRA394-1.html.

26. Mark Cozad, Jeffrey Engstrom, Scott W. Harold, Timothy R. Heath, Sale Lilly, Edmund J. Burke, Julia Brackup, and Derek Grossman, *Gaining Victory in Systems Warfare: China's Perspective on the U.S.-China Military Balance*, RAND Corporation, 2023, https://www.rand.org/pubs/research_reports/RRA1535-1.html.

27. Andrew F. Krepinevich, "How to Deter China: The Case for Archipelagic Defense," *Foreign Affairs*, February 18, 2015, https://www.jstor.org/stable/24483484; and Terrence Kelly, David C. Gompert, and Duncan Long, *Smarter Power, Stronger Partners*, 1: *Exploiting U.S. Advantages to Prevent Aggression*, RAND Corporation, 2016, https://apps.dtic.mil/sti/tr/pdf/AD1018936.pdf.

Chapter Eight

The Denial Dilemma in the Taiwan Strait and South China Sea

Zack Cooper

If the United States and China go to war, the first spark is likely to ignite in either the Taiwan Strait or South China Sea. These two flashpoints are combustible for several reasons. First, they involve conflicting interests often labeled vital by China, the United States, and US allies or partners. Second, the military balance around Taiwan and in the South China Sea has been deteriorating quickly, with Beijing frequently probing for ways to leverage its growing military and paramilitary advantages in the gray zone below open conflict. Third, each flashpoint exhibits a high risk of miscalculation, due to uncertainty about how far the parties involved might go to pursue their objectives. The result is a combination of growing tensions, changing power balances, and rising unpredictability—all the makings for a crisis that could escalate into a major conflict.

The situations in the Taiwan Strait and South China Sea are also shifting due to the Trump administration's distinctive foreign policy and defense approaches. On one hand, President Donald Trump and his top advisors have insisted that US allies and partners must do more for their own defense. On the other hand, some senior administration officials have embraced "denial strategies" that would require allies to stop investing in traditional means of power projection. The result is that US allies and partners will be asked to do more to defend themselves but

Zack Cooper is a senior fellow at the American Enterprise Institute and a lecturer at Princeton University. He is the author of *Tides of Fortune: The Rise and Decline of Great Militaries* from Yale University Press.

will also be pushed to divest some of the ships and aircraft that are most valuable in so-called gray zones below the threshold of open warfare.

This creates a particularly tricky paradox for Taiwan and the Philippines: the denial dilemma. Denial capabilities such as anti-ship missiles, aerial drones, and naval mines may help repel a Chinese invasion. But they are less useful in the gray zones, where countries are usually jockeying for control of maritime zones with ships and aircraft. If US allies and partners follow Washington's dictate to shift toward denial capabilities, they could find themselves less capable of responding in the gray zones. Although a number of Trump administration officials have insisted that the United States should be less focused on responding to China's gray-zone coercion campaign, US policies could make Taiwan and the Philippines more reliant on the United States in this area.

One potential answer would be for the United States to deploy its own legacy power-projection forces to deter China's aggressive actions in the gray zone. But this appears unlikely, given the Trump administration's insistence that allies and partners do more for themselves, as well as Washington's desire to avoid getting entrapped in conflict. And yet, if the United States does not take on more of the burden in the gray zones, then Taiwan and the Philippines will have to either cede control of maritime areas to China or rebuff the Trump administration's insistence on denial capabilities.

This denial dilemma will prove to be one of the central strategic challenges to the Trump administration's defense policies. It will prove particularly thorny in East Asia, given the potential for crises and conflict in the Taiwan Strait and South China Sea. Understanding the roots of this dilemma and the possible options for addressing it will be crucial to avoiding US decoupling with allies and partners, and to bolstering regional deterrence in the years ahead.

Flashpoints in the "Near Seas"

China's desire to alter the status quo by asserting control over a large swath of the maritime zone within East Asia's First Island Chain lies at the root of many regional tensions. The two most likely flashpoints for a larger conflict are the Taiwan Strait and South China Sea, each of which Chinese leadership asserts must be under Beijing's control. Chinese General Secretary Xi Jinping asserts that Taiwan must be "reunified" with mainland China, and the Chinese government also claims "historic rights" to a vast swathe of the South China Sea.

It should not be surprising that China is attempting to increase its control over Taiwan and the South China Sea. Most rising powers seek to exert greater control over their near abroad, whether on land or at sea. In China's case, disputes over Taiwan and the South China Sea have been increasingly tied to the Communist Party's own domestic legitimacy. Taking control of Taiwan has been a key objective of the Communist Party going back to 1949. But Xi Jinping has stepped up pressure in recent years and characterized China's aims as central to its rejuvenation. In late 2024, for example, Xi said: "The people on both sides of the Taiwan Strait are one family. No one can sever our family bonds, and no one can stop the historical trend of national reunification."[1] Whether Xi has a specific timeline for "reunification" is a hotly debated issue, but it is clear that the Communist Party sees control over Taiwan as a central political objective. Xi himself has insisted that "these issues cannot be passed on from generation to generation."[2]

The South China Sea is an equally complicated issue. Chinese leaders have at times referred to the South China Sea as a "core issue" akin to Taiwan, raising the risk of conflict over disputed waters and shoals. But China has no strong legal basis for asserting control over the expanse of the South China Sea. International law makes clear that only archipelagic states can include the islands and waters within archipelagic baselines as internal waters. Even though China is not an archipelagic state, Beijing has asserted nebulous "historical rights" to much of the South China Sea, including high-seas areas and foreign exclusive economic zones, in contravention to international law. China's control of individual features in the South China Sea is generally not contested by the United States or most other non-claimants, but its claims to the waters within China's so-called nine-dash line are out of line with international legal rules and norms. Equally problematic are China's efforts to undermine the control of features held by other claimants and to interfere in their exclusive economic zones.

What makes this situation more combustible is that China is rising into a regional order that is fortified by US alliances and partnerships, which are themselves backed in some cases by US extended nuclear guarantees. This dynamic is historically unique, since no other great power has even risen into a world characterized by extended nuclear guarantees. This makes the regional system more difficult to overturn without risking a broader conflict that could potentially endanger a large portion of the world's population. This in turn heightens the tensions in the Taiwan Strait and South China Sea, implying that even a small skirmish could potentially escalate into a larger military conflict with global ramifications. Central to this contest is the degree to which the United States will support its allies and partners, and how it will decide to act if and when its commitments are challenged.

Although the United States is not a direct party to either dispute, Washington has made legal and political commitments to both Taiwan and the Philippines. The Taiwan Relations Act asserts that "the United States decision to establish diplomatic relations with the People's Republic of China rests upon the expectation that the future of Taiwan will be determined by peaceful means."[3] It also requires that the United States maintain the capacity "to resist any resort to force or other forms of coercion that would jeopardize the security, or the social or economic system, of the people on Taiwan." Thus, the United States explicitly opposes efforts by China to use force or coercion to undermine Taiwan.

The US commitment to the Philippines is even sharper. Under the US-Philippines Mutual Defense Treaty, Washington has agreed to respond to "an armed attack in the Pacific Area on either of the Parties," which "is deemed to include an armed attack on the metropolitan territory of either of the Parties, or on the island territories under its jurisdiction in the Pacific or on its armed forces, public vessels or aircraft in the Pacific."[4] In 2019, the first Trump administration clarified for the first time that an armed attack "in the South China Sea will trigger mutual defense obligations."[5] Several recent incidents between China and the Philippines have nearly crossed this line.

What makes Taiwan and the Philippines more attractive targets of Chinese coercion is the fact that neither is strong enough to rebuff Beijing on its own, and both have had uneven relationships with the United States over the years. This sets them apart from Japan and South Korea, which both have more robust defense capabilities and substantial forward-stationed US military forces. The fact that the United States abrogated its alliance to Taiwan in 1979 and was forced to withdraw most of its forces from the Philippines in 1991–1992 meant that Taipei and Manila have been left more vulnerable to Chinese force and coercion for decades. Although the United States does have some military trainers in Taiwan as well as more frequent rotational deployments through Enhanced Defense Cooperation Agreement sites in the Philippines, the presence of US military forces in both countries remains limited.

Taiwan and the Philippines also do not have the military capabilities to compete with China on their own, at least not on a symmetrical basis. Although Taiwan's per capita income is several times higher than that of China, its overall gross domestic products is less than one twentieth that of China. The Philippines is in an even more disadvantageous position, accounting for just one fortieth of China's gross domestic product. As a result, even if Taiwan and the Philippines spent nearly all of their economic production on defense, they might still find themselves at a disadvantage militarily. Clearly, Taipei and Manila's efforts at internal balancing through domestic military spending must be amplified by external balancing through alliances and partnerships with other powers.

The presence and commitment of the United States have helped to stabilize the military balance in the First Island Chain. But even a robust American presence is no longer sufficient to provide a guarantee against possible Chinese military action. For most of the last 80 years, China was not strong enough to forcefully alter the status quo vis-à-vis Taiwan and the Philippines. Several decades ago, in the 1995–1996 Taiwan Strait Crisis, many military experts assessed that two US carrier strike groups would have been sufficient to protect Taiwan and defeat the bulk of China's navy and air force, given the limited power-projection capabilities of the People's Liberation Army.[6] Today, however, that situation has changed. China now fields a larger navy than that of the United States. It is also building power-projection systems, including amphibious vessels, designed for forcible entry. Taiwan and the Philippines have not been able to keep up. The stage is thus set for a crisis or conflict in what China terms its "Near Seas."

The Denial Dilemma

A central challenge for the Trump administration will be aligning its alliance strategy with its military strategy. President Trump is asking allies to do more for their own defense, including dealing with lower-level coercion in the gray zones. But at the same time, his team is trying to reshape US and allied military forces by embracing the concept of denial. The result is that US allies and partners are likely to be advised that they must be more responsible for responding to gray-zone coercion on their own, while simultaneously being instructed to disinvest in those capabilities most useful for rebuffing China's gray-zone coercion.

The second Trump administration's approach to defense policy is still emerging, but it is clear that the administration is likely to identify the Indo-Pacific theater as one of two priority theaters (along with the US homeland). Secretary of Defense Pete Hegseth reinforced this message in his initial trip to the Indo-Pacific region when he commented that, "in the interim National Defense Strategy from the DOD [Department of Defense], we'll focus—make sure we're defending the homeland, including the homeland OCONUS [Outside the Contiguous United States] here in Hawaii, and that we're postured to focus on the Indo-Pacific."[7] Elsewhere, Hegseth has asserted that "the Indo-Pacific is the region of consequence," and that the United States "will work with our allies and our partners to deter the communist Chinese and their aggression in the Indo-Pacific. Full stop."[8] Although he has described allies and partners as being "at the forefront of deterring aggression," Hegseth has also noted "we need each and every one of our friends and partners and our allies to do their part as well . . . That has to be a two-way street."[9]

Thus, it is clear that the Indo-Pacific will be a priority theater for Trump administration, but also that a dominant feature of its regional approach will be insisting that allies and partners do more for their own defense. Various US officials have insisted that ally and partner spending should be above 3% of gross domestic product (for Japan), 5% of GDP (for NATO), or even 10% of GDP (for Taiwan).[10] In both public and private settings, administration officials have sent signals that although US forces will remain prepared to deter major escalations, US allies and partners should expect less focus on escalations below that threshold. Bridge Colby, Trump's Under Secretary of Defense for Policy, has argued bluntly that "Taiwan needs to [be] laser focusing on implementing a denial defense against invasion. The gray zone won't kill you. Invasion would."[11] One might logically expect that Trump administration officials would be similarly skeptical of the importance of gray-zone conflicts for the Philippines. Indeed, Andrew Byers, the Pentagon's Deputy Assistant Secretary of Defense for Southeast Asia, has asserted, "The United States might begin a cooperation spiral with China by proposing to remove US military forces or weapons systems from the Philippines in exchange for the China Coast Guard executing fewer patrols."[12]

Meanwhile, the central theme of the second Trump administration's military strategy is likely to be greater reliance on "denial" capabilities. Colby is the architect of the administration's forthcoming National Defense Strategy and has written a book on the advantages of denial. He argues that "a denial defense strategy generates a minimum military standard of being able to prevent China from seizing and holding the key territory of our allies—essentially, the core political and economic areas of a country."[13] Now advocated by a range of Trump administration officials appointed to the Defense Department, such a strategy of denial would emphasize the importance of more expendable systems, such as uncrewed aircraft, uncrewed undersea vehicles, and cheaper missile systems. As one political appointee at the Pentagon has argued, "Taiwan does not require high-end combat aircraft, surface vessels and other prestige systems and platforms to deter and repel a Chinese military invasion. What it needs most critically are [anti-access / area denial] systems, like maritime mines and anti-aircraft batteries."[14] The logic is that smaller, cheaper, and more expendable systems are more effective on the modern battlefield. Trump administration officials have thus insisted that US allies and partners should invest more in these capabilities and forgo many of their legacy investments in larger platforms designed to project power.

The focus on defending the "core" regions of ally and partner territory, and putting less emphasis on gray zones, suggests a redefinition of the recent US approach to the Indo-Pacific region. Unlike the European theater, which is likely to be downgraded in priority by the Trump administration, the Indo-Pacific is set to receive higher billing and more resources. But those resources are likely to be devoted primarily to avoiding the invasion of the central economic and metropolitan zones in ally and partner states, rather than their outlying islands. For US allies and partners such as Japan, the Philippines, and Taiwan, this could put at risk areas such as the Senkaku Islands (controlled by Japan), Second Thomas Shoal (controlled by the Philippines), and Pratas Island (controlled by Taiwan).

This shift is in some ways reminiscent of the Nixon administration's Guam Doctrine. In 1969, Richard Nixon asserted, "as far as the problems of military defense, except for the threat of a major power involving nuclear weapons, that the United States is going to encourage and has a right to expect that this problem will be handled by, and responsibility for it taken by, the Asian nations themselves."[15] Nixon was focused primarily on devolving responsibility for domestic communist insurgencies in allied countries, but the Trump administration might be on the verge of adopting a version of the Guam Doctrine for escalations against outlying islands and other lower-level escalations in the gray zones.

If this proves to be the Trump administration's strategy, then it will create a denial dilemma. Denial capabilities are well-suited to defend against an outright invasion, since they can bring to bear asymmetric weapons that can more cheaply inflict damage against a stronger adversary. But denial capabilities are of little value in the gray zone, where the competition is often over the ability to maintain presence in distant waters or airspace without firing a shot. Most cheap unmanned systems cannot maintain presence in distant areas for long. Furthermore, uncrewed systems do not convey the same risk of escalation as crewed platforms, since political leaders and their publics are more likely to overlook the loss of weapons systems if there is no accompanying loss of life involved. As a result, uncrewed systems create less of a risk of escalation, less of what Thomas Schelling called the "threat that leaves something to chance," and therefore less of an effective trip wire for deterring gray-zone coercion. Thus, spending a greater share of a country's military funds on denial capabilities can better defend against invasion while providing little value in gray-zone scenarios. This has major implications for not only America's division of roles and missions with its allies and partners, but also the continued viability of their territorial and maritime claims and control.

Ally and Partner Options

The dilemma caused by the Trump administration's unique approach to alliances and military capabilities cannot easily be resolved. Allies and partners are likely to find themselves on their back foot in gray-zone competitions. This is problematic because US allies and partners—particularly Taiwan and the Philippines—are already under pressure in the gray zone and losing ground.

In recent years, China has increased gray-zone coercion against Taiwan through multiple channels. Most notable, Beijing has established a new normal in the aftermath of now-former House Speaker Nancy Pelosi's visit to Taipei, escalating the frequency and intensity of its operations around Taiwan. This has included higher numbers of ships and aircraft operating closer to Taiwan. Operations such as the Joint Sword exercises have demonstrated the People's Liberation Army's ability to coordinate assets surrounding Taiwan in complex operations.[16] In addition, China has attempted to erode the median line between China and Taiwan, while also surging fishing vessels, maritime militia, and coast guard ships into the surrounding waters.

China's gray-zone pressure on the Philippines has also increased, particularly since President Ferdinand "Bongbong" Romualdez Marcos took power. Beijing has engaged in escalatory behavior repeatedly, including particularly dangerous operations near Second Thomas Shoal and Sabina Shoal. China's efforts to block the resupply of Philippine forces and stop Filipino fishers in traditional fishing areas well within the Philippines' exclusive economic zone have only accelerated in recent years. Some of these tensions have gotten uncomfortably close to invoking Articles IV and V of the US-Philippines Mutual Defense Treaty. In 2024, for example, a Philippine armed forces member lost a finger in hand-to-hand fighting after Chinese paramilitary forces intercepted a Philippine resupply effort.

The fact is that these rising tensions are not purely military issues. If the political leadership in Taiwan and the Philippines appear to be helpless in the face of Chinese pressure, then Taiwanese and Philippine voters may reconsider support for political leaders who support pushing back against Chinese coercion. Indeed, before entering the Trump administration, Bridge Colby argued exactly that, in a passage worth quoting at length:

The key for Beijing is to strike at the coalition's center of gravity: perceptions of Washington's willingness to come to the stout defense of those to which it has committed. Only if they believe Washington can and will stand with them will Asian countries judge it prudent to take the risks necessary to check Beijing's ambitions. If they do not have this confidence, they will fear being isolated and punished by China and thus will likely cut a deal with Beijing. If Beijing can pick off enough countries in this fashion, it could achieve regional hegemony without having to fight World War III. Indeed, given how sensitive Asian countries are to China's strength and how lucrative it is to be in its good graces, Beijing may not have to fight many—or even any—wars to attain regional dominance.[17]

What remains unclear is how the United States can reassure allies and partners that "Washington can and will stand with them" if the United States is sitting idly by as gray-zone coercion erodes their positions. Members of the Trump administration argue that reputation is unique to specific theaters or alliances, so the United States choosing to cease support for Ukraine should not undermine ally and partner confidence in the Indo-Pacific. But it is not clear how a decrease in US support for those same allies and partners in the gray zone would not undermine their confidence in the United States more generally. As Colby warns, this might lead many in the public to vote for leaders who would be more willing to "cut a deal with Beijing."

There are several potential options to address this concern. First, the United States could choose to deter China's gray-zone activities itself. If the Trump administration is insisting that allies and partners should focus more on denial capabilities and less on the gray zone, then the natural division of labor would be for the United States to use its own power-projection forces to deter and respond to China's coercion of US allies and partners. This would likely be the most logical way to square the circle and solve the denial dilemma. Unfortunately, this option cuts directly against the political instincts of the Trump administration. If anything, the message to US allies and partners has been that the United States will be less—not more—involved in gray-zone contingencies. This has been particularly true in Europe but is also likely to apply in the Indo-Pacific region. After all, how could the United States justify stepping in to the breach to assist Taiwan and the Philippines when it has been publicly berating leaders in both capitals about their lack of sufficient defense spending? Thus, although using US power-projection capabilities to deter Chinese gray-zone operations would make logical sense, it is unlikely to be an attractive option for the Trump administration.

A second alternative would be for US allies and partners to simply forgo their interests in the gray zone. From an American perspective, this might have some benefits. It would decrease the likelihood that the United States would be pulled into a conflict "over rocks"—as gray-zone operations have sometimes been labeled. But for Taiwan, this would mean essentially sacrificing Taiwanese positions in the Kinmen, Matsu, Wuchiu, Pratas, and Taiping Islands. Even larger features with substantial populations, such as the Penghu Islands, might find themselves outside the defense perimeter in this case.[18] Taiwan would also have to stop enforcing fishing and energy exploration rights in its surrounding waters and permit China to operate immediately off its coast.

The Philippines would likewise have to effectively give up its claims to numerous features in the South China Sea. This would include Second Thomas Shoal, Sabina Shoal, Scarborough Shoal, Commodore Reef, Flat Island, Loaita Cay, Loaita Island, Nanshan Island, Northeast Cay, West York Island, and most importantly Thitu Island. Moreover, Manila would have to stop enforcing its exclusive economic-zone claims and the fishing (and energy) rights that are so vital to much of its coastal population. An arbitral tribunal ruled in the Philippines' favor on most of these issues in 2016, so this shift in approach would be a drastic change in policy. It is hard to imagine how political leaders in either Taipei or Manila could sell such decisions to their publics yet remain in office, so this option also appears unlikely.

If the United States is unwilling to step in the gray-zone breach, but US allies and partners are unable to concede in the gray zone, then how might an American strategy predicated on denial maintain deterrence? The answer to this question is unclear. But what is clear is that China would likely be emboldened to test Taiwan and the Philippines in the gray zone, and to probe for ways to wedge Washington away from Taipei and Manila. Potential results could include either the erupting of conflict or a decoupling of the US partnership with Taiwan or alliance with the Philippines. So how might US allies and partners respond to the US insistence to invest in denial capabilities and forgo gray-zone contestation?

One possibility is that US appeals could simply fall on deaf ears in friendly capitals. Foreign militaries might purchase more denial systems but also continue to invest in larger platforms to maintain presence and conduct deterrence operations in the gray zones. This would put the Trump administration on the horns of another dilemma. Leaders in Washington could threaten to abandon the ally or partner in question, essentially ending the relationship. Or they could capitulate and allow the ally or partner to continue business as usual. Neither would be appealing to the Trump administration, but which direction they might go remains unclear.

Alternatively, the ally or partner could realign away from the United States. Theoretically, they could attempt to pursue greater independence by developing more sovereign defense capabilities. This is more feasible for large countries like Japan, but it is not realistic for Taiwan and the Philippines, which are at a more significant military disadvantage. Taipei and Manila might also look to other foreign partners for assistance, but it is unlikely that any consortium of countries that would come to Taiwan's or Manila's aid would be sufficient to deter a concerted coercive campaign by China. This leaves the last, and perhaps least palatable option: accommodating China and effectively abandoning Washington in favor of Beijing. Leaders in Taiwan and the Philippines might not want to do so, but they might be left with few other options in the case of a breakdown of relations with the United States.

This is the backdrop in which the Trump administration finds itself in East Asia. Denial capabilities are quite appealing for defending against an invasion. But they can only be one part of a larger political strategy. The United States will have to be attuned to the denial dilemma if it is to come with a practicable regional strategy. How might the Trump administration blend its desire to bolster deterrence with the immediate need to sustain ally and partner cooperation in the gray zone? The best answer is a new division of labor between Washington and friendly capitals in East Asia.

Toward a New Division of Labor

If the Trump administration is determined to force allies and partners to invest more in denial capabilities, then the best solution to the denial dilemma is for the United States to propose a new division of labor with Taiwan, the Philippines, and other front-line friends. The administration is right that allies and partners should invest more of their resources into denial capabilities such as anti-ship missiles, uncrewed submersibles, aerial vehicles, and mines. Yet the United States will also have to work with these countries to jointly respond to China's gray-zone operations.

How might this work in practice? If Taiwan and the Philippines agree to invest more in denial capabilities, then the United States (ideally alongside other allies and partners) should agree to act more frequently to deter Chinese gray-zone coercion. When Chinese aircraft enter into the airspace near Taiwan or the Philippines, the United States should periodically scramble jets to monitor the Chinese operations. Similarly, when Chinese ships enter into the exclusive economic zone (and especially territorial waters) near Taiwan and Philippine territory, the United States should periodically send ships to monitor those operations. Obviously, given the different political and military relationships that Taipei and Manila have with Washington, these operations would have to be careful handled. But doing so would have several benefits.

First, it would demonstrate to the publics in Taiwan and the Philippines that they are not standing alone in the gray zone against Chinese aggression. It would therefore increase confidence in the United States in both places, helping to offset concerns about Taiwan and the Philippines' own decreased military capabilities to meet gray-zone coercion. It could also guard against any decrease in confidence in the United States caused by a US withdrawal of support for allies and partners in the European theater, including Ukraine. War is politics by other means, so US leaders must recognize that domestic political dynamics in Taiwan and the Philippines are central to maintaining security in East Asia.

Second, increased US operations would also demonstrate to China that there is a real downside to continuing to push and probe in the gray zones. Beijing has long been wary of operations that bear a risk of escalation with the United States (but much less so against smaller and weaker regional players). So one of the only ways to deter China in the gray zone is to introduce more risk of direct escalation with the United States. Moreover, increased American engagement would demonstrate to China that the more it presses Taiwan and the Philippines in the gray zone, the more it pushes them closer together with the United States.

This is not to minimize the risks that deeper US engagement in the gray zone would incur. Direct US involvement in the gray zone would raise the risk of direct conflict with China. This is a real risk and one that should be taken seriously. But in international politics, one cannot get something for nothing. It should be clear by now that attempting to avoid risk in the gray zone is tantamount to allowing China to coerce US allies and partners in their maritime zones. This comes with its own risks, not only to those relationships, but to the stability of the broader regional and global order.

An additional downside is that this mission would add yet another burden to US forces. That being said, the Trump administration has committed to shift more attention to the Indo-Pacific region, which could free up additional assets to conduct missions of this sort. Many in the Trump administration are skeptical of the value of legacy forces—particularly surface ships and tactical fighter aircraft—for conducting operations against China. This, however, would be a valuable use of these forces in peacetime. And they need not respond to every Chinese escalation to change Beijing's risk calculus and reassure regional allies and partners, so concerns about US operational tempo could be integrated into response plans. Combined with the uptick in presence created by shifting forces to the Indo-Pacific, adding this mission to that of some legacy forces seems a trade-off worth considering, particularly given the lack of better options for simultaneously maintaining deterrence and keeping US alliances and partnership intact.

In conclusion, the denial dilemma leaves the United States with some tough tradeoffs in the Indo-Pacific. Although the Trump administration's prioritization of the Indo-Pacific is welcome across most of the region, its emphasis on denial capabilities and high-end scenarios has left leaders in ally and partner capitals in a difficult spot. Denial systems are useful primarily for high-intensity warfighting, rather than low-intensity contests of will in the gray zone. Therefore, efforts to shift toward denial-focused capabilities will have to be accompanied by political and military strategies to deter China from applying more gray-zone pressure. The denial dilemma means that Washington will likely have to embrace a new division of labor with both Taiwan and the Philippines—it will have to do more, not less, in the gray zone.

NOTES

1. "Xi Says No One Can Stop China's 'Reunification' with Taiwan," *Reuters*, December 31, 2024, https://www.reuters.com/world/china/xi-says-no-one-can-stop -chinas-reunification-with-taiwan-2024-12-31/.

2. "China's Xi Says Political Solution for Taiwan Can't Wait Forever," *Reuters*, October 6, 2013, https://www.reuters.com/article/world/chinas-xi-says-political-solution -for-taiwan-cant-wait-forever-idUSBRE99503Q/.

3. Taiwan Relations Act, H.R. 2479, 96th Cong. (1979) (enacted). https://www .congress.gov/bill/96th-congress/house-bill/2479/text.

4. Mutual Defense Treaty, U.S.-Phil., Aug. 30, 1951, T.I.A.S. No. 2529. https://avalon .law.yale.edu/20th_century/phil001.asp.

5. Karen Lema and Neil Jerome Morales, "Pompeo Assures Philippines of US Protection in Event of Sea Conflict," *Reuters*, March 1, 2019, https://www.reuters.com /article/world/pompeo-assures-philippines-of-us-protection-in-event-of-sea-conflict -idUSKCN1QI3O7/.

6. John Culver and Jonathan A. Czin, "Understanding China's Military: A Q&A with New Brookings Expert John Culver," Brookings Institution, March 31, 2025, https://www.brookings.edu/articles/understanding-chinas-military-a-qa-with-new -brookings-expert-john-culver/.

7. Pete Hegseth, "Secretary of Defense Pete Hegseth Holds Media Availability in Honolulu, Hawaii," March 25, 2025, transcript posted by US Department of Defense on

Defense.gov website on March 26, 2025, https://www.defense.gov/News/Transcripts /Transcript/Article/4136055/secretary-of-defense-pete-hegseth-holds-media-availability -in-honolulu-hawaii/.

8. Pete Hegseth, "Secretary of Defense Hegseth Delivers Remarks in Hawaii, March 25, 2025," press conference, video posted on Facebook March 25, 2025, https://www.facebook.com/watch/?v=1351585442763865.

9. Hegseth, "Hegseth Delivers Remarks in Hawaii."

10. Elbridge Colby (@ElbridgeColby), "Correct. So then why isn't Japan spending 3% of GDP on defense *now*? And Taiwan 5 or even 10%?," Twitter (now X), April 8, 2025, https://x.com/ElbridgeColby/status/1844335747622633782; Brian Vaughn, "Trump Says NATO Nations Should Spend 5% of GDP on Defense," *Bloomberg News*, January 7, 2025, https://www.bloomberg.com/news/articles/2025-01-07/trump-says-nato-nations-should -spend-5-of-gdp-on-defense; Marc A. Thiessen, "Trump Wants to Make Deterrence and (Really) Legal Immigration Great Again," *Washington Post*, September 30, 2024, https://www.washingtonpost.com/opinions/2024/09/30/donald-trump-2024-interview -immigration-ukraine/.

11. Elbridge Colby (@ElbridgeColby), "The lack of urgency and effort on Taiwan's part described here are deeply concerning. Taiwan needs to laser focusing on implementing a denial defense against invasion. The gray zone won't kill you. Invasion would," Twitter (now X), April 8, 2025, https://x.com/ElbridgeColby/status /1666949240994791424.

12. Andrew Byers and J. Tedford Tyler, "Can the United States and China Forge a Cold Peace?" *Survival* 66, no. 6 (2024): 67–86, https://www.tandfonline.com/doi/full/10 .1080/00396338.2024.2432202.

13. Elbridge Colby, "A Strategy of Denial for the Western Pacific," *Proceedings* 149, no. 3 (March 2023), https://www.usni.org/magazines/proceedings/2023/march/strategy -denial-western-pacific.

14. Byers and Tyler, "Can the United States and China Forge a Cold Peace?"

15. US Department of State, "Document 29: Editorial Note," in *Foreign Relations of the United States, 1969–1976*, ed. Louis J. Smith and David H. Herschler, vol. 1, *Foundations of Foreign Policy, 1969–1972* (Government Printing Office, 2003), https://history .state.gov/historicaldocuments/frus1969-76v01/d29.

16. Dan Blumenthal, Frederick W. Kagan, Alexis Turek, Matthew Sperzel, Daniel Shats, Alison O'Neil, Karina Wugang, and Will Pickering, "China–Taiwan Weekly Update, December 12, 2024," American Enterprise Institute, December 12, 2024, https://www.aei.org/articles/china-taiwan-weekly-update-december-12-2024/.

17. Colby, "Strategy of Denial."

18. Andrew Chubb, "Taiwan Strait Crises: Island Seizure Contingencies," Asia Society Policy Institute, February 22, 2023, https://asiasociety.org/policy-institute /taiwan-strait-crises-island-seizure-contingencies-0.

Chapter Nine

Shifting Nuclear Postures and US-China Rivalry

Francis J. Gavin

China is expanding and improving its nuclear capabilities, after decades of comparatively modest effort. Concurrently, the United States is devoting considerable resources to modernizing its own nuclear forces. This is happening against a backdrop of marked global turbulence, highlighted by Russia's invasion of Ukraine and its threat to use nuclear weapons. How should we understand these developments—in particular, China's shifting nuclear posture and profile—and what are the range of responses available to the United States?

These are difficult questions to answer with confidence. China's military and grand strategic decision-making processes are opaque. Even if they were more transparent, nuclear policy is especially difficult to assess. Perhaps more than with other aspects of strategy, public statements and official doctrines surrounding nuclear weapons may not tell us as much as we hope. Nuclear weapons have different qualities and consequences for state behavior than other kinds of military capabilities.

One way to gain some insight into China's choices is to assess our stock of theories about nuclear behavior, as well as identify and explore historical episodes where shifting nuclear postures may have played a role in driving strategic decisions and

Francis J. Gavin is the Giovanni Agnelli Distinguished Professor and the director of the Henry A. Kissinger Center for Global Affairs at the School of Advanced International Studies of Johns Hopkins University. His latest book is *Thinking Historically: A Guide to Statecraft and Strategy*.

shaping outcomes. This method is far from perfect, however: the insights derived from these theories and history are often contested. Nor is it clear that theories and historical episodes that largely emerged from the Cold War rivalry between the Soviet Union and the United States provide full purchase on the strategic interactions between China and the United States in the mid/late-2020s and beyond. Indeed, this comparison is likely to reveal as many variations as similarities, and there is some danger that simply importing "lessons from the past" into the present might blind us to important differences in contemporary circumstances and context.

While modest, however, this exercise can identify the key questions that analysts and policymakers should focus on as they try to make sense of and develop responses to China's nuclear expansion. Three sets of questions are especially important. First, what do theory and history reveal about how nuclear weapons advance a state's interests? Does a state's nuclear posture—what kinds of weapons it possesses and how they are deployed—affect those goals? Second, what does China hope to achieve with its nuclear build-up? Third, what are the options available to the United States to respond?

Explaining Nuclear Behavior

A state faces any number of consequential choices when it comes to nuclear weapons. It must first decide whether to pursue nuclear weapons in the first place, either by acquiring them from others or building its own nuclear weapons program.[1] The answer is not always obvious; nuclear weapons are expensive and expose one to vulnerabilities. Far fewer states possess nuclear weapons that most analysts would have predicted at the start of the nuclear age, while far more have accepted nuclear guarantees and extended deterrence from more powerful patrons. When a state such as China does acquire its own nuclear forces, it must determine what kinds of capabilities it should acquire, how to deploy them, and to what grand strategic end.

There are several reasons why a country may acquire nuclear weapons and pursue different nuclear postures. Its nuclear behavior could be driven by a desire for prestige or to demonstrate its technological prowess. A bureaucracy or organization might embrace certain nuclear strategies to increase their sway within a particular government. The most compelling reason for a state to acquire nuclear weapons and construct particular strategies, however, is to advance its grand strategic interests in the world.

Our theories and history suggest that nuclear weapons can be used to advance a state's national security interests in at least three ways. The bomb can be used as a weapon to win a battle or war. A state may believe it can use or threaten to use nuclear weapons coercively to obtain a political goal or end it might not otherwise achieve. Furthermore, possessing nuclear weapons and embracing particular nuclear postures may deter or prevent an adversary from doing something drastic.

None of these nuclear missions are without controversy. Nuclear use, except perhaps under the direst circumstances, would be understood by most as a grievous crime. If used against a state with survivable nuclear weapons, it could be suicidal folly. Whether nuclear threats can successfully compel or coerce a state into doing something it wouldn't otherwise is deeply contested. Most analysts believe nuclear weapons are best used to deter, but even here, there are questions: Deter what? Possessing nuclear weapons should prevent an adversary from attacking you with nuclear weapons or trying to invade and conquer you. What is less clear is whether nuclear weapons can deter an adversary from launching an attack short of an all-out invasion, or dissuade your rival from attacking your friends and allies.

Which goal you choose—to win, to coerce, to deter—and how easy or hard it is to achieve that goal will shape your nuclear posture. A nuclear posture consists of two key components: (1) what kinds and how many nuclear weapons you possess, and (2) how you deploy those weapons in a strategy. Your strategy includes where you will deploy your nuclear weapons, who or what will be targeted, and guidelines for what circumstances will commence their launch.

A state's nuclear posture will be shaped by the specific goal it is trying to accomplish, as well as the country it intends to take action against. But other variables and questions invariably come into play. One factor includes whether you believed the nuclear balance to be "sensitive" and opportunities to achieve politically meaningful nuclear "advantage" existed. This might affect your investments to deliver nuclear weapons or defend against them with increased accuracy, speed, and stealth. Your attitude toward "escalation" dynamics would also play a role: Do you believe it is possible to achieve political goals by employing or credibly threatening to employ nuclear weapons in a way other than a large-scale nuclear attack against a competitor's homeland?

A piece of conventional wisdom long-held by nuclear analysts is that the extraordinarily destructive nature of nuclear weapons makes them different than other military tools. Since few political objectives are worth risking a catastrophic nuclear attack upon yourself, according to this view all a state needs are enough nuclear forces to survive an adversary's first strike and deliver unacceptable damage in return. During the Cold War, there was an intense debate over what nuclear posture you needed to establish and stabilize this state of mutual vulnerability, or "how much is enough."

The "nuclear revolution school" think this condition of mutually assured destruction is relatively easy to achieve and virtually impossible to escape.[2] Other political theorists, however, believe nuclear advantage, even nuclear primacy, is achievable and a state has a responsibility to try to attain it. Perhaps nuclear primacy would allow something approaching a first strike, where you wipe out your rival's ability to retaliate—or at least hold their nuclear deterrent at risk. This nuclear advantage might be converted into political leverage, perhaps forcing an adversary to think twice during a crisis. Even if a obtaining a successful first strike capacity is elusive, possessing a clear comparative advantage, some believe, matters and can convey political benefits. You might emerge from a conflict with less damage, which may allow you to take greater risks and demonstrate greater resolve. Perhaps you can achieve "escalation dominance," or meaningful advantages below the strategic level. These advantages, according to some analysts, may signal greater confidence and resolve to an adversary, conveying important benefits.[3]

What weapons you have is only one part of the equation; how you think about the sensitivity of the nuclear balance and escalation dynamics may shape how you plan to use your weapons. If you believe in and accept a world of mutual vulnerability with nuclear rivals, you can be relatively relaxed in your posture. There is little advantage in going first, and your posture can be structured to respond at your own pace and to target population centers instead of military assets, a far less demanding assignment. If, however, you seek nuclear advantage and/or flexibility, and think these characteristics matter, you may do more than seek more sophisticated nuclear capabilities than your adversary. You may place your weapons in more forward-leaning, riskier strategies. A state seeking nuclear advantage may construct a posture that allows you to use your weapons preemptively, targeting the adversary's nuclear capabilities. It may plan to launch its weapons first, fast, and massively, or in a more controlled, flexible manner. These postures require superior intelligence and advanced sensors to track a rival's military assets, as well as its command, control, communications, and intelligence capabilities (C3I), which may be mobile or in the air, sea, or space. Choosing this posture would demand you invest a lot in the speed, stealth, and accuracy of your nuclear weapons and defenses, as well as in C3I, so that your attack could hit its targets before the adversary had a chance to respond.

This gets to the question of technological change. Though the science and engineering of fission and fusion weapons are old, new technologies to deliver and/or track these weapons appear all the time. From the development of inter-continental missiles in the 1950s and 1960s, to the dramatically improved targeting, stealth, and launch capabilities in the 1970s and 1980s, to more recent advances in sensors and hypersonics, the nuclear enterprise has undergone (and will likely continue to undergo) dramatic changes. Recent technologies, such as artificial intelligence applications, could affect the nuclear mission in the future. How much these changes affect a state's grand strategies and international political outcomes, however, remains unclear. These technologies are expensive, and investments in the nuclear mission may crowd out expenditures in more useable military forces. They can be destabilizing and initiate arms races. Perhaps most critically, there is the question of credibility: how believable is the threat to launch a nuclear attack, short of the direst circumstances? Arguments that nuclear advantage can convince an adversary you were willing to either launch a preemptive strike or initiate more limited options are fiercely contested. If neither threat is credible, will such a nuclear posture still generate political advantages, both before and during crises?

Whether nuclear forces can and should be made more useable is also hotly contested. As weapons become more accurate and stealthy, possessing lower yields and fallout, there are some who believe the taboo against or restraints imposed on nuclear use can be lowered.

While few believe the threat to launch a massive strategic nuclear assault is credible, perhaps nuclear weapons could be deployed tactically either to gain advantage on the battlefield or to signal resolve against an adversary. Throughout the nuclear age and continuing today, planners have tried to construct postures that allow nuclear weapons to be employed flexibly in ways that are tailored to specific circumstances. Critics of this approach argue that there is no reason to think nuclear weapons can be controlled and limited to lower levels of use. Any nuclear use, they suggest, may easily escalate in a terrifying manner to a strategic nuclear exchange, regardless of the wishes of either combatant. Escalation dynamics may be the most important variable in assessing any nuclear posture, yet neither theory nor history provides conclusive answers.

How have varying nuclear postures affected outcomes in world politics? Most states, such as France, Great Britain, and others, built modest arsenals arrayed in relatively relaxed postures motivated by a mixture of basic deterrence (to prevent being conquered) and desire for the perceived prestige and sway nuclear weapons are believed to provide. During the Cold War, the superpowers pursued more ambitious nuclear postures, a strategy many believe is most relevant to the

US-China rivalry today. Both the Soviet Union and the United States saw nu-clear weapons as the touchstone of power during their 40-year-plus rivalry. They sought larger and more sophisticated forces, extended their nuclear umbrella to members of their respective alliances, and viewed efforts to limit these weapons as the primary avenue of diplomatic interaction.

Some have argued that nuclear weapons had a stabilizing effect on world poli-tics during the Cold War, preventing a world war between the Soviet Union and the United States. There are several problems with this view. First, it assumes that in the absence of nuclear weapons, the rivalry between the superpowers would have been more dangerous, inevitably resulting in a war. This counterfactual is, of course, unknowable. Second, the Cold War *was* in fact very dangerous, wracked by crises, and shadowed by the possibility of global war. Third, the most danger-ous crises of the Cold War involved nuclear standoffs. The Cuban Missile Crisis, arguably the most frightening confrontation of the postwar period, is hard to imagine in a world without nuclear weapons. The United States and its allies would have been unlikely or unable to protect West Berlin—another sharp, dangerous crisis—without the threat of nuclear weapons. This leads to my fourth point: whether the nuclear balance affected these crises is fiercely contested.

There is historical evidence to support a variety of views. The Soviet Union, it could be argued, pursued its most aggressive policies in the first years of the Cold War, when it possessed no nuclear weapons, and again in the late 1950s and early 1960s, when it threatened West Berlin and placed medium-range nuclear missiles in Cuba despite arguably being in a position of strategic nuclear inferiority versus the United States. On the other hand, America's strategic nuclear superiority in the 1950s may have allowed the United States to pursue more aggressive policies, such as promoting West German rearmament. Whether or not America's strate-gic nuclear advantage mattered in ending the Cuban Missile Crisis on terms favorable to the United States is an open question, though some policymakers in Moscow and Washington certainly believed it mattered.

Examining the last two decades of the Cold War nuclear rivalry is both reveal-ing and confusing. The superpowers achieved relative equality of forces by the 1970s. They both appeared to accept mutual vulnerability as the cornerstone of strategic stability, best reflected by their decision to negotiate limits on defensive weapons (the Antiballistic Missile Treaty, or ABM) and offensive forces (the Stra-tegic Arms Limitation treaties, or SALT). Embracing mutual assured destruction appeared to be both the policy of the superpowers and an accepted fact. Despite that, decisionmakers in both countries remained highly sensitive to perceived shifts in the strategic nuclear balance. In the aftermath of the ABM and SALT trea-ties, the United States increased its expenditures on counterforce capabilities—the MX missile, the Trident D-5, the B1 and B2 aircrafts, Pershing II missiles, cruise missiles, and improved command, control, and intelligence capabilities—that made little sense for a nuclear posture that accepted mutual vulnerability. Decision-makers in the Soviet Union appeared alarmed by America's investments in these capabilities, which may have affected their larger political calculations.

The history of the Cold War nuclear arms race reveals a puzzle. Official policy in both capitals involved accepting mutual vulnerability as a cornerstone of stra-tegic stability. Few analysts believed this condition was escapable, even with great effort, or that nuclear weapons could be used tactically without the grave risk of escalation. Yet both the Soviet Union and the United States invested in capabili-ties and pursued nuclear postures that went well beyond what was needed for (and instead threatened) strategic stability. They also sought flexible nuclear options. These shifts in the strategic nuclear balance, as well as the two countries' differ-ent nuclear postures, certainly played into political calculations in both capitals, though in uncertain ways.[4]

What lessons would China have taken from this history? China's leaders look at Soviet policies, both domestically and abroad, with a certain level of scorn. While this is speculative on my part, Chinese leaders may have evaluated Moscow's reactions to America's post-ABM/SALT investments seeking nuclear advantage with skepticism. They might have concluded that nuclear advantage is difficult if not impossible to achieve, and even if it was obtainable, what matters is a state's resolve. In other words, nuclear advantage may only exist if you let it affect your own perceptions and policies. Consider again the Cuban Missile Crisis. In the 1960s, the United States possessed an enormous advantage in nuclear capabili-ties over the Soviet Union; indeed, it may have had enough nuclear weapons to launch a first strike and cripple Russia's ability to respond, a capability that Presi-dent John F. Kennedy knew would disappear soon. Yet President Kennedy went to great lengths to defuse the crisis and avoid actions that could escalate to nuclear war. He demonstrated this caution when memories of surprise attack and fully mobilized wars of total conquest were still fresh, and where eventual conflict with the Soviets was seen by many as likely if not inevitable. If the United States dem-onstrated nuclear caution in 1962, during a grave crisis 90 miles from its home-land where it possessed an enormous if wasting advantage, why would anyone think they'd be more willing to risk nuclear war in more recent, less threatening times over issues of less immediate concern when nuclear advantage was arguably harder to obtain?

China's leaders could have calculated that ignoring your rival's investments in expensive, unusable forces might free you to spend your defense monies on conventional military capabilities that would actually shape the outcome of a conflict. While unknowable, this may explain why China, until recently, made relatively modest investments in nuclear capabilities compared to its conventional military investments and the nuclear capabilities of both Russia and the United States.

Recent nuclear history might be even more confusing.[5] Russian officials made nuclear threats—some veiled, others less so—during the war it launched against Ukraine in February 2022. Neither the United States nor other North Atlantic Treaty Organization (NATO) countries were deterred from supplying critical intelligence and massive military supplies to aid Ukraine. But the Biden administration made it very clear it was deterred from intervening directly in the conflict by Russia's nuclear forces.[6] Russia was not deterred from invading Ukraine, but did not attack any of the supply lines or depots in NATO countries or use nuclear weapons against Ukraine. While there was much discussion about tactical nuclear use, the question of the strategic nuclear balance between Russia and the United States was rarely mentioned and it was unclear what effect, if any, the nuclear balance had on the various players. Some have suggested this is evidence of the stability-instability paradox, where strategic nuclear deterrence makes military conflict at the conventional, sub-strategic level more permissible and likely. It is hard to know what lessons China has drawn from this, though it weighed in publicly and (it is believed) privately to dissuade Russia from using nuclear weapons.

China's Expansion and America's Response

Why is China now investing in significant increases in the number and quality of its nuclear forces?[7] According to a recent report of the Federation of American Scientists, "Within the past five years, China has significantly expanded its ongoing nuclear modernization program by fielding more types and greater numbers of nuclear weapons than ever before."[8]

In my opinion, China pursues this vigorous effort from a comparatively low base. Interestingly, China's original decision to build nuclear weapons did not reveal what kind of nuclear posture it would eventually have. Chinese efforts to build nuclear weapons in the mid-1950s were likely driven by America's implied or explicit nuclear threats during the Korean War and the Taiwan Strait crises. It received considerable assistance from the Soviet Union until Nikita Khrushchev and Mao Zedong's relationship deteriorated in the late 1950s. China detonated a nuclear device in October 1964 and developed and tested increasingly sophisticated missile delivery systems in the decade that followed. Mao's terrifying rhetoric about nuclear weapons and erratic foreign and domestic policies worried both the United States and Soviet Union, and both considered attacking China's nuclear forces in the 1960s. Surprisingly, however, China did not try to keep pace with either the Soviet Union or the United States during the Cold War.[9] Even after China's economy began its massive expansion during the first decades after the end of the Cold War, China built far fewer nuclear weapons than it was capable of, displaying what appeared to be a relatively relaxed posture. In other words, the People's Republic of China's (PRC's) recent massive investments in nuclear capabilities represent a dramatic policy turn that needs explaining.

There are several possibilities for this shift. First, China's leaders could feel that recent improvements in America's nuclear capabilities put China's assured retaliatory capabilities at risk. The United States began its nuclear modernization program over a decade ago, with America investing in systems that possessed improved accuracy, mobility, and stealth. Meanwhile, the United States has also pursued improved defensive and conventional military capabilities. These advanced capabilities appear matched to America's military strategies that have long seemed preemptive in nature, and target an adversary's command, control, communication, and intelligence capabilities to blind and limit a rival's ability to fight. China might conclude that the United States plans to paralyze China's strategic capabilities early in a conflict, leaving it without a robust retaliatory capability and forcing it to back down. Beijing could also worry that America's investments will produce novel, advanced technologies that threaten it and may want to keep pace. Or China's larger expenditures might be meant to simply protect, strengthen, and ensure its ability to respond to an attack by the United States.[10]

A second possibility is that China, viewing itself as a great power equal to the United States, seeks nuclear capabilities on par with its rival. It already views itself as an equal or better in other forms of power—economics, innovation, sociocultural appeal, space (outer and cyber), conventional military tools—and simply wants to close the gap in terms of the only form of power where China is clearly behind: nuclear capabilities. Looking to the past, China might conclude that the United States only took the Soviet Union seriously as an equal in the 1970s, when it caught up to and in some ways surpassed America's nuclear forces. China might also note that this mutual recognition of equality led to a period of détente, which saw the superpowers sign arms control agreements and resolve many unsettled questions in Europe through the Helsinki accords.

A third possibility is that China seeks meaningful strategic nuclear advantage over the United States. China may want to expel America from its forward military presence in East Asia and incorporate Taiwan into its state. The United States vigorously opposes both positions, and its conventional military capabilities, backed by its nuclear forces, may give China's leaders pause as they pursue their goals. If China believes it can achieve meaningful nuclear advantage, America's position in the region may become less tenable. Perhaps a China possessing a nuclear advantage can reduce or even eliminate America's power position in the region. In a crisis over Taiwan, China's leaders may believe that attaining a nuclear advantage might deter the United States from intervening or escalating once a conflict began.

Though China's motivations for its massive investments in nuclear capabilities are obscure, they are likely based on some mix of all three reasons. Indeed, the overall goal of these improved forces might be to simply complicate America's calculations in the region, to generate a greater sense of uncertainty and unease. China may also be motivated by other geopolitical concerns. Its relations with nuclear Russia and North Korea appear fine today, though in the past, there has been tension and acrimony, which could return in the future. It has long-standing border disputes with nuclear India. China may seek nuclear advantage to influence the decisions of other neighbors, including non-nuclear states.

How should the United States respond to China's dramatic enhancements in nuclear capabilities? The answer likely depends on how American policymakers evaluate the various arguments made for and against nuclear advantage. If the United States believes that the nuclear balance is both sensitive and consequential, and that shifts could affect America's grand strategic position in East Asia and its calculations during a crisis over Taiwan, it will want to respond vigorously to China's improvements and continue and perhaps expand its nuclear modernization plans. If, on the other hand, American leaders think that the nuclear balance is stable, that meaningful nuclear advantage is elusive, and that responding to China's investments with its own effort will spur an expensive arms race that conveys no political advantage, it may be less inclined to do more.

There are, however, two crucial considerations that confound these calculations. The first involves America's grand strategy of inhibition.[11] Since the start of the nuclear age but accelerating in the mid-1960s, America has sought to inhibit the rise of independent nuclear states around the world. The United States pursues inhibition for a variety of reasons, but at heart, it believes that the lower the number of nuclear weapons states (and the smaller the number of nuclear weapons there are), the more freedom of action the United States has to do what it wants. A world with many nuclear states complicates America's behavior: a small nuclear weapons state can deter the United States, despite its overwhelming superiority in economic, technological, and conventional military power. A world with more nuclear weapons states might also risk the United States being pulled catalytically into conflicts it would rather avoid. There are several elements to America's strategies of inhibition, including the Nuclear Nonproliferation Treaty regime, but the most important element is Washington's provision of security agreements, including the protection of its nuclear forces, to allies who might otherwise seek their own nuclear weapons.

On its face, the promise to protect another state, up to and including the use of its own nuclear weapons, seems far-fetched. If an ally is threatened by a nuclear armed enemy, such as China, why would the United States risk a nuclear attack on its own soil to protect another country, no matter how friendly? To make this promise credible and assure its ally, the United States cannot simply accept mutual vulnerability or a relaxed nuclear posture. Instead, many believe it should pursue nuclear advantage and more flexible options, no matter how elusive, while enmeshing these advantages in dynamic, forward-leaning strategies that may envision using nuclear weapons first, flexibly, and perhaps preemptively. America's strategies of inhibition are especially salient in East Asia, with its history of conflict and geopolitical rivalry. At different points during the nuclear age, a number of countries, including South Korea, Japan, Australia, and even Taiwan explored acquiring their own nuclear capabilities. If America's nuclear advantage was challenged or undermined—either by China's nuclear posture or by America's unwillingness to respond—America's allies (in addition to unaligned countries like Vietnam) might seek their own independent nuclear forces.

The fact that the region's proliferation dynamics are tied to America's nuclear strategies highlights an important, ironic consideration for China: increased nuclear proliferation in the region would be a far sharper challenge to China's geopolitical interests than the United States. A nuclear South Korea, Japan, Australia, Vietnam, or Taiwan would dramatically complicate China's freedom of action in its own neighborhood. Ironically, if China successfully undermined the credibility of America's extended deterrent—or if the United States would make its own choice to remove it—China's geopolitical position would arguably be the most harmed. During the Cold War and after, the United States suggested to the Soviet Union and Russia that it was in their interests to have a strong American military presence in West Germany / Germany, backed by its nuclear umbrella, lest it seek its own nuclear weapons. Is China willing to pay the cost of a nuclear South Korea, Japan, and others to reduce or eliminate America's power position in the region?

The second consideration: Russia more than China has been the main focus of America's strategic nuclear posture. If China achieves nuclear parity or superiority, does the United States possess enough capability to deter both?[12] The United States has never had to develop a nuclear posture to counter two peer rivals. This would be a problem even if China and Russia did not coordinate their nuclear plans (as the United States does with Great Britain, and to a lesser extent, France). But both rivals have deepened their political and strategic cooperation in recent years. Even in the absence of formal coordination, American policymakers must ask whether a nuclear posture oriented toward one nuclear peer will be sufficient to deal with two. This question is even sharper in a world that may see both new nuclear weapons states and increased capabilities by the states that already possess nuclear weapons.

The Future of the China-US Nuclear Relationship

The most important variable shaping both China and the United States nuclear posture and behavior will be its grand strategic goals and the two countries' relations with each other. China-US relations have deteriorated dramatically over the past decade or so, with little sign they will improve. Disagreements on issues ranging from human rights to intellectual property to economic policies are fiercely contested. China's desire to reduce the US's military and political presence in East Asia and to take over Taiwan sharply clashes with America's stated grand strategic interests and policies. Each side will likely tailor their nuclear postures in ways they believe best help them achieve their goals.

Within this general framework, however, there is a lot of uncertainty about how nuclear weapons will influence the China-US relationship, both generally and during a crisis. Much will depend upon the specific scenario. A crisis wherein China threatens a disputed territory with a treaty ally, like Japan or the Philippines, might be more likely to engage an American military response and call into play nuclear postures than other situations. The most dangerous and unfortunately likely crisis scenario is a showdown between China and the United States over the status of Taiwan. How will nuclear weapons shape the "if" and "when" that comes and fixes the outcome? A lot might be determined by how the crisis unfolds: a massive amphibious invasion, where Taiwan is directly aided by American forces, may be more likely to bring nuclear weapons into play than a PRC blockade or slower strangulation strategy. In this scenario, the very fact that China initiated such a crisis means that at some level deterrence has failed and that it doubts America's nuclear weapons will come into play.

Two interconnected variables would be crucial if this happens. First, China might calculate that its increasingly robust conventional advantages in its near abroad would provide the upper hand in any military conflict, forcing the United States to choose whether to fight and lose before being forced to choose whether or not to go nuclear. Even if the United States engaged initially and successfully in a conventional struggle, China might believe that the flexible nuclear options its buildup appears to be focusing on (such as tactical nuclear weapons) might prevent the United States from escalating a crisis to the strategic nuclear level. While it is impossible to know what the United States would do, either if China won with conventional forces or after using tactical nuclear weapons, the PRC leadership might calculate that it possesses enormous advantages in the key variable—resolve, both to initiate the crisis and to see it through to what it considered a successful completion. Taiwan is far closer to the PRC and its status of far greater interest to China than the United States. China might believe the United States was bluffing, that it would not respond militarily to a PRC incursion, and that even if the United States did initially respond with conventional weapons, it would be unwilling to go so far as to use nuclear weapons. It might look to the history of a previous era, the Cold War, when the whole idea of nuclear use was not only seen as more permissible but likely. Yet China would note that the United States avoided dropping the bomb on the Soviet Union (or a far weaker, more aggressive China), despite greater stakes and at times nuclear advantage. It might be reasonable for Chinese leaders to discount America's nuclear posture in a future Taiwan contingency, where Washington's other pressing concerns gave it little appetite for a war that risked nuclear escalation against a resolved China whose nuclear capabilities increase by the day.

That said, neither theory nor history provides clear comfort, as resolve is a notoriously difficult quality to measure ex ante. It is hard to imagine either side backing down or accepting a loss if a war starts. Once a great power war breaks out, escalation dynamics may be hard to predict or control. Worryingly, this uncertainty takes place in an environment where Beijing and Washington have fewer formal and informal avenues to discuss political tensions, to say nothing of nuclear relations, than the superpowers did during much of the Cold War. Then again, a strategy that doubles down on this uncertainty, that attempts to complicate Beijing's calculations, while dangerous, may be the United States' best deterrent option.

Nuclear behavior is riddled with tensions and contradictions. American policymakers, for example, recognize that mutual vulnerability is a reality and a key element of strategic stability, a cherished policy goal. Still, Americans have vigorously pursued nuclear systems within nuclear postures that arguably seek to lessen and escape mutual vulnerability. China seeks to blunt America's nuclear advantage, which could undermine the nuclear umbrella the United States extends to its allies in East Asia and unleash increased proliferation in China's near abroad. Both sides desire an international environment where nuclear weapons have less salience and emphasize that nuclear weapons should never be used, all while investing in flexible capabilities that appear to make these weapons more useable. For both countries, shifting nuclear postures generate uncertainty and increase risk, while also being a form of expensive insurance that hopefully prevents the worst outcomes in international politics. Both China and the United States will likely continue to make massive investments in their nuclear capabilities, despite mixed evidence that such spending will generate the grand strategic outcomes they seek.

NOTES

1. Vipin Narang, *Seeking the Bomb: Strategies of Nuclear Proliferation* (Princeton University Press, 2022).

2. Robert Jervis, *The Meaning of the Nuclear Revolution: Statecraft and the Prospect of Nuclear Armageddon* (Cornell University Press, 1989).

3. There is a vigorous debate about whether meaningful nuclear superiority is obtainable or worth it. For a sample, see Matthew Kroenig, *The Logic of American Nuclear Strategy: Why Strategic Superiority Matters* (Oxford University Press, 2020); and Todd Sescher and Matthew Furhmann, *Nuclear Weapons and Coercive Diplomacy* (Cambridge University Press, 2017).

4. For great insight into this, see Brendan Rittenhouse Green, *The Revolution that Failed: Nuclear Competition, Arms Control, and the Cold War* (Cambridge University Press, 2017).

5. Francis J. Gavin, "Nuclear Lessons and Dilemmas from the War in Ukraine," in *War in Ukraine: Conflict, Strategy, and the Return of a Fractured World*, ed. Hal Brands (Johns Hopkins University Press, 2023), 173–196, https://muse.jhu.edu/pub/1/oa_edited _volume/chapter/3881924.

6. Joseph R. Biden Jr., "What America Will and Will Not Do in Ukraine," *New York Times*, May 31, 2022, https://www.nytimes.com/2022/05/31/opinion/biden-ukraine -strategy.html.

7. A good analysis of the debate around this question can be found in Joshua Rovner and Caitlyn Talmadge, "The Meaning of China's Nuclear Modernization," *Journal of Strategic Studies* 46, no. 6–7 (2023): 1116–1148.

8. Hans M. Kristensen, Matt Korda, Eliana Johns, and Mackenzie Knight, "Chinese Nuclear Weapons, 2025," *Bulletin of Atomic Scientists* 81, no. 2 (2025): 125–160, https://www.tandfonline.com/doi/epdf/10.1080/00963402.2025.2467011?needAccess=true.

9. M. Taylor Fravel and Evan S. Medeiros, "China's Search for Assured Retaliation: The Evolution of Chinese Nuclear Strategy and Force Structure," *International Security* 35, no. 2 (Fall 2010): 48–87.

10. Henrik Stålhane Hiim, M. Taylor Fravel, and Magnus Langset Trøan, "The Dynamics of an Entangled Security Dilemma: China's Changing Nuclear Posture," *International Security* 47, no. 4 (Spring 2023): 147–187.

11. Francis J. Gavin, "Strategies of Inhibition: US Grand Strategy, the Nuclear Revolution, and Nonproliferation," *International Security* 40, no. 1 (Summer 2015): 9–46.

12. The Biden administration originally appeared sanguine about facing two peer nuclear competitors. See Jake Sullivan, "Remarks by National Security Advisor Jake Sullivan for the Arms Control Association Annual Forum," speech, National Press Club, Washington, DC, June 2, 2023, https://www.armscontrol.org/events/2023-06/remarks-national-security-advisor-jake-sullivan-arms-control-association-aca-annual. This view seemed to shift a year later; see Vipin Narang, "Nuclear Threats and the Role of Allies: A Conversation with Vipin Narang," interview by Heather Williams, Center for Strategic and International Studies, August 1, 2024, https://www.csis.org/analysis/nuclear-threats-and-role-allies-conversation-acting-assistant-secretary-vipin-narang.

PART III / Politics, Strategy, Intelligence, and Values

Chapter Ten

The Asia First Debate

Kori Schake

The United States has been pivoting to Asia since at least 1821. Threats to American territory and interests by foreign powers from across the Pacific were the origin of the Monroe Doctrine. The 1898 Spanish-American War occasioned major strategic gains in Asia, making the US a power in the Pacific theater. President Franklin D. Roosevelt's prioritization of the European theater was contested by the military throughout much of World War II. Accusations of "who lost China" politicized an "Asia First" debate during the Korean War. Each of those historical precedents to our current Asia First debate faced significant opposition, from within the government and from the American public. And there is one more important historical antecedent to the current debate over which geographic region to give precedence to in planning: the inter-war America First movement.

The strategy and resource mismatch that is the foundation of the current Asia First strategy began as the Cold War ended and was exacerbated across the subsequent 30 years. With budgets constricting and strategies multiplying military missions, levels of ambition declined and risk increased. What began with the Base Force in 1992 as two major regional contingencies for the force-planning construct slunk down to winning in one theater while holding in another. This imbalance

Kori Schake leads the foreign and defense policy team at the American Enterprise Institute. She is the author of *Safe Passage: The Transition from British to American Hegemony.*

continued with outright abandonment of major wars as the guide to developing the force during the Rumsfeld and Gates Pentagons, return to an implausible two regional wars (plus a pivot to Asia in the Obama years), and subsequent strategies more focused on China but reliant on spending increases that didn't materialize.

Asia First advocates are correct that US defense spending is inadequate to need, that the defense enterprise has absorbed an untenable amount of risk that it can carry out the strategy, and that America's allies can and should do more for their own defense. But their proposed solutions excuse political leaders accepting those constraints as fixed instead of building support for what is necessary for American security.

Moreover, the approach ignores the antibodies the Trump administration's approach is activating, by discouraging other countries from providing help that will be essential to producing the outcomes that the United States needs. Without allied assistance, the United States cannot adequately surveil and protect its networks or physical infrastructure, orchestrate an effective economic penalties campaign, project power across the vast Pacific Ocean, launch high-intensity combat operations, resupply its forces, or produce necessary munitions. The advocates for the Trump administration's Asia First strategy are no more likely than were those of his first term to constrain Donald Trump's behavior—and they are destroying 80 years of effective allied cooperation that made the United States safer and more prosperous than their alternative.

Historical Precedents

Daniel Walker Howe, author of the *What Hath God Wrought: The Transformation of America, 1815–1848*, considers the Monroe Doctrine "the moment when Americans no longer faced eastward across the Atlantic and turned to face westward across the continent."[1] The first use of both the language and the diplomatic intent by the Monroe administration to limit European claims on American security interests came in 1821 from Russian incursion into the Pacific Northwest: it was in response to the establishment of Russian trading outposts in what was then newly independent Mexico's Alta California that Secretary of State John Quincy Adams proclaimed, "the American continents are no longer subjects for any new colonial establishments."[2]

The debate about whether American interests are better served by prioritization of Europe or Asia has been ongoing in the US strategy community since at least the Spanish-American War in 1898. In that conflict, as in the campaigns of the American Civil War, most of the attention was riveted on the Atlantic sea-board, when the moves of greatest strategic importance occurred in the Pacific theater.

True, President William McKinley's request that Congress "authorize and em-power the President to take measures to secure a full and final termination of hostilities between the government of Spain and the people of Cuba" made no mention of Spain's Pacific possessions.[3] Yet division of scarce combat power bal-anced and tailored the force for the respective theaters of operations, prioritizing firepower for the Caribbean but speed and maneuverability for the Pacific. The Navy's Caribbean squadron consisted of four battleships and two armored cruis-ers, while the Asiatic squadron was accorded four armored cruisers, two gun-boats, an armed revenue cutter, and two supply steamers.

Military action against Spain in the Pacific was central to US planning for the war: From 1896 the Navy planned to blockade Cuba and attack Spanish forces in the Philippines, ostensibly to prevent Spain's naval forces in the Pacific from re-inforcing and resupplying operations in Cuba. But given the extensive transit time from the Western Pacific to the Caribbean before the 1914 opening of the Panama Canal, the Navy would either have to have assessed a war of long duration that was inconsistent with its assessments of Spain's maritime weakness or was ambi-tious for control of the seas.

Both the Navy's assessment and its prowess were validated in combat, with the Pacific squadron under Commodore George Dewey sinking the Spanish fleet in under an hour with only a single American fatality. The Congress that had refused to annex Hawaii and only supported McKinley's declaration of war with the Teller Amendment—precluding US colonization of Cuba—quickly acculturated itself to an American empire of colonies both actual (Guam, Hawaii, Wake Island, the Philippines, Puerto Rico) and virtual (Cuba). The United States became a Pacific power with the Spanish-American War.

The American military has been struggling with apportionment of scarce com-bat power among the competing Atlantic and Pacific theaters ever since. The most demanding circumstances attending on the apportionment occurred during World War II, when the United States was engaged in total war in both theaters against two dominating empires. While the US military dramatically expanded from 200,000 personnel in 1939 to more than 12,000,000 in 1945, the forces were inadequate to the demands of the war effort.

The War Department's rainbow suite of war plans from the late 1930s antici-pated multitheater wars against coalition opponents. Although three of the five scenarios outlined by Chief of Naval Operations Admiral Harold Stark to President Roosevelt in November of 1940 on the basis of the rainbow plans were Pacific-focused (the fourth was US neutrality), Stark advocated for prioritizing the European theater. His argument was that early support to Britain and committing troops to fight Germany in Europe and Africa best positioned the US to eventually defeat both Germany and Japan. Stark concluded: "If Britain wins decisively against Germany, we could win everywhere; but that if she loses the problem confronting us would be very great; and while we might not lose everywhere, we might, possibly, not win anywhere."[4]

Army Chief General George Marshall endorsed Stark's recommendation, and in January 1941, President Roosevelt adopted the approach, committing to maintaining supply lines to Britain by US naval escort.[5] Military historian Joseph Micallef concludes, "what the Rainbow plans implicitly recognized was that the European and Asian theaters were already tied together and what happened in one theater, especially in Europe, would affect the other."[6]

Within two weeks of Italy and Germany declaring war on the United States, Roosevelt's Arcadia conference with British Prime Minister Winston Churchill cemented priority of the European theater in US war efforts. The United States, the United Kingdom, and Canada formally adopted the policy in March 1941 of establishing a "strategic defensive" in the Far East, with priority for "the early defeat of Germany as the predominant member of the Axis with the principal military effort of the United States being exerted in the Atlantic and European area."[7] Although more resources flowed toward the Pacific than the Atlantic until 1943, President Roosevelt's strategy remained unequivocally Europe First throughout the war.

Once the wars commenced, the American military leadership equivocated on the Europe First strategy, both because the US was attacked by Japan and because of disagreements with Britain over how to prosecute the war in Europe. Chief of Naval Operations Ernest King (who replaced Stark in March 1942) openly advocated for shifting focus to the Pacific, while Army Chief of Staff George Marshall, in exasperation, wanted to threaten Britain with abandonment to gain agreement for a cross-channel invasion. Prime Minister Churchill's obduracy in advocating a Mediterranean focus for the first Allied landings in Europe cemented the American military leaders' suspicion that Britain was using US power to preserve its imperial holdings rather than the narrower focus on defeat of Germany. So skeptical were the American military leaders that both Admiral Ernest King and General Douglas MacArthur declined Britain's offer of subordinated forces to their commands.

In July 1942, the American military chiefs of staff formally objected to the president's strategy of prioritizing the European theater. President Roosevelt responded formally. In one of a very few written instructions—and the only one in which he pulled rank, signing it as Commander in Chief—he replied:

> I have carefully read your estimate of Sunday. My first impression is that it is exactly what Germany hoped the United States would do following Pearl Harbor. Secondly: it does not in fact provide use of American troops in fighting except in a lot of islands whose occupation will not affect the world situation this year or next. Third: it does not help Russia or the Near East. Therefore, it is disapproved as of the present.[8]

Admiral King was never reconciled to the Europe First strategy. Although he complied with the president's direction, he agitated throughout the war for greater resourcing to the Pacific theater.

There was a postwar push by Republicans for an Asia First strategy—largely for partisan reasons of opposing President Harry S. Truman's deepening commitment to Europe and the success of China's Communist Party conquest—but it availed little internationally. It did have a coherent set of organizing principles that still resonate in the debate over American strategy: sovereignty, selective military intervention, strident anticommunism, and the promotion of a technological defense state.[9]

The final historical precedent—an uncomfortable one but unquestionably also a precursor to elements of the current debate—is the America First movement between the two world wars. The idea of neutrality in international affairs grew in popularity between the wars as privations from the depression hit hard in America, and authoritarian governments advanced in both Europe and Asia. And while the 1930s version of America First opposed US involvement in Asia and Europe, both it and the current incarnation have an undercurrent of isolationism that is likely to create a dangerous gap between declaratory policy and actual willingness to carry out the strategy when confronted—whether by Chinese aggression or allied actions deemed undeserving.

Evolution of the Strategy-Resources Mismatch

Contemporary rebalancing of US strategy to weight Asia more heavily started in the late 1980s as the Cold War thawed. NATO allies, including the United States, took deep peace dividends: the US reduced spending by 10% and force structure by 25%.[10] While the 1992 Base Force was intended to be a floor for US spending and forces, it quickly became a ceiling. Without the Soviet threat, determining force sizing became both an analytic and political challenge. The 1991 Gulf War provided one framework, that of two major regional contingencies. But that was quickly swept away by William (Bill) Clinton's administration relaxing the assumption of two simultaneous wars and doubling the George H. W. Bush administration's budget cuts. Defense Secretary Les Aspin's Bottom-Up Review was predicated on a "win-hold-win" strategy for potential wars in Northeast and Southwest Asia, translating into cuts of two divisions, six fighter aircraft wings, 102 battle force ships, a carrier battle group, and 190,000 personnel. Since at least that time, 1993, the United States has not had a military force capable of truly carrying out its defense strategies. While mission sets expanded, forces contracted.

The Bush administration initially all but abandoned the two-war construct in a stampede to "transformation" of warfare. Secretary of Defense Rumsfeld concluded: "We will place greater emphasis on deterrence in four critical theaters, backed by the ability to swiftly defeat two aggressors at the same time, while preserving the option for one massive counteroffensive to occupy an aggressor's capital and replace the regime."[11] The Bush administration provided budgets nowhere near encompassing those objectives. It also went further, attempting to employ planning that drove force modernization by what was possible in innovations for US forces instead of by adversary military capabilities. The associated force structure for the 2003 Quadrennial Defense Review eliminated another active-duty division but retained other major elements of the Bottom-Up Review force. Which is to say that the plan further expanded missions and objectives but reduced the forces for carrying them out.

By 2006, with wars in Afghanistan and Iraq going badly and obviously underresourced, the Department of Defense (DOD) updated the force sizing construct to relax the need for "decisive" victory in the second theater, combined with defending the homeland and deterring attacks in four regional theaters. But these expansive aims were only achievable by accepting additional risk. Secretary Robert Gates considered the additional risk prudent, asking, "It is true that the United States would be hard pressed to fight a major conventional ground war elsewhere on short notice, but as I've said before, where on Earth would we do that?"[12]

Like Secretary Rumsfeld before him, Secretary Gates believed the American way of war had been transformed. But while Rumsfeld believed that the driving force was technology, Gates considered it the difficulty of winning the wars the US was involved in, saying, "any future defense secretary who advises the president to again send a big American land army into Asia or into the Middle East or Africa should have his head examined."[13] They both, in their different ways, collapsed confidence that the US needed a military capable of fighting an equally capable military in an extended war. Which is to say both defense secretaries of the Bush administration extending into the Barack Obama administration failed to anticipate what would be needed in the force within the coming five years of the defense program.

The 2010 Quadrennial Defense Review explicitly discarded the two-war construct: "It is no longer appropriate to speak of 'major regional conflicts' as the sole or even the primary template for sizing, shaping, and evaluating US forces."[14] What US officials would replace it with was unclear until the 2012 Budget Control Act forced their hand by cutting an additional $500 billion across a decade—this after Secretary Gates got the military services to offer $500 billion in cuts on the promise that the money would be reinvested but was instead reclaimed by the Obama White House. What they replaced it with was greater risk associated with execution of the strategy . . . and a pivot to Asia.

The 2017 National Security Strategy is credited with getting serious about the China threat, but it was actually the 2018 National Defense Strategy (NDS) where the emphasis comes through. Yet even there, the NDS producing the force adequate to the strategy of containing China was premised on a 3%–5% year-on-year real spending increase that did not materialize beyond the first two years.

Nor did defense spending keep pace with inflation in any of the four years of the administration of Joe Biden. The 2022 National Defense Strategy purports to consider China the "pacing challenge"—but so inadequate were both the funding and the force that President Biden's defense secretary ended his tenure by disavowing the four budgets he supervised, claiming, "I have not wavered in my assessment that meeting the demands of our strategy requires real growth" to the tune of $55 billion more in the coming year alone.[15]

There are ways the DOD can resolve misalignment of strategy, budgets, and force structure: Curtail what you expect of the force in strategy; increase spending; or accept greater risk that the force will fail to be able to execute the strategy.

Since 1991, mission sets have expanded to include new domains of warfare (cyber, space, hybrid), and new types of operations (peacekeeping, homeland defense, terrorism prevention). Adversaries have burgeoned and now include a China that has a larger navy than the US, an aggressive Russia, a North Korea with an inventory of at least 32 nuclear weapons and missiles of long range, and an Iran that teeters on the brink of nuclear possession, in addition to various extremist groups.

By 1997, defense spending had been reduced by a full 33% from 1991. As Mackenzie Eaglen has argued, the damage done by the Obama bait and switch and the Budget Control Act has never been repaired. In 2016, Chairman of the Joint Chiefs of Staff General Joe Dunford, described the strategy-to-funding gap as the DOD's greatest challenge.[16] And Congress has exonerated itself from its Article I obligation to authorize and appropriate funding, relying repeatedly—11 of the past 13 years—on continuing resolutions that sap DOD buying power and prevent program adjustments.

Failing to restrain the demand signal of strategy or to match spending to strategy, the US has allowed the gap between strategy and resources to grow and be absorbed as risk. The 1997 Quadrennial Defense Review concluded the strategy could be executed with "moderate risk," which represented the secretary of defense's view; the chairman of the Joint Chiefs of Staff put risk as "moderate to high." By 2014, the chairman's risk assessment sounded more concerned: "the US military will be capable of executing the 2014 QDR strategy but with higher risk in some areas. In fact, our military risk will grow quickly over time if we don't make the types and scope of changes identified in the report."[17] Neither the 2018 nor the 2022 National Defense Strategies included a chairman's risk assessment.

Although there have not been adequate budgets or forces for the strategy in the past 30 years, the US cannot credibly purport to defend its interests and its allies to whom it has undertaken treaty obligations on opposite sides of the globe without committing to being able to protect both.

The Current Debate

The major impetus for an Asia First strategy has been the dramatic increase in China's military capabilities and international assertiveness over the past decade. Xi Jinping has directed the Chinese military to be capable of winning a war over Taiwan by 2027. China's defense budget adjusted for buying power now tops $700 billion, bringing it into the ballpark of US spending.[18] It now leads the US in crucial areas of military technology. China has achieved the world's largest navy (at 370 ships) while the US Navy lags behind (with only 291) and is programmed for further reduction. China's shipbuilding capacity is *230 times* what US industry could produce, making for a decisive wartime advantage. It has more than doubled its nuclear weapons to 600 and is aiming to have a force of over a thousand nuclear weapons by 2030.[19] In addition to its conventional and nuclear force buildup, China has developed cyber tools that are active, political, and strategic: "It does not just spy and steal anymore; it has also laid the ground for hugely disruptive cyber operations against western critical infrastructure."[20]

Advocates of an Asia First strategy in recent years are on solid ground to argue that the US is choosing not to purchase the military forces it needs to carry out a strategy requiring commitments across the globe. The budgeting and force planning of the past thirty years bear them out. But they conclude that irrespective of what American security requires, spending levels will remain unresponsive. This removes responsibility from both elected leaders and appointed defense officials from doing the hard work of changing public attitudes. Russia's invasion of Ukraine in 2014 began changing attitudes in NATO Europe; the full-scale attack in 2022 has solidified public support for higher defense spending in European countries that are derided by Vice President J. D. Vance and Secretary of Defense Pete Hegseth as incurably soft, so how is it that the US administration, brimming with "broligarch" masculinity, cannot shift public attitudes to spend what is needed?

Asia First advocates are also on solid ground in arguing that the US has accepted dangerous levels of risk associated with carrying out its strategy with the forces it has purchased. Much earnest creativity has gone into compensating for too-few forces in the Pacific with posturing those forces more expansively—which, while necessary, only marginally reduces risk. The Asia First solution is to further reduce risk by amputating American support for Europe and the Middle East in order to husband resources for Asia.

But their monomaniacal focus on China belies that it is not the only country with the ability to destroy the United States, nor is it the only region in which hostile actors can affect American interests. Sole focus on China accrues risk in other regions, and without stabilizing participation by the US, regional allies are rarely able to contain problems that affect American interests—as President Obama found in expecting regional allies to contain ISIS, and the Trump administration is implicitly acknowledging by rushing forces to the Red Sea to campaign against the Houthis.

The Asia First approach assumes that countries will have no option but to bend to our demands or that other countries, if abandoned by us, will nonetheless make choices advantageous to us. That has not been the pattern in wartime coalitions in the 1991 Gulf, mid-1990s Balkan, 2001 Afghanistan, and 2003 Iraq wars—nor the anti-ISIS campaign, Syrian civil war, or the fight against Houthi dominance of Yemen. When we step back, allies step back further, and they often make suboptimal choices for themselves that are damaging to our interests because they lack confidence that they can achieve good outcomes without American assistance.

Severing support to Europe would allow Russia to achieve many of its war aims in Ukraine. The Asia First advocates say that war distracts effort from confronting China and is expending valuable and scarce stockpiles of munitions needed for potential war with China. Leaders of Japan, South Korea, Taiwan, Australia, and the Philippines—the frontline countries facing Chinese aggression—do not agree. Those leaders consider capitulation to Russian invasion an encouragement for China to act similarly. Rather than adjust strategy to the concerns of frontline states, the reaction of Asia First advocates has been to redefine "Chinese dominance of Asia" as though Taiwan was unimportant.[21] This is where the undercurrent of isolationism in both the 1930s and 2020s America First movements becomes visible: Their purported support collapses when pressed to deliver.

But could or would the United States actually be unaffected by the collapse of security in Europe? That has not been the experience of either the 20th or 21st centuries—and not just the world wars, but the struggles for freedom by Eastern Europe and former Soviet states, the dismemberment of Yugoslavia, and terrorist attacks in Europe including by Russia (the US expelled more Russian operatives than even Britain did after the Skripal attack). Europe going up in flames doesn't prevent American involvement, but it does dramatically increase the price of restoring what our aloofness as the order corroded allowed.

Moreover, the US cannot attain the economy of scale it needs to manage China alone. Without cooperation from European states, the United States will not have the economic, technological, or industrial heft to compete with Beijing. Nor will it have the help if it abandons its long-standing commitment to defend European states. Would Europe destroy its political and economic relationships with China to protect US interests in Asia?

The administration's ruthlessness in forcing Ukrainian concessions by turning off US weapons and intelligence and humiliating Ukrainian President Volodymyr Zelensky gives pause to countries reliant on US security support. The Trump administration is particularly vituperative toward Europe, where our self-defeating behavior is driving even our allies into cooperation with China. Nor is it just the case in Europe. For example, Japan, South Korea, and China indicated they might act in unison by retaliating against US tariffs, and that may portend cooperation in other areas.[22] And we will want all those allies to fight with us if a war should break out in Asia, but the shocking rudeness and ominous threats from the Trump administration's officials toward allies will preclude them contributing to our fights or grieving with us our losses.

The Asia First strategy assumes allies have no option other than to comply with US demands, when in fact they can simply opt out—and that choice enfeebles US efforts. Sanctions, regimes, and export controls will be ineffectual without European participation; US power projection will be impeded without European ports, overflights, and medical facilities; and preferential access to weapons stockpiles for US forces are unlikely to materialize.

While it's true that US military service chiefs and combatant commanders are nervous about the diminished munitions stockpiles—even if nothing had been provided to Ukraine—US forces fighting China would very quickly (certainly within a month) have exhausted our own holdings. What aiding Ukraine has done is allow the US and its allies to understand their defense industrial deficiencies and seek funding to redress the deficiencies.

Another element of the Asia First approach is a thirst to "create some distance between Beijing and Moscow." This was illusory in 2020 and is even more fantastical now that China, Russia, Iran, and North Korea have pulled into close and collaborative alignment to support Russia's 2022 invasion of Ukraine. While there may be some discomfort in Moscow with the degree of dependence on Beijing, there is strong alignment among China, Russia, North Korea, and Iran that the American-led order is not just invidious to their interests but dangerous to regime control in their countries. The histrionic dysfunctionality of the US has created the opportunity to collapse or at least corrode the international order into one more conducive to them.

America's allies in Asia understand that our deepest security relationships are in Europe. There is a reason that the other regional treaty organizations established in the 1950s withered: None but NATO have the ideological, economic, and political webbing to make credible such deep commitments. Allowing the security order in Europe to be collapsed by extracting ourselves from support to Ukraine wouldn't just make Europe unsafe; it would call all other US security guarantees into question. If the US won't defend Europe, both allies and adversaries will rightly wonder whether the US will defend any security partner.

Early Indications

The interim national defense guidance issued in March 2025 provides an early window into the Trump administration's strategy. The guidance is, as it should be, responsive to the security issues most animating the president: border security and drug trafficking. Not only are those issues important to the president, but also most Americans would not understand why a large and capable American military is not in the business of defending the borders of our territory.

The interim guidance is in large part consistent with the Asia First approach dominating Trump administration thinking. It reportedly states clearly that countering China is the "sole pacing threat," and identifies the "potential invasion of Taiwan as the exclusive animating scenario that must be prioritized over other potential dangers."[23] But the administration's adamance that Taiwan needs to spend 10% of GDP on defense in order to merit American support undercuts the reliability of US support to Taiwan. The countermanding directions suggest it is setting up a test designed for Taiwan to be blamed for an Asia First US strategy collapsing when called on to be carried out.

The main change from the 2018 National Defense Strategy guidance is suggesting the US contribution to NATO would be composed entirely of nuclear deterrence but would not provide conventional forces to support to NATO allies if attacked by Russia. That would be a major diminishment of the US commitment, and the reliability of extended nuclear deterrence would be questionable without US conventional forces in the fight. The guidance is likely to revisit 1950s debates about extended deterrence that tortured logic to make the threat of escalation from conventional to nuclear war credible without an extended phase of conventional war in Europe. Without American troops involved in the conventional fight, neither allies nor enemies believed that the US would put its own territory at risk by launching nuclear weapons. Now, the US homeland is much more vulnerable than it was then to both nuclear and cyberattacks. This would amplify the risk between declaratory policy and willingness to carry out our strategy.

The guidance assumes risk in the Middle East and East Asia, directing force sizing to a single major war. This portends significant cuts to the Army in particular but is out of alignment with the administration's mantra of peace through strength. The guidance is also out of alignment with the administration's actions in its first three months, which have conducted operations against the Houthis (with the president threatening attacks against Hamas and Iran in the Middle East) and involved threats against Greenland, Panama, and Canada.

The administration is telegraphing deficit reduction as its overarching priority, so the DOD is unlikely to get the budget necessary to enact its guidance. Nor does it portend well that both Republicans and Democrats on Capitol Hill describe the approach as confusing. Congress really runs defense policy and will have to both authorize these moves and appropriate the funds for it. The secretary cannot even effectuate the 8% cuts to existing budgets to internally redirect funds to presiden-

tial priorities without congressional approval. In addition, President Trump's actions in the first term were very little influenced by either his own National Security Strategy or departmental strategy documents—and there is reason to be
skeptical that he will be more disciplined in the second term.

The shortcomings of the Asia First approach in its current Asia-almost-solely
form make it unlikely to be an adequate strategy for defending, much less advancing, American interests in Asia or beyond. That would be the case even if fully
funded—which it is not—or rigorously executed by an administration of adroit or-
chestrators of the US government apparatus and allied activity—which the
Trump administration is palpably unlikely to be. Instead of narrowing the objectives of US strategy or matching resourcing to the strategy, the administration
looks to be on track to accrue even greater risk associated with US ability to carry
out its strategy. We will be incredibly fortunate if adversaries don't make us prove
we are willing and able to redress what we are so loudly declaring the Asia First
approach is the answer to.

NOTES

1. Daniel Walker Howe, *What Hath God Wrought: The Transformation of America,
1815–1848* (Oxford University Press, 2007), 115.

2. John Quincy Adams, *Memoirs*, ed. Charles Francis Adams, vol. 6 (J.B. Lippincott
& Co, 1875), 163. See also Samuel Flagg Bemis, *John Quincy Adams and the Foundations of
American Foreign Policy* (Knopf, 1949), 368.

3. William McKinley, "Message to Congress Requesting a Declaration of War with
Spain," April 11, 1898. The text of the speech is available online at The American
Presidency Project, https://www.presidency.ucsb.edu/node/304972.

4. Admiral Harold Stark, Memorandum for the Secretary, November 12, 1940,
Franklin D. Roosevelt Presidential Library and Museum, Hyde Park, New York. The
document is digitized and available in the FRANKLIN digital collections, http://docs
.fdrlibrary.marist.edu/psf/box4/a48b01.html.

5. Waldo H. Heinrichs. *Threshold of War: Franklin D. Roosevelt and American Entry
into World War II* (Oxford University Press, 1988), 38.

6. Joseph V. Micallef, "Why 'Germany First?' The Origins of the WWII Policy,"
Military.com, June 22, 2020.

7. Louis Morton, *Strategy and Command: The First Two Years. The United States Army
in World War II* (Government Printing Office, 1962), 88.

8. Franklin Delano Roosevelt, quoted in Mark A. Stoler, "The 'Pacific-First'
Alternative in American World War II Strategy," *International History Review* 2, no. 3
(1980): 436–452, 451; Geoffrey C. Ward, *The Roosevelts: An Intimate History* (Knopf
Doubleday, 2014), 402.

9. Joyce Mao, *Asia First* (University of Chicago Press, 2015).

10. Lorna S. Jaffe, *Development of the Base Force, 1989–1992* (Department of Defense, Joint History Office, 1993), 36.

11. Donald Rumsfeld, "21st Century Transformation," remarks at the National Defense University, Washington, DC, January 31, 2002.

12. Robert M. Gates, speech at the National Defense University, Washington, DC, September 29, 2008.

13. Robert M. Gates, remarks at the US Military Academy, West Point, New York, February 25, 2011.

14. US Department of Defense, *Quadrennial Defense Review Report*, February 2010, p. vi.

15. Tony Capaccio, "Austin Tells OMB $926 Billion Defense Budget Needed, $55 Billion over Current Plan," *MSN*, January 13, 2025, https://www.msn.com/en-us/money/markets/austin-tells-omb-926-billion-defense-budget-needed-55-billion-over-current-plan/ar-BB1rlrGq.

16. General Joe Dunford, quoted in James Kitfield, "'Our Greatest Challenge,' CJCS Gen. Dunford," *Breaking Defense*, August 12, 2016, https://breakingdefense.com/2016/08/our-greatest-challenge-cjcs-gen-dunford/.

17. Chairman's Risk Assessment, US Department of Defense, Quadrennial Defense Review 2014, April 2014, https://history.defense.gov/Portals/70/Documents/quadrennial/QDR2014.pdf?ver=tXH94SVvSQLVw-ENZ-a2pQ%3d%3d.

18. Mackenzie Eaglen, "Setting the Record Straight on Beijing's Actual Military Spending," American Enterprise Institute, August 8, 2023, https://www.aei.org/foreign-and-defense-policy/setting-the-record-straight-on-beijings-actual-military-spending/.

19. US Department of Defense, *Military and Security Developments Involving the People's Republic of China*, 2024.

20. Ciaran Martin, "Typhoons in Cyberspace," Royal United Services Institute, March 20, 2025.

21. Elbridge Colby, "The US and Taiwan Must Change Course," *Wall Street Journal*, September 2, 2024, https://www.wsj.com/opinion/us-taiwan-china-defense-elbridge-colby-64ef679c.

22. "China, Japan, South Korea Will Jointly Respond to US Tariffs, Chinese State Media Says," *Reuters*, March 31, 2025, https://www.reuters.com/world/china-japan-south-korea-will-jointly-respond-us-tariffs-chinese-state-media-says-2025-03-31/.

23. Alex Horton and Hannah Natanson, "Secret Pentagon Memo on China, Homeland Has Heritage Fingerprints," *Washington Post*, March 29, 2025, https://www.washingtonpost.com/national-security/2025/03/29/secret-pentagon-memo-hegseth-heritage-foundation-china/.

Chapter Eleven

The US-China Intelligence Competition

A Preliminary Assessment

Peter Mattis

The strategic rivalry between the United States and the People's Republic of China (PRC) may be a contest between systems; however, individuals will make the decisions that determine the ebb and flow of the rivalry. What those individuals know about the other side, how they interpret the other's moves, and their ability to act will be informed by intelligence. Both the United States and the PRC have large, well-established intelligence systems. These systems also operate within a broader context of national understanding that determines in part what leaders need from intelligence. Both countries have deliberately cultivated international networks that inform or assist policy. They are politically engaged but operate more freely than their governmental counterparts. Beijing and Washington also leverage international partners to bolster their intelligence capabilities.

The PRC almost certainly maintains an intelligence edge over the United States because of the capability of its systems to engage in collection and counterintelligence that support leaders who are generally more aware of the United States. The US Intelligence Community, however, probably maintains an edge in the way that it can integrate different intelligence disciplines and provide focused support

Peter Mattis is the president of The Jamestown Foundation and coauthor of *Chinese Communist Espionage: An Intelligence Primer* (Naval Institute Press, 2019). He started his government career as a counterintelligence analyst at the Central Intelligence Agency and was Senator Marco Rubio's staff director at the Congressional-Executive Commission on China.

The author would like to thank Peace Ajirotutu for her research assistance and editorial support.

to policymakers. These capabilities are bolstered by the United States' ability to work with any potential intelligence partner anywhere in the world at any time.

The question of whether the political systems can exploit and act on their intelligence support to the fullest extent is beyond the scope of this chapter. The Chinese Communist Party (CCP) possesses ideological blinders that limit the flow of objective information and may even prevent a proper understanding of information in their possession. US leaders often demand a high level of specificity from intelligence, and few presidents have provided the kind of steady, structured policymaking process that makes the best of the US Intelligence Community's capabilities.[1] But, for both countries, the relationship between intelligence and decision-making is generally opaque, even more so than intelligence as a subject of study.

The comparison of intelligence systems is useful for gauging the strategic effectiveness of the United States and the PRC because the move and countermove that each side will make depends a great deal on intelligence. Policymakers can plan for contingencies and prepare different options, but they might not be prepared to act until they know what the other side is doing. Although the role of intelligence is sometimes controversial,[2] one side's intelligence failure may, in fact, reflect the intelligence superiority of the other, which decided to act in a way that the other side could not detect or anticipate. From the US perspective, Beijing is a revisionist power, and warning is (and will be) required to deter the PRC from acting. From the PRC perspective, the United States is a powerful, if declining, hegemon whose power must be respected and restrained. Intelligence can help Beijing's leaders operate more effectively, and influence can be used to shape Washington's understanding. In a protracted global rivalry with repeated points of contestation, intelligence cannot help but play a role.

This chapter proceeds in five parts that assess different aspects of the intelligence contest. The first part outlines the differing levels of national understanding between the United States and the PRC to frame the kind of support intelligence provides. The second part explores the shape of the engaged networks each side supports. The third part offers some observations on the two intelligence systems and their respective strengths and weaknesses. The fourth part provides some analysis of how both countries use intelligence partners to supplement their capabilities. The fifth part addresses some of the ways in which the intelligence contest plays out apart from the national intelligence systems to support leadership decision-making, because other key decision-makers in each country are not the president or the CCP general secretary.

National Understanding

Leaders' intuitive understanding and level of knowledge about their competitors and the nature of the rivalry are key contextual factors for intelligence services. Over time, leaders may become familiar with issues or rivals, and their needs will evolve respectively. In a systems confrontation or rivalry like that between the United States and the PRC, important national decision-makers are spread across the country. They may be corporate leaders, university presidents, or technologists. Moreover, the US political appointment system and the CCP united-front system provide avenues for others to contribute directly to leaders' decision-making or even become governmental officials. Understanding the adversary, however, is only one part of the contextual story.

The shared understanding of the other side's political leadership, national purpose, and strategy also shapes the intelligence context. Intelligence support for decision-making works best when that process is stable, and both the users and providers of intelligence know what is relevant. This is a point emphasized in official intelligence textbooks for PRC officials. One of the key features of intelligence is "selectivity," according to Chinese intelligence writers, because the totality of information cannot be conveyed to decision-makers if that information is to help guide action in a timely fashion.[3]

In both categories of national understanding—knowledge of the rival and of one's own purpose—the PRC almost certainly maintains a significant edge over the United States. More CCP leaders and Chinese people, generally, have spent time in the United States outside of their routine government duties than vice versa. They have seen how Americans act in their natural habitat, but few Americans are able to have a similar experience in the PRC. Fewer still are eligible to work in national security positions that require a clearance.[4]

At the very top level, at least 15 PRC elites in the last three Central Committees (including alternates and senior provincial leaders) have US or other English-speaking degrees relevant to understanding the United States, according to the China Data Lab hosted by the University of California, San Diego.[5] Although this number may seem small, no comparable US policymakers have this experience in the PRC, including Hong Kong and Macao. Only a handful of senior US officials at a political level have had any meaningful, direct China experience that they gained outside of their government roles. Official engagements are highly stylized affairs that restrict the ability of either side to get a genuine sense of who the other officials are and how they live their lives.[6] President Donald Trump's first-term deputy national security advisor, Matthew Pottinger, is probably the most notable and influential recent official with extended, nongovernmental China experience. He spent several years in China as a student and a journalist. These experiences matter because they suggest senior policymakers' literacy level about the other country and help them develop a more instinctual understanding of the other. In an interview after his service as then–Vice President Joseph Biden's deputy national security advisor, Ely Ratner noted that US leaders continually needed to be reminded about maritime features and national interests amid Beijing's island-building campaign in the South China Sea after 2012. These same leaders, however, knew geographic features in Syria and Ukraine almost as well as the locals.[7]

Using long-term residents as a proxy for national understanding supports the notion of a wide gap between the two countries' knowledge of the other. Chinese students who study in the United States may not rise to the political system's highest ranks, but they work in other key party-state institutions and can contribute at the working levels. The number of Americans studying in the PRC has been steadily declining over the last decade, and the ratio of PRC students in the US compared with American students studying in the PRC was greater than 750 to 1 for the 2023–2024 academic year.[8] The number of US students in the PRC peaked in 2012 at 14,887 and has since sunk to approximately 300–400 students currently studying in the PRC. By contrast, more than 277,000 PRC students were studying in the United States for the 2023–2024 academic year, which is the lowest number since the 2013–2014 academic year.[9] The gap in experience is also quite substantial in terms of the number of nonstudent residents in the other country. For the last decade, approximately two million PRC nationals have possessed residency permits in the United States. In contrast, the State Department reports that only 130,000 Americans reside inside the PRC.[10] The result is that the United States has a substantially smaller pool of individuals who can inform or work for the US government with direct knowledge of how things work in the PRC, the stakes of everyday life, and the ways in which Chinese people relate to their government as subjects or officials.

The CCP's internal political processes also deliver a high degree of awareness among the party cadre in government, state-owned and private enterprises, universities and research institutes, and anywhere else the CCP maintains itself. The process through which the Party prepares the report delivered by the general secretary at the party congress every five years requires inputs from across government. The resulting report is, in many ways, the final deliverable of a political process and not an aspirational document.[11] Ahead of the 19th Party Congress in 2017, this author met with a range of officials in Beijing who noted that being assigned to foreign delegation meetings was relaxing compared with the relentless tasking occurring daily in preparation of the report. One official noted that they would know that the party congress would be announced soon once the taskings stopped. Particularly under General Secretary Xi's leadership, the CCP has expanded and experimented with ideological indoctrination to ensure political materials reached as many people as possible. For example, the Party produced an app called "Learning Power" (学习强国), also known as "Study Xi, Strong Nation," to teach Xi Jinping's "Thoughts" in an accessible and gamified method. It is the Party's attempt at a modern-day "Little Red Book." At its peak, it was the number one app on China's Apple Store, with over 900 million downloads.[12]

The US government process for developing a national security strategy does not compare with the CCP's indoctrination process as a means for ensuring common awareness across the relevant decision-makers and organizations. Even if the process ensures that senior US policymakers and staffers share a common purpose, there is no mechanism to build that shared understanding throughout the government, including in elements that rarely deal in national security strategy, and throughout the wider society. If the rivalry is truly a system-on-system competition, then such shared awareness of the stakes and objectives is a crucial animating feature that is missing from the United States. This is always a difficult process for democracies and, arguably, has required a national crisis if not a war to deliver such clarity and consensus.

Engaged Networks

The United States and the PRC build and leverage networks outside the official state governmental apparatus. In the United States, these are nongovernmental civil society organizations. In the PRC, the CCP operates a vast network under the aegis of the united front policy system. For both countries, these networks are not really about intelligence as much as for promoting desirable political outcomes. Beijing almost certainly has an edge in these engaged networks, largely because the CCP plays a much more active role in cultivating and guiding the united front system. Moreover, the united front system draws upon or is connected to every part of the state apparatus. The US side, however, draws on these organizations more informally, and the organizations focus more on their own priorities than those of the US government. In the Cold War, these organizations worked quite closely with the US government, but that connectivity began drifting by the 1970s.[13]

The US system of engaged networks can be described as having three major elements: the National Endowment for Democracy (and related organizations), grant-giving organizations, and general civil society or nongovernmental organizations. At its peak going into the second Trump administration, the National Endowment for Democracy, along with its four related organizations,[14] operated on more than $300 million, including a significant congressional appropriation and support from the State Department and the US Agency for International Development. They had offices, staff, contractors, and recipient organizations in more than 100 countries worldwide.[15] In many parts of the world, office directors and program officers developed close personal relationships with local politicians and others around the political process. These relationships have proven to be a source of strength for the United States because they facilitated connections, provided on-the-ground perspectives, and sometimes substituted for US government action. Grant-giving organizations, like the Ford Foundation and the Open Society Foundation, added millions of dollars of support to local civil society organizations, including inside the PRC. Other US-based or US-supported nongovernmental organizations worked inside the PRC to promote the rule of law, protect marginalized groups, support town and village elections, and other liberalizing programs.

These organizations have consistently played a far more limited role in the PRC than they have played elsewhere in the world. When these organizations entered China in the 1980s, the Ministry of State Security (MSS) often co-opted the Chinese participants in their programs. The American foundations may have had a positive impact on the administrative state, but their programs were managed in such a way as to build state capacity without creating political problems for the Communist Party—or, in some cases, taken over by the Ministry of State Security (MSS).[16] The space for such organizations steadily shrank throughout the 1990s and 2000s before CCP General Secretary Xi Jinping introduced a comprehensive set of security laws beginning in 2014. The Foreign NGO Law provided dramatic transparency requirements for any NGO conducting business inside the PRC, including staff traveling there for a conference or Track II dialogue. Moreover, these organizations did not produce the kind of deep connections with PRC political leaders that characterized their other work elsewhere. Arguably, Beijing's view that the National Endowment for Democracy and other foundations were trying to promote regime change and fomenting unrest precluded such meaningful relationships.[17]

The CCP's united front system, by contrast, is a professional Party endeavor and a routine part of its day-to-day operations.[18] It is always led by the Politburo Standing Committee, the CCP's highest decision-making body. In nearly every way, it is different from the American approach to civil society—partly because the engaged network is carefully controlled by the CCP as part of its rejection of independent civil society. The purpose of the united front work, to paraphrase Mao Zedong, is to identify and mobilize friends to isolate and strike at the Party's enemies. Where the American civil society and National Endowment for Democracy might directly support US policy as individuals saw fit, the united front system creates resources for Beijing to draw upon, including for intelligence. While united-front cadres understand their history as a means of helping the Party secure its objectives, their US counterparts no longer see themselves engaged in political warfare or advancing US interests against a rival as part of a broader campaign of action.

The size and resourcing of the united front system far exceed that of their US counterparts. United front work departments exist at every level of the CCP, from the national to the local. Such departments also can be attached to party committees wherever they reside, including in labs, academic institutions, PRC and foreign corporations, and nearly any other organization where the Party has established a formal structure. Another key institution of the united-front system is the Chinese People's Political Consultative Conference, which includes more than 700,000 members of PRC society who can be leveraged as a kind of united front militia to support efforts to organize and mobilize non-party collaborators for Beijing. Based on an internal Jamestown Foundation database, no fewer than 1,000 people are actively working through community organizations, Chinese chambers of commerce, and other nongovernmental organizations on the Party's behalf in the United States. They have demonstrated access to US federal and state governments.[19]

The Intelligence Contest

The publicly available information about the direct intelligence competition, be it spy versus spy or hacker versus hacker, is insufficient to be used to provide an authoritative assessment. Almost all of the public information comes from failed or disrupted operations. Americans know about the PRC intrusions into Guam's infrastructure, US phone networks, and the Microsoft Exchange hack because US intelligence or corporate security identified those operations and then worked to mitigate the effects.[20] Similarly, the PRC side only became aware of how effective US intelligence could be at targeting it because former National Security Agency contractor Edward Snowden dumped thousands of documents into the public realm and because the MSS was reportedly able to exploit a technical error and US overuse of a covert communications system.[21] In the absence of more complete information, a different approach is required. The visible activities and structure of intelligence systems and official assessments of intelligence performance provide the basis for making general observations about each system.

From this perspective, the PRC intelligence system is arguably better prepared to support a long-term rivalry against the United States than the US Intelligence Community is prepared to do the same against the PRC. The greater national understanding the CCP leadership has about the United States and its objectives reduces the burden on intelligence to provide precise information through exquisite sourcing. Beijing also benefits from a highly resilient system due to the sheer number of people involved and the strong counterintelligence capabilities of PRC security and intelligence services. The US Intelligence Community can provide greater specific insights on issues of concern by creating inventive intelligence access based on its history of combining human and technical operations in a way that has not yet been seen in the PRC intelligence system.

PRC Strengths and Weaknesses

The PRC intelligence system is a vast national system, including civilian and defense components. There are no authoritative figures on the size of the intelligence systems, but circumstantial evidence suggests that the MSS and its subordinate elements number at least 100,000. These include intelligence officers tasked with foreign intelligence, counterintelligence, administration, and technology.[22] The Ministry of Public Security (MPS) also has an estimated 1.9 million officers, with only a relatively small fraction of them focused on domestic intelligence, political security, or overseas law enforcement operations.[23] Both the MSS and MPS are organized with a central ministry, 31 provincial-level departments and bureaus, approximately 300 prefecture-level bureaus, and many other local offices. In some cases, these can be quite sizable. The Shanghai State Security Bureau, for example, has office space for an estimated 20,000 people, and it is one of the more active sub-national elements in conducting foreign intelligence operations.[24]

The numbers, structure, and rigorous compartmentation make the intelligence system a difficult target for US exploitation. US intelligence officials cannot simply dismiss parts of this system. Recent espionage cases in the United States indicate that the MSS, the Shanghai State Security Bureau, the Guangdong State Security Department, and the Jiangsu State Security Department have all run successful operations against the United States.

This leads directly to the second strength of the system: counterintelligence and counterespionage. The PRC has an incredible ability to trace the movement of people and data across the PRC. When the MSS reportedly broke into US covert communications systems in the early 2010s, it was able to combine human and technical investigative means to identify over 20 alleged US assets. According to US media, those assets were then killed or imprisoned by the Chinese government, making it the worst breach of US intelligence services in decades.[25]

Despite the PRC's strengths in counterintelligence and counterespionage, Party corruption remains an enduring weakness worth exploiting by the United States. Xi Jinping's ongoing anti-corruption campaign, launched shortly after he assumed power in 2012, remains a signature of his leadership. Framed as necessary to restore public confidence in the CCP and enforce internal discipline, the campaign has targeted a wide range of officials partly because of the fear that foreign powers would exploit this corruption. *The New York Times* reported that at least one of the alleged CIA agents arrested in the PRC between 2010 and 2012 had been given money they could use to pay for their promotion.[26] The fact that the corruption campaign continues to purge CCP officials and military officers suggests that corruption can continue to be exploited.

US Strengths and Weaknesses

The US Intelligence Community is arguably the most effective system in the world at combining intelligence disciplines to exploit specific intelligence targets. Combining human and technical intelligence methods allows the US Intelligence Community to access sensitive air-gapped networks, collect measurements and signatures intelligence, and other seemingly inaccessible information, such as leadership communications. Countless examples exist or are hinted at in publicly available materials and international media. These range from the efforts to find and confirm Osama Bin Laden's whereabouts to covert actions against Iran's terrorist network and nuclear program.

However, US policy toward the PRC probably has undermined US intelligence collection over the long term. Human intelligence sources can provide specific intelligence reports and stolen documents; moreover, they are valuable as interpreters of how their own system works. Good sources, especially if and after they are exfiltrated, and defectors can help build national understanding. Treason against one's country or defecting is quite serious and requires a significant psychological break. Most examples include elements of ego and rationalization. People want to believe that their actions will make a difference and that they did not really betray their country or, sometimes more importantly, their people. In some cases, like that of Polish Colonel Ryszard Kukliński, who provided the United States with intelligence at a critical moment in the Polish Crisis of the early 1980s, spies believed their espionage was an act of patriotism to protect their people against the real enemy.[27] US policy toward the PRC since its opening in 1971 probably has not offered the consistency and clarity needed for would-be PRC spies to believe that helping Washington would, in turn, be helping the Chinese people.

A way of illustrating this issue with US intelligence collection is to compare the seniormost human sources who were recruited or who defected from the Warsaw Pact with the known equivalents from the PRC. The highest-level source that the CIA reportedly ever recruited inside the CCP system was Yu Qiangsheng, who was a senior MSS officer from a politically well-connected family. Additional scattered reports suggest that there have been other high-level sources, possibly including the private secretary to an MSS vice minister.[28] The list of senior spies and defectors from Warsaw Pact countries, however, includes a number of incredibly senior officials, such as Romania's acting intelligence chief Ion Mihai Pacepa, UN Undersecretary-General for Political Affairs Arkady Shevchenko, and Soviet military intelligence officer Major General Dmitri Polyakov. The US inability to find, recruit, handle, and then exfiltrate similar sources in the CCP in sufficient numbers to justify publicizing their knowledge of the Party's inner workings—as was done for other defectors or exfiltrated spies in the Cold War—suggests an ongoing weakness in the US intelligence system and its ability to support the wider, nongovernmental needs to be aware of the US-PRC rivalry.

Intelligence Partnerships

A truism of the intelligence profession is that services are best where they focus, often locally. Intelligence cooperation—or liaison—benefits any intelligence service because they cannot be good at everything, everywhere in the world. Some intelligence services develop specialties, such as the Cuban intelligence service Dirección de Inteligencia's long history of targeting the United States and perfecting the collection tradecraft against their primary targets. In some cases, informing liaison services of counterintelligence problems relating to a third-party country, like French intelligence informing the United States about Soviet economic espionage, can provide a competitive advantage by blinding the rival.[29]

This is an area where the United States possesses a clear advantage over the PRC intelligence services. Since the origin of the modern US intelligence system in World War II, international collaboration has been baked into the system. The Five Eyes intelligence alliance, including Australia, Canada, New Zealand, and the United Kingdom, offers global capacity and presence. Cooperation among the five countries' intelligence services is a part of their day-to-day routine. The North Atlantic Treaty Organization (NATO) as a military alliance necessarily includes an intelligence element, and, to varying degrees, each of the other US alliances also has intelligence embedded in its structure.

The United States can use these structural incentives in the alliances or with partners concerned about PRC ambitions to cooperate with intelligence services. The US Intelligence Community can offer global insights and technological acumen in exchange for superior local knowledge. Most intelligence systems are not international, and their capabilities reflect their country's immediate priorities. The US system, however, developed in an international rivalry with the Soviet Union to compete globally against that adversary. Today, while bits and bytes can be accessed from nearly anywhere, signals, electrical emanations, and other physical signatures have to be gathered locally. US intelligence today can leverage that legacy.

By contrast, the PRC has relatively few intelligence relationships of any importance, in part due to the international isolation of the Mao Zedong era. Until the last 15 or so years, Beijing's most important partnership was arguably with the United States. The intelligence relationship reportedly began sometime around the normalization of relations, as Washington searched for alternative locations for signals intelligence equipment to replace the lost Iranian facilities.[30] However, since the early 2000s, Russia seems to have emerged as the PRC's most important partner. US media reported the two countries cooperated on exploiting a compromised US covert communications system used by the CIA's human assets.[31] There also have been some indications of building greater intelligence sharing into the Shanghai Cooperation Organization (SCO) and with Southeast Asian countries, but it is unclear whether this is a genuine exchange or an attempt to dominate these partners.[32]

Intelligence Support for National Competitiveness

Beijing[33] and Washington[34] have heavily emphasized the scientific and technological aspects of the strategic rivalry. Both countries recognize that new technologies offer enormous opportunities and that whoever achieves dominance in these emerging technologies is likely to shape the global order. The scientific and technological dimension of the rivalry, however, requires thinking about decision-makers outside of their traditional national security roles. For over a century in the US system, national defense has been the animating logic of how intelligence, counterintelligence, and security operate, even though US laws and executive orders have recognized that other decision-makers, including the private sector, might be key intelligence consumers.[35]

While the United States is debating how best to support a broad base of relevant decision-makers, the PRC has continued operating a well-established professional system for collecting and analyzing foreign scientific and technical information. The Institute for Scientific and Technological Information of China (ISTIC) is China's foremost civilian institution dedicated to the collection, analysis, and dissemination of open-source science and technology intelligence.[36] Established in 1956, ISTIC was created in response to Premier Zhou Enlai's call for a formal intelligence mechanism to support scientific advancement. Initially named the "Institute of Scientific Information," it became a foundational pillar in the PRC's scientific intelligence system, supporting strategic development initiatives through the systematic monitoring of global scientific trends. In 1992, its Chinese name was modified to use "information" instead of "intelligence" to avoid negative connotations, although its core mission remained unchanged.

Structurally, ISTIC operates under the Ministry of Science and Technology and plays a leading role in the National Engineering and Technology Library and the broader National Science and Technology Library system. It employs approximately 850 staff across multiple divisions, and its operations include maintaining massive physical and digital collections of scientific materials, offering analytical services for government decision-making, and supporting technology transfer efforts. ISTIC not only serves as a data aggregator but also directly contributes to national planning, such as five-year plans and major research and development programs, and helps train China's scientific intelligence workforce, including embassy-based science counselors.

ISTIC is part of a vast and highly professionalized science, technology, and innovation network in China, which is unmatched globally in size and capability. The broader system includes over 100,000 personnel across civilian and military branches, organized in a tiered structure from national to local levels. ISTIC alone provides access to millions of documents, maintains proprietary databases, and has developed international partnerships to access foreign materials. Its services include data verification, patent application support, and customized intelligence for key stakeholders. This highly integrated framework, based on an open-source model, is central to the PRC's science and technology strategy and is a crucial tool for guiding national innovation and policy.

The PRC's engaged networks and intelligence operations bolstered this scientific and technological intelligence effort. The united front system runs a network of organizations facilitating technology transfers, like the Chinese Association for Science and Technology and the Western Returned Scholars Association. In some cases, companies, universities, and other labs leverage these international front organizations to acquire scientific know-how. On the intelligence side, the case of Jiangsu State Security Department officer Xu Yanjun offers an interesting example of how an intelligence officer sat at the center of a network of state-supported researchers at the Nanjing University of Aeronautics and Astronautics, contracted hackers, and recruited human sources for the MSS. Xu was organizing an effort to steal specific aerospace technologies from the US company GE Aviation to provide to the university researchers.[37] Similar cases have been observed in other parts of the PRC, including where the MSS provided support to state-owned enterprises to steal secrets and cultivate American scientists.

This is an area where the CCP's advantage has not been challenged by the United States because the US Intelligence Community interprets the principle of fairness in commercial activity as barring it from collecting and providing such secrets to the private sector. Because these PRC collectors rely almost entirely on open sources—except where the intelligence services get involved—it is essentially an area that US counterintelligence overlooks. Americans have evinced some interest in analysis of global technology competition or techno-economic intelligence, but the reality is that this element of intelligence remains a focus of a small range of analysts and rarely a priority of collectors.[38] Moreover, even if the United States substantially expanded its capacity to collect and analyze technology-related intelligence, the focus would be on supporting a narrow set of senior US government decision-makers rather than supporting the full range of corporate and scientific practitioners who could best make use of foreign technological information.

Conclusion

The intelligence rivalry between the United States and the PRC reveals a broader contest of capabilities, systems, and strategic cultures. While both nations possess formidable intelligence apparatuses, the PRC's edge in counterintelligence, national understanding, and long-term systemic resilience grants it significant advantages in sustaining a rivalry with the United States. These strengths may enable Beijing to camouflage its actions, up to and including an invasion of Taiwan and the start of a devastating global war, from Washington. US policymakers may require specific, exquisitely acquired intelligence to believe that the CCP would really launch such a war. Similar dynamics could be at play elsewhere in the world, where both sides compete for influence and access. Beijing is revisionist; Washington protects a status quo. US officials may not see derailing PRC actions and inroads as their primary responsibility, and therefore may be late to seeing their counterparts' moves. The strengths and dispersion of the Chinese party-state, however, makes it difficult to anticipate its moves.

Conversely, the US Intelligence Community continues to leverage its strengths in technical integration, global partnerships, and the ability to deliver highly specific intelligence to support policy. However, the relative lack of China expertise among American decision-makers and the underutilization of intelligence insights beyond traditional national security roles remain enduring liabilities. The lower the level of knowledge, the higher the bar for intelligence to equip US policymakers with decision advantage. Beijing may feel confident that it is capable of hiding its moves until it is too late for Washington to act, but these human and technical capabilities should give PRC policymakers pause. Although many PRC initiatives may go undiscovered, PRC leaders should never feel at ease because their biggest moves, like an invasion of Taiwan, create indicators across the vast space of the PRC government, society, and military and are anticipatable developments.

The differences between the two systems are also reflected in their respective approaches to influence and engagement. The CCP's united front system and the PRC's professionalized network of scientific and technological intelligence reflect a coherent, state-led strategy for integrating intelligence support into broader national competitiveness. In contrast, the United States has a more decentralized approach, relying on civil society organizations, grant-making institutions, and a historical legacy of global collaboration. While this model has strengths in flexibility and innovation, it lacks the tight integration seen in China's whole-of-state approach. Moreover, Beijing's prioritization of information collection as a strategic national function, supported by a deeply rooted infrastructure like the ISTIC, enables it to respond to global challenges and opportunities with increasing agility.

Ultimately, the intelligence competition between the United States and the PRC is about more than tradecraft or technology—it reflects deeper asymmetries in how each country organizes knowledge, power, and strategy. As this rivalry continues to unfold, both nations will need to grapple with internal limitations as much as they confront each other. For the United States, narrowing the experiential and informational gap with China will be essential, requiring a more structured and sustained intelligence integration into decision-making across the spectrum—from national security to science and technology. For the PRC, ideological rigidity and limited partnerships may pose long-term challenges despite current advantages. The outcome of this contest may well hinge not on who collects more secrets but on who better understands and adapts to the rapidly changing rivalry as it plays out worldwide.

NOTES

1. Intelligence historian Christopher Andrew noted that few US presidents made best use of intelligence, including George Washington, Dwight Eisenhower, and George H. W. Bush. These presidents possessed both direct experience with intelligence, and the latter two were known for their structured policymaking process. See Christopher Andrew, *For the President's Eyes Only* (Harper Perennial, 1995).

2. John Keegan, *Intelligence in War: Knowledge of the Enemy from Napoleon to al-Qaeda* (Alfred A. Knopf, 2003), 25.

3. Zhang Xiaojun, *Junshi qingbao xue* [The Science of Military Intelligence] (Beijing: Academy of Military Science, 2001), 112.

4. Peter Waldman and Andre Tartar, "Mistrust and the Hunt for Spies Among Chinese Americans," *Bloomberg*, December 10, 2019, https://www.bloomberg.com/news/features/2019-12-10/the-u-s-government-s-mistrust-of-chinese-americans; Peter Waldman, "Suspected of Spying for Just Being Chinese: US Government Rejects Security Clearance for Chinese-Americans," *South China Morning Post*, June 2, 2020, https://www.scmp.com/magazines/post-magazine/long-reads/article/3048091/suspected-spying-just-being-chinese-us; Edward Wong and Amy Qin, "Asian American Officials Cite Unfair Scrutiny and Lost Jobs in China Spy Tensions," *New York Times*, January 2, 2024, https://www.nytimes.com/2023/12/31/us/politics/china-spy-asian-americans.html.

5. Victor Shih, "CCP Elites Data Catalog," UC San Diego, 2021, https://chinadatalab.ucsd.edu/resources/ccp-elites-database/.

6. The PRC also made meaningful engagement more difficult by employing diplomats for whom intelligence and united-front work had been their formative experience in the Chinese Revolution. Interlocutors, like Zhou Enlai, Xiong Xianghui, and Li Kenong, became the face of Beijing's diplomacy because they were adept manipulators at an individual level.

7. "Jaw-Jaw: How America Got China Wrong," War on the Rocks, January 22, 2019, https://warontherocks.com/2019/01/jaw-jaw-how-america-got-china-wrong/.

8. "All Destinations," Institute of International Organization, accessed April 7, 2025, https://opendoorsdata.org/data/us-study-abroad/all-destinations/.

9. "All Places of Origin," Institute of International Organization, accessed April 7, 2025, https://opendoorsdata.org/data/international-students/all-places-of-origin/; Li Yawei, "China No Longer Top Source of International Students in US, Political Atmosphere, Opportunities at Home Among Reasons: Expert," *Global Times*, November 19, 2025, https://www.globaltimes.cn/page/202411/1323416.shtml.

10. Madeleine Greene and Jeanne Batalova, "Chinese Immigrants in the United States," Migrant Policy Institute, January 15, 2025, https://www.migrationpolicy.org/article/chinese-immigrants-united-states.

11. Wu Guogang, *China's Party Congress: Power, Legitimacy, and Institutional Manipulation* (Cambridge University Press, 2015), esp. 294–313.

12. "The National Immigration Administration Held a Meeting to Promote the Use of the "Learning Power" Learning Platform" [国家移民管理局召开运用"学习强国"学习平台推进会], National Immigration Administration, July 17, 2020, https://www.nia.gov.cn/n794014/n794021/c1320627/content.html; Jordan McGillis, "The Chinese App We Should Really Be Talking About," Foundation for American Innovation, August 31, 2020, https://www.thefai.org/posts/the-chinese-app-we-should-really-be-talking-about. For a broader perspective, see John Dotson, "The CCP's Renewed Focus on Ideological Indoctrination, Part 1: The 2019 Guidelines for "Patriotic Education," *China Brief*, The Jamestown Foundation, December 10, 2019.

13. David C. Engerman, *Know Your Enemy: The Rise and Fall of America's Soviet Experts* (Oxford University Press, 2009), 235–308.

14. The four organizations are the Center for International Private Enterprise, International Republican Institute, National Democratic Institute, and the Solidarity Center.

15. "About the National Endowment for Democracy," National Endowment for Democracy, accessed April 7, 2025, https://www.ned.org/about/.

16. Alex Joske, *Spies and Lies: How China's Greatest Covert Operations Fooled the World* (Hardie Grant, 2022), 8–16.

17. "The National Endowment for Democracy: What It Is and What It Does," Ministry of Foreign Affairs of the People's Republic of China, August 9, 2024, https://www.fmprc.gov.cn/eng/xw/wjbxw/202408/t20240809_11468618.html; "Document 9: A ChinaFile Translation," *ChinaFile*, November 8, 2013, https://www.chinafile.com/document-9-chinafile-translation.

18. Alex Joske, *The Party Speaks for You: Foreign Interference and the Chinese Communist Party's United Front System*, Report No. 32 (Australian Strategic Policy Institute, 2020), 4–9.

19. Alan Suderman and Sam Metz, "Amid Strained US Ties, China Finds Unlikely Friend in Utah," *Associated Press*, March 27, 2023, https://apnews.com/article/china-foreign-influence-utah-legislature-mormon-church-921526d0c8e-da2732c361488d20dd1b4; Didi Kirsten Tatlow, "Chinese Foreign Agent Was Behind New York Parade with Eric Adams, Emails Show," *Newsweek*, March 12, 2024, https://www.newsweek.com/eric-adams-china-new-york-xi-jinping-influence-asian-parade-united-states-1897424.

20. Rebecca Falconer, "Chinese Hackers Hit Critical US Infrastructure, Intelligence Agencies Warn," AXIOS, May 24, 2023, https://www.axios.com/2023/05/25/chinese

-hackers-critical-infrastructure-us-guam; "Chinese Nationals with Ties to the PRC Government and 'APT27' Charged in a Computer Hacking Campaign for Profit, Targeting Numerous US Companies, Institutions, and Municipalities," US Department of Justice, March 5, 2025, https://www.justice.gov/usao-dc/pr/chinese-nationals-ties-prc -government-and-apt27-charged-computer-hacking-campaign-profit.

21. Daniel McKivergan, "How Edward Snowden's Leaks Benefited China," Hudson Institute, February 11, 2025, https://www.hudson.org/foreign-policy/how-edward -snowdens-leaks-benefited-china-dan-mckivergan; Zach Dorfman, "Botched CIA Communications System Helped Blow Cover of Chinese Agents," *Foreign Policy*, August 15, 2018, https://foreignpolicy.com/2018/08/15/botched-cia-communications -system-helped-blow-cover-chinese-agents-intelligence/.

22. A. J. Bakari, "Ministry of State Security: China's Intel Machine in High Gear," Grey Dynamics, February 22, 2025, https://greydynamics.com/ministry-of-state -security-chinas-intel-machine-in-high-gear/; Minxin Pei, "Piercing the Veil of Secrecy: The Surveillance Role of China's MSS and MPS," *Chinese Leadership Monitor*, February 29, 2024, https://www.prcleader.org/post/piercing-the-veil-of-secrecy-the -surveillance-role-of-china-s-mss-and-mps

23. Pei, "Piercing the Veil of Secrecy"; "Senior Communist Official Extends Greetings to Police," *Xinhua*, February 8, 2008, http://www.china.org.cn/english/GS-e /242398.htm.

24. Peter Mattis, "Everything We Know About China's Secretive State Security Bureau," *The National Interest*, July 10, 2017, https://nationalinterest.org/feature /everything-we-know-about-chinas-secretive-state-security-21459; Alex Joske, *Spies and Lies: How China's Greatest Covert Operations Fooled the World* (Hardie Grant, 2022), 175.

25. Dorfman, "Botched CIA Communications System"; Mark Mazzetti, et al., "Killing C.I.A. Informants, China Crippled US Spying Operations," *New York Times*, May 20, 2017, https://www.nytimes.com/2017/05/20/world/asia/china-cia-spies -espionage.html.

26. Mazzetti et al., "Killing C.I.A. Informants."

27. Benjamin Weiser, *A Secret Life: The Polish Colonel, His Covert Mission, And the Price He Paid To Save His Country* (PublicAffairs, 2004).

28. "Exclusive: Arrested Spy Compromised China's US Espionage Network: Sources," *Reuters*, June 15, 2012 https://www.reuters.com/article/us-china-usa -espionage-idUSBRE85E06G20120615.

29. Gus W. Weiss, "Duping the Soviets: The Farewell Dossier," CIA, 1996, https:// www.cia.gov/resources/csi/studies-in-intelligence/1996-2/the-farewell-dossier/.

30. Geogre Lander Jr and R. Jeffrey Smith, "Intelligence Ties Endure Despite US-China Strain," *Washington Post*, June 25, 1989, https://www.washingtonpost.com /archive/politics/1989/06/25/intelligence-ties-endure-despite-us-china-strain/f8b2789d -0f0c-4ea7-932b-9f4267a994a3/; Phillip Taubman, "US and Peking Join in Tracking Missiles in Soviet," *New York Times*, June 18, 1981, https://www.nytimes.com/1981/06/18 /world/us-and-peking-join-in-tracking-missiles-in-soviet.html.

31. Dorfman, "Botched CIA Communications System"; John C. K. Daly, "Feature: US, China—Intel's Odd Couple," United Press International, February 24, 2001,

https://www.upi.com/Archives/2001/02/24/Feature-US-China-intels-odd-couple/6536982990800/.

32. Peter Mattis, "Zhou Yongkang's Trip Highlights Security Diplomacy," *China Brief*, The Jamestown Foundation, October 5, 2012; Roger McDermott, "SCO Summit in Tashkent: Breakthrough in Practical Cooperation," *China Brief*, The Jamestown Foundation, June 17, 2004, https://jamestown.org/program/sco-summit-in-tashkent-breakthrough-in-practical-cooperation/.

33. Xi Jinping, "Xi Jinping: Keep Key Technologies in Your Hands" [习近平: 把关键技术掌握在自己手里], Cyberspace Administration of China, June 9, 2014, https://www.cac.gov.cn/2014-06/10/c_1112674083.htm; Xi Jinping, "Xi Jinping: Speech at National Science and Technology Conference, National Science and Technology Award Conference and Academician Conference of the Two Academies" [习近平: 在全国科技大会、国家科学技术奖励大会、两院院士大会上的讲话], The State Council of the People's Republic of China, June 24, 2024, https://www.gov.cn/yaowen/liebiao/202406/content_6959120.htm.

34. For example, The White House, "A Letter to Michael Kratsios, Director of the White House Office of Science and Technology Policy," March 26, 2025, https://www.whitehouse.gov/briefings-statements/2025/03/a-letter-to-michael-kratsios-director-of-the-white-house-office-of-science-and-technology-policy/; The White House, "Remarks by National Security Advisor Jake Sullivan at the Special Competitive Studies Project Global Emerging Technologies Summit," September, 16, 2022, https://bidenwhitehouse.archives.gov/briefing-room/speeches-remarks/2022/09/16/remarks-by-national-security-advisor-jake-sullivan-at-the-special-competitive-studies-project-global-emerging-technologies-summit/.

35. Peter Mattis and Katherine Kurata, "From National Defense to National Competitiveness," Special Competitive Studies Project, March 22, 2023.

36. The following paragraphs draw from William Hannas and Huey-Meei Chang, "China's STI Operations" (Center for Security and Emerging Technology, January 2021), https://doi.org/10.51593/20200049.

37. "Chinese Government Intelligence Officer Sentenced to 20 Years in Prison for Espionage Crimes, Attempting to Steal Trade Secrets from Cincinnati Company," Department of Justice, November 16, 2022, https://www.justice.gov/archives/opa/pr/chinese-government-intelligence-officer-sentenced-20-years-prison-espionage-crimes-attempting.

38. For example, Special Competitive Studies Project "Intelligence: Interim Panel Report," October 2022, 28–34, https://www.scsp.ai/wp-content/uploads/2022/10/FINAL-Intelligence-Panel-IPR.pdf.

Chapter Twelve

The Battle for Soft Power
US-China Ideological Competition in the 2020s

Larry Diamond and Frances Hisgen

> As bridges are burning, new bridges are being formed.
> —GHANAIAN PRESIDENT JOHN MAHAMA
> AT THE 2025 MUNICH SECURITY CONFERENCE[1]

It has been widely and correctly argued that "soft power"—to quote the inventor of the term, Joseph Nye—"was essential in winning the Cold War."[2] Soft power operates through persuasion and attraction to shape the preferences of others, often incrementally over time. It "can be a force multiplier," helping to set the agenda and "getting others to want the outcomes you want," because they are attracted to your power and performance or because they share your values and see the world the way you do.[3]

As the People's Republic of China (PRC)[4] has risen as a world power, it has not only dismissed the soft power of Western democracies as fragile, hubristic, and overrated, but it has also sought to compete with a different type of soft power, devoid of the universalism and thus judgementalism that come with liberal norms.[5] The PRC recognizes that its contest with the United States for global preeminence will not be determined by technological prowess and economic and military might alone—or it would not be spending an estimated $10 billion annually

Larry Diamond is a senior fellow at the Hoover Institution and the Freeman Spogli Institute for International Studies at Stanford University. He cofounded the Hoover Institution's Project on China's Global Sharp Power and currently co-leads Hoover's Project on Taiwan in the Indo-Pacific Region.

Frances Hisgen is the senior research program manager for the Program on the US, China, and the World at the Hoover Institution, Stanford University, where she also serves as key personnel for the National Science Foundation's SECURE program. She holds degrees in Chinese history from Harvard College and the University of Cambridge.

on global information operations and billions more on exchanges, scholarships, and expanding diplomatic representation.[6]

This chapter assesses how the competition for soft power is faring. To some considerable extent, as Nye argues, soft power is not zero sum. Some countries admire or at least appreciate both the US and the PRC. Others may resent and distrust both great powers (an incipient trend). But ideologically, there is a zero-sum quality to this global competition, in that the values each country is projecting are substantially incompatible. The US and its fellow democracies advance and defend the liberal norms of freedom, individual rights, rule of law, and the ability of citizens to choose and replace their leaders in free and fair elections. These countries do not consider sovereignty absolute when it tramples on these norms. The PRC does consider sovereignty (at least its own) absolute—and does trample on these norms. Its leaders can dress up the normative battle as one between different "forms" of democracy—liberal versus "whole process"; universal or with "Chinese characteristics." But once again, the rivalry is between two systems of government and two ways of thinking. If the PRC does not push Marxism-Leninism globally the way the Soviet Union did, it still promotes a PRC "line" on governance, development, security, and world order that is very different from the American one.

The battle for soft power is an important dimension of the larger global contest between the two great powers. And its parameters are fluid, probably more so than at any time since the end of the last Cold War. The PRC is having some success in projecting its line into the media bloodstream of other countries. But somewhat to our surprise, its enormous investments in overseas aid, diplomacy, and propaganda are not having a commensurate impact on global public opinion. Rather, publics are wary of what the PRC is pushing. At the same time, however, they are losing confidence in the US. This erosion was discernible in the first Trump administration and appears to be accelerating in the second one. Thus, while the PRC may not win the struggle for global hearts and minds, the US could well lose it.

We proceed in this chapter as follows: First, we summarize the PRC line and illustrate how it seeks to propagate these ideas in global dialogue and information flows. Next, we examine whether and how the PRC line is resonating, through a snapshot of global media content from November 2024 through March 2025. Specifically, we look at how the PRC and the US are each being portrayed, and how this is changing in the second Trump administration. Third, we examine public opinion survey data to assess what, if any, impact the PRC is achieving with its campaigns. We conclude with a few thoughts about the future.

The PRC Line and How It Is Projected

Other chapters in this volume elucidate key PRC concepts, including the Belt and Road Initiative (BRI), the Global Development Initiative (GDI), the Global Security Initiative (GSI), the Global Civilization Initiative (GCI), and the Community of Common Destiny. These initiatives are central to the vision of governance, development, security, and world order that the PRC advances globally. Its conception of democracy is also core to that vision. It hails its system of governance as a "Whole Process People's Democracy" (全过程人民民主) that brings rapid development, poverty reduction, scientific and educational advances, and improvements in human welfare, in contrast to chaotic and sclerotic liberal democracies like the US.[7] The PRC insists that Western modes of democracy are not the only legitimate ones and that the US and Europe do not have standing to critique alternative political systems as undemocratic. Consider a famous 2021 metaphor from the Ministry of Foreign Affairs: "Democracy is not Coca-Cola, which has the same taste across the world" (民主不是可口可乐, 全世界一个味道).[8]

The Xi Jinping era has also stressed the party-state's priority of "telling China's story well" (讲好中国故事), a concept coined by Xi in a 2013 speech to the National Propaganda and Ideology Work Conference.[9] "International discourse power" (国际话语权), the concept goes, "is foundational to comprehensive national power" (综合国力).[10]

Between November 2024 and March 2025, we asked a team of research assistants to monitor legacy and social media in 32 countries in Africa, Asia, Europe, and Latin America to observe the PRC's efforts to tell China's story to international audiences.[11] We documented how the PRC has developed local-language versions of PRC state media outlets, pursued content-sharing agreements to publish PRC-originated content in local media outlets, and provided funding and operational support to develop new media organizations in many nations. These outlets disseminate the PRC's vision of global order. A March 2024 piece by China Radio International's Portuguese arm underscored such themes as the degradation and hypocrisy of the "rules-based order," the need for south-south cooperation, the principle of non-interference in foreign affairs, the right to development, and the importance of whole-process democracy or democracy "with Chinese characteristics."[12] The PRC's practical contributions to global development are also a focus. CPEC Portal, a Pakistani news site that publishes original content by local writers with partial support from the PRC's Central Propaganda Department, maintains infographics highlighting the benefits of PRC investment in Pakistan, including thousands of local jobs created by PRC hydropower plants and solar parks.[13]

Fostering this media ecosystem, especially through commitments to strengthen media cooperation, is a central goal of PRC diplomacy. A recent agreement between China Media Group (the state-owned radio and TV arm known as the "Voice of China") and the Brazilian public broadcaster committed the partners to publish each other's "journalistic text and materials . . . without alteration to [their] structure or coherence."[14] With content-sharing agreements, translated materials from PRC sources appear alongside material created by local journalists. As Joshua Kurlantzick has documented for Southeast Asia, "readers don't really notice where [PRC content] comes from"; the difference between independent journalism and content produced to further state aims does not register.[15]

In 2024, the Taiwan-based think tank Doublethink Lab catalogued at least 76 countries (of 101 surveyed) where "media outlets have delivered content provided by PRC state-funded media, or under content-sharing agreements with PRC state-funded media."[16] In many regions, material from content-sharing agreements accounts for a significant portion of local news coverage about the PRC.[17] In Indonesia, Antara News, the country's national news agency and most popular online news source, signed cooperation agreements with Xinhua in 2019 and 2021.[18] While not transparent, part of the collaboration involves translating Chinese-language news into Bahasa Indonesia and tailoring Xinhua content to appeal to Indonesians.[19] The stories published in Antara include glowing portrayals of the PRC system that echo its propaganda lines. A March 2025 piece praises the PRC's "whole process people's democracy model . . . a consultative system that ensures legislation reflects the people's aspirations."[20]

PRC diplomats also communicate directly through both legacy and social media. In Argentina, PRC ambassador Wang Wei has published repeatedly in *La Nación*, a right-leaning newspaper of record. In November 2024, he lauded the PRC's twin pillars of engagement with Latin America, the "China-Latin America Community with a Shared Future" and the "Belt and Road Initiative." He also saluted the PRC-Argentina partnership as two "members of the Global South and fellow travelers in defending sovereignty and independence."[21] PRC diplomats often attempt to frame arguments about the PRC's international aims that resonate with local populations. The PRC consul general in São Paulo, Yu Peng, celebrated the "essence of vitality and passion for life" shared by the Brazilian Carnival and the Chinese New Year as a metaphor for Brazil-PRC relations.[22]

PRC diplomats in Latin America are also adept social media users: The ambassador to Colombia, Zhu Jingyang, with close to 60,000 followers (as of March 2025), tweets and replies in fluent Spanish—and not always politely. Responding on March 23, 2025, to an online debate about whether the PRC respects private property, Zhu's account tweeted, "Poor thing, the complex reality of China overwhelms his very mediocre cognitive capacity."[23] In Mexico, the PRC embassy Twitter, with close to seventy thousand followers, assertively defends the PRC's policies in the region while denouncing American policies. On February 13, 2025, it posted a long message condemning US Secretary of State Marco Rubio for saying that he wants to counter PRC influence in the region: "The US claims to be 'strengthening alliances' and 'diversifying supply chains,' [but it] brutally interferes in the internal affairs of Latin American and Caribbean countries, arbitrarily abuses illegal unilateral sanctions, frequently shifts blame for issues such as drugs and migration onto other countries, and recklessly threatens them with tariffs."[24]

The PRC also communicates at the subnational level through international communication centers (ICCs) operated by provincial-level jurisdictions.[25] A December 2024 cybersecurity analysis documented more than one hundred ICCs established by PRC provincial, city, and county governments. These ICCs perform such global information functions as "explaining China to the world, developing external propaganda capabilities, . . . operating foreign social media accounts, training external propaganda talent, monitoring international public opinion, building networks of foreign influencers, [and] organizing trips by foreigners around China."[26] ICC accounts project PRC propaganda in more granular fashion, cultivating relationships with specific overseas subnational jurisdictions to promote trade ties, investment opportunities, and a positive image of the PRC. A June 2023 effort to coordinate among the ICCs via a nationwide association forged a division of labor geographically.[27] The Twitter account of Harbin pursues closer bonds with Russian-speaking audiences,[28] as do Shandong's ICC with Kyrgyzstan and other Central Asian nations and Hebei's Great Wall ICC with Brazil.[29]

Global Media Commentary on US-PRC Ideological Competition

We searched legacy and social media in 32 countries for news, editorials, and commentaries indicative of how the PRC and the US are being portrayed and perceived. Two key themes emerged.

First, perhaps surprisingly, the PRC's efforts to project its vision of global order and to promote a positive image globally have met with only mixed success. While recent media discussion in many countries has engaged themes that resonate with the PRC's vision of global order, it has also voiced considerable criticism of the PRC as a potentially exploitative, and even neocolonial, power. The PRC's development model remains attractive for many countries looking to move up the global value chain, but there is growing mention about the trade-offs of partnering with the PRC, including poor treatment of local workers, exploitation of natural resources, and lack of respect for local sovereignty.

Second, since Donald Trump became president again, the global conversation has featured widespread anxiety about the ability of the US to serve as a moral leader and reliable partner on the global stage. There is growing concern about the state of American democracy, particularly as Trump escalates assaults on checks and balances and the rule of law. Even longtime US friends increasingly doubt its ability to serve as a model of democracy or to provide leadership on these issues. Commentators cite the Trump administration's cuts to foreign aid, aggressive tariff and trade policy, and disrespect for multilateral institutions and the sovereignty of countries like Panama and Denmark (Greenland). Global discourse often deems this moment a turning point, where countries must consider adopting new global postures in response to the Trump administration's defection from norms of human rights, democracy, multilateralism, and international cooperation. As a result, the PRC is seen as a more stable force in the international system, even if its specific concepts for restructuring the international system are not entering the conversation. In other words, people may be frustrated and frightened by the recent stunning turn in American foreign policy, but they have not (yet) embraced the PRC's "community of common destiny" as an alternative.

The PRC as Discussed Abroad

The PRC's energetic promotion of its economic and governance models as exemplars has resonated in many countries. One Pakistani article gushed, "Developing countries can also walk the Chinese path to middle- and higher-income levels by following the Chinese model of development and modernisation."[30] A January 2025 report in Sri Lanka's main newspaper lauded the PRC's "effective poverty eradication strategies."[31] A February 2025 article in Tanzania's state newspaper praised the PRC for demonstrating "alternative paths to industrialisation for African countries. As the Western powers imposed their neoliberal model on the Global South, leading to deindustrialisation in many developing countries, China followed a different path by adhering to its own characteristics."[32] The leftist Mexican newspaper *La Jornada* hailed the GDI for its "people-centered approach, inclusivity, benefits for all, development driven by innovation, harmony between humanity and nature, and result-oriented actions," calling these "dreams amid the neoliberal nightmare."[33] In Benin, a piece on the GSI concluded, "Between peace and war, China resolutely chooses peace."[34] An article in Madagascar praised the GCI for presenting "new avenues for mutual learning between Chinese and African civilizations" and opportunities to "contribute to [their] harmonious coexistence."[35]

Articles also tout the economic benefits of ties to the PRC. A piece in Zimbabwe's *Sunday Mail* observed: "The sheer scale of what China is offering, and the direction it is steering its own economy, makes it a no-brainer for Africa to pivot East."[36] In Argentina, the Buenos Aires daily *Página 12* attributed lagging Latin American growth to over-reliance on the West and advocated closer ties with the PRC.[37] In his annual press conference, influential Mexican billionaire Carlos Slim made a similar appeal for Mexico to strengthen its economic relations with the PRC.[38]

Articles also stress the technological benefits of closer relations with the PRC, citing, for example, DeepSeek, the open-source and comparatively affordable AI model. Brazilian commentary viewed DeepSeek as an example of the PRC's superiority to the US in AI innovation, while Costa Rican commentary contrasted DeepSeek's open-source nature and the PRC's willingness to share technological innovation with a stingier US approach that approves "measures that are beneficial only to them, thereby hindering the development of countries like ours."[39]

Not all global commentary about the PRC, however, was positive. Senegalese commentators criticized the PRC for "winning markets and executing projects without any transfer of technology."[40] They also challenged the PRC's self-portrait as a paragon of development, noting, "It is the most brutal capitalism that exploits workers to the maximum. . . . There are far too many people left behind by Chinese growth."[41]

One finds criticism of the PRC even in nations trying to draw closer to it. In Sri Lanka, where the PRC has implemented massive infrastructure projects, public discourse is increasingly wary, despite the government's embrace of Chinese investment.[42] The BRI is widely dismissed as a failed promise, with unfinished projects, high-interest loans, and mounting debt stoking fears of economic entrapment. Beijing's slow response to Sri Lanka's 2022–2023 financial crisis cemented its reputation as an opportunistic rather than benevolent partner. An editorial in Colombo's *Daily Mirror* cited the BRI's mixed results as "a powerful reminder that genuine international development requires transparency, mutual benefit, and respect for sovereignty—principles that appear increasingly absent from China's global infrastructure strategy."[43] Editorial cartoons caricature Sri Lanka as overly reliant on Chinese loans, with officials signing agreements under pressure.[44]

In some countries, the PRC's attempts to promote its governance ideology and build closer ties are backfiring. While Thailand's prime minister met with Xi Jinping and praised the PRC's development model, Thai university students at an annual soccer game satirized Thailand's submissiveness to the PRC with banners reading "Welcome to Taiguo [Thailand in Chinese]."[45] Brazil's netizens criticized their government's signing of memoranda with the PRC during Xi Jinping's state visit in November 2024: "Brazil is little by little being bought by the dictatorship, and no one says anything."[46] The PRC's pursuit of a relationship with Singapore based on ethnic ties has been firmly rebuffed in Singaporean social media, with one Redditor declaring: "I have had so many interactions where they expect us to be 'one of them,' simply because of race. And that felt really quite demeaning to my identity as a Singaporean."[47] In a 2022 National Day address, then–Prime Minister Lee Hsien Loong responded archly to the PRC push to "Tell China's Story Well": "Chinese Singaporeans have sunk their roots here in Singapore and have our own unique stories to tell."[48]

The US as Discussed Abroad

Some global discourse during the Biden administration portrayed the US as lacking a vision for a mutually beneficial world order. The Biden administration's theme of "democracy vs. autocracy" and the broader conception of the "liberal international order" are increasingly criticized as selective, disingenuous, and even hypocritical. In many countries (especially Muslim-majority ones, including in Asia), this view intensified in response to American support for Israel's war in Gaza after the October 7 Hamas attacks. A November 2024 opinion in *El Pais*, Spain's most influential center-left paper, argued that the West needs to present a "better offer to the countries of the Global South."[49]

Negative perceptions of the US intensified with Trump's return to the White House in January 2025. Globally, many media commentaries view Trump as a threat to democratic norms, both at home and abroad. A February 11, 2025, editorial in France's venerable *Le Monde* warned of the dangers of an "imperial presidency" as Trump seeks to "reshape the architecture" of American democratic institutions for the sole purpose of enabling the president to "escape the system of checks and balances."[50] Trump's February 2025 bid for US ownership of the Gaza Strip provoked this bitter condemnation in *Dawn* (Pakistan's most influential

English-language newspaper) from the former head of the BBC Urdu Service: "Of late, dozens of examples of flawed democracy have shaken—all but shattered—my faith in the system. . . . Both Trump and [Israeli Prime Minister Benjamin] Netanyahu are not freaks but *products of a flawed democratic order* where the hard right's capture of the narrative allows it to manipulate public opinion to its advantage."[51]

Global concerns about the state of American democracy have been building for some time. They accelerated sharply with Trump's first presidential election and administration and then with the January 6, 2021, assault on the US Capitol. But they did not fully subside during the Biden administration. After engaging a range of Kenyan elites in 2022, *New York Times* writer Farah Stockman was struck by "the heavy geopolitical cost of American political dysfunction." Kenyan elites "spoke of American power in the past tense." In their view, the "American political model has not produced the results that Africans have been hoping for and now seems to be failing America itself." Some think "the Chinese system of meritocratic autocracy is a better route to middle income status for countries such as Kenya."[52] However, many in the Global South who share this critique of the US are liberal democrats who worry about its implications for freedom in their own countries.

Global discourse is further critical of the impacts of four Trump administration foreign policy initiatives: the "America First" trade policy with higher tariffs; the dissolution of US foreign aid commitments; the assaults on the sovereignty of friendly nations, particularly Canada, Panama, and Denmark; and the pullback of American support for Ukraine.

An article on US-Mexico tariff negotiations in *El Universal* condemned Trump for instituting "a new way of negotiating with [foreign] counterparts . . . , imposing the logic of the powerful in an aggressive manner and without respect for international agreements," while sowing "chaos."[53]

Around the world, newspaper commentaries condemned the abrupt cutoffs in US foreign aid. In Thailand, a piece reported that the cuts have "damaged the United States' image as a global leader" and "hurt vulnerable communities around the world."[54] A Tanzanian public health specialist said the US had "done amazing work to approve PEPFAR and USAID funding that has saved millions of lives. In such an abrupt disruption, it is telling those people you can now die."[55] The head of the Africa Centers for Disease Control declared the aid cuts a "total disaster" for public health in Africa, threatening "to undo 20 years of progress in maternal and child health, infectious disease control, and poverty reduction."[56] Some African commentators have taken the aid cuts as a challenge to seek greater self-reliance,[57] but they are daunted by the immediate pain and warn that African countries may look increasingly to the PRC. Ghanaian President John Mahama observed, "America loses soft power because USAID is a well-known brand of America and it intervenes in very critical areas" where "other countries might decide to fill that gap."[58]

In Spain, a horrified *El Pais* editorial wrote that, for the United States, "it would no longer be a question of exposing their civilizing or democratic model across the continent or the planet—'liberal' values—but rather the opposite: taking what they believe belongs to them by right with an imperial aftertaste, from the Panama Canal to Greenland."[59] Around the world, Trump's lust for these two territories has been widely condemned as imperialistic. In the aftermath of the contentious Oval Office meeting between Trump and Volodymyr Zelensky on February 28, 2025, the conservative South Korean paper *Chosun Ilbo* compared Trump to a "mafia" boss, while Poland's esteemed *Gazeta Wyborca* compared Trump and Vance to "Hitler and Göring" in "forcing the proud Ukrainian nation to accept the status of a protectorate—because it's more convenient for the aggressor."[60]

Taken together, these reactions underscore the US's declining reliability as a partner. "America First" isolationism is contrasted with the PRC's message of cooperation, shared development, and multilateralism. Many countries have even begun to consider that the PRC may be a better partner than the US. A February 2025 commentary in Spain's *El Mundo* argued that "it seems inevitable that the MAGA philosophy will fuel distrust toward the US to the benefit of Xi Jinping's government strategy. Thus, it could lead to countries in Latin America and the Asia-Pacific region accelerating their ties and trade relations with China to reduce dependence on the world's leading power."[61] That same month, a column in Peru's *El Comercio* offered a devastating assessment of the "decline of the US" under the second Trump administration, noting that "the Chinese, for their part, are already seeing the enormous window of opportunity that has been left for them to capitalize on."[62] Sri Lanka's *Daily Mirror* editorialized: "China is projecting itself in the Global South as a non-interventionist aid giver, unlike Western democracies, which have the promotion of their form of democratic government as the ideal for all."[63] Such commentaries echo the PRC line that it offers aid without imposing arrogant political conditions, while the US and its allies push their liberal norms.

The policies of the second Trump presidency are prompting many nations to readjust the balance of their postures toward the US and the PRC. In the wake of Trump's push to reclaim the Panama Canal, Costa Rica's President Rodrigo

Chaves explained his quest for a middle ground between the US and the PRC: "When elephants fight, one must be careful where they stand because they can cause a lot of damage."[64] Mexico's former ambassador to the PRC urged his country to look away from the US after Trump's tariffs and diversify its trade relationships, especially to "the Asian market, which in China alone amounts to more than 400 million middle-class people."[65]

What Publics Think

Given that global attitudes toward the US and the PRC may have shifted dramatically since Donald Trump's return to the White House, pre-2025 public opinion data should be taken with a grain of salt. Still, we can glean important insights from such surveys into how the battle for soft power is faring.

In the 14 East Asian countries surveyed in Wave 5 (2018–2019) and Wave 6 (2021–2023) by the Asian Barometer, average attitudes toward the PRC changed little in these years, with slightly more people having clearly positive views of the PRC's impact (26%) than clearly negative ones (about 21%). By contrast, views about the US impact were much more positive, with only 12% in Wave 5 and 7% in Wave 6 feeling clearly negative toward the US, compared with 32% in Wave 5 and 39% in Wave 6 feeling clearly positive. Thus, the US advantage over the PRC in the average net-positive sentiment went from a 15-point advantage in Wave 5 to a 28-point advantage in Wave 6, probably owing mainly to the change in administrations from Trump to Joseph R. Biden. This US advantage has likely shrunk again since 2023, due not only to Trump's new policies but also to US support for Israel's war in Gaza, which drew great concern in Malaysia and Indonesia.[66]

The Latinobarómeter showed a similar change in attitudes toward the US and the PRC. During the last year of the first Trump administration (2020) and the third year of the Biden administration (2023), Latin Americans were much more favorable (in net terms) to the US than to the PRC, and this US advantage sharply increased between 2020 and 2023, from 26 to 44 percentage points.

In Africa as well, the US advantage over the PRC in net-favorable views improved during the Biden years by 15 points (compared with a survey conducted during the first Trump administration). Both China and the US declined over time in the relative balance of positive views, but the PRC did so much more than the US. The PRC's net favorability dropped dramatically in some African countries: by 22 points in Kenya, 33 in Nigeria, 26 in Senegal, and 64 in Ghana. Such big changes cannot be explained purely by changes in the nature or scale of PRC propaganda. More likely, they reflect direct experience with the PRC as the positive impacts of

BRI infrastructure projects are eroded by the heavy-handedness of PRC diplomats and businesspeople.

The 2024 Pew Research Center's global survey of attitudes toward the US and the PRC also showed a sizable advantage for the US. Among 18 high-income countries, the PRC's median level of favorable attitudes was just 24%, compared with 53% for the US.[67] However, across the total of 34 high- and middle-income countries surveyed, the median percentage agreeing that "democracy in the US is a good example for other countries to follow" was only 24%. The modal response was that American democracy "used to be a good example but has not been in recent years."[68]

A poll of Europe following the November 2024 US election uncovered "a newly pessimistic and transactional view of the transatlantic partnership."[69] While many more Europeans (37% on average) view the PRC as a rival or adversary than view the US as such (11%), the emerging European view is of a "less ideals- and values-based" relationship with the US "in which Europe must more often defend its interests when they come under pressure from American actions."[70]

What about global attitudes toward democracy? Given that democracy has been receding for two decades, popular support for it has not declined as much as one might expect. Over the last two decades, the preference for democracy has held up consistently in Japan, Korea, and Taiwan, and (more or less) in Thailand, Malaysia, and Indonesia, while equivocating or eroding in the Philippines and Mongolia. More fleeting almost everywhere is satisfaction with the way democracy is working.[71] The 2021–2023 round of the Afrobarometer finds that "support for democracy remains robust: Two-thirds (66%) of Africans say they prefer democracy to any other system of government, and large majorities reject one-man rule (80%), one-party rule (78%), and military rule (66%)."[72] In Latin America in 2024, a weaker majority still prefers democracy over any other system, and a regional average of 69% (up from 63% in 2020) agree that "democracy may have its problems, but it is still the best form of government."[73] Globally, Pew finds: "People around the world generally believe that representative democracy is a good way to govern their countries," but they are increasingly dissatisfied with how it is working in practice.[74] Citizens of democracies believe their systems need reform and reinvigoration. However, there is no evidence that the PRC model of "whole process," fake democracy holds any attraction for them.

Conclusion

The relative prestige of the US and the PRC has been contested and in flux over the past two decades, and the battle has accelerated since Donald Trump's reelection, to the advantage of the PRC. This trend could have significant implications for global norms and the balance of global power. Ghanaian President John Mahama's reaction to the USAID freeze suggests the stakes: "This is a disruption that is happening, maybe a new world order will be born out of it."[75] Nigerian political scientist and publisher Jideofor Adibe warned: "Trumpism could lead to an acceleration in the prestige of institutions such as BRICS, whose avowed objectives include the creation of a multipolar world that will either drastically reduce or overthrow the current American-led Western system of global governance and security."[76] A Spanish economist predicted that the PRC could displace the US in much of the nonaligned world and suggested that the PRC had "already done this in many African countries."[77]

Yet there is growing wariness of the PRC, too. Despite its enormous investments in aid and information flows, the PRC is not winning the battle for global soft power. But the US could lose it. In the near term, people around the world do not seem inclined to simply throw in their lot with autocracy and certainly not with the PRC's version of it. The PRC says it favors "multipolarity," but what growing proportions of global opinion perceive is a potential new hegemony. Moreover, in most countries, there is still considerable popular sentiment behind the liberal idea of democracy—political freedom, pluralism, and accountability—as opposed to the bastardized "democracy with Chinese characteristics."

However, doubts are growing about the United States as an exemplar of (or even legitimate voice for) that model. To the extent that the US pursues a global path of isolationism, unilateralism, hyperrealism, and arrogant bullying, it will lose two massive advantages it had in its competition with the Soviet Union and in an earlier era of its competition with the PRC: its historically unique system of alliances built on common liberal values and its moral advantage in appealing to publics that value freedom, truth, and dignity. Without these two advantages, the United States is much less likely to prevail in this new era of competition to shape which way the world will go.

NOTES

1. Rob Merrick, "Ghana on US Aid Cuts: 'As Bridges are Burning, New Bridges Are Formed,'" *Devex*, February 14, 2025, https://www.devex.com/news/ghana-on-us-aid -cuts-as-bridges-are-burning-new-bridges-are-formed-109405.

2. Joseph S. Nye Jr., "Soft Power and Public Diplomacy Revisited," *The Hague Journal of Diplomacy*, April 22, 2019, p. 7, https://brill.com/view/journals/hjd/14/1-2 /article-p7_2.xml.

3. Nye, "Soft Power," 7–8.

4. We prefer to call China by its formal name, to stress that soft-power competition is between two states and two political systems more than between two peoples.

5. Eric Li, "The Rise and Fall of Soft Power," August 20, 2018, *Foreign Policy*, https://foreignpolicy.com/2018/08/20/the-rise-and-fall-of-soft-power/.

6. "China Is Spending Billions to Make the World Love It," *The Economist*, March 23, 2017, https://www.economist.com/china/2017/03/23/china-is-spending-billions-to-make-the-world-love-it. The dollar estimate is from David Shambaugh and is probably greater now.

7. The PRC constitution defines the state as a "people's democratic dictatorship" (人民民主专政). Conceptually, the CCP argues that democracy and dictatorship are not inherently opposed to each other and that the PRC can claim to be democratic despite possessing authoritarian characteristics.

8. "王毅: 民主不是可口可乐, 全世界一个味道 希望美国尊重中国自主选择的道路和制度 (Wang Yi: Democracy is not Coca-Cola, with the same taste all over the world; We hope the United States will respect China's independently chosen path and system)," Ministry of Foreign Affairs of the People's Republic of China, https://www.mfa.gov.cn/wjbz_673089/xghd_673097/202104/t20210424_9175221.shtml.

9. China Media Project, "Telling China's Story Well," April 16, 2021, https://chinamediaproject.org/the_ccp_dictionary/telling-chinas-story-well/.

10. China Media Project, "Telling China's Story Well."

11. Argentina, Benin, Brazil, Bulgaria, Colombia, Costa Rica, Democratic Republic of the Congo, El Salvador, France, Germany, Ghana, Guinea, India, Indonesia, Kenya, Kyrgyzstan, Madagascar, Mexico, Nigeria, Pakistan, Panama, Poland, Peru Senegal, Singapore, South Africa, South Korea, Spain, Sri Lanka, Tanzania, Thailand, and Zimbabwe.

12. China Media Group, "A democracia chinesa é um contributo fundamental para a paz no mundo [Chinese democracy is a fundamental contribution to world peace]," Portuguese China Radio International, March 19, 2024, https://archive.ph/LMqLi.

13. "CPEC Info," China Pakistan Economic Corridor, accessed April 12, 2025, https://cpecinfo.com/.

14. "Atos adotados por ocasião da visita de estado ao Brasil do Presidente da China, Xi Jinping—20 de novembro de 2024 [Acts adopted on the occasion of the state visit to Brazil by the President of China, Xi Jinping—November 20, 2024]," Ministério das Relações Exteriores, accessed April 12, 2025, https://www.gov.br/mre/pt-br/canais_atendimento/imprensa/notas-a-imprensa/atos-adotados-por-ocasiao-da-visita-de-estado-ao-brasil-do-presidente-da-china-xi-jinping-2013-20-de-novembro-de-2024-1.

15. Quoted in Liam Scott, "How China Became a Global Disinformation Superpower," *Coda*, December 6, 2022, https://www.codastory.com/disinformation/kurlantzick-book-china-global-media-offensive/.

16. DoubleThink Lab, "Media Indicator 07—China Index," accessed March 25, 2025, https://china-index.io/indicator/question07.

17. Freedom House, "Beijing's Global Media Influence: Indonesia," https://freedomhouse.org/country/indonesia/beijings-global-media-influence/2022.

18. Freedom House, "Beijing's Global Media Influence: Indonesia."

19. Devianti Faridz, "China Expands Media Influence in Indonesia," *Voice of America*, February 7, 2024, https://www.voanews.com/a/china-expands-media-influence-in-indonesia/7473675.html.

20. Xinhua, "Pakar sebut kemajuan inovasi China jadi inspirasi bagi Global South [Experts say China's innovation progress is an inspiration for the Global South]," *Antara News*, March 4, 2025, https://www.antaranews.com/berita/4687409/pakar-sebut-kemajuan-inovasi-china-jadi-inspirasi-bagi-global-south.

21. Wang Wei, "China y América Latina, de la mano hacia un mundo más justo de desarrollo común [China and Latin America, hand in hand toward a more just world of common development]," *La Nación*, December 1, 2024, https://www.lanacion.com.ar/opinion/china-y-america-latina-de-la-mano-hacia-un-mundo-mas-justo-de-desarrollo-comun-nid30112024/.

22. Yu Peng, "Opinião—Yu Peng: Celebramos o Ano-Novo do Patrimônio Cultural e construímos pontes entre China e Brasil [Opinion—Yu Peng: We celebrate the New Year of Cultural Heritage and build bridges between China and Brazil]," *Folha de S.Paulo*, February 13, 2025, https://www1.folha.uol.com.br/mundo/2025/02/celebramos-o-ano-novo-do-patrimonio-cultural-e-construimos-pontes-entre-china-e-brasil.shtml.

23. Zhu Jingyang (@zhu_jingyang), "Pobrecito, la compleja realidad de China desborda su muy mediocre capacidad cognitive [Poor thing, the complex reality of China overwhelms his very mediocre cognitive capacity]," Twitter, March 23, 2025, https://archive.ph/xy9dL.

24. Embajada de China en México (@EmbChinaMex), "Instamos a EE.UU. a Renunciar a su Orgullo y Prejuicio [We urge the US to renounce its pride and prejudice]," Twitter, February 13, 2025, https://archive.ph/TYCnm.

25. David Bandurski, "More Local Centers for Global Propaganda," China Media Project, June 12, 2024, https://chinamediaproject.org/2024/06/12/more-local-centers-for-global-propaganda/.

26. Insikt Group, "Breaking the Circle: Chinese Communist Party Propaganda Infrastructure Rapidly Expands," December 10, 2024, https://www.recordedfuture.com/research/breaking-the-circle-chinese-communist-party-propaganda.

27. Bandurski, "More Local Centers."

28. Dreamlike Harbin (@DreamlikeHarbin), "【中俄双语】当亚冬会遇见元宵节｜冰雪大世界赏月 [When the Asian Winter Games meets the Lantern Festival | Moon Viewing at Ice and Snow World]," Twitter, February 13, 2025, https://archive.ph/Kl2Xl.

29. Insikt Group, "China's Propaganda Expansion."

30. "Chinese Economic Growth Model Path to Modernisation, Says Mushahid," *Dawn*, May 29, 2023, https://www.dawn.com/news/1756480; Adeel Raza, "Attempt to Undermine Pakistan-China Cooperation Will Yield No Result," *Dawn*, October 19, 2024, https://www.dawn.com/news/1866091.

31. Editor, "President on State Visit to China," *Daily News*, January 17, 2025, https://www.dailynews.lk/2025/01/18/local/706517/president-on-state-visit-to-china-2/.

32. George Muntu, "How China Contributes to Africa's Industrial Development," *Daily News*, January 4, 2025, https://dailynews.co.tz/how-china-contributes-to-africas-industrial-development/.

33. José Blanco, "Bretton Woods vs. BRICS," *La Jornada*, October 29, 2024. https://www.jornada.com.mx/noticia/2024/10/29/opinion/bretton-woods-vs-brics-6848.

34. Héribert-Label Elisée Adjovi, "Gouvernance mondiale: Les trois initiatives chinoises (La vision du Président XI Jinping)," November 14, 2024, https://lanation.bj /actualites/gouvernance-mondiale-les-trois-initiatives-chinoises-la-vision-du-president-xi -jinping.

35. Julian Rakotoarivelo, "Chine-Afrique: L'Initiative pour la civilisation mondiale pour l'apprentissage mutuel entre civilisations chinoise et africaine [China-Africa: The Global Civilization Initiative for Mutual Learning between Chinese and African Civilizations]," *Midi Madagasikara*, September 19, 2024, https://midi-madagasikara.mg /chine-afrique-linitiative-pour-la-civilisation-mondiale-pour-lapprentissage-mutuel-entre -civilisations-chinoise-et-africaine/#google_vignette.

36. "China in Africa: Who Is Fooling Who?," *Sunday Mail*, October 3, 2024, https://www.sundaymail.co.zw/new-china-in-africa-who-is-fooling-who.

37. Néstor Restivo, "Los BRICS Marcan El Ritmo Mundial Del Crecimiento [The BRICS set the pace of global growth]," *Página 12*, January 4, 2025, https://www .pagina12.com.ar/792989-los-brics-marcan-el-ritmo-mundial-del-crecimiento.

38. Mariana Allende, "Carlos Slim Urges Investment, Stronger US-China Trade Ties," *Mexico Business News*, February 11, 2025, https://mexicobusiness.news/trade-and -investment/news/carlos-slim-urges-investment-stronger-us-china-trade-ties.

39. Marcelo Ninio, "Jantando Com o Premier Da China [Dining with the Premier of China]," *O Globo*, April 2, 2025, https://oglobo.globo.com/blogs/marcelo-ninio/post/2025 /02/jantando-com-o-premier-da-china.ghtml; Esteban Arrieta, "China es el mejor aliado para desarrollar tecnología porque evita políticas restrictivas [China is the best ally to develop technology because it avoids restrictive policies]," *La República*, January 29, 2025, https://www.larepublica.net/noticia/china-es-el-mejor-aliado-para-desarrollar-tecnologia -porque-evita-politicas-restrictivas.

40. "Nouveaux partenaires Faire attention au tandem Indo-Chinois (Économiste) [New partners: Pay attention to the Indo-Chinese tandem (economist)]," Seneweb.com, February 10, 2025, https://www.seneweb.com/news/Economie/nouveaux-partenaires -faire-attention-au-_n_462846.html.

41. Awa Faye, " 'La Chine ne dépassera jamais les États-Unis': La réponse Pékin à l'affirmation de Joe Biden ['China will never overtake the United States': Beijing's response to Joe Biden's claim]," January 17, 2025, https://www.seneweb.com/news /International/laquo-la-chine-ne-depassera-jamais-les-e_n_460741.html.

42. Vaisali Basu Sharma, "Belt and Road Initiative: China's Ambitious Project Faces Growing International Skepticism," *Daily Mirror*, March 3, 2025, https://www .dailymirror.lk/international/Belt-and-Road-Initiative-Chinas-ambitious-project-faces -growing-international-skepticism/107-303531.

43. Vaisali Basu Sharma, "Sri Lanka's China Dilemma: Strategic Partnerships and the Risk of Overdependence," *Daily Mirror*, January 16, 2025, https://www.dailymirror .lk/international/Sri-Lankas-China-dilemma-Strategic-partnerships-and-the-risk-of -overdependence/107-300205.

44. *Daily FT*, Cartoon 17.01.2025, accessed April 13, 2025, https://www.ft.lk/cartoon /Cartoon-17-01-2025/10494-771857.

45. "Paethongtarn Discusses with Xi Jinping, China Supports Thailand's Entry into 'BRICS' to Develop the Economy," *Bangkok BizNews*, November 16, 2024, https://www.bangkokbiznews.com/business/economic/1153831; "Traditional Football Match 'Thammasat-Chula' Teases Politics After a 5-Year Absence, 'Political Satire' Is Back!," *Channel 7 News*, February 15, 2025, https://news.ch7.com/detail/785118?fbclid=IwY2xjawIf TURleHRuA2FlbQIxMAABHdQU3FRCHiA331cvMMLgjoIEMkq7-bClhn3w7rNyv N9wPPLOd3wjnxU7ig_aem_rTrtsHpPN0n1gBSajgaCGg.

46. @GeopolPt, "Hoje em Brasília, os presidentes Lula da Silva e Xi Jinping assinaram um total de 37 acordos bilaterais entre o Brasil e a China," X, November 20, 2024, https://archive.ph/ISN0K; @brasilscenes, "Pé de Chinesa? Band e China Media Group estreitam relações com visita do presidente Xi Jinping ao Brasil durante o G20," X, November 24, 2024, https://archive.ph/2HndV.

47. r/singapore, "Youth must see China beyond its major cities, Singapore beyond its majority: Chan Chun Sing," Reddit, February 6, 2025, https://www.reddit.com/r/singapore/comments/1iiyfgr/youth_must_see_china_beyond_its_major_cities/.

48. *National Day Rally 2022—PM Lee's Malay and Mandarin Speeches*, 2022, https://www.youtube.com/watch?v=fmXY3FnXJSw.

49. Alicia García Herrero, "Los BRICS se fortalecen para cambiar el orden global [The BRICS are strengthening their position to change the global order]," *El País*, November 5, 2024, https://elpais.com/opinion/2024-11-05/los-brics-se-fortalecen-para-cambiar-el-orden-global.htmlAlic.

50. "Etats-Unis : le danger d'une présidence impériale [United States: The Danger of an Imperial Presidency]," *Le Monde*, February 11, 2025, https://www.lemonde.fr/idees/article/2025/02/11/etats-unis-le-danger-d-une-presidence-imperiale_6541822_3232.html.

51. Abbas Nasir, "Democratic Ethnic Cleansing," *Dawn*, February 9, 2025, https://www.dawn.com/news/1890765.

52. Farah Stockman, "Kenya's Political Elite Talk About American Power in the Past Tense," *New York Times*, August 3, 2022, https://www.nytimes.com/2022/08/03/opinion/kenya-presidential-elections.html.

53. Eunice Rendón, "Sheinbaum, Trump y la diplomacia que pone en riesgo el equilibrio global [Sheinbaum, Trump, and the diplomacy that jeopardizes global equilibrium]," *El Universal*, March 11, 2025, https://www.eluniversal.com.mx/opinion/eunice-rendon/sheinbaum-trump-y-la-diplomacia-que-pone-en-riesgo-el-equilibrio-global/.

54. "Trump's Aid Cuts Take Effect, Ends Medical Treatment in Shelter Centers on Both Thai and Burmese Sides, Over 90,000 Refugees Abandoned Along Border, Fears of Overflowing into Thai Hospitals," *TransBorder News*, January 27, 2025, https://transbordernews.in.th/home/?p=41212.

55. Michel Martin, Majd Al-Waheidi, and Reena Advani, "'You Can Now Die': The Human Cost of America's Foreign Aid Cuts in Africa," *National Public Radio*, March 13, 2025, https://www.whqr.org/2025-03-13/you-can-now-die-the-human-cost-of-americas-foreign-aid-cuts-in-africa.

56. "Africa CDC Says Millions of Lives in Africa Are at Risk due to US Aid Cut," *Premium Times* (Nigeria), March 21, 2025, https://www.premiumtimesng.com/news/top-news/782438-africa-cdc-says-millions-of-lives-in-africa-are-at-risk-due-to-us-aid-cut.html.

57. Ken Opalo, "African Countries Must Urgently Start the Process of Ending Aid Dependency," *An Africanist Perspective* (blog), March 2, 2025, https://www .africanistperspective.com/p/african-countries-must-start-the; Ebenezer Obadare, "The End of USAID Is an Opportunity for Africa," *Foreign Policy*, March 21, 2025, https:// foreignpolicy.com/2025/03/21/usaid-africa-foreign-aid-development/.

58. Jennifer Zabasajja, "US Aid Freeze Is Costing It Soft Power, Ghana's President Says," *Yahoo News*, February 15, 2025, https://www.yahoo.com/news/us-aid-freeze -costing-soft-060000334.html?guccounter=1.

59. Pablo R. Suanzes, "Trump y el Destino Manifiesto [Trump and Manifest Destiny]," *El Mundo*, February 4, 2025, https://www.elmundo.es/economia/2025/02/04 /67a10eeffc6c83355c8b4581.html.

60. Kim Dae-jung, "Trump's 'Ukraine Solution' and the Korean Peninsula," *Chosun Ilbo*, March 3, 2025, https://www.chosun.com/opinion/column/2025/03/04/CMZVW 6MFEBA6FCE74GIKMOPOEE/; Sergiusz Michalski, "Dzięki Bogu Wołodymyr Zełenski nie jest Emilem Hachą, zaś 40 milionów Ukraińców . . . [Thank God Volodymyr Zelensky is not Emil Hacha, and 40 million Ukrainians . . .]," *Wyborcza.pl*, March 2, 2025, https://wyborcza.pl/7,162657,31734512,dzieki-bogu-wolodymyr-zelenski-nie-jest -emilem-hacha-zas-40.html.

61. Alicia Coronil, "El arancel como arma de consecuencias incalculables [The tariff as a weapon of incalculable consequences]," *El Mundo*, February 9, 2025, https://www .elmundo.es/economia/macroeconomia/2025/02/09/67a60403e85ece24538b45b7.html.

62. Augusto Townsend Klinge, "El Declive de U.X.A. [The Decline of the USA]," *El Comercio Perú*, February 15, 2025, https://elcomercio.pe/opinion/columnistas/el-declive -de-uxa-por-augusto-townsend-klinge-noticia/#google_vignette.

63. P. K. Balachandran, "Trump's Disdain for Soft Power Opens Doors to China," *Daily Mirror*, March 2, 2025, www.dailymirror.lk/opinion/Trumps-disdain-for-soft -power-opens-doors-to-China/172-30348.

64. Lucia Astorga and Ángela Ávalos Rodríguez, "Marco Rubio Advierte de Sanciones a Funcionarios de Costa Rica Que Colaboren Con Actores Extranjeros Contra La Ciberseguridad [Marco Rubio Warns of Sanctions for Costa Rican Officials Who Collaborate with Foreign Actors Against Cybersecurity]," *La Nación*, February 4, 2025. https://www.nacion.com/politica/marco-rubio-advierte-de-sanciones-a-funcionarios /IVR44JWTTZAZTPUH2OHOUSS7RE/story/.

65. Braulio Carbajal, "Crecen Exportaciones a Asia; Es Opción para Diversificar Mercados [Exports to Asia Grow; It's an Option to Diversify Markets]," *La Jornada*, March 2, 2025, https://www.jornada.com.mx/noticia/2025/03/02/economia/crecen -exportaciones-a-asia-es-opcion-para-diversificar-mercados.

66. David Hutt, "Some Southeast Asians are Turning Against America over Gaza. It Likely Won't Last," *The Diplomat*, April 17, 2024, https://thediplomat.com/2024/04/some -southeast-asians-are-turning-against-america-over-gaza-it-likely-wont-last/.

67. Laura Silver, "More People View the US Positively than China Across 35 Surveyed Countries," Pew Research Center, July 9, 2024, https://www.pewresearch.org /short-reads/2024/07/09/more-people-view-the-us-positively-than-china-across-35 -surveyed-countries/.

68. Richard Wike et al., "Is US Democracy a Good Example to Follow?," Pew Research Center, June 11, 2024, https://www.pewresearch.org/global/2024/06/11/is-u-s-democracy-a-good-example-to-follow/.

69. Jana Puglierin, Arturo Varvelli, and Pawel Zerka, "Transatlantic Twilight: European Public Opinion and the Long Shadow of Trump," European Council on Foreign Relations Policy Brief, February 12, 2025, https://ecfr.eu/publication/transatlantic-twilight-european-public-opinion-and-the-long-shadow-of-trump/#the-china-conundrum.

70. Puglierin, Varelli, and Zerka, "Transatlantic Twilight."

71. Larry Diamond, "Trends in Support for Democracy in East Asian Democracies," in Yun-han Chu et al., *How Asians View Democratic Legitimacy* (National Taiwan University Press, 2023), 36–53.

72. "African Insights 2024, "Democracy at Risk: The People's Perspective," https://www.afrobarometer.org/feature/flagship-report/.

73. Informe 2024, "La Democracia Resiliente," Corporación Latinbarómetro, https://www.latinobarometro.org/lat.jsp.

74. Richard Wike and Janell Fetterolf, "Satisfaction with Democracy Has Declined in Recent Years in High-Income Nations," Pew Research Center, June 18, 2024, https://www.latinobarometro.org/lat.jsp; Richard Wike, "Why the World Is Down on Democracy," *Journal of Democracy* 36 (January 2025): 109–122.

75. Zabasajja, "US Aid Freeze Is Costing It Soft Power."

76. Jideofor Ajibe, "Will Trump Accelerate the End of the American Century?," *Premium Times* (Nigeria), February 11, 2025, https://www.premiumtimesng.com/opinion/773624-will-trump-accelerate-the-end-of-the-american-century-by-jideofor-adibe.html.

77. Inmaculada Martínez-Zarzoso, "La cooperación internacional, en entredicho [International cooperation is in question]," *El Pais*, March 1, 2025, https://elpais.com/economia/negocios/2025-03-02/la-cooperacion-internacional-en-entredicho.html.

Chapter Thirteen

China, Domestic Politics, and America's Global Role

Peter Feaver and William Inboden

Over the span of American history, perhaps no foreign country has loomed as large in the popular mind, for as long, and in as many different incarnations as China. Americans—and American policymakers—have alternately viewed China as a friend or foe, an alluring market or economic rival, an object of pity or source of threat, and a burden or an opportunity. Throughout, US policy on China has been shaped by three separate but interwoven threads of logic and action. In turn, the interplay of these threads has produced three important consequences for the often-fractious domestic debate over the US-China relationship.

The first thread shaping US policy is economic—an impulse born of the recognition of the enormous potential for commercial exchange with China. From the earliest days of the republic, China has been an important trading partner with the United States. But the real allure was always the promise of much more, if only the full potential of US-Chinese relations could be realized. American leaders believed that these economic interests would lead the country to "the Orient"—

Peter Feaver is a professor of political science and public policy at Duke University, where he directs Duke's Program in American Grand Strategy and is also a co–principal investigator of the America in the World Consortium. His most recent book is *Thanks for Your Service: The Causes and Consequences of Public Confidence in the US Military* (Oxford University Press, 2023).

William Inboden is the director of the University of Florida's Hamilton School of Classical and Civic Education and before that was the executive director of the Clements Center for National Security at the University of Texas–Austin. He previous service includes serving on the staff of the National Security Council and the State Department's Policy Planning Staff.

and US business leaders frequently pressed that possibility forward. More recently, as China has come to pose as much economic peril as promise, the underlying logic has remained the same: Get economic relations with China right, and the US economy flourishes; get it wrong, and it flounders.

The second thread is a security-based impulse that views China as a great power in global affairs and an essential actor in the regional balance of power. Here again, China often benefited from a strategic promise that exceeded the strategic reality, such as during its decades of internal weakness and civil war in the nineteenth and early twentieth centuries. Likewise, even when it did not enjoy diplomatic relations with the United States, China nevertheless managed to cast an enormous shadow over US strategy during the Mao era. And once the Soviet Union collapsed, China returned to the forefront of long-term US grand strategy debates.

The third thread is a values-based impulse that has viewed China's vast population as a mission field. In the 19th and early 20th centuries, American Protestants made China their highest-priority nation for sending missionaries to spread the Christian Gospel as well as new civilizational norms. In turn, these missionaries provided the lens through which many Americans viewed China. After the communist victory in the civil war and the expulsion of nearly all missionaries, this values impulse shifted from a spiritual to a more political framing in the second half of the 20th century. Similarly, debates about engaging China in the post–Cold War era were inextricably tied up in debates about the universal, and perhaps inexorable, attractiveness of the civic religion of Western values.

Of course, these impulses have often been in tension with one another, subject to continual trade-offs, compromises, and debates between hawks, who were bearish about US-China conflict, and doves, who were bullish on cooperation. Any policy that tried to completely ignore one of these impulses would have a short shelf-life, as would any policy that overemphasized any one aspect.

These three impulses, in turn, have had three primary implications for the domestic debate over China. First, since World War II, China has been the specter haunting many of the key divides and controversies in American grand strategy. It is difficult to identify a national security issue of substance that has not had a China angle. Even those that seemed remote, such as debates over terrorism in the September 11th era, questioned whether these near-term problems were distractions from the bigger long-term problem of China.

Second, China has figured prominently in domestic debates over American foreign policy. The Truman administration faced a debilitating critique—not over who lost Eastern Europe, but over who lost China. General Douglas MacArthur posed the gravest threat to civilian control in the Cold War era over how to manage the threat from China—not the threat from the Soviet Union. Donald Trump leveled a scorched-earth attack on US grand strategy in his rise to power, fueled by the allegation that China had hoodwinked all other American leaders and that he alone perceived the Chinese threat realistically.

Third, over the last several decades, China has become the strategy topic most likely to frustrate and wrong-foot a presidency. Bill Clinton campaigned by mocking George H. W. Bush for cozying up to the "butchers of Beijing," yet concluded his presidency seeking concessionary terms for China's entry into the World Trade Organization. George W. Bush promised to confront the long-term threat from China, only to make early concessions after China downed an American spy plane, and ultimately granted those very concessionary terms his predecessor had proposed. Barack Obama at first embraced a "G-2 condominium" with China only to pivot later to a more hawkish posture. Trump revived the "Who lost China?" debate with get-tough rhetoric but then botched the early handling of the pandemic spreading from China because of his desire for a favorable soybean trade deal in the early months of 2020. Joe Biden never resolved the strategic incoherence of imploring China to cooperate on climate change while also framing Beijing as the pacing threat on national security. The Trump 2.0 administration will be no exception given how narrow a governing majority it enjoys, how conflicted its coalition is on all things (but especially China), and how complex the set of challenges are that it faces.

Two other observations bear mentioning. First, while China has often been a divisive political issue domestically, it has less often been a purely partisan one. Rather, debates over US-China relations have usually provoked divisions *within* the main political parties more than *between* them. Overall, public opinion has evolved from markedly negative in the early days of polling, to near-neutral during the key shift under Nixon, to actually positive during Reagan, and back to sharply negative in the last decade.[1]

Second, there is a complex interplay between political leadership and public opinion. While voters with strong views on China sometimes pressure political leaders to adopt policy stances aligned with those views, in other instances, ordinary citizens often take their cues on China policy from political leaders.

The Deep Roots: The Early Republic Until World War II

As Michael Green details in his magisterial survey of US strategy in Asia, *By More than Providence*, the lure of commercial ties with China predates even the

US Constitution. In 1784, a commercial ship named the *Empress of China* sailed from New York to China and back, proving that intercontinental trade was physically possible and raising hopes that it might be a bonanza. Alongside the profits of Mammon came the prophets of God. Throughout most of the first century of US-China relations, missionaries were as important as government or commercial figures. Ships carrying missionaries from American ports to China might then carry Chinese laborers on the return voyage.

This first century of US-China relations culminated in the Open Door Notes, issued by Secretary of State John Hay in 1899 and 1900, which outlined a US policy demanding equal access to China on the same terms as the European great powers. President Theodore Roosevelt made the ambition of the Open Door Notes a reality. Roosevelt's vision—of an America that could profit handsomely from trade in the Pacific while also preserving regional stability—lasted a few decades until the rise of Japanese aggression and the Great Depression provoked a bloody upending of the balance of power. Japan's invasion of Manchuria in 1931 disoriented all Pacific powers: the young ones (Japan and the United States) sought greater status, and the old ones (China, Russia, and the European imperial powers) tried to prevent the loss of territorial privileges as their powers waned. When Japan overreached by attacking Pearl Harbor, President Franklin D. Roosevelt led the American response—one that, by war's end, established the United States as the preeminent power in Asia.

The domestic politics of US-China policy during this era were not as stormy as they would become in the decades that followed. But there were harbingers of what was to come in the fractious debates over how to handle Chinese migrant laborers in the West and how to balance looming threats in Europe versus Asia during the post–World War I era.[2]

Dawn of the Superpower Era and Early Cold War: Roosevelt to Johnson

As Franklin D. Roosevelt balanced the grand strategy demands of waging a global war and planning for the peace to follow, one factor loomed especially large: how to restore China's status as a great power—as one of the Big Four, alongside the US, Britain, and the Soviet Union. The tantalizing hope that China could play a constructive global role vied in American strategic debates with the dispiriting reality that the Nationalist government in China was too weak to be an effective counterweight to Japan—or even to vanquish its own internal Communist rivals. Despite heroic attempts, the US military was not able to make the alliance with the Nationalists a successful enterprise, and the eventual island-hopping campaign to reach Japan's shores eschewed the pathways that might have strengthened America's hand in China after Japan's surrender.

In 1949, the Nationalists fled to Formosa in defeat, a victorious Mao Zedong established the People's Republic of China, and the United States was consumed with the question "Who lost China?" This debate served as a proxy for a larger strategic debate over whether the United States should prioritize Europe or Asia in the emerging Cold War.

The China debates sharpened the following year, when China's massive military intervention in the Korean War decisively turned the battlefield balance against the United States and its allies. After using nuclear threats to induce a settlement, breaking the Korea stalemate in 1953, the Eisenhower administration also had to address Beijing's ongoing threats to Taiwan, exemplified by the Taiwan Strait Crises of 1954 and 1958. The People's Republic of China's bombardments of Taiwan's offshore islands—Quemoy and Matsu—brought the US and the PRC to the brink of war and led to the Eisenhower administration again resorting to nuclear threats to get Beijing to back down.

The Korea stalemate and Taiwan crises together shaped the tenets of US grand strategy in Asia for the next several decades. First, the United States believed it could not afford to allow more nations to fall prey to an expanding communist axis headed by the Soviet Union and China. Second, the United States believed it could not afford to commit the resources to win these fights decisively, as it had against Japan in World War II. Third, the United States believed it had to finesse the logical tension between these two tenets by a strategy of bluffs (brinksmanship), self-deceptions (such as the One China policy and the myth that the Nationalists in Taiwan were destined to retake control of mainland China), heavy-handed alliance management (e.g., refusing to "unleash Chiang" against the mainland), and a frustrating "not enough to win, but enough to postpone defeat" commitment wherever China or its allies were ascendant. Fourth, the United States was slow to exploit the tensions within the Sino-Soviet alliance—in part because the US focused more on the genuine threat that Mao posed to the region, and his ghastly torment of his own people through the disastrous Great Leap Forward and the Cultural Revolution.

The Heyday of Rapprochement: Nixon to Reagan

The calamity of the Vietnam War—itself a partial consequence of US-China tensions and the aforementioned tenets—contributed to the most significant shift in US-China relations in the entire 250-year history: the "Nixon goes to China" gambit. America's struggles in Vietnam and eroding posture in the strategic competition with the Soviet Union convinced President Richard Nixon and National Security Advisor Henry Kissinger that the balance of power had shifted markedly against the United States—and that US policy needed to adjust in a similarly marked fashion. The simultaneous rift within the Communist Bloc between the Soviet Union and China presented an opportunity to shift from bipolarity to a triangular dynamic—albeit an imbalanced triangle given China's weaker stature in comparison with the US and the USSR. The challenge, of course, was that this would require abandoning a core tenet of early Cold War US strategy in Asia: isolate Communist China through a network of bilateral strategic partnerships.

In this way, Nixon and Kissinger's bold move was based both on a novel sense of American weakness—at home and abroad—and, simultaneously, on an old sense that China offered an opportunity, if only we could grab it. Nixon also appreciated that he was one of the few American leaders with the political capital to craft an entente with China. He had forged his earlier political career as an ardent anti-communist, and his hardline credentials gave him the latitude within the Republican party—and the American public more broadly—to extend the outreach to Beijing, such that "Nixon goes to China" soon became a colloquialism for any political gamble that entailed a course reversal from a prior fervently held position. Domestic opinion responded in kind: A critical mass of American voters embraced Nixon's move and began to view China in a more favorable light.

While the gambit may have been born out of strategic weakness, it was also shaped by a desire—driven by domestic politics—to counter that very perception of weakness. Notwithstanding their diplomatic boldness, Nixon and Kissinger faced limits on how far they could travel on the road to Beijing. They could not afford—or chose not to pay the price of—a clean break that would "lose" Taiwan to "win" the bigger China.

The Carter administration extended the framework of US-China cooperation by switching formal diplomatic recognition from Taiwan to China. This move further provoked Ronald Reagan, then a leading GOP presidential candidate, who lacerated Jimmy Carter's abandonment of Taiwan as a "betrayal of a longtime friend and ally." Meanwhile, Congress, believing that Carter had leaned too far toward Beijing, passed the Taiwan Relations Act in 1979, ensuring that détente with Communist China would be balanced by continuing support for the Republic of China's security needs. The compromise—messy as it was—succeeded over the subsequent decades in preserving Taiwan's autonomy and semi-official partnership with the United States, while also facilitating a deepening American engagement with China.

As president, Reagan's main foreign policy priority was confronting and weakening the Soviet Union. In Asia, he focused on shifting the US-Japan relationship from economic rivalry to upgraded strategic partnership, while repairing other US regional alliances, such as with South Korea. In one of history's ironies, these priorities—which did not seem to include China—actually created the conditions for deepened US cooperation with China based on shared security and economic interests. Reagan's efforts to upgrade US alliances with Japan and South Korea, while locking in the US commitment to Taiwan, helped induce Beijing to adopt a more congenial posture toward the US. Similarly, Reagan's harder line toward Moscow coupled with America's economic revival made the US a more attractive security and economic partner for China.

The initial China policy question Reagan faced was how to resolve—or at least manage—the ambiguities in the vexed triangle of the US-China-Taiwan relationship that he inherited from Carter and Congress. In his first 18 months in office, Reagan orchestrated an elaborate web of agreements to both reinforce America's security commitment to Taiwan and to upgrade the US-China partnership. Neither Taipei nor Beijing felt fully satisfied with the outcomes. But the compromises in the "Third Communiqué" and its associated codicils and side deals gave all parties just enough reassurances and incentives to stabilize cross-Strait relations and cement US-China ties.[3]

Reagan articulated a strategic assumption that would be shared by every American president from Richard Nixon to Barack Obama: "a strong, secure and stable China can be an increasing force for peace, both in Asia and the world."[4] However, Reagan was not unmindful of the repressive system of the Chinese Communist Party (CCP). While he promoted the first two threads of historic American interests in China with his security and economic outreach, he also reintroduced the third thread of values (which had otherwise been neglected in China policy by Nixon, Ford, and Carter) through public and private advocacy for human rights and democratic reform in China. In balancing the three threads, Reagan presided over what Jim Mann would later describe as the "golden years" in US-China relations.[5]

The good times were not to last, but nor were they to dissipate altogether. When George H. W. Bush succeeded Reagan, he entered the White House as the most seasoned "China hand" in the history of the American presidency. Bush had previously served as the first de facto US Ambassador to the PRC, and had worked extensively on China policy during his eight years as Reagan's vice president. As president, Bush planned to continue the cooperative relationship the US enjoyed with China.

Less than five months into his presidency, the Tiananmen Square massacre of June 4, 1989, disrupted Bush's plans. It did not disrupt his strategic paradigm, however. As ghastly as the CCP's butchery of thousands of peaceful democracy demonstrators was, Bush was determined to maintain US engagement with China rather than isolate the CCP. While imposing some punitive measures—such as economic sanctions and suspension of military cooperation—less than a month after the massacre Bush sent National Security Advisor Brent Scowcroft on a secret mission to Beijing to reassure Deng Xiaoping that the US still desired to maintain a strategic partnership.[6]

Realizing that the CCP had rejected the political liberalization then being pioneered by Soviet leader Mikhail Gorbachev and flowering in Eastern Europe, Bush instead put in place the strategic framework that would guide his administration and the next three presidencies. The framework assumed that continued economic and political engagement with China would induce political liberalization at home and more responsible conduct abroad. There was a security logic to this as well. The US enjoyed sufficient military overmatch against the PRC such that Washington could indulge continued appeasement of Beijing based on American strength, not weakness. In turn, a China that reformed its economy and became more prosperous would, in time, reform its political system, moderate its military ambitions, and integrate into the international system. Or so the theory hoped.

From the outset, this framework faced dissent. In the two decades before Tiananmen Square, the executive branch had largely shaped both China policy and US public opinion toward China. But after the crackdown, Congress reasserted itself as a major factor in shaping policy when a new coalition of China hawks hatched on Capitol Hill. Notably, this congressional concern was—and remains—bipartisan. Led in the Senate by liberal Democrats such as George Mitchell and conservative Republicans such as Jesse Helms, and in the House of Representatives by liberal Democrats such as Nancy Pelosi partnered with conservative Republicans such as Frank Wolf and Chris Smith, this cohort put human rights at the center of US-China relations. They marshalled sustained opposition to efforts by successive presidencies to forge closer economic ties with Beijing. In short, the executive branch maintained the economic and security threads of the tradition, while Congress held fast to the values thread.

As such, the new Clinton administration soon found itself buffeted by the cross-currents of this China engagement paradigm and its skeptics. As a presidential candidate in 1992, Bill Clinton campaigned on a promise to revoke China's Most Favored Nation (MFN) trading status and memorably denounced the "butchers of Beijing" for the Tiananmen massacre. Once in office, he reversed himself, and, under substantial pressure from an American business community eager for access to the world's largest emerging market, decided to grant MFN to China. A furious debate ensued in Congress that split both the Democratic and Republican caucuses—a divide replicated among the American people writ large. The labor movement, human rights, and religious freedom advocates opposed MFN, while the business community and agricultural interests strongly favored it. The commercial engagement side prevailed, and Congress upheld Clinton's MFN decision.

Clinton soon went a step further and supported China's membership in the new World Trade Organization under concessionary terms that gave Beijing permanent MFN status and reified the strategic engagement paradigm. This framework held that China's continued economic growth and integration into the international order would bring about greater political openness at home and more pacific behavior abroad.

While the failures and errors of this strategy are now abundantly known and endlessly lamented (including by the authors), at the time it was a very plausible paradigm. Consider how the world looked to policymakers in the late 1990s. The previous decade had witnessed the peaceful dissolution of communist regimes across the Soviet Union and Eastern Europe, many of which had successfully transitioned to market democracies. In Asia, growing economies and emerging middle classes in South Korea, Taiwan, and the Philippines had all led to peaceful transitions from dictatorships to market democracies. In short, it was not at all imprudent to expect that China could follow a similar path of an Asian communist authoritarian state with a growing middle class and exposure to the communications revolution evolving into a peaceful market democracy.

There were frictions and security tensions, even at the time, but American geopolitical muscle gave Washington the upper hand. Thus, during the Taiwan Strait Crisis of 1995–1996, the United States could simultaneously anger a humiliated Beijing by sending two carrier battle groups through waters China deemed within its sovereign claim, while also angering domestic pro-Taiwan interest groups by conceding China's input on whether Washington could allow a Taiwanese leader to visit the US. Playing a strong hand in this way convinced both Chinese and Taiwanese actors that they needed to shuffle the deck in the hopes of generating more favorable conditions in the future. Thus, hawks within mainland China drove a steady military buildup to ensure that they would never face an adverse tactical balance of power again, while hawks in Taiwan pushed the republic further away from the One China policy fiction—even as Beijing's clumsy aggression toward the island sparked a growing Taiwanese identity and sense of autonomy among its citizens.

The Gradual Shift to a Pivot to Asia: Bush and Obama

As a presidential candidate, George W. Bush campaigned on getting a generational jump on the arms race with China as the most likely (but little mentioned) adversary, yet Bush otherwise took office still holding to the strategic engagement paradigm.

The apotheosis of the engagement model came with Deputy Secretary of State Robert Zoellick's famous 2005 speech urging China to become a "responsible stakeholder" in the international system. This exhortation, coupled with continued economic integration, sought to secure China's future ambitions in a constructive direction. These efforts deepened under Treasury Secretary Hank Paulson's leadership of the Strategic Economic Dialogue with China during Bush's second term. The symbolism of the treasury secretary helming the dialogue indicated the policy substance of putting the economic thread first in the relationship. Bush also encouraged China to play a constructive role in regional security, exemplified by including Beijing in the Six-Party Talks, a diplomatic initiative to curtail North Korea's nuclear weapons program.

But the Bush administration did not neglect the other two threads of security and values. The Pentagon began adapting its force posture to more assertively deter potential Chinese aggression. Bush's strategic opening to India, exemplified by the civil-nuclear deal, sought to hedge against a belligerent China by bringing India into a regional balancing coalition as a de facto US ally. On the values thread, Bush did arguably more to support human rights in the PRC than any other president before or since. For example, he became the first US president to host a White House meeting with Chinese dissidents still active in China (unlike other presidential meetings with exiled activists such as Wei Jingsheng and the Dalai Lama), and as his 2006 *National Security Strategy* showed, he prioritized human rights, religious freedom, and democratic values in his public remarks and private diplomacy with Chinese leaders.

President Barack Obama similarly entered the White House believing in the strategic engagement paradigm with China. Taking office during the global financial crisis, Obama and Secretary of State Hillary Clinton vocally eschewed human rights or security concerns while flirting with Beijing's notion of a "G-2 condominium"—of the US and China partnering as equals to oversee the world economy. In the process the Obama administration also elevated climate change to a strategic priority that assumed even deeper cooperation with the CCP.

These lofty ambitions and hopes, however, did not avail. Even before Xi Jinping took power in China at the start of Obama's second term, the CCP resisted the administration's blandishments while continuing its military buildup, assertive colonization in the South China Sea, genocide against its Uighur minority, massive theft of American technology and intellectual property, and other malign activities.

Midway through his presidency, Obama and his team began to shift their rhetoric, although a policy change lagged. Secretary Clinton announced a "pivot" to Asia—with a more skeptical posture toward China the clear implication—but her successor Secretary John Kerry refused to implement the policy.

Moreover, even architects of the pivot acknowledged problems. It was poorly explained in the rollout and under-resourced in the implementation. Most fundamentally, it suffered from internal contradictions. Its proponents stressed that it was not an effort to contain China, and yet it clearly was a hedge against the bet that China would inexorably evolve in a direction favorable to US interests. They never explained what the difference was between containing and hedging.[7]

In over-hyping the pivot, the Obama team also missed a chance to build a surer bipartisan foundation. Moreover, they botched the domestic politics of the Trans-Pacific Partnership (TPP)—a key adjustment to the concessionary trade policies that Clinton, Bush, and Obama had all followed, but at increasing domestic cost—and thus left the establishment defending an easily caricatured China policy against a populist who could say anything and promise anything without any responsibility for results.

The mistaken strategic assumptions and policy failures of Obama's approach to China meant that, whoever won the presidency in 2016, a big change was afoot. Indeed, skepticism toward China was one of the few policies on which candidates Hillary Clinton and Donald Trump seemed to agree.

Not a New Cold War but a New Hot Competition: Trump 1.0 to Trump 2.0

Domestic politics demanded a change not only in how leaders talked about the topic but also in the policies they pursued. China was now a hostile competitor—a rival, or worse, an outright adversary in a "New Cold War." However one described it, the change was unmistakable: China went from being seen as a land of economic opportunity to a land of economic and security threat.

The shift was not due exclusively to US domestic politics. Rather, the primary driver was China's aggressive turn toward "wolf-warrior diplomacy" and other bellicose policies once Xi Jinping took power in 2012. Beijing unleashed a steady drumbeat of geopolitical shocks—from openly defying international law in colonizing the South China Sea, to belligerent brinkmanship with Taiwan, South Korea, Japan, and Australia—all pushing the relationship in a conflictual manner. If the default trajectory from 1989 until 2012 was one of peaceful co-development, occasionally punctuated by crises, the default trajectory since then has been hostile rivalry, occasionally punctuated by episodes of fitful cooperation.

Even in this shift, however, the patterns and dilemmas that emerged from earlier periods reappeared, albeit in a reverse photo-negative kind of way. First and most obviously, the shift from China as an economic opportunity to China as an economic threat was incomplete since the economic opportunity was impossible to ignore and decades of trade had inseparably entangled the economies. Thus, even as Trump was imposing tariffs to launch a trade war that none of his predecessors dared to attempt, he was also loudly signaling that he was open to a deal none of his predecessors could land. Even in January and February 2020, when the menace from China was looming from the COVID-19 virus that would become the worst global pandemic in a century, Trump hesitated in protecting the homeland in the hope of landing a bilateral trade deal on soybeans that would give him a "win" for the reelection campaign. Unlike every president before him, Trump was willing to risk a global economic meltdown to confront China; but just like every president before him, Trump was tantalized by the prospect of an economic windfall, if only he could get China right.

The values-based impulse that historically complicated attitudes toward China also played a key role in driving US-China policy over the past decade. Indeed, in an era of intense polarization, where every single issue seemed to divide Americans, one issue united them: China was an increasingly bad actor abroad and at home. The PRC's genocide against its Uighur population was one of the few human rights issues that Trump 1.0 championed. Biden's rhetoric was a bit more ambivalent, but still followed the traditional liberal playbook of lamenting China's authoritarian excesses. Meanwhile his fellow party leaders, especially Speaker Nancy Pelosi, went further in their full-throated denunciations. Indeed, the reason the mass public lost confidence in the post–Cold War consensus on the US approach to China was based mainly on economics and the exaggerated (but not entirely mistaken) belief that it caused trade-induced job-loss at home. But elites nevertheless lost their enthusiasm for the China policy mostly for a values-based reason: Xi Jinping made it impossible to believe that China would grow more democratic and more liberal as it grew wealthier.

Likewise, the long-held trope of China as the impossible-to-ignore actor who held the balance in regional affairs was as true over the past decade as it ever was—and gradually became truer in a global and not just a regional sense. Biden confronted this more directly than did Trump 1.0 in two ways that had a curious intersection with domestic politics. From the start, Biden embraced a contradictory logic, as articulated in his *National Security Strategy*. On the one hand, China was the "pacing challenge" that posed the gravest security and economic problems, and thus was the measuring stick for all of Biden's efforts to restore American standing after the decline of the Trump years. It provided the rationale for a bold re-embrace of industrial policy through trillions of dollars of stimulus and massive clean energy subsidies. On the other hand, China was indispensably part of any conceivable successful policy to confront a different existential threat that Democratic voters cared a lot about: climate change. Biden thus called for his team to pursue economic and security policies that would give the United States a competitive edge on China in the medium to long term while also pursuing cooperative, if politically painful (for China) climate-related policies that would produce results immediately. The strategy may have seemed coherent in the Situation Room, but China made it clear that it would not make concessions to the United States on climate change while watching the US steal a competitive advantage in other areas. When Russia, emboldened by China's "unlimited partnership," invaded Ukraine, China became the spoiler of US policy in Europe as well as in Asia. Forced to choose, China chose Russia over good relations with the United States, and Biden chose progress on meeting China's security threat (notably AUKUS and other policies advocated by Biden's able Asia czar, Kurt Campbell) rather than progress on addressing climate change.

Trump 2.0 has inherited this complex and internally contradictory policy—and thus far has added a few more levels of incoherence and complexity. At its root, Trump 2.0 seems to embody an extreme form of the tensions that bedeviled earlier administrations. His professed appetite for the risks of confronting China exceeds that of any previous administration—as does his appetite for cutting a deal. Trump talks about building a position of strength in China to ensure that the United States can never be intimidated in the region—but also talks about Taiwan's precarious geography and claims its only real strategic value is as a chip manufacturing facility based on ideas it "stole" from the US. He seems to regard China as America's main adversary, yet has been unilaterally disarming in key areas of asymmetric advantage such as slashing or eliminating the United States' institutions of democracy promotion and international broadcasting. These incoherencies also manifest in the area of "personnel is policy," with a spectrum of top advisors, some among the most hawkish in the Republican party, others advocating for a retreat from everywhere else so as to prioritize all resources for a China confrontation, a third group who has become rich by doing business with China and want to maintain that economic access, and still others talking about spheres of influence that would keep the United States focused narrowly on the Western Hemisphere.

In the present moment, China poses more direct threats to American security interests than at any time since the Vietnam War; and China has further entrenched its authoritarianism and undermining of democracies abroad—including American democratic institutions. Similarly, China has become a partner to every other security threat the US faces, from North Korea to Iran to Russia to Venezuela and Cuba.

At the same time, while the rise of Trump and the poisoning of American domestic politics cannot be entirely blamed on China, it is nevertheless the case that China issues played a big role. Trump's anti-institutional narrative in the 2024 campaign—and his early approach to governing—owes a great deal to the populist fury he helped stoke by making China the scapegoat for lost jobs and a perceived decline in American power.

And just as the China issue became a stumbling block for multiple administrations over the past century, China may prove to be the issue that splits apart the incoherence of the Trump coalition, with its many camps and tribes as described above. Each of those seams could be ripped apart by the China challenge.

One can draw a straight line from Trump's rhetoric and personnel choices that leads directly to an early war with China over Taiwan; or one can just as easily anticipate the opposite outcome, a rapprochement with China that abandons Taiwan. These dynamics in the aggregate may point to another China reckoning—one that exposes the flaws in the current apparent consensus, just as the earlier one exposed the flaws in the responsible stakeholder consensus.

Indeed, one can observe a new trend from the past 15 years that is an ominous harbinger for the future. Starting with President Obama, each president has handed over to his successor a US-China relationship that was in worse shape than the one he inherited from his predecessor. There is nothing in what the Trump team has shown in the first few months of office—nor anything in US domestic politics—that gives any reason for optimism that this pattern will improve in the foreseeable future. Over the past 250 years, China has consistently been one of those grand strategy topics that frustrates and wrong-foots administrations, and America's current travails make the future look particularly foreboding.

NOTES

1. See Faith Laken et al., "American Attitudes Toward Japan and China, Decades of Polls," *Asian Journal for Public Opinion Research* 2, no. 1 (November 2014): 52–70; and Craig Kafura, "American Views of China Hit All-Time Low," *Chicago Council on Global Affairs*, October 2024.

2. Michael J. Green, *By More than Providence: Grand Strategy and American Power in the Asia Pacific Since 1783* (Columbia University Press, 2019).

3. William Inboden, *The Peacemaker: Ronald Reagan, the Cold War, and the World on the Brink* (Dutton, 2022), 169–171.

4. NSDD-140. Folder: China Foreign Relations President Reagan's Trip to China (1) RAC box 14, box 3, David Laux Files. Reagan Presidential Library.

5. Inboden, *Peacemaker*, 278–282.

6. James Mann, *About Face: A History of America's Curious Relationship with China, from Nixon to Clinton* (Vintage Books, 2000), 205–209.

7. Kurt M. Campbell, *The Pivot: The Future of American Statecraft in Asia* (Twelve, 2016), 11, 26, 32, 290.

PART IV / America and China in a Shifting Global Order

Chapter Fourteen

China's Global Governance Gambit

Elizabeth Economy

Over the course of his more than decade-long tenure as general secretary of the Chinese Communist Party (CCP) and president of China, Xi Jinping has signaled his intention to transform the international system, as well as China's position within it. Xi's bold calls for the "great rejuvenation of the Chinese nation" and his pronouncements that epochal changes in the world order are underway are matched by equally bold initiatives to realize these objectives. China is actively working to reshape international norms and institutions to reflect Chinese values, interests, and policy priorities.

China's approach to reordering the world order has evolved over decades but has accelerated in recent years. Beijing has developed a preferred political lexicon—including "a shared future for mankind," "common security," "multipolarity," and "system diversity"—that is now commonplace in international discourse. It has created grand-scale programs, such as the Belt and Road Initiative (BRI), Global Security Initiative (GSI), Global Development Initiative (GDI), and Global Civilization Initiative (GCI), which China is weaving into multilateral arrangements and international institutions. The objectives are explicit: end the

Elizabeth Economy is the Hargrove Senior Fellow and the co-director of the Program on the US, China, and the World at the Hoover Institution, Stanford University. She is a member of the Aspen Strategy Group and the Council on Foreign Relations. Her most recent book is *The World According to China* (Polity, 2022).

The author would like to thank Declan Herrera for his excellent research assistance.

US-led alliance system, erode dollar dominance in the global economy, and undermine the legitimacy of universal human rights. And China has moved beyond even these ambitions to try to assert leadership in governance over the still uncharted frontiers of space, oceans, and the Arctic.

To date, however, China has achieved only limited success. Countries support China where the cost to them is lowest: providing rhetorical support for China's normative discourse and welcoming China's financial largesse. Beijing struggles, however, to gain support either for fundamental change to the international system or for leadership in areas where norms and rules have yet to be fully defined. Its successes derive from its ability to maneuver within the system as opposed to its ability to change the system itself. The current system has demonstrated more resilience than many might appreciate. Nonetheless, the United States should not be complacent. China's growing political, economic, and military influence, along with its long-term commitment to transforming the system and its willingness to invest substantial human and financial capital to achieve its objectives, may well over time make significant advances in eroding the system from within.

Words Matter

The basic building blocks of China's vision emerged well before Xi Jinping came to power. Since the founding of the PRC in 1949, Chinese leaders have espoused principles such as mutual trust, mutual benefit, and equality; advocated for the primacy of sovereignty and a multipolar world; and opposed formal alliances. China's 1997 New Security Concept (NSC) crystallized many of these concepts, calling for common security—for countries to resolve their disputes through diplomacy rather than military force, to respect sovereignty, and to address not only military but also economic and human security—as well as system diversity, the notion that countries will determine their own political and economic development path based on their own cultures and historical experiences. The NSC also used system diversity to criticize alliances, noting: "security cooperation is not just something for countries with similar or identical views and mode of development, it also includes cooperation between countries whose views and mode of development differ."[1]

At the same time, China's growing economic and military prowess gave credibility to nationalist voices who called for China to become "a leading power in the world," "replacing the dominant position of the West in the world" and "making the twenty-first century a Chinese century."[2] These voices rejected universal principles and underscored the vast gap between Western models and that of

China.[3] By the late 2000s, China's successful hosting of the 2008 Olympics and the US's economic failings in the 2008 global financial crisis had spurred an even greater sense of national pride and ambition. Leading Chinese scholar Hu Angang predicted that, by 2020, China would surpass the US as the world's largest economy and, by 2030, would lead the world in global transformation.[4] The head of the People's Bank of China, Zhou Xiaochuan, also called for a new world reserve currency.[5]

Xi Jinping has championed these ideas and ambitions—the NSC, Chinese global leadership, and the rise of the East over the West—and made them an acceptable part of global discourse. The NSC's terms—common security, multipolarity, sovereignty, reform of the international financial and economic system, and system diversity—are common reference points in multilateral and UN discussions.

Chinese centrality is reinforced through leadership of a multiplicity of multilateral arrangements, such as the Forum on China-Africa Cooperation (FOCAC) and the Asian Infrastructure Investment Bank (AIIB). And Xi has expressed his confidence in the inevitable rise of China and decline of the United States across several dimensions: a revolution in technology, demographics, climate, and power that favors China—often described as "great changes unseen in a century";[6] a shift from West to East that is reflected in the "chaos of the west" and "governance of China";[7] and the "eventual demise of capitalism and the ultimate victory of socialism."[8]

Words Become Action

Chinese officials like to argue that their conception of the global order has evolved from a "Chinese initiative" to an "international consensus."[9] Their proof is in the international community's acceptance of China's global initiatives, including the 2013 BRI, the 2021 GDI, the 2022 GSI, and the 2023 GCI.

The BRI links China's market to Europe, Asia, and the Middle East, as well as the east coast of Africa through hard infrastructure, such as ports, railways, and roads. It also promotes the coordination of trade and investment standards and trade settlement in local currencies. Over time, the BRI has expanded to include individual silk roads for infrastructure related to information and communications technologies, health, and the environment. And the notion of trade settlement in local currencies has expanded to a much more explicit effort to move the world economy away from its reliance on the dollar.[10] In contrast to the BRI's large-scale infrastructure projects, the GDI prioritizes small-scale development projects and is designed "not only to give people fish but also to teach them how to fish."[11] Underpinning the GDI, however, is a Chinese principle that economic development is the foundation for political development; Chinese government documents describing the GDI claim that other countries marginalize development issues by emphasizing human rights and democracy.[12] Together, the GDI and BRI serve to entrench China's digital, health, and clean technology ecosystems globally; advance its development model; and support the use of its currency.

The GSI reflects concepts found in the NSC, such as respect for sovereignty, system diversity, opposition to bloc confrontation, and resolution of interstate differences through dialogue and consultation.[13] It also embraces indivisible security, the principle that one country's security is linked to that of the countries around it, and if a country feels threatened, it has the right to take preemptive action. Underlying the pacifist rhetoric, however, are China's ambitions to end US alliances and to justify Russia's invasion of Ukraine as well as potential Chinese military action against Taiwan.

Xi's most recent initiative, the GCI, reflects China's commitment to system diversity. It also makes clear that individual states determine their rights and that no single country has the right to control the global discourse on human rights. As former Foreign Minister Qin Gang put it: "There is no one-size-fits-all model in the protection of human rights."[14]

Chinese leaders have had significant success in encouraging other countries to sign on to these various initiatives, particularly the BRI, GDI, and GSI. Approximately 150 countries have joined the BRI; more than 70 have signed on to a "Group of Friends of the GDI"; and over 100 countries, regional organizations, and international organizations have announced support for the GSI.[15] Both the BRI and GDI have also helped realize significant gains for Chinese companies globally; Chinese enterprises and technologies now dominate in construction, clean energy, and digital projects in many parts of the world. For example, China has laid 80,000 km of fiber optic cables in Africa, Southeast Asia, and the Middle East, and invested in 117 ports across 43 countries, including 16 of the top 20 countries for shipping connectivity—improving efficiency in many of them.[16] In one 2024 survey, 38% of officials from 129 countries chose China as their preferred infrastructure partner, and slightly more than half stated that BRI projects had contributed to gains in their countries' connectivity and technology access.[17] China has also made progress in de-dollarizing the global economy. It settled over half its 2024 payments in RMB, marking a new high;[18] the energy trade is increasingly settled in non-USD currencies, and the US's share of foreign exchange reserves has diminished over the past decade.[19] Beijing also claims that the 2023 Iranian-Saudi rapprochement it helped broker is evidence of GSI success.[20] Finally, China's success in blocking debate of its human rights abuses in Xinjiang within the UN Human Rights Council in 2022—marking only the second time in the Council's history that it has voted against holding a debate[21]—could be understood as a victory for the GCI.

Translating these successes into meaningful support for systemic change, however, has been difficult. The BRI has encountered growing skepticism as many countries have expressed wariness of these projects: they do not pay off economically;[22] they engender new environmental, labor, and even criminal activities;[23] and they crowd out host countries' nascent industries.[24] Some countries choose instead to actively pursue investment by US, Japanese, and EU companies rather than China. A study of global media reports on the BRI revealed that while there is significant variation in sentiment across regions, overall sentiment toward the BRI deteriorated across all regions during 2017–2022.[25] China has also not managed to effect a global consensus to move away from the dollar, although its actions have contributed to the erosion of its use around the margins. In addition, the primary objectives of the GSI remain unrealized; during 2022–2024, the US-led alliance system deepened rather than weakened through the addition of two new members in NATO and the establishment of the AUKUS security arrangement between Australia, the UK, and the US. Moreover, the lopsided February 2023 vote in the United Nations to condemn Russia's invasion of Ukraine was a clear rebuke of the GSI's principle of indivisible security.[26] China's notion of system diversity has similarly not manifested in a shift within the international community toward acceptance of state-determined human rights. A 2022 Lowy Institute study revealed that there has been no significant shift in the number of countries aligning with China's human rights votes in the United Nations since 2015, despite Beijing's deepening engagement on these issues through its global initiatives.[27]

China has proved masterful at advancing its political, economic, and security interests within the confines of the current international system. However, its ability to reshape current international norms and institutions in new ways is less compelling. And, as the discussion below suggests, even when the rules of the road are not clearly defined—as in ocean, space, and Arctic governance—China's success emerges not in writing those rules but in benefiting its own narrow economic and security interests.

China's Stake in the Great Unknown

Chinese leaders have long recognized the strategic importance of frontier domains: oceans, polar, and outer space. As early as 1957, after the Soviet launch of Sputnik, Mao Zedong declared that China would also launch satellites as a means of maintaining pace with the great powers.[28] In 2000, Jiang Zemin raised the prospect of China becoming a "maritime great power."[29] And Hu Jintao not only mentioned the importance of developing Chinese economic and military capabilities for securing Chinese interests in the maritime and space domains[30] but also worked to raise China's status in the Arctic.[31] Unlike his predecessors, however, Xi Jinping has a vision to assert Chinese leadership.[32] Speaking on the topic of global governance before an audience of Chinese academicians in 2014, Xi stated, "We can play a major role in the construction of the playgrounds even at the beginning, so that we can make rules for new games."[33]

Beneath the Deep Blue Sea

"The deep sea contains treasures that remain undiscovered and undeveloped," stated Xi Jinping before an audience of Chinese scientists in 2016, "and in order to obtain these treasures, we have to control key technologies in getting into the deep sea, discovering the deep sea, and developing the deep sea."[34] Xi intends for China to lead in the exploration and exploitation of the seabed, which contains significant reserves of the oil, gas, cobalt, copper, nickel, and rare earth elements that are essential to his technological, economic, and national security ambitions.

As early as the late 1980s, China started working on applications for exploration, and in 1990, it established the state-controlled China Ocean Mineral Resources Research and Development Association (COMRA), which authorizes the prospecting and mining of the seabed in international waters. In 1996, China acceded to the United Nations Convention on the Law of the Sea (UNCLOS) and became party to the International Seabed Authority (ISA)—which is responsible for governance of deep-sea resources outside national jurisdictions. In 2001, COMRA signed its first contract with the ISA.[35] Xi further enhanced China's commitment by enacting the 2016 Deep Seabed Law,[36] prioritizing seabed mining and deep-sea equipment manufacturing in China's five-year plans, and conducting extensive research and exploration missions.[37]

China has also become one of the most powerful players in the ISA. It is the largest funder of the organization, and its officials lead and participate in ISA bodies at a high rate to try to ensure that Beijing's views are reflected in deep-sea mining codes, environmental standards, and financial frameworks for resource exploitation. In partnership with the ISA, Beijing also established a Joint Training and Research Center (JTRC) in Qingdao, where it provides free training opportunities for developing countries;[38] and in June 2024, China hosted the ISA secretary-general for a five-day visit to discuss draft regulations for the exploitation of seabed minerals, meet with Chinese seabed mining companies, and deliver a keynote address at a symposium.[39] As a result of China's commitment, its companies now hold more deep-sea mining permits than any other country[40] and cover the largest geographical area—approximately the size of the United Kingdom.[41]

China's participation within the ISA is not without controversy, however. There are concerns over China's influence, its weak environmental standards, and its revenue-sharing approach. Smaller island nations and some Western countries have expressed concern that China is using its economic and diplomatic leverage to dominate ISA policymaking and seabed mining. In addition, Germany, Costa Rica, and the Pacific island states have pushed back against China's efforts to implement weak environmental standards. China opposes legally binding environmental protections before mining begins[42] and any stand-alone inspection regime.[43] In 2023, it blocked discussion of an agenda item at the ISA Assembly meeting put forth by Chile, Costa Rica, France, Palau, and Vanuatu to hold a discussion on the protection of the environment, including a pause on deep-sea mining.[44] Moreover, China, along with Russia and India, has advocated for mining nations to keep a larger percentage of the profits from the mining and to lower mining company fees, on the grounds that high fees will discourage investment in seabed mining projects. Other countries, such as Brazil and South Africa, have pushed for a stronger revenue-sharing system. (This resistance from Brazil and South Africa may have contributed to China's announcement in October 2024 that it would create a BRICS Deep Sea Resources International Center.)[45]

The United States has a limited voice in these deliberations; it is not party to UNCLOS and thus cannot participate in ISA negotiations. However, US officials have raised concerns about the military applications of China's deep-sea activities. Chinese military strategists have identified the deep seabed as a future warfare domain, noting the potential for a "military struggle in the deep sea."[46] As retired US Navy captain and former US Pacific Fleet director of intelligence James Fanell stated in an interview: "The PRC's deep seabed survey operations have two purposes. One, and the one most publicized, is to find and exploit natural resources and the other is to collect oceanographic data for the Chinese Communist Party's strategic goal of expanding the geographic area and lethality of the

People's Liberation Army (PLA) Navy's blue-water submarine force." In 2021, a China Minmetals research vessel took an unexplained detour from its exploration zone, spending five days in the waters near Hawaii, in the area of US military bases.[47] According to Fanell, the PLA Navy will gain access to a wealth of oceanographic data that will enable it to neutralize the US's longtime advantage of control over the undersea domain.[48]

The Final Frontier

Alongside the deep seabed and the Arctic, Xi Jinping views space as a relatively ungoverned and unregulated arena, where China can be at the forefront of scientific research, exploitation of resources, and national security. China's 2021 white paper on space opens with a quotation by Xi: "To explore the vast cosmos, develop the space industry, and build China into a space power is our eternal dream."[49]

Mao's call to launch a satellite in order to compete with the Soviet Union and United States precipitated a decades-long commitment to investing in a Chinese space program. In 2000, China published its first white paper, "China's Space Activities," which mapped out its plans to advance China's technological, commercial, and security priorities. Chinese scientist Ouyang Ziyuan argued that "China's long-term aim and task is to set up a base on the moon to tap and make use of its rich resources."[50] (The moon holds rare earth elements like platinum, titanium, scandium, and yttrium.) And by 2019, experts estimated the benefits of a Chinese "space economic zone" at $10 trillion.[51] More recently, China released a 25-year road map for space exploration, space station expansion, and space-related science with the goal of becoming a world leader in space science and technology by 2049.[52]

The 2021 white paper reinforced Xi's desire to become a leader in space governance. In 2017, together with Russia, China proposed an International Lunar Research Station (ILRS)—a base on the south pole of the moon—that would serve as an "expandable platform for scientific research and resource use" for the international community.[53] China has encouraged emerging and middle-income economies to join the ILRS, advancing the idea through regional organizations, such as the China-Community of Latin American and Caribbean States (CELAC), the Asia-Pacific Space Cooperation Organization (APSCO), and the Arab Union for Astronomy and Space Sciences (AUASS). As part of BRICS, China also launched the Joint Committee on Space Cooperation in May 2022. However, establishing space cooperation has been an uphill battle. Only 13 countries have signed on to the ILRS, and several of those, such as Azerbaijan, Belarus, Pakistan, and Venezuela have no space program or only a nascent one.[54] In contrast, the US-led

Artemis Accords for space exploration, introduced in 2020, have attracted 53 states as signatories. Notably, many are emerging and middle-income economies such as Ecuador, India, Mexico, Nigeria, Panama, Peru, and Uruguay.[55] The Artemis Accords are rooted in principles such as transparency, interoperability, scientific data-sharing, and peaceful use. Analysts assert that China's challenge in attracting countries may be due to its lack of transparency—it has not made public the terms of participation in ILRS—as well as others' fears that China will dominate in the decision-making.[56]

China's space-related military ambitions have also produced friction with other countries. For example, in December 2022, the United States sponsored a resolution in the UN that called for a moratorium on tests of direct ascent anti-satellite weapons. The final vote—155 for, 9 against, and 9 abstentions—overwhelmingly supported the US position. (China and Russia both voted against the resolution.)[57] The militarization of China's space program—245 of its 700 satellites are for military purposes—has also cost the nation in other ways. In 2020, the Sweden Space Corporation announced that it would no longer renew contracts for Chinese access to its ground stations within Sweden, Australia, and Chile.[58]

A Strategic Melt

The road forward for China to shape Arctic governance is more challenging than for the deep seabed or space. Unlike in those domains, China does not have a seat at the Arctic decision-making table—only states that border the Arctic, as well as representatives of the Indigenous peoples of the region, are part of the governing Arctic Council. That has not deterred China, however, from trying to influence the rules around exploration, exploitation, and security in the Arctic.

China already stands as a powerhouse center of Arctic research and leader in Arctic expeditions. It established the State Oceanic Administration (SOA) in 1964 with part of its mandate being to "engage in polar expeditions in the future."[59] Over the next decades, the SOA began to build its research capabilities: it created the Shanghai-based Polar Research Institute of China with a staff of over 200 to serve as the country's command post for international collaborative research; constructed research stations in Norway, Iceland, and Finland; joined the International Arctic Science Committee (as of 2025, there were two or more Chinese officials or scholars in every one of the Committee's working groups);[60] and invested heavily in cutting-edge equipment for surveying and monitoring, including three nuclear-powered icebreakers, which allow for year-round exploration and travel. (The United States has none.)

In 2018, China published its first Arctic white paper, which claimed that non-Arctic nations, including China, have rights in the region.[61] This assertion was both a recognition of China's multi-decade march to insinuate itself into the process of Arctic governance, as well as a declaration that China would continue to push for the right to shape how the spoils of the region were protected, distributed, and utilized. Like the seabed, the Arctic is rich in mineral resources (as well as fish and hydrocarbons) and provides a geography that offers claimant states opportunities to advance their military security priorities. Since 2012, Beijing has embarked on an aggressive investment spree in the region: mining projects and airports in Greenland; natural gas, mining, railroad, and ports in Russia; and energy projects in Iceland.[62] And already Chinese companies have become among the most frequent users of the Northern Sea Route—accounting for approximately 30% of trips—primarily bringing oil and gas to Chinese markets from Russia.[63] Still Sweden, Denmark, and Iceland have all rejected high-profile potential Chinese investments over national security concerns.[64]

China has also staked out a strong national security imperative in the Arctic, describing the region as the "new commanding heights of global military competition."[65] *The Science of Military Strategy*, a 2020 textbook published by the Chinese National Defense University, emphasizes that "military-civilian mixing is the main way for great powers to achieve a polar military presence" and urged the government to "leverage military forces in supporting polar scientific research and other operations."[66] There is a satellite receiver station in Norway, for example, that provides access for the operation of China's BeiDou Satellite system, which enables Chinese military and cyber communications and could be used to guide strike weapons and other operations.[67] Beijing has also taken advantage of its close ties with Russia to begin to realize its military ambitions in the Arctic. In July 2024, Chinese and Russian long-range bombers patrolled the Arctic Ocean near Alaska, and in October 2024, the two countries' coast guards undertook their first joint patrol in the Northern Sea Route.[68]

China's leaders assert that China is a near-Arctic or polar power[69] and desire an Arctic governance framework that grants them rights. Chinese researchers have suggested that climate change and the melting of the Arctic have made the region a global commons issue necessitating China's engagement.[70] Others have proposed that the absence of a dedicated Arctic treaty offers China the opportunity to assert influence by "filling the white parts" of the normative framework with principles aligned to Chinese interests.[71] And Shanghai Institutes for International Studies scholar Cheng Baozhi has argued more straightforwardly: "It is unimaginable that non-Arctic states will remain users of Arctic shipping routes and consumers of Arctic energy without playing a role in the decision-making process, and an end to the Arctic States' monopoly of Arctic affairs is now imperative."[72] To date, these arguments have not opened the door to direct Chinese participation in Arctic governance. Moreover, while China has expanded its economic and security footprint through partnerships with Arctic Council countries, the United States and other Arctic Council members have begun to develop new investment screening and research guidelines that will likely make it more difficult for China to make further progress in these areas.[73]

The US Response

The United States has developed neither a coherent vision for a revitalized international system nor a consistent strategy to meet the challenge China presents to that system. Instead, it has veered wildly from a Biden administration that largely prioritized US primacy and defense of the status quo to a Trump administration that is itself challenging the system and seeking to reduce its global footprint.

The Biden administration's global vision reflected traditional foreign policy values and international arrangements. It advocated for democracy and human rights as underpinnings for a stable and just international order and working with allies and partners in the United Nations to try to hold China to account for its domestic human rights abuses. (Yet it also lost credibility internationally with its unwillingness to more directly criticize and punish Israel for its human rights abuses in Gaza.) The Biden administration maintained and bolstered US military partnerships in the Indo-Pacific through AUKUS and minilateral defense arrangements and helped welcome two new countries—Finland and Sweden—into NATO. Yet it failed to deter or quickly resolve Russia's invasion of Ukraine or the Israeli-Palestinian conflict. The Biden administration also failed to advance a clear strategy for trade or continued dollar dominance, although it built new arrangements around technology, economics, and defense, such as the US-EU Trade and Technology Council (TTC) and the Indo-Pacific Economic Framework for Prosperity (IPEF). And while its position as a leader in space governance was extended, it did not make much headway in advancing a long-term, competitive Arctic strategy or joining UNCLOS to earn a seat in the negotiations over the deep seabed.

The Trump administration, in contrast, downplays the value of democracy, alliances, and international institutions, while elevating US economic and security interests. It withdrew the United States from the United Nations Human Rights

Council (UNHRC) and eliminated the US Agency for International Development (USAID), which supported democracy promotion, as well as small-scale economic development programs, and humanitarian assistance globally. Uncertainty surrounds the US global security commitments to NATO and its Asian allies. President Trump has threatened to withdraw from NATO, although others in his administration have been vocal in their support of traditional US-led military alliances.[74] In addition, the president's global tariffs, levied on April 2, 2025, have undermined the United States' standing as a reliable trade and investment partner and signaled an overall devaluing of allies and partners. The Trump administration has yet to articulate a strategy for governance of the seabed, Arctic, and space. However, its focus on securing access to critical minerals for its technological and military needs (including its radical suggestion to purchase Greenland), as well as its support for a domestic shipbuilding industry, and first-term emphasis on competition in space and the Arctic suggest that the Trump administration will continue to press for US leadership in defining the rules in both domains.

Conclusion

Chinese leader Xi Jinping has advanced a vision of an international order premised on Chinese values, norms, and interests. It reflects the transformation of the current international system from unipolar to multipolar, from dollar-dominated to multi-currency, from US alliances to common security, and from universal values to system diversity. Xi also envisions China as the rule-setter for the world's frontier regions, where he perceives significant economic and security benefits. Xi's strategy is straightforward. He outlines the challenges before the world and provides a benign-sounding and broadly appealing framing for proposed solutions. He invests significantly in China's domestic expertise and capabilities to promote Chinese leadership, deploys significant human and financial capital to international organizations and other stakeholders to create a sense of alignment with accepted norms and values, and uses multilateral arrangements and organizations to advance China's preferences.

The Trump administration's early policy moves present both new opportunities and challenges to China in the latter's efforts to reshape global norms. If the United States no longer advocates for universal human rights, China's push for system diversity will gain greater salience; if the US unilaterally withdraws from NATO and weakens its alliances in Asia, China's GSI will have accomplished its primary objective; and if the Trump administration's tariffs are not resolved quickly, de-dollarization of the global economy will certainly accelerate. To date, China has succeeded primarily in advancing its own political, economic, and security interests within current international norms and rules. It has not managed to realize its larger objectives of transforming the international system to reflect its values and interests. However, the Trump administration initiatives, if left unmoderated, may provide China the keys to the castle of global leadership.

NOTES

1. Ministry of Foreign Affairs of the People's Republic of China, *China's Position Paper on the New Security Concept*, August 6, 2002, https://www.mfa.gov.cn/eng/wjb /zzjg_663340/gjs_665170/gjzzyhy_665174/2612_665212/2614_665216/202406 /t20240606_11404682.html.

2. Suisheng Zhao, "Chinese Nationalism and Its International Orientations," *Political Science Quarterly* 115, no. 1 (Spring 2000): 1–33, https://doi.org/10.2307/2658031.

3. Zhao, "Chinese Nationalism and Its International Orientations."

4. Institute of International and European Affairs, "Professor Hu Angang on China in 2030," YouTube video, May 12, 2012, https://www.youtube.com/watch?v=nTZrTddiISY.

5. Tania Branigan, "China Calls for End to Dollar's Reign as Global Reserve Currency," *The Guardian*, March 24, 2009, https://www.theguardian.com/business/2009/mar /24/china-reform-international-monetary-system.

6. Alicja Bachulska et al., *The Idea of China: Chinese Thinkers on Power, Progress, and People* (European Council on Foreign Relations, 2024), 28, https://ecfr.eu/publication /idea-of-china/.

7. "習近平：「東升西降」鮮明對比 面對圍堵打壓應理直氣壯鬥爭," *Sing Tao*, January 3, 2025, https://std.stheadline.com/realtime/article/2044891.

8. Tanner Greer, "Xi Jinping in Translation: China's Guiding Ideology," *Palladium Magazine*, May 31, 2019, https://www.palladiummag.com/2019/05/31/xi-jinping-in -translation-chinas-guiding-ideology/.

9. Xiaodong Chen, "Jointly Acting on the Global Security Initiative and Building a Community with a Shared Future for Mankind That Enjoys Universal Security," Speech presented at the 11th Beijing Xiangshan Forum, Beijing, China, September 15, 2024, Ministry of Foreign Affairs of the People's Republic of China, https://www.fmprc.gov.cn /eng/wjb/zzjg_663340/swaqsws_665306/xgxw/202409/t20240915_11491406.html.

10. Robert Greene, "The Difficult Realities of the BRICS' Dedollarization Efforts— and the Renminbi's Role," Carnegie Endowment for International Peace, December 5, 2023, https://carnegieendowment.org/research/2023/12/the-difficult-realities-of-the -brics-dedollarization-effortsand-the-renminbis-role?lang=en.

11. Xinhua Institute, *The Practical Achievements and Global Contributions of the Global Development Initiative*, October 18, 2023, https://english.news.cn/20230920/2a3237e2b9 a04e61b14d245f26e73c89/d5135b8a244a4e269121535a85af6817 _%E3%80%90dingbandaifengmian-yingwen%E3%80%91GDIbaogao.pdf.

12. Xinhua Institute, *The Practical Achievements and Global Contributions of the Global Development Initiative*.

13. Ministry of Foreign Affairs of the People's Republic of China, "Xi Jinping Delivers a Keynote Speech presented at the Opening Ceremony of the Boao Forum for Asia Annual Conference, 2022," April 21, 2022, https://www.mfa.gov.cn/eng/zy/jj /2020zt/kjgzbdfyyq/202204/t20220421_10671083.html.

14. Gang Qin, "Forging Ahead on the New Journey Toward a Community with a Shared Future for Mankind," Speech presented at the China Development Forum 2023, Beijing, China, March 27, 2023, http://mv.china-embassy.gov.cn/eng/zgyw/202303 /t20230329_11051025.htm.

15. Chen, "Jointly Acting on the Global Security Initiative and Building a Community with a Shared Future for Mankind that Enjoys Universal Security."

16. Daniel F. Runde et al., "Responding to China's Growing Influence in Ports of the Global South," Center for Strategic and International Studies, October 30, 2024, https://www.csis.org/analysis/responding-chinas-growing-influence-ports-global-south.

17. Sarina Patterson, "The BRI at 10: A Report Card from the Global South," *AidData Blog*, March 26, 2024, https://www.aiddata.org/blog/the-bri-at-10-a-report-card -from-the-global-south.

18. Robert Greene, "China's Dollar Dilemma," Carnegie Endowment for International Peace, October 3, 2024, https://carnegieendowment.org/research/2024/10/chinas -dollar-dilemma?lang=en.

19. "De-Dollarization: Is the US Dollar Losing Its Dominance?" J.P. Morgan, October 8, 2024, https://www.jpmorgan.com/insights/global-research/currencies/de-dollarization.

20. Amrita Jash, "Saudi-Iran Deal: A Test Case of China's Role as an International Mediator," *Georgetown Journal of International Affairs*, June 23, 2023, https://gjia .georgetown.edu/2023/06/23/saudi-iran-deal-a-test-case-of-chinas-role-as-an -international-mediator/.

21. Emma Farge, "UN Body Rejects Debate on China's Treatment of Uyghur Muslims in Blow to West," *Reuters*, October 6, 2022, https://www.reuters.com/world /china/un-body-rejects-historic-debate-chinas-human-rights-record-2022-10-06/.

22. "How Is the Belt and Road Initiative Advancing China's Interests?," *ChinaPower*, Center for Strategic and International Studies, https://chinapower.csis.org/china-belt -and-road-initiative/.

23. Paul Antonopoulos, "Growing Concerns Around Chinese Investments in European Seaports, Especially Piraeus," *Greek City Times*, August 31, 2024, https:// greekcitytimes.com/2024/08/31/concerns-chinese-investment-piraeus/.

24. Xue Gong, "The Challenges Behind China's Global South Policies," Carnegie China, December 11, 2024, https://carnegieendowment.org/posts/2024/12/the -challenges-behind-chinas-global-south-policies?lang=en.

25. Alicia García-Herrero and Robin Schindowski, "Global Trends in Countries' Perceptions of the Belt and Road Initiative," Bruegel, April 25, 2023, https://www.bruegel .org/working-paper/global-trends-countries-perceptions-belt-and-road-initiative.

26. "UN General Assembly Calls for Immediate End to War in Ukraine," *UN News*, United Nations, February 23, 2023, https://news.un.org/en/story/2023/02/1133847.

27. Courtney J. Fung and Shing-hon Lam, "Mixed Report Card: China's Influence at the United Nations," Lowy Institute, December 18, 2022, https://www.lowyinstitute.org /publications/mixed-report-card-china-s-influence-united-nations.

28. "China's Long March into Space," China National Space Administration, April 26, 2016, https://www.cnsa.gov.cn/english/n6465652/n6465653/c6480475/content.html.

29. Andrew Chubb, "Xi Jinping and China's Maritime Policy," Brookings, January 22, 2019, https://www.brookings.edu/articles/xi-jinping-and-chinas-maritime-policy/.

30. "Full Text of Hu's Report at 18th Party Congress," *China Daily,* November 18, 2012, https://www.chinadaily.com.cn/china/19thcpcnationalcongress/2012-11/18/content_29578562_4.htm.

31. Kevin Rudd, "Continuity and Change in Chinese Worldviews: An Historical Survey," in *On Xi Jinping: How Xi's Marxist Nationalism Is Shaping China and the World,* (Oxford University Press, 2024), 77–80.

32. Camilla T. N. Sorensen, "The Polar Regions as New Strategic Frontiers for China," in *Mapping China's Strategic Space,* ed. Nadège Rolland, NBR Special Report no. 111, September 12, 2024, https://strategicspace.nbr.org/the-polar-regions-as-new-strategic-frontiers-for-china/.

33. Xi Jinping, *The Governance of China* (Foreign Languages Press, 2014), 135–136.

34. Alexander B. Gray, "The Deep Seabed Is China's Next Target," American Foreign Policy Council, July 15, 2021, https://www.afpc.org/publications/articles/the-deep-seabed-is-chinas-next-target.

35. Wang Yan, "China's Deep-Sea Mining, a View from the Top," Dialogue Earth, October 18, 2019, https://dialogue.earth/en/ocean/10891-china-deep-sea-exploration-comra/.

36. Chelsea Zhaoxi Chen, "China's Domestic Law on the Exploration and Development of Resources in Deep Seabed Areas," in chapter 15 *The Law of the Seabed* (Brill, 2020), 335–370, https://doi.org/10.1163/9789004391567_017.

37. Xinhua, "China's Submersible and Research Vessels Fine-Tuned for Future Deep-Sea Missions," Xinhuanet, February 2, 2025, https://english.news.cn/20250202/2c9aa8468efb44b1add4110a85f88bd3/c.html.

38. Yan, "China's Deep-Sea Mining, a View from the Top."

39. International Seabed Authority, "ISA Secretary-General Concludes High-Level Visit to China Resulting in Renewed Cooperation in Support of the Mandate of ISA and the Implementation of Its Global Deep-Sea Research Agenda," June 7, 2024, https://www.isa.org.jm/news/isa-secretary-general-concludes-high-level-visit-to-china/.

40. Anna Fleck, "Who's Leading the Race to Mine the Deep Sea?," Statista, March 27, 2024, https://www.statista.com/chart/31999/where-isa-contractors-for-deep-sea-mining-are-based/.

41. Lily Kuo, "China Is Set to Dominate the Deep Sea and Its Wealth of Rare Metals," *The Washington Post,* October 19, 2023, https://www.washingtonpost.com/world/interactive/2023/china-deep-sea-mining-military-renewable-energy/.

42. Angus Soderberg, "Drilling Deep on Chinese Deep-Sea Mining," American Security Project, January 25, 2023, https://www.americansecurityproject.org/drilling-deep-on-chinese-deep-sea-mining/?utm_source=chatgpt.com.

43. Regina Lam, "China's Push into Deep-Sea Mining Gathers Speed." Dialogue Earth, August 5, 2024, https://dialogue.earth/en/ocean/chinas-push-into-deep-sea-mining-gathers-speed.

44. Sabrina Skelly, "Wins and Outcomes of July Meetings at the International Seabed Authority," Sustainable Ocean Alliance, August 9, 2023, https://www.soalliance .org/soablog/recap-isa-july-23.

45. The State Council Information Office of the People's Republic of China, "Full Text: Address by Chinese President Xi Jinping at the 16th BRICS Summit," October 24, 2024, https://english.www.gov.cn/news/202410/24/content _WS67196533c6d0868f4e8ec3b9.html.

46. Gray, "The Deep Seabed Is China's Next Target."

47. Kuo, "China Is Set to Dominate the Deep Sea and Its Wealth of Rare Metals."

48. Gray, "The Deep Seabed is China's Next Target."

49. The State Council Information Office of the People's Republic of China, "Full Text: China's Space Program: A 2021 Perspective," January 28, 2022, https://english.www .gov.cn/archive/whitepaper/202201/28/content_WS61f35b3dc6d09c94e48a467a.html.

50. Namrata Goswami, "The Strategic Implications of the China-Russia Lunar Base Cooperation Agreement," *The Diplomat*, March 19, 2021, https://thediplomat.com/2021 /03/the-strategic-implications-of-the-china-russia-lunar-base-cooperation-agreement/.

51. Andrew Jones, "From a Farside First to Cislunar Dominance? China Appears to Want to Establish 'Space Economic Zone' Worth Trillions," *SpaceNews*, February 15, 2020, https://spacenews.com/from-a-farside-first-to-cislunar-dominance-china-appears -to-want-to-establish-space-economic-zone-worth-trillions/.

52. Na Chen, "China Releases Space Science Development Program for 2024– 2025," Chinese Academy of Sciences, October 15, 2024, https://english.cas.cn /newsroom/cas_media/202410/t20241015_691782.shtml.

53. Andrew Jones, "China Adds New Moon Base Project Partners, but Struggles to Attract National-Level Participation," *SpaceNews*, March 28, 2024, https://spacenews .com/china-adds-new-moon-base-project-partners-but-struggles-to-attract-national-level -participation/.

54. Jones, "China Adds New Moon Base Project Partners, but Struggles to Attract National-Level Participation."

55. "The Artemis Accords," NASA, https://www.nasa.gov/artemis-accords/.

56. Güneş Ünüvar and Xueji Su, "International Legal Governance of Space Resources and the Role of National Frameworks: The Case of China," *Chinese Journal of International Law* 23, no. 3, (September 2024), 499–545, https://doi.org/10.1093 /chinesejil/jmae024.

57. Laura Delgado López, "BRICS+ from Above: Why the Space Dimension of the Expanded Alliance Matters," CSIS, October 2, 2023, https://www.csis.org/analysis/brics -above-why-space-dimension-expanded-alliance-matters.

58. Jonathan Barrett and Johan Ahlander, "Exclusive: Swedish Space Company Halts New Business Helping China Operate Satellites," *Reuters*, September 21, 2020, https://www.reuters.com/article/world/exclusive-swedish-space-company-halts-new -business-helping-china-operate-satell-idUSKCN26C1ZS/.

59. Ties Dams et al., "Presence Before Power: China's Arctic Strategy in Iceland and Greenland," *Clingendael Report*, June 2020, https://www.clingendael.org/pub/2020 /presence-before-power/2-presence-before-power-why-china-became-a-near-arctic-state/.

60. International Arctic Science Committee, "IASC Working Groups," https://iasc .info/our-work/working-groups.

61. The State Council Information Office of the People's Republic of China, "Full Text: China's Arctic Policy," January 26, 2018, https://english.www.gov.cn/archive /white_paper/2018/01/26/content_281476026660336.htm.

62. House Committee on Foreign Affairs, "China Regional Snapshot: Arctic," October 25, 2022, https://foreignaffairs.house.gov/china-regional-snapshot-arctic/.

63. Tiago Tecelão Martins, "Arctic Ambitions: China's Engagement with the Northern Sea Route," *The Diplomat*, November 24, 2023, https://thediplomat.com/2023 /11/arctic-ambitions-chinas-engagement-with-the-northern-sea-route/.

64. Marc Lanteigne, "Greenland's Airports: A Balance Between China and Denmark?," *Over the Circle*, June 5, 2018, https://overthecircle.com/2018/06/15 /greenlands-airports-a-balance-between-china-and-denmark/; Omar Valdimarsson, "Iceland Rejects Land Deal with Chinese Tycoon," *Reuters*, November 25, 2011, https://www.reuters.com/article/business/iceland-rejects-land-deal-with-chinese-tycoon -idUSL5E7MP21G/.

65. Rush Doshi et al., *Northern Expedition: China's Arctic Activities and Ambitions*, Brookings, April 2021, https://www.brookings.edu/wp-content/uploads/2021/04/FP _20210419_china_arctic_handout.pdf.

66. Anne-Marie Brady, "Facing Up to China's Military Interests in the Arctic," *China Brief* 19, no. 21 (December 10, 2019), https://jamestown.org/program/facing-up-to -chinas-military-interests-in-the-arctic/.

67. Brady, "Facing Up to China's Military Interests in the Arctic."

68. Michael Paul, "China's Arctic Turn," Stiftung Wissenschaft und Politik (SWP), Comment 2025/C 08 (February 13, 2025), https://www.swp-berlin.org/10.18449 /2025C08/.

69. Bonnie S. Glaser and Elizabeth Buchanan, *China Global*, podcast, episode 21, "China in the Arctic: Ambitions and Strategy," GMF, March 8, 2022, https://www .gmfus.org/news/china-arctic-ambitions-and-strategy.

70. Stephanie Pezard et al., *China's Strategy and Activities in the Arctic*, RAND, December 23, 2022, https://www.rand.org/content/dam/rand/pubs/research_reports /RRA1200/RRA1282-1-v2/RAND_RRA1282-1-v2.pdf.

71. Matti Puranen and Sanna Kopra, "China's Arctic Strategy—a Comprehensive Approach in Times of Great Power Rivalry," *Scandinavian Journal of Military Studies*, (December 26, 2023), https://sjms.nu/articles/10.31374/sjms.196.

72. Cheng Baozhi, "Arctic Aspiration," *Beijing Review*, no. 34 (August 22, 2011), http://www.bjreview.com.cn/world/txt/2011-08/22/content_385386_2.htm.

73. Didi Kirsten Tatlow, "China's Arctic Presence Worries US Ahead of Trump's Return," *Newsweek*, January 8, 2025, https://www.newsweek.com/us-diplomats -strongly-concerned-about-china-science-arctic-2011527.

74. Kawala Xie, "Trump Security Pick Waltz Pledges China Strategy That Reinforces Indo-Pacific Ties," *South China Morning Post*, January 15, 2025, https://www.scmp .com/news/china/diplomacy/article/3294804/trumps-security-pick-pledges-china -strategy-reinforces-indo-pacific-ties.

Chapter Fifteen

Great Changes

Xi, Trump, and the Remaking of Global Order

Jude Blanchette

Throughout history, significant shifts in national governance and domestic politics have propelled great changes in the structure of the international system, from the rise of competing imperial systems in the 19th century to the post–World War II emergence of American hegemony following the New Deal transformations. Currently, significant and potentially enduring political transformations occurring within the United States under President Donald Trump and in China under General Secretary Xi Jinping are reshaping not only domestic politics and institutions but also helping to accelerate the collapse of the post–Cold War international order.

Under Donald Trump's leadership, the United States has witnessed significant domestic change characterized not only by his own leadership style but also by fundamental institutional recalibrations: the adoption of populist governance challenging establishment elites, the systematic disruption of bureaucratic autonomy, the realignment of party coalitions along educational and cultural divides, and the dismantling of administrative and legal norms in favor of personalized executive authority.[1] This internal reconfiguration has directly shaped his "Amer-

Jude Blanchette is the Distinguished Tang Chair in China Research and the inaugural director of the RAND China Research Center. Previously, he held the Freeman Chair in China Studies at the Center for Strategic and International Studies and served as engagement director at the Conference Board's China Center for Economics and Business in Beijing.

ica First" foreign policy doctrine, which represents a distinct revisionist vision challenging the liberal internationalist order that the United States itself largely constructed since World War II. Trump's approach to international affairs rejects multilateralism in favor of bilateral deal-making, prioritizes short-term transactional gains over long-term institutional investments, and views global relations primarily through the lens of zero-sum competition rather than positive-sum cooperation. Trump's domestic vision of strong executive power unconstrained by institutional checks directly translates to his foreign affairs approach, where he seeks to liberate American action from multilateral constraints, treats international organizations as impediments rather than enablers of American influence, and applies the same transactional approach to diplomatic relationships. Just as his domestic approach prioritizes loyalty and personal relationships over established processes, his international strategy elevates direct leader-to-leader engagement over traditional diplomatic channels, reflecting his fundamental belief that both domestic governance and world affairs are best managed through strongman politics rather than rules-based systems.

Similarly, since assuming power in late 2012, Chinese leader Xi Jinping has overseen a profound shift in China's overall trajectory that extends far beyond his individual leadership preferences. This transformation encompasses a comprehensive expansion of the powers of the Communist Party, a restructuring of party-state relations, a recalibration of center-periphery dynamics strengthening Beijing's Leninist control over far-flung localities, fundamental shifts in elite recruitment prioritizing loyalty over technocratic expertise, and the dismantling of succession norms that had institutionalized leadership transitions. In place of the decades-long pursuit of economic growth, Xi has prioritized political control, national security, and ideological conformity as the defining objectives of the Chinese state.[2] Xi's predecessors from Deng Xiaoping onward largely emphasized pragmatic economic growth and incremental global integration, whereas Xi has repositioned economic priorities within a broader framework of national rejuvenation that elevates Communist Party authority, technological self-reliance, and China's unquestioned standing as a comprehensive global power. This fundamental reordering of priorities represents not merely a tactical adjustment but a strategic recalibration that privileges regime security and international dominance over the wealth-maximization strategies that characterized the bulk of China's reform era.[3]

Xi's domestic vision of centralized party control and state-directed development directly shapes his approach to international affairs, where he seeks to establish

China as a rule-maker rather than a rule-taker in global governance, promotes the principles of sovereignty and non-interference to shield China's political model from external criticism, and advances a state-centric vision of international order that contrasts sharply with traditional (if now currently evolving) Western liberal norms. Just as his domestic governance emphasizes disciplined hierarchy and long-term planning, his foreign policy boldly pursues advantage through initiatives like Belt and Road and military modernization, reflecting his conviction that China's domestic stability and international ascendance are inseparable facets of the same national rejuvenation project.[4]

Despite fundamental differences in their respective political systems—with Trump presiding over a populist shift within a democratic framework and Xi overseeing authoritarian consolidation within a Leninist structure—their strategic approaches exhibit notable similarities, as both administrations prioritize economic self-reliance, employ economic coercion, demonstrate territorial assertiveness, and view "entangling alliances" skeptically. These internal transformations are accelerating the erosion of the post–Cold War international order through shared skepticism toward multilateralism and preference for bilateral dealmaking, directly contributing to a now-visible fracturing of the international system already under strain from a buckling global trading regime, Russia's shattering of taboos against territorial conquest in Europe, mounting legitimacy crises in multilateral institutions, technological fragmentation, and compounding disruptions from climate change, mass migration, and global pandemics—all creating a volatile context that amplifies the global consequences of governance transformations in Washington and Beijing.

These parallel domestic transformations create a paradoxical dynamic in the US-China competition: as each power pushes massive change at home and adopts increasingly assertive and revisionist international postures, they simultaneously introduce critical vulnerabilities into their own governance systems. Trump's distrust of institutionalized partnerships coupled with his undermining of unbiased expertise and counsel undermines America's traditional strategic advantages in diplomatic coordination and alliance management, while Xi's centralization of authority and ideological rigidity fuels international backlash and limits China's diplomatic and economic influence that have long given it significant global advantage. The resulting competition thus features two powers whose domestic transformations may be undercutting the very foundations of their prior international influence, suggesting that long-term strategic success may hinge not only on outmaneuvering the other but also on mitigating the self-imposed constraints of their current styles of governance.

Internal political shifts within major powers—whether rising, status quo, or declining—are both shaped by, and fundamentally reshape, the international landscape. These domestic reconfigurations often translate into profound foreign policy realignments that reverberate throughout the global system.[5]

The Bolshevik Revolution of 1917 transformed Russia from a traditional empire into the world's first revolutionary communist state, triggering not just a new ideological competition that would reverberate for 70 years but also fundamentally altering Western security calculations and eventually leading to a bipolar world order. This profound transformation within Russia had immediate international consequences. The Bolsheviks' withdrawal from World War I through the Treaty of Brest-Litovsk disrupted the Allied strategy and released German divisions for the Western Front. More significantly, Lenin's establishment of the Communist International (Comintern) in 1919 institutionalized revolutionary ideology as a component of Soviet foreign policy, creating a transnational movement dedicated to promoting similar domestic transformations around the globe.[6] Western responses were equally dramatic—from military interventions during the Russian Civil War to the diplomatic isolation of the Union of Soviet Socialist Republics throughout the 1920s and the formation of anti-communist alliances.

Similarly, Germany's internal collapse and the Nazi rise to power in the 1930s directly precipitated World War II. For Germany, the domestic political collapse manifested through hyperinflation, political violence, and democratic breakdown, which created conditions for Adolf Hitler's ascendance. The Nazi regime's subsequent reordering of German society—subordinating institutions to party control, militarizing the economy, and implementing a racial ideology that underpinned the Holocaust—directly shaped its revisionist international behavior. Hitler's repudiation of Versailles constraints, remilitarization of the Rhineland, and expansionist "Lebensraum" policy stemmed directly from internal political transformations.

These domestic revolutions produced lasting structural changes in the international system. Stalin's "socialism in one country" policy led to Soviet industrialization and military buildup that established the foundation for its emergence as a superpower after World War II. Meanwhile, the Nazi regime's regional aggression triggered a global conflict that accelerated imperial decline, particularly for Britain and France, whose domestic economic exhaustion and political transformations rendered their colonial empires unmanageable and unsustainable. The United States and Soviet Union, shaped by their distinctive internal political systems, emerged as competing architects of rival international orders—democratic capitalism versus state socialism—that would define global politics for nearly half a century.

Significant domestic political changes in the United States and China during the 20th century also contributed to a reordering of international politics.

In the US, the New Deal revolution established the foundation for America's postwar international leadership by creating both institutional capacity and ideological frameworks that shaped the liberal order. The expansion of federal authority through agencies like the Tennessee Valley Authority provided templates for postwar development programs including the Marshall Plan, while New Deal financial regulations informed the creation of global financial architecture at Bretton Woods in 1944. This transformation generated the administrative expertise needed for complex international commitments, with the Export-Import Bank exemplifying how domestic economic policy became linked to international engagement. Franklin D. Roosevelt's "Four Freedoms" speech and the Atlantic Charter explicitly connected domestic values to international principles, repositioning American exceptionalism toward global leadership.[7]

The institutional impact was significant—wartime mobilization leveraged New Deal administrative systems while producing a generation of officials versed in economic planning who subsequently designed the postwar order. Key figures like Dean Acheson and George Marshall, shaped by New Deal governance principles, helped created international institutions that essentially globalized American domestic governance approaches to address worldwide challenges.[8]

In China, Deng Xiaoping's ascension in the years following Mao Zedong's death in 1976 marked a pivotal domestic transformation with profound global impact. His "reform and opening up" policy reoriented China's international engagement while preserving Communist Party control. By decollectivizing agriculture, establishing special economic zones, and liberalizing trade, Deng and his leadership group created a development model that challenged Western assumptions about the necessary link between economic and political liberalization. This recalibration transformed the global economic order, with China eventually becoming the world's manufacturing powerhouse and fundamentally reshaping international supply chains while maintaining distinctive state-capitalist principles. Diplomatically, Deng's "hide your strength and bide your time" approach positioned China, for a time, as a participant in the existing order rather than a perceived challenger.[9] China integrated into institutions like the World Bank, International Monetary Fund, and World Trade Organization on its own terms—accepting certain economic norms while rejecting political ones that it felt undermined its domestic control and authority.

The historical patterns of domestic governance transformations reshaping international systems provide crucial context for understanding today's fracturing global order and the growing intensity of the US-China strategic competition. While previous cases—from the Bolshevik Revolution to the New Deal and the post-Mao reforms in China—demonstrate this dynamic, the contemporary parallel transformations of China under Xi Jinping and the United States under Donald Trump represent a particularly consequential inflection point in world politics. These simultaneous domestic reconfigurations in the world's two most powerful states are not merely coincidental but are mutually reinforcing drivers of systemic change.[10]

Xi Jinping's comprehensive remodeling of China's domestic governance system since 2012 represents perhaps the most significant departure from established patterns in Chinese politics since Deng's initial and piecemeal reforms. This internal transformation has fundamentally altered China's international posture and directly contributed to escalating strategic competition with the United States. Xi has methodically bent or broken the norms that bounded Chinese politics in the post-Mao era, systematically dismantling core elements of the political architecture established by Deng Xiaoping and subsequent leaders.[11] The predictable political calendar, retirement norms, succession planning, and informal agreements against targeting top officials have all been eroded or eliminated entirely.[12]

Xi's restructuring of China's political system has gone far beyond tactical maneuvers to consolidate personal authority. He has fundamentally altered how power operates within the Chinese Communist Party, replacing the relatively stable collective leadership model with a hyper-centralized and personalized system. The establishment of the Central National Security Commission (CNSC) signaled a profound expansion of the scope, scale, and capabilities of China's national security apparatus guided by his Overall National Security Outlook.[13]

Xi's governance revolution has fundamentally recalibrated China's economic model, subordinating development to political and security objectives. The formalized "new-style whole-country system" (新型举国体制) approach mobilizes national resources behind strategic priorities, as seen in the electric vehicle sector, where subsidies, tax incentives, and regulatory advantages created protected markets allowing Chinese companies to build scale domestically before targeting exports.[14] This transformation prioritizes technological self-reliance, industrial capacity, and strategic resilience over a long-standing fixation on economic growth, with national security now taking precedence over a narrower focus on GDP in Xi's vision of China's future. The resulting export-driven solution to domestic overcapacity directly externalizes China's internal economic contradictions, particularly in clean technology sectors where state-supported firms, having achieved technological competitiveness through government backing, aggressively pursue international markets. These patterns have generated trade tensions that reflect fundamental divergences between China's state-directed capitalism and market-based economic systems rather than mere commercial competition.

Xi's domestic political transformation has profoundly reshaped US-China relations over the past decade by exacerbating old structural tensions and creating new ones that transcend traditional diplomatic frictions. His centralization of power—dismantling collective leadership norms, establishing new security institutions like the CNSC, and expanding the party's disciplinary apparatus—has systematically eliminated moderating voices and institutional constraints that previously tempered aspects of Chinese foreign policy. Meanwhile, Xi's recalibration of China's economic model toward technological self-reliance and state-directed development has generated systemic trade tensions with the United States that reflect fundamental governance incompatibilities rather than mere commercial disputes.[15]

Compared to his predecessors, Xi's approach to foreign policy is more assertive and confident in projecting power globally, demonstrating less concern about creating friction with other nations. He has expanded China's diplomatic influence through a network of global partnerships, established alternative international institutions like the Asian Infrastructure Investment Bank, significantly increased military spending, and deepened strategic ties with countries that share grievances against the United States, particularly Russia. Xi's foreign policy is explicitly tied to his vision of "national rejuvenation," with China no longer focused on reassuring others about its peaceful rise but instead on accelerating toward becoming a central global power. This approach combines economic integration, military modernization, and ideological confidence, while accepting the reputational costs of increased domestic repression and nationalism.[16]

Just as Xi Jinping's domestic governance revolution has reshaped China's international posture, Donald Trump's time in the White House, beginning with his first term in 2017 and now accelerating in his second term, has ushered in a profound internal reconfiguration of American politics with far-reaching consequences for US-China relations and the international order. Trump and Trumpism represent not merely a clear shift in policy preferences but a fundamental challenge to long-standing governance norms that have undergirded American global leadership since 1945.[17]

Donald Trump's 2015–2016 presidential campaign emerged at a critical moment of economic and social disquiet, directly addressing deep-seated frustrations stemming from the 2008 global financial crisis and the perception of a "China shock." The dramatic surge in Chinese imports following China's World Trade Organization entry was seen by many as decimating manufacturing communities across America's industrial heartland and was believed to have caused significant job losses and wage depression in regions that felt abandoned by traditional political establishments. While subsequent research has questioned the conclusions of the original "China shock" research, the perception of trade as a destabilizing force for American families had already become near-consensus.[18] Trump's electoral strategy uniquely capitalized on these economic anxieties by breaking from previous candidates' pro-globalization consensus and explicitly linking trade policy to economic insecurity. His "America First" message, promising to confront China's trade practices and bring back manufacturing jobs, resonated strongly in swing states like Pennsylvania, Michigan, and Wisconsin. By directly addressing the economic wounds perceived to be inflicted by import competition, Trump transformed widespread regional discontent into a powerful political movement that successfully challenged existing long-standing political certainties.[19]

The "America First" foreign policy that emerged after Trump assumed office in January 2017 was fundamentally an extension of his domestic political ideology, rooted in a narrative of national revitalization and economic protectionism. His worldview cast the United States as a nation under siege—economically exploited by global competitors and undermined by international agreements that he believed sacrificed American workers' interests. This perspective transformed diplomacy into a zero-sum game, where international relationships were viewed primarily through the lens of immediate economic gains and a series of transactions that would yield better "deals" for the US. By challenging existing multilateral frameworks, Trump sought to reposition the United States as an unrestrained economic power, directly challenging the post–World War II liberal international order that had long been a cornerstone of American global leadership.

The practical manifestation of this approach was both radical and unprecedented in modern American foreign policy. Trump's administration systematically dismantled long-standing diplomatic conventions, imposing tariffs unilaterally, questioning the value of well-established alliances, and reframing international negotiations as purely transactional business deals. His withdrawal from critical multinational agreements like the Paris Climate Agreement and the Trans-Pacific Partnership was not merely a policy shift but was a symbolic repudiation of globalist approaches that he argued had weakened American economic sovereignty. By targeting not just economic rivals like China, but also traditional allies in NATO, Canada, Mexico, and the European Union, Trump signaled a fundamental reimagining of international engagement—one where national self-interest was paramount and multilateral compromise was viewed with deep skepticism.

Trump's domestic governance strategy was equally transformative, characterized by a systematic attempt to refashion the federal bureaucracy and implement economic nationalist policies. At the core of his approach was a radical reimagining of the administrative state, driven by a belief that entrenched bureaucratic institutions had become disconnected from the interests of working-class Americans. Since the start of Trump's second term, this initiative has intensified markedly. President Trump established the Department of Government Efficiency, led by Elon Musk, to spearhead aggressive cuts across the entirety of the federal government. These actions reflect a concerted effort to realign the administrative state with the administration's economic nationalist vision, emphasizing streamlined governance and a focus on traditional economic priorities.

President Donald Trump's recent foreign policy approach has been characterized by open hostility toward traditional alliances, strategic alignment with illiberal powers, and unprecedented territorial ambitions. His administration has severely damaged transatlantic relationships by imposing punitive tariffs on European allies and repeatedly questioning NATO's value, explicitly threatening to withhold defense commitments from members not meeting spending thresholds. Most controversially, Trump initially pursued a remarkable rapprochement with Russia, dismissing intelligence concerns about election interference while advocating for Russia's readmission to the G7 and scaling back sanctions imposed after the Ukraine invasion. Vice President J. D. Vance intensified these tensions through pointed criticism of European leadership for allegedly suppressing dissent and undermining democratic norms, while actively courting far-right parties including Germany's Alternative for Germany. Breaking with all diplomatic precedent, Trump aggressively pursued Greenland's annexation—offering financial incentives to residents while hinting at possible military action—provoking immediate and forceful objections from Greenlandic and Danish officials who condemn this as a clear violation of sovereignty. Simultaneously, his administration adopted an increasingly confrontational stance toward Canada, combining economic threats with provocative suggestions about Canadian statehood, driving Canadian leadership to seek alternative security partnerships and emphatically assert their national independence.

Similarly striking is Trump's aggressive use of trade policy as an instrument of economic restructuring. Tariffs became the primary weapon in his re-industrialization strategy, with particular focus on Chinese imports. The administration imposed unprecedented tariffs on Chinese goods, with rates escalating to as high as 25% on hundreds of billions of dollars' worth of imports. These tariffs were explicitly designed to challenge China's trade practices and create protective conditions for domestic manufacturing. In a significant escalation of his trade policy, President Trump announced on April 2, 2025, a series of sweeping tariffs during what he termed the "Liberation Day" speech. This new policy introduced a baseline 10% tariff on all imports, with substantially higher rates for specific countries—quickly reaching 145% on many Chinese goods. These measures were framed as a "declaration of economic independence," aiming to rectify perceived trade imbalances and bolster domestic manufacturing.

Unlike previous administrations' approach to trade, Trump's strategy is unabashedly interventionist and designed to smash the existing international trade order. He views economic policy through a mercantilist lens, believing that trade deficits were a direct measure of national economic weakness. The tariffs have been accompanied by a broader set of policies designed to incentivize domestic manufacturing, including tax breaks for companies that reshored production, regulatory rollbacks targeting environmental and labor regulations, and direct presidential interventions pressuring corporations to maintain or expand domestic manufacturing facilities. While it is too soon to evaluate their impact, what is clear is that they are designed to fragment the existing global trading system and, in its place, to create a more bilateral, transactional framework where American economic leverage can be maximized through one-on-one negotiations. This approach rejects multilateral institutions and rules-based trade in favor of a system where economic might dictates terms, national sovereignty over economic policy is reasserted, and the United States can selectively enforce its advantages without being constrained by global trade norms that Trump views as disadvantageous to American interests.

What, then, do these twin domestic political transformations in the US and China under Trump and Xi, and their resultant impact on the deteriorating international order, portend for the future of the US-China strategic competition? Building on the above analysis of the domestic changes ushered in by Donald Trump and Xi Jinping over the last decade, several tentative conclusions are offered here.

Donald Trump's presidency exemplified a dramatic departure from institutional foreign policy norms, notably through his unconventional diplomacy with North Korea's Kim Jong Un and his apparent disdain for traditional diplomatic preparations. Trump's preference for direct, personalized diplomacy echoes Xi Jinping's consolidation of foreign policy decision-making within a small, trusted inner circle. Xi's centralization of authority, meanwhile, mirrors Josef Stalin's emphasis on personal control, limiting the influence of professional bureaucratic expertise and raising the risk of miscalculation and misunderstanding due to insulated decision-making.

As leadership in Washington and Beijing grows increasingly personalist, bilateral relations become volatile, dependent heavily on individual leaders' temperaments, perceptions, and personal rapport. Rather than systemic, institutionally moderated conflicts, relations increasingly hinge on unpredictable and subjective elements of personal diplomacy. This personalization introduces capricious and unpredictable variables precisely when stability and predictability are critically necessary, potentially magnifying the risk of escalation during crises.

In the evolving strategic landscape, diplomatic breakthroughs and breakdowns will likely occur with diminished predictability and increased suddenness. Direct summit diplomacy will increasingly overshadow routine diplomatic exchanges, generating cycles of heightened expectations followed by abrupt disappointments. While this personalization occasionally yields surprising moments of cooperation when leaders find fleeting common ground, it also dangerously raises the stakes during tense periods, potentially bypassing established crisis management protocols. Without institutional safety nets, crises may rapidly escalate through impulsive or misjudged leader-to-leader interactions, echoing the perilous historical experiences under Stalin and Mao.

Additionally, both leaders are currently pursuing visions of "national rejuvenation" that extend domestic illiberalism into the international arena. While this has long been the case with Beijing, a world in which the United States disdains multilateralism, actively employs economic coercion, and threatens the territorial integrity of neighboring states signals a dangerous new phase in global politics. President Trump's explicit threats to annex territories such as Greenland and Canada exemplify this shift. The simultaneous embrace of illiberal approaches by the United States and China fundamentally reconfigures the strategic landscape of international relations, with profound implications for bilateral engagement and global governance. While the US and China continue to compete fiercely, their rivalry increasingly revolves around pure national interests rather than competing values or ideologies. The departure from established norms of international law creates a strategic environment that incentivizes opportunistic behavior by regional powers. By adopting a transactional approach to international relations—where territorial sovereignty and multilateral commitments are treated as negotiable—the United States inadvertently provides a strategic template that may embolden nations with expansionist ambitions.

Finally, the simultaneous pursuit of economic nationalist strategies by both China and the United States will continue to fundamentally reshape the global economic and technological landscape. As both powers pursue strategies to enhance economic security, seek to boost technological innovation, and strengthen the resilience of their domestic manufacturing capacity through an admixture of inducements, incentives, and coercion, they will further drive significant changes to global economic and technological governance and supply chains.

The competitive deployment of industrial policies will likely accelerate technological innovation in targeted sectors but may also create significant market distortions that undermine key, broader aspects of national competitiveness. China will continue to "steer" massive resources into strategic technologies like semiconductors, artificial intelligence, quantum computing, and clean energy. This investment surge will lead to global leadership or near-leadership in strategically vital sectors but also create overcapacity that will continue to aggravate trade and geopolitical tensions for Beijing. The US will likely remain less wedded to Chinese-style industrial policy and instead seek its own "steerage with Trumpian characteristics," through presidential arm-twisting to direct more corporate capital into key sectors, or at least industries that have political salience owing to their impact on Trump's base.

Intensified economic nationalism will further erode multilateral trade institutions and norms as both Xi and Trump pursue nakedly mercantilist and quasi-autarkic approaches to economic and trade governance. The World Trade Organization, already on life support, will be further marginalized as a mediator of inter-state disputes, not only between the US and China, but likely across the entire global landscape. Smaller economies will face growing pressure to align their regulatory frameworks with either the American or Chinese model, further fragmenting the global economic system into competing regulatory spheres. Regional trade agreements like the Regional Comprehensive Economic Partnership will continue to exist, and under China's influence, it may potentially expand as it seeks to further bind middle powers to its own economic might.

Ultimately, economic nationalism pursued simultaneously by the world's two largest economies carries significant risks. It could undermine global productivity growth, accelerate inflation, and reduce living standards by fragmenting efficient global supply chains. It may also increase international tensions by securitizing previously routine economic interactions. However, competition could drive innovation and create opportunities for third countries, if managed properly. The challenge will be finding limited areas for cooperation on global challenges even as competition intensifies in strategic sectors.

The irony of the current US-China strategic competition lies in how each power's domestic transformations may ultimately undermine their respective international ambitions. In China, Xi's centralization of authority and subordination of economic pragmatism to political control has delivered short-term stability but introduced profound vulnerabilities. The elimination of internal dissent and alternative viewpoints has created an echo chamber that constrains adaptive policymaking. Meanwhile, the reassertion of state control over the economy has dampened innovation and entrepreneurship—the very forces that powered China's meteoric rise. Xi's governance revolution has triggered unprecedented international backlash, culminating in coordinated Western responses from investment screening to export controls that threaten to limit China's access to the global innovation ecosystem it still requires for continued development.

Similarly, in the United States, the erosion of institutional norms and expertise under Trump has compromised America's traditional strategic advantages. The systematic dismantling of bureaucratic competence and policy consistency has undermined the credibility and effectiveness of US diplomacy. America's unilateral approach to international relations has weakened alliance structures that historically multiplied American power, while the embrace of economic nationalism has alienated partners whose cooperation remains essential for addressing transnational challenges. The abandonment of the rules-based order that the US itself constructed has inadvertently diminished American influence by removing the institutional architecture through which it exercised global leadership for decades.

The resulting competition thus increasingly resembles a contest between two powers whose domestic transformations may be undercutting the very foundations of their prior international influence. As the international system continues to evolve under these twin pressures, long-term strategic success will likely hinge not only on outmaneuvering the other but also on each power's ability to mitigate the self-imposed constraints of its own governance model—adapting domestic institutions to preserve the sources of national strength while navigating an increasingly complex and fragmented global landscape.

NOTES

1. Steven Levitsky and Lucan A. Way, "The Path to American Authoritarianism: What Comes After Democratic Breakdown," *Foreign Affairs*, February 11, 2025.

2. Kevin Rudd, *On Xi Jinping: How Xi's Marxist Nationalism Is Shaping China and the World* (Oxford University Press, 2024).

3. Carl Minzner, *End of an Era: How China's Authoritarian Revival Is Undermining Its Rise* (Oxford University Press, 2018).

4. Ryan Hass, "From Strategic Reassurance to Running Over Roadblocks: A Review of Xi's Foreign Policy Record," *China Leadership Monitor*, no. 73 (September 2022), https://www.prcleader.org/post/from-strategic-reassurance-to-running-over-roadblocks -a-review-of-xi-jinping-s-foreign-policy-recor.

5. Helen V. Milner, *Interests, Institutions, and Information: Domestic Politics and International Relations* (Princeton University Press, 1997).

6. Kevin McDermott and Jeremy Agnew, *The Comintern: A History of International Communism from Lenin to Stalin* (Bloomsbury Publishing, 1996).

7. Elizabeth Borgwardt, *A New Deal for the World: America's Vision for Human Rights* (Belknap Press of Harvard University Press, 2007).

8. David Ekbladh, *The Great American Mission: Modernization and the Construction of an American World Order* (Princeton University Press, 2011).

9. Ezra F. Vogel, *Deng Xiaoping and the Transformation of China* (Harvard University Press, 2011).

10. This chapter largely sidesteps a lengthy discussion of the buildup to, and the current dimensions of, the US-China strategic rivalry in order to focus on a narrower argument. To better understand the full context of US-China great-power competition, see Evan Medeiros, ed., *Cold Rivals: The New Era of US-China Strategic Competition* (Cambridge University Press, 2023); Rush Doshi, *The Long Game: China's Grand Strategy to Displace American Order* (Oxford University Press, 2021); Thomas J. Christensen, *The China Challenge: Shaping the Choices of a Rising Power* (W. W. Norton, 2015).

11. Jonathan Czin, "Burying Deng: Xi Jinping and the Abnormalization of Chinese Politics," *China Leadership Monitor*, no. 83 (March 2025), https://www.prcleader.org/post /burying-deng-xi-jinping-and-the-abnormalization-of-chinese-politics.

12. Of course, this "agreement" had limits, as was evidenced in the purge of Chen Liangyu in 2006 and the Yang brothers in 1992. But purge actions were relatively limited when compared with the size and scale of Xi's subsequent anti-corruption campaign.

13. Jude Blanchette, "The Edge of an Abyss: Xi Jinping's Overall National Security Outlook," *China Leadership Monitor*, no. 73 (September 2022), https://www.prcleader.org /post/the-edge-of-an-abyss-xi-jinping-s-overall-national-security-outlook.

14. Angang Hu, Shaojie Zhou, and Yize Xie, "A New National System: Background, Basic Features and Applicable Fields," in *Study on the National Conditions of Modernization with Chinese Characteristics* (Springer Nature Singapore, 2024), 155–172, https://doi .org/10.1007/978-981-97-7447-0_5.

15. See Mark Wu, "The 'China, Inc' Challenge to Global Trade Governance," *Harvard International Law Journal* 57 (2016): 1001–1063.

16. Bates Gill, *Daring to Struggle: China's Global Ambitions Under Xi Jinping* (Oxford University Press, 2022).

17. Alexander Cooley and Daniel H. Nexon, "How Hegemony Ends: The Unraveling of American Power," *Foreign Affairs* 99, no. 4 (June 9, 2020): 143–156.

18. For an excellent summary of the original "China shock" research and the subsequent critiques, see Center for Strategic and International Studies, "The China Shock: Reevaluating the Debate," CSIS China Power Project, October 14, 2022, https://bigdatachina.csis.org/the-china-shock-reevaluating-the-debate/.

19. David Autor, David Dorn, Gordon Hanson, and Kaveh Majlesi, "Importing Political Polarization? The Electoral Consequences of Rising Trade Exposure," *American Economic Review* 110, no. 10 (October 2020): 3139–3183.

Chapter Sixteen

Competitive Antiliberalism

How Geoeconomics, Security, and Values Define Chinese and American Worldviews in the 2020s and Beyond

Rana Mitter

O nly two powers will be able to exercise full-spectrum geopolitical power in the 2020s and beyond: the US and China. Power, in this context, is the capacity to exploit military and economic resources to achieve overall geopolitical ends. Up to the mid-2020s, there was a fairly clear distinction between the overall US global project that emerged from World War II, the "liberal leviathan" as characterized by John Ikenberry, and the Chinese project, which stressed a combination of national interest and a strategy to increase "authoritarian welfarism" as a global norm.[1]

As of 2025, it is no longer immediately obvious that one should characterize the US competition with China in terms of an economically or politically liberal "Western" project versus a Chinese "authoritarian" one. Instead, there are two geopolitical/geoeconomic projects that are nominally opposed, and start from different political premises and systems, but that also share some aspects of their worldviews. This is a new formation that can be defined as *competitive antiliberalism*: a contest between nonliberal global projects that veer between isolation and self-defined communitarianism. The framing has implications for the nature of political economy, international security, and divergence of worldviews between the US and China into the later 2020s and beyond.

Rana Mitter is S. T. Lee Chair in US-Asia Relations at the Harvard Kennedy School. He is the author of several books, most recently *China's Good War: How World War II Is Shaping a New Nationalism* (Harvard University Press, 2020).

There is a similarity and difference—and a powerful contradiction—at the heart of the American and Chinese projects. The Chinese project speaks in terms of creating a sense of global community but, in practice, also stresses economic self-sufficiency (*zili gengsheng*). The American project, in contrast, has shifted, rather than trying to square the circle between global and national interests. Having previously broadly embraced a policy of seeking to create global community, in significant part based on ideas of economic interdependence, the US has, as of 2025, embarked on an explicit policy of as much self-sufficiency as possible. In 2023, Xi Jinping declared at the National People's Congress that "China should work to achieve greater self-reliance."[2] Meanwhile, in his inaugural speech on January 20, 2025, Donald Trump declared: "We will protect our farmers, our cowboys, and everyone who works to feed our great nation. No more reliance on foreign goods and resources—America will once again be self-sufficient."[3]

These projects of self-sufficiency are, as of 2025, distinctive to the United States and China. The EU, and European actors more broadly, along with NATO members apart from the US, generally find themselves still preferring to use language more ideologically oriented toward global interaction, with a strongly values-driven element. Other significant geoeconomic groupings with limited security responsibilities, such as ASEAN, also still tend toward a language of interaction, albeit with less emphasis on values. India, a relatively isolationist state in terms of its actual security and geoeconomic choices, has nonetheless moved away from the language it used in the 1970s and 1980s, which emphasized import substitution and homemade products.

The current Chinese geopolitical project styles itself a "community of common destiny" at a global level.[4] Its characteristics include an attempt to create an economic model ("dual circulation"), which separates the domestic and international aspects of the Chinese economy; a broad sense that Chinese foreign direct investment will create a wider penetration for Chinese economic power in Asia and beyond; and a rhetorically strong embrace of the language of global free trade.[5] Its latest manifestation (as of 2025) is to combine three global initiatives, on development, security, and (the least well-defined) civilization. It aims for "democratization" of international society, by way of claiming that an emergent multipolarity is the best outcome for the new global order. An official Chinese source cites Xi stating that the Global Civilization Initiative "advocates respect for the diversity of civilizations, the common values of humanity, the importance of inheritance and innovation of civilizations, as well as robust international people-to-people exchanges and cooperation."[6] Yet the bottom line is clear: none of these terms are used to define a political or economic system that is liberal. "Democratization" of the international system means multipolarity. It does not refer to liberalization of domestic Chinese politics.

The American project of the second Trump administration is characterized by its fluidity. But it has already showcased a range of ideas that contrast strongly with the previous liberal hegemony (which was perhaps a "community of common destiny" by another name). It explicitly rejects ideas of free trade, instead advocating the use of tariffs as an incentive to concentrate as much investment as possible within the United States. The project is dependent on electoral democracy for its legitimacy but rejects traditionally liberal or pluralist outcomes in both political and economic terms. It stresses the importance of outcomes for the American people first, with international consequences (positive or negative) placed at a lower order of salience.

How do the two projects regard each other? China seems both bemused at and wary of the new US settlement.[7] The first few months of the Trump administration were marked by heavy tariffs on Chinese imports into the US, but the new administration had given little indication of its attitude toward issues such as Taiwan or ways in which China would be treated differently in principle (if at all) from any other trading partner if a trade deal were to be reached. Certainly, human rights issues have been no part of any confrontation with China, an undoubted source of relief for Beijing. There are also opportunities for China in the new uncertainty. But overall, Beijing has reacted with issue-specific fury over the issue of tariffs specifically, combined with a cautiousness on any broader geopolitical issues.[8] There are Chinese thinkers who draw comparisons with their own history. Xiao Gongqin, one of China's most influential "neo-authoritarian" thinkers, has approvingly compared the initial actions of the second Trump administration with Deng Xiaoping's actions in 1989.[9]

Likewise, there are distinctly mixed signals toward China in the Trump era. The all-out rhetorical hostility of the second half of the first Trump term is absent, for now. Instead, there is a range of views within the administration and in the penumbra around it: traditional policy hawks who regard China as a major challenge, tech libertarians who have significant connections with China, and isolationists who have no love for Beijing but are not sure that containing its ambitions is a primary American interest. Meanwhile, the attitude of Donald Trump himself is still unclear when it comes to issues such as Taiwan's future status or what the final trading relationship between China and the US should be. Meanwhile, long-standing US-driven geopolitical narratives about the importance of liberal democracy and free trade have also disappeared, at least for now, into the realms of history.

The Long Trajectory

Although competitive antiliberalism only became evident as the framing of the US-China relationship in 2025, its origins have been much longer in the making. The competition between ideologies defined the 20th century in a way that was explicit and confrontational. The 21st century is marked by an ideological conflict just as fierce as that of the 20th but much less stated or indeed formed. It is also a contest that has been shifting during the course of the 2020s, with China and the US both central to the global shift, while other actors, Europe most notably, follow uneasily in the slipstream.

In the interwar period, European politics was divided between liberal and communist states and movements, as well as their fascist opponents. During the Cold War, fascism was discredited, but communism and liberal capitalism continued to vie for supremacy. The ending of the Cold War, for some, became the end of ideology.

Yet, it is now clear that the 21st century's ideological reformulation was alive and well. The US story has become well-known. In retrospect, the increasing unhappiness of former industrial workers in the 2010s (in the aftermath of the 2008 financial crisis) and the longer-running displacement of jobs to China, Mexico, and other countries with cheaper labor costs since the 1990s has fueled discontent. This has led to the rise of nationalistic politics that combine communitarianism with economic protectionism. (Make America Great Again, or MAGA, is the most recent and successful manifestation, but the campaigns of Pat Buchanan and Ross Perot in the 1990s were part of the longer trajectory). The era of global free trade restarted in 1945 after the tariffs of the 1930s, but it may be coming to an end if high tariffs now become normal in the 2020s.

The Chinese story reflects a wider historical underpinning in which trade and sovereignty are closely intertwined. The "unequal treaties" that arrived in the aftermath of the Opium Wars gave rise to a near-century of compromised trade sovereignty. From 1854 until 1930, when China regained tariff autonomy, successive Chinese governments (the Qing dynasty and then successive Republican governments) had to deal with a tariff regime controlled by the Maritime Customs Service, an agency technically under Chinese government control but in practice run by Britons at the senior level. China participated in a global socialist trade system in the 1950s but became increasingly isolated from world trade after the

Sino-Soviet split. From the 1970s onward, however, it cast its lot with the American-dominated global trade environment instead and achieved spectacular economic results, leading to its entry into the World Trade Organization in 2001 and its rise to the status of the world's second-biggest economy.[10]

Just as the Cold War involved severe conflicts over ownership of the same turf of Enlightenment politics—that is, ideas of rationality, scientific progress, and peaceful cooperation—so does the current moment involve a fierce conflict, in which the US and China are dominant players, over a new welfarist communitarianism. In the case of China, this ideology combines autocratic politics with limited consultative elements (in some sense drawing on classic Maoist ideas of the "mass line"), and in the US, it is legitimized by democratic electoral politics, but with a vastly significant shift toward executive power and personal fiat.

Worldviews That Underpin Competitive Antiliberalism

There has been considerable academic work in recent years to identify intellectual antecedents both for the Trump project and that of the Chinese Communist Party (CCP). One interpreter who has useful insights on both is the German politico-legal theorist Carl Schmitt (1888–1985).

Schmitt's thought is complex, but there are some elements that broadly apply across his thinking. One is the division of political actors into the categories of friends and enemies. Schmitt's thinking is profoundly antiliberal and regards the idea of argued and acknowledged difference in politics as being a pious fiction that masks the real nature of power relations. "The political enemy is the other, the stranger," Schmitt noted, "and it is sufficient for his nature that he is, in a specially intense way, existentially something different and alien, so that in the extreme case conflicts with him are possible."[11]

There have been analyses that draw on Schmitt to explain Trump, and to explain the CCP. However, few have sought to compare the two. Yet both are notable in that they seek to define international relationships (both in security and economic terms) via definitions of friends and enemies, which are exactly the terms that Schmitt used. Still, the usage of the terms differs in the American and Chinese ideological framing.

The Trump project seeks to redefine how the two terms are used. Speaking of tariffs in late March 2025, Trump declared: "They've taken so much out of our country, friend and foe. And frankly, friend has been often times much worse than foe."[12] This could, at first glance, be seen as a way to declare that there is no meaningful distinction between the two terms "friend" and "foe." In geoeconomic terms, this seems broadly correct. The value of the economic relationship is being judged in this statement purely on its importance to the US (usually in terms of a positive trade balance for America). However, there are other areas, related much more to the support of national conservatism across boundaries, where an affinity or definition of friends and enemies is much more values-driven and clearly differentiates between the two. Senior administration figures have praised the actions and worldviews of national conservative figures in India, Hungary, and Germany, among other places. There are relatively few liberal/centrist figures who have received praise, although Britain's Keir Starmer has in general been treated with respect, if not extensive warmth.[13]

The CCP, in contrast, has long had a formally constituted framing for understanding friends and enemies, which is the idea of the United Front (*tongyi zhanxian*). The origins of the United Front lie in the alliance between the Nationalists (Guomindang) and Communists in 1923–1927, but in its contemporary form, it has proved one of the most powerful ideological tools for international political influence, seeking either to create committed supporters of CCP positions in other countries or at least to neutralize those who might otherwise be hostile.[14]

Few, if any, Trump advocates explicitly use Schmitt to illustrate their arguments (whereas there are certainly liberal critics who use Schmitt to critique Trump).[15] In contrast, Schmitt's work is openly discussed and admired in parts of the Chinese policymaking community. The "Schmitt Fever" that emerged in the 1990s in Beijing circles certainly included active discussions of the question of who were friends and who were enemies.[16] One prominent analyst of Schmitt, Jiang Shigong of Peking University Law School's faculty, was also key to the formulation of the 2020 Hong Kong National Security Law.[17]

Still, how is any sense of China having friends or enemies meaningful in terms of policymaking? China makes frequent claims that it does not seek to spread ideology or influence across borders. The corollary of this statement (regardless of whether it is accurate) is that China has also not formulated a universalist proposition in terms of its external relations, other than a largely economic one. Under Mao Zedong, China claimed specific ideological affinities with the Union of Soviet Socialist Republics, at least until the 1960 split. In more recent years, it has spoken of its relationship with Russia as a "friendship without limits." But this seems more a formulation of the moment than the kind of deep and emotionally grounded affinity that marked much of the relationship between Britain and the US or France and Germany, during the 20th century and into the 21st.

There are other aspects of the worldviews of both projects that are (perhaps surprisingly) similar. Both worldviews are ambivalent about their relationship with the wider world. The Trump project is strongly against ideas of free trade. Former US Trade Representative Robert Lighthizer, who served in the first Trump administration, discussed this formulation in his book *No Trade Is Free*.[18] To that extent, trade is not part of a wider vision of global community-building in the Trump formulation as it is, at least rhetorically, in the Chinese formulation. The US is also not keen to stress traditional security coalitions in Europe, although the links with Asian allies have not been subject to active questioning in the same way. In a visit to Manila in March 2025, Defense Secretary Pete Hegseth made sure to state that the US commitment to the security of longtime ally the Philippines was "ironclad."[19]

Yet in practice, China's openness to trade and cooperation has immense and obvious limits. Perhaps the most obvious is the cybersphere. The US retains free access to the internet, whereas China is now decades into its use of a "Great Firewall" that limits access to outside information. China also maintains multiple nontariff barriers to trade, including limiting access to data, conflating academic and business due diligence with national security violations, and creating doubts around rule of law. Problems with these issues also exist in the US, but this should not obscure the reality that throughout the history of the People's Republic of China, these barriers have been everyday practice at a much more intrusive level, even during its most open periods.

A term that both the US and China avoid, but which shapes their views of global order, is hierarchy. The Trump view of the world is one where America, famously, comes first, and which also characterizes that primacy as part of a hierarchy.[20] The term "America First" is double-edged: it can refer both to placing the interests of the US and American citizens first and also to making sure that the US stands ahead of any other countries. China does not use the term "China First." However, aspects of that worldview are visible in some of its actions. Perhaps one of the most famous occurred at an ASEAN meeting in Hanoi in 2010, where then–foreign minister Yang Jiechi declared to the representatives of other Asian states: "China is a big country and you are small countries, and that is a fact."[21]

Yang's mindset can be interpreted in a more consensual way. Some years ago, the political theorists Daniel A. Bell and Pei Wang wrote of a "just hierarchy" in which China would be acknowledged as the primary leader in Asia, as opposed to an equal sovereign state, but where that role would mean, in Confucian style, a duty to offer protection of patronage to states lower down in the hierarchy.[22] Both the US and China now show signs of following such a norm in reshaping global society, without explicitly talking about it as being hierarchical. China speaks of offering *ren*, or benevolence, to other states but is clear that it expects those states to conform to Chinese geopolitical needs, although not to its political system. The US has also started to be explicit about other states needing to conform to US needs, with some exceptions, notably Russia. However, the US no longer makes the case for liberal governance or democratic norms as goods in their own right in other societies.

This does not, mean, however, that the US is neutral in all aspects of other states' domestic politics. But in an innovative development, the US has chosen to comment on the domestic politics of traditional allies rather than adversaries or competitors. For instance, significant figures such as Vice President J. D. Vance have expressed approval of a range of national-conservative figures globally (Javier Milei, Narendra Modi, Viktor Orban). To that extent, there is a communitarian values-driven aspect of the wider political project, if not an economic one.[23]

Less noticed, however, have been the emotional and values-driven elements with echoes of each other in both countries. For instance, the value system associated with both the American national conservative and the Chinese Communist settlements stresses masculinity as an important part of the construction of a reconstituted national and international values-driven order. This is not an entirely new phenomenon. In the early 20th century, Social Darwinist rhetoric was common in the West and Asia. Politicians such as Theodore Roosevelt stressed masculine activity as a means of boosting their image, and in China, Mao Zedong argued for the importance of physical exercise as a means of combating the supposed indolence of traditional Confucian values.

In the 2020s, manhood and its discontents has become a powerful part of the American political discourse, with terms such as "bro" (which operate on left as well as right) and concerns about attacks on masculinity becoming commonplace in domestic politics. In Xi's China, there has also been a growing pushback against perceived political femininity. In 2021, there was a pushback by the CCP against the supposed social dominance of "niangpao," or "sissy boys," in popular culture (such as boy-band members perceived as effeminate). Early on in his rise to power, Xi noted that there was no "real man" who had risen up to offer resistance to the collapse of the Communist Party of the Soviet Union.[24] Meanwhile, feminist movements are subject to heavy censorship.[25]

There is very little, if any, direct connection between the culture of political masculinity in the US and that in China. Yet the politics of both places are shaped by personalistic leaders who stress the importance of such values in a way that suggests similar worldviews. Perhaps oddly, this aspect of political culture is one where there is more direct connection between the US and Russia than with China. Although very close to Russia politically in the 2020s, China shows very little cultural connection with the country these days, as opposed to during the Cold War prior to 1960. Instead, it is the US, where there are significant media and cultural figures who see a link between the culture of contemporary Russia and one that would benefit the US. Prominent figures such as the media personality Tucker Carlson have spoken of Russia as a society that is "thriving" under Putin's leadership.[26]

It may sometimes appear that the emergent world order is, to use a word of the moment, transactional, with few values. But it may instead be the case that there are still values, both in the US and China, that are very different from those of the dominant liberal era. In particular, one aspect of politics that has become evident in both states is a shift by the dominant political actors to make political discourse more homogenous. This, too, is an aspect of the era of competitive antiliberalism.

Competitive Antiliberalism—to What End?

If the US and China find themselves pursuing competitive antiliberalism, what is the likelihood of a stable end state? Both projects are underpinned by political worldviews that draw on unconventional economic thinking, which make it challenging to plan what comes next.

First, there is a contradiction at the heart of the Chinese economic proposition. It demands that China should move toward self-sufficiency, while also positing a global role for Chinese trade.

The main theoretical framing for this idea is the "dual circulation" economic policy, which seeks to separate the global and domestic "circuits" of the economy. The policy's priorities, however, demand three elements that will be hard to coordinate simultaneously: a maintenance of China's trade surplus, an increase in domestic consumption, and keeping the capital account closed. In practice, this has meant that domestic consumption has not grown at the level it needs to, as the other factors constrain it. China has been speaking—for more than two decades—about the need for greater consumption but does not put the policy measures in place to achieve it.

However, the sociology of the current era is forcing China to think again about how it deals with economic policy. The demographic shift in China is now well-known, and it is also clear that the change is real, but not instant. However, the state needs to make plans now for the upcoming economic pressures that this demography brings. China's pension systems, which are a mosaic rather than a fully coordinated entity, will likely go bankrupt if pension ages are not increased into the 2030s. The property boom crashed in part because of the slowing demand for housing, as China started to run out of younger families buying properties.

Meanwhile, younger people are suffering from the alternative problem: the information technology revolution does not currently provide the kind of jobs that they need, and there is chronic youth under- and unemployment.[27]

The US is, at the time of writing, at a much earlier stage of reorienting its economic policies. However, it appears that tariffs are likely to play a very significant role in the new economic strategy, a tactic that has not yet found favor with the majority of economic analysts but that has a political mandate, not least as tariff policy was explicitly placed before voters in 2024 as part of the Republican platform. Unlike the Chinese proposition, the US does not make a particular virtue of being embedded in the global trading system. But its model shares the idea that domestic economic production can make any dependence on wider global trade less important, or even irrelevant.

The debate over "weaponized interdependence" in the late 2010s was a harbinger of the shift away from globalization, not just as economic reality but as rhetorical good.[28] During the presidency of Joe Biden, numerous actions were taken to make sure that the US was not dependent on technology or parts from China. Yet these actions have in turn raised complex questions about how far decoupling or self-sufficiency is really possible, despite the rhetoric.

During the earlier period of US shift from globalization to decoupling, there was increased discussion of "friendshoring": the idea that liberal states might cooperate on technology to the exclusion of China. As of early 2025, there is less discussion of this term, with Western allies of the US (Canada and the EU among them) preoccupied with protecting themselves from tariffs and other trade barriers from the US. It is unclear whether the friendshoring strategy can be sustained in the form identified during the Biden years, as the term "friends" becomes ambiguous in a way that "Schmittians" might not have anticipated.

Another geoeconomic area where key terms are in flux is in international development. The ending of most programs of the United States Agency for International Development, with the status of the US as a major aid donor, actually creates a more level playing field between the US and China as geoeconomic actors on global development. Other major players (EU, Japan, UK) continue to advocate the award of donations and grants for international development. Even they are constrained financially (the UK recently reduced its spending on aid from 1.7% to 1.3% of GDP). However, the explicit US statement that it will no longer be a major player on grants for international assistance forces comparison with a less-mentioned reality: that China has never been a major donor of international aid as grants, but rather of loans, often at high interest rates.[29]

The ecology of international lending and infrastructure projects by the US and China may well become more similar; competitive antiliberalism certainly suggests that "loans not grants" is a preferred strategy for governments, whether in Washington or Beijing. China's private sector has been encouraged to contribute strongly to the Global Development Initiative, the successor of sorts to the Belt and Road Initiative, but very much in areas where China seeks to create long-term path dependency. Examples include 5G, life sciences, and green energy infrastructure. Meanwhile, the US business sector, particularly in areas such as technology, has become more explicitly tied to government priorities, with prominent business-people coordinating their priorities with the administration and in some cases serving in it.

In areas where both the US and China cannot be self-sufficient, both have sought to create areas of exclusive control of key resources. Thus, China has long invested in ways that dominate the supply of rare earths. However, the US has become more explicit in its interest in creating mineral deposit rights of its own, for instance in negotiations over the ending of Russia's war of invasion of Ukraine. As things stand, both China and the US promote these largely as national projects; in other words, there is little ostensible attempt to create a collective sense of alliance behind these projects of resource capture.

The current US dialogue on minerals explicitly suggests a division of control with Russia, another key player in the newly emergent world of competitive antiliberalism. While current discussions are on the contested territory of Ukraine, another contemporary issue shows the growing concern about control of resources. The insistence by the second Trump administration on greater control over Greenland, which began in earnest in late 2024, reflects a longer-standing sense that there is a struggle for control of the Arctic and its minerals. In this area, the US may be in competition with Russia and China, while the EU is ignored.

However, there are other areas emerging in the 2020s where China can show itself as contributing to the global commons. One area of significance divergence is energy transition technology. Here, China has become a key actor in terms of global dominance, particularly in solar and wind technology. The dynamics of climate change have the potential to provide ballast for Chinese claims that collective action on climate means that individual liberties need to be restrained, an antiliberal discourse that may find little purchase in Europe but a potential audience in the Global South, where the problems of providing enough energy to power growth may encourage the support of authoritarian politics. China is more likely to promote such language if there is no longer a hegemonic state actively promoting an alternative liberal discourse but rather a different (fossil fuel based) antiliberal alternative.

The Chinese project's potential success is highly dependent on continued economic stability in its own region. One of the greatest threats to that stability would be efforts by Beijing to use coercion to take Taiwan, or possibly areas of the South China Sea.

Would such Chinese actions over Taiwan and the South China Sea be ignored by the US? It seems hard to imagine that could be the case, not least as the follow-on effects of withdrawing the US from its security role in the Pacific would be so serious. Nuclear proliferation in the region would expand. South Korea and Japan might be the first, but not last, to develop weapons. Domestic economies would be oriented toward defense spending, and consumption in the region could be heavily constrained; one of the most economically vibrant regions in the world would necessarily rethink the predictability around economic and political decisions. As noted above, early language from the new administration is much more unequivocal about US partnerships in Asia than with Europe. But Asian partners are wary about how unstable the region might become.

How Will the Power Competition Be Defined in the Age of Competitive Antiliberalism?

The central dilemma faced by all US and Western governments since the 1990s remains the same, even under the significantly changed international system emerging under the second Trump administration. What is the version of China that the wider world can coexist with? And is the answer to that question different if the US is no longer the liberal hegemon of the past but rather a competitive antiliberal one instead? Singapore's Minister for Defense Ng Eng Hen stated at the 2025 Munich Security Conference that the US role in Asia had shifted from being an actor that drew on ideas of "moral legitimacy" to something akin to "a landlord seeking rent."[30]

If the United States no longer draws on a competition of values as the reason for rivalry with China or a reason to be wary of Chinese dominance, then what becomes the basis of the contest? Simply put, it may be the continued primacy of the US in its own right and the wider sense that Chinese dominance in Asia and beyond is still a worse bargain for the other Asian powers than is acceding to a more transactional US. The global exercise of geopolitical power across the economic and military spheres remains the province of the US and China. Even if their worldviews show relatively more convergence than could have been imagined a decade ago, they are still inexorably rival projects.

Other powers in the region will make their judgments according to the level of flexibility and maneuver that their partnerships provide with one of the great powers. To use Ng's analogy: Landlords are rarely loved, but still, those who want to stay housed usually pay the rent. They move only if another option proves more attractive. Beijing's house has an attractive market attached to it. But it has not yet persuaded potential residents that they want to hire China to cover the residence's security needs. As long as that remains the case, the US's new antiliberalism will not be enough to stop it being competitive in Asia—if it chooses to be.

Is the world of competitive antiliberalisms permanent? That may not be the case. A future US might swing back in the direction of internationalism. More speculatively, even though any future China is likely to be authoritarian, it might be more willing to allow limited pluralism at home, as happened in the 1990s, which in turn might influence its global stance toward a more liberal authoritarianism (a paradoxical but increasingly common political variant). But you can't go home again. The US's turn toward antiliberalism in the short term means that potential partners will start to think in more instrumental ways in the long term about how a pro-US foreign policy will play at home. The natural post-1945 willingness to join in with a US project or campaign because of shared values will be much harder to recover.

Ironically, this might make it harder for the US to create a coalition against China, even with countries that share the antiliberal worldview. Hungary may decide that it likes Chinese investment more than it values ideological affinity with an antiliberal US. The US may have to work harder to demonstrate to partners what the benefits they gain from such a coalition really are; it may need to provide assurance that any such benefits have a long-term worth that justifies the investment of partners' commitment. An antiliberal US declines to be taken for granted. The corollary is that it will need to work harder to be taken on trust.

NOTES

1. G. John Ikenberry, *Liberal Leviathan: The Origins, Crisis, and Transformation of the American World Order* (Princeton University Press, 2011).

2. Francois de Soyres and Dylan Moore, "Assessing China's Efforts to Achieve Self-Reliance," *VoxEU*, January 4, 2024, https://cepr.org/voxeu/columns/assessing-chinas-efforts-increase-self-reliance.

3. "The Inaugural Address," The White House, January 20, 2025, https://www.whitehouse.gov/remarks/2025/01/the-inaugural-address/.

4. China Media Project, "The CMP Dictionary Community of Common Destiny for Mankind," August 25, 2021, https://chinamediaproject.org/the_ccp_dictionary/community-of-common-destiny-for-mankind/.

5. Hung Tran, "Dual Circulation in China: A Progress Report," Atlantic Council, October 24, 2022, https://www.atlanticcouncil.org/blogs/econographics/dual-circulation-in-china-a-progress-report/.

6. Xinhua, "3 Things to Know About China's Global Civilizational Initiative," State Council Information Office of China, April 3, 2024, http://english.scio.gov.cn/in-depth/2024-04/03/content_117103205.htm.

7. See comments by Zhou Bo in Amy Hawkins, "America Is Going Down," *The Guardian*, March 2, 2025, https://www.theguardian.com/world/2025/mar/02/america-is-going-down-china-can-capitalise-on-damage-caused-by-trump-former-pla-colonel-says.

8. Jude Blanchette, "China Sees Opportunity in Trump's Upheaval," *Foreign Affairs*, March 27, 2025, https://www.foreignaffairs.com/china/china-sees-opportunity-trumps-upheaval.

9. "Xiao Gongqin on Trump 2.0," trans. David Ownby, *Reading the China Dream* (blog), https://www.readingthechinadream.com/xiao-gongqin-on-trump-20.html.

10. On the Maritime Customs Service, see Hans J. van de Ven, *Breaking with the Past: The Maritime Customs Service and the Global Origins of Modernity in China* (Columbia University Press, 2014). On China in the socialist economy, see William C. Kirby, "China's Internationalization in the Early People's Republic: Dreams of a Socialist World Economy," *China Quarterly* 188 (December 2006): 870–890. On the Deng Xiaoping period, see Julian Gewirtz, *Unlikely Partners: Chinese Reformers, Western Economists, and the Making of Global China* (Harvard University Press, 2017).

11. Peter Michael Gratton, "Why Liberals Must Confront Schmitt and the Logic of Trumpism," *Liberal Currents*, March 20, 2025, https://www.liberalcurrents.com/why-liberals-must-confront-carl-schmitt-and-the-logic-of-trumpism/.

12. Stephen Collinson, "A Warning Sign Flares as the Trump White House Refuses to Moderate Its Shock Politics," *CNN*, March 28, 2025, https://www.cnn.com/2025/03/27/politics/trump-white-house-stefanik-hegseth-tariffs/index.html.

13. Ryan Patrick Jones, "Trump Says He Doesn't Care If Liberals Beat Conservatives in Canada," *Reuters*, March 18, 2025, https://www.reuters.com/world/americas/trump-says-he-doesnt-care-if-liberals-beat-conservatives-canada-2025-03-19/.

14. Matt Schrader, "Friends and Enemies: A Framework for Understanding Chinese Political Interference in Democratic Countries," GMF US, April 22, 2020, https://

securingdemocracy.gmfus.org/friends-and-enemies-a-framework-for-understanding -chinese-political-interference-in-democratic-countries/.

15. A partial exception is the writer Curtis Yarvin, who is influential in MAGA circles and has cited Schmitt explicitly.

16. Kai Marchal and Carl K. Y. Shaw, eds., *Carl Schmitt and Leo Strauss in the Chinese-Speaking World* (Lexington Books, 2017); Xie Libin and Haig Patapan, "Schmitt Fever: The Use and Abuse of Carl Schmitt in Contemporary China," *International Journal of Constitutional Law* 18, no. 1 (January 2020): 130–146, https://doi.org/10.1093/icon/moaa015.

17. "Jiang Shigong, 'Probing the Imaginary World,'" trans. David Ownby, *Reading the China Dream* (blog), https://www.readingthechinadream.com/jiang-shigong-probing -the-imaginary-world.html.

18. Robert Lighthizer, *No Trade Is Free: Changing Course, Taking on China, and Helping America's Workers* (Broadside Books, 2023).

19. Jim Gomez, "Hegseth Tells Philippines the Trump Administration Will Ramp Up Deterrence Against China," *Associated Press*, March 28, 2025, https://apnews.com /article/pete-hegseth-philippines-south-china-sea-8d77bd438667895aca30a86f2e07d1b2.

20. "President Trump's America First Priorities," The White House, January 20, 2025, https://www.whitehouse.gov/briefings-statements/2025/01/president-trumps -america-first-priorities/.

21. Ian Storey, "China's Missteps in Southeast Asia: Less Charm, More Offensive," The Jamestown Foundation, December 17, 2010, https://jamestown.org/program/chinas -missteps-in-southeast-asia-less-charm-more-offensive/.

22. Daniel Bell and Wang Pei, *Just Hierarchy: Why Social Hierarchies Matter in China and the Rest of the World* (Princeton University Press, 2022).

23. Ishan Tharoor, "J. D. Vance's Vocal Admiration for Orban's Hungary Tells Its Own Story," *Washington Post*, July 17, 2024, https://www.washingtonpost.com/world /2024/07/17/trump-vance-project-2025-orban-hungary/.

24. Rana Mitter, "The Super-Rich, 'Sissy Boys,' Celebs—All Targets in Xi's Bid to End Cultural Difference," *The Guardian*, September 5, 2021, https://www.theguardian .com/commentisfree/2021/sep/05/super-rich-sissy-boys-celebs-all-targets-in-xis-bid-to -end-cultural-difference.

25. Natalie Xu, "China's Feminists Walk a Tightrope," Index on Censorship, February 14, 2024, https://www.indexoncensorship.org/2024/02/chinas-feminists-walk-a -tightrope/.

26. Justin Bargona, "Tucker Carlson Says He's 'Definitely More Sympathetic to Putin than Zelensky' Because Russia Is 'Thriving,'" *The Independent*, March 7, 2025, https://www.the-independent.com/news/world/americas/us-politics/tucker-carlson -putin-zelensky-b2711134.html.

27. On the Chinese economy, see Zongyuan Zoe Liu, "China's Real Economic Crisis," *Foreign Affairs*, August 6, 2024, https://www.foreignaffairs.com/china/chinas -real-economic-crisis-zongyuan-liu.

28. Henry Farrell and Abraham L. Newman, "Weaponized Interdependence: How Global Economic Networks Shape State Coercion," *International Security* 44, no. 1 (July 2019): 42–79, doi: https://doi.org/10.1162/isec_a_00351.

29. Yun Sun, "Can China Fill the Void in Foreign Aid?," Brookings Institution, March 11, 2025, https://www.brookings.edu/articles/can-china-fill-the-void-in-foreign-aid/.

30. Philip J. Heijmans, "Singapore Says Asia Sees US as 'Landlord Seeking Rent,'" *Bloomberg*, February 16, 2025, https://www.yahoo.com/news/singapore-says-asia-now-views-021334719.html.

Chapter Seventeen

US-China Rivalry in a Shifting International System

Michael Beckley

For much of the post–Cold War era, US-China competition played out within a stable international framework. China's rise powered global growth and integration, while the United States underwrote a liberal order through military presence, open markets, and alliance leadership. That system is now breaking down. China's economy is stalling and its leaders are expanding military power, escalating territorial disputes, and aligning with other authoritarian regimes. The United States, meanwhile, is not working to restore the old order—it is moving away from liberal internationalism and adopting a more unilateral, interest-driven approach to global power. These shifts are not just altering the balance between two rivals; they are reshaping the structure of the international system itself.

This chapter makes four arguments. First, China is no longer a stabilizing force in the global economy or international politics. As its growth slows and influence fades, it is relying more on coercion than commerce, triggering military buildups and regional counterbalancing. Second, the United States is moving beyond its postwar role as system manager—instead using its dominance in finance, technology, and defense to secure advantage without assuming the burdens of liberal leadership. Third, a loose but increasingly coordinated authoritarian bloc—

Michael Beckley is an associate professor of political science at Tufts University, a nonresident senior fellow at the American Enterprise Institute, and the director of the Asia Program at the Foreign Policy Research Institute.

anchored by China, Russia, Iran, and North Korea—is forming through shared weapons systems, diplomatic support, and aligned efforts to weaken the US-led order. Finally, these political shifts are unfolding alongside deeper structural disruptions—demographic decline, uneven technological change, and growing instability in the developing world—that are compounding the volatility of great-power competition.

The result is a more fragmented and dangerous international environment. The wars in Ukraine and the Middle East have already strained US capacity and revealed cracks in global deterrence. With tensions building in the Taiwan Strait and South China Sea, the risk of simultaneous conflicts across Eurasia is growing. US-China rivalry over the next decade will not follow the trajectory of the past 10 years. It will unfold within a fractured system, shaped by the behavior of declining powers and the breakdown of old assumptions about order and restraint.

The End of China's Economic Rise

From the 1980s through the 2010s, trade networks, supply chains, and international institutions were reoriented around the promise of China's booming economy and peaceful rise. That era is over. China's economy is slowing, and its leaders are responding not with restraint but with rearmament—escalating territorial disputes, expanding military capabilities, and deepening ties with other revisionist regimes. Given the scale of China's economy, population, and strategic ambitions, this is not just a national adjustment but a systemic shift. A country that once helped stabilize the global order is now contributing to its unraveling, accelerating a broader transition from cooperation to confrontation.

The signs of China's economic slowdown are becoming harder to ignore. For the first time in decades, its share of global GDP—measured in dollar terms—is shrinking, down from over 18% in 2021 to about 16% in 2024.[1] Its economy has also slipped relative to the United States, falling from nearly 75% of US GDP to just 64%—and those figures rely on official data that likely overstate both size and growth. Independent estimates suggest China's real GDP could be 20% smaller than reported, with actual growth stuck between 0% and 2%.[2]

Currency depreciation and deflation have contributed to the decline, but the underlying problems are structural: weak domestic demand and an exhausted growth model. Productivity growth—the engine of long-term prosperity—has been flat or negative for much of the past decade.[3] Capital-output ratios have surged, meaning China is investing more to produce less. The property sector—once a quarter of the economy—has collapsed, wiping out an estimated $18 trillion in household wealth since 2021. Despite massive subsidies, emerging sectors like electric vehicles and solar panels still account for just 3.5% of GDP—far too small to drive a broad recovery. Debt has ballooned with total liabilities across government, households, and businesses now exceeding 300% of GDP.[4] Youth unemployment recently surpassed 20% before the government stopped releasing the data. What once appeared to be an unstoppable economic miracle now resembles a classic middle-income trap.

Public sentiment reflects this shift. Between 2021 and 2024, Chinese citizens illicitly moved hundreds of billions of dollars out of the country and became the fastest-growing group of migrants at the US southern border, with their numbers surging 50-fold.[5] Survey data point to growing disillusionment: more citizens report declining economic prospects and attribute inequality to corruption rather than merit.[6]

Looking ahead, China's downturn is likely to deepen. The forces that once powered its rise—favorable demographics, open markets, political pragmatism, and abundant resources—are now moving in reverse. The country is projected to lose nearly 200 million working-age adults and gain a comparable number of retirees by mid-century. It is facing severe environmental and resource constraints, including water shortages, degraded farmland, and growing dependence on energy and food imports. Externally, access to foreign capital and markets is narrowing amid rising global protectionism. Internally, the political system has ossified as Xi Jinping has centralized authority, prioritized loyalty over competence, and diverted capital from the private sector to state-connected firms.

This marks a sharp reversal.[7] For nearly two decades, China powered global growth—accounting for over 40% of worldwide GDP gains between 2008 and 2021, fueling commodity booms, anchoring supply chains, and lending more than a trillion dollars to become the world's largest bilateral creditor. Beijing used that economic weight to extend its geopolitical reach, financing infrastructure across Eurasia and becoming the top trading partner for more than half the world. But that era is ending. Imports have dropped from 30% of GDP in 2007 to just 17% today. Overseas development lending has collapsed—from over $80 billion in 2016 to $4 billion by 2021—and net foreign direct investment turned negative in 2023 for the first time in decades.

As China's economic magnetism fades, it is transforming from an opportunity to a threat for many countries. To save its economy Beijing has doubled down on industrial policy, pouring hundreds of billions into sectors like electric vehicles, solar panels, steel, and advanced manufacturing—more than any other country, both in absolute terms and relative to GDP. But with domestic demand still weak, much of this output is being dumped abroad, saturating global markets. Between 2019 and 2023, China's manufacturing trade surplus grew by $775 billion, and its overall export surplus hit a record $1.7 trillion. Emerging economies have borne the brunt: China's surplus doubled to 6% of ASEAN's GDP and rose to nearly 4% of Mexico's. From steel and chemicals to batteries and cars, Chinese overcapacity is undercutting industries across both the developing and developed world.

The global backlash has been swift. As of early 2025, G20 countries had imposed over 4,600 import restrictions since 2009—most targeting Chinese goods. The United States has raised average tariffs above 25%; the European Union is preparing broad duties on Chinese EVs, steel, and solar panels. South Korea and Vietnam have penalized Chinese steel; Mexico is probing dumping in plastics and chemicals; Indonesia is taxing Chinese nylon; even Russia has curbed Chinese vehicle imports. With the World Trade Organization (WTO) sidelined and trade rules fraying, governments are embracing protectionism on a broad scale.

The fallout is not just economic. As growth slows and market leverage fades, Beijing is relying more heavily on military coercion to achieve what it once pursued through commerce. Defense spending is rising 7%–10% annually, even as GDP growth struggles to exceed 2%. China's military budget—estimated between $450 billion and $700 billion—is now approaching US levels. The result is the most ambitious peacetime military buildup since World War II. China is producing ships, aircraft, and munitions at five to six times the US rate, has tripled its operational nuclear warheads since 2020, and is on pace to field 1,500 by 2035. The People's Liberation Army (PLA) is rehearsing missile strikes on mock-ups of US and Taiwanese bases, while expanding capabilities in space, cyber, and electronic warfare, and integrating them into joint operations.

With fewer economic incentives to offer and a growing arsenal of military tools, Beijing is increasingly turning to coercion—nowhere more visibly than in the Taiwan Strait. For decades, China pursued unification through economic integration, betting that trade and investment would gradually bind Taiwan to the mainland. That strategy has failed. Nearly two-thirds of Taiwanese now identify exclusively as Taiwanese, while just 2.5% identify solely as Chinese. Although most still prefer to preserve the status quo, a majority say they would opt for independence if forced to choose. In January 2024, despite mounting threats from Beijing, Taiwanese voters handed the pro-independence Democratic Progressive Party a third consecutive presidential victory. Even the traditionally Beijing-friendly Kuomintang has shifted course, pledging to strengthen Taiwan's defenses and deepen ties with the United States.

Beijing has responded with escalating pressure. It has codified the right to use force against Taiwan, expanded missile deployments and conducted large-scale encirclement drills. In 2022, following a senior US visit to Taipei, China launched live-fire exercises and ballistic missile tests around the island. In 2023, it carried out "Joint Sword" exercises simulating a blockade and precision strikes. By 2024, the PLA was conducting its largest drills in decades and deploying amphibious landing craft designed to support potential beach assaults. These actions suggest that China is not only posturing—it is systematically preparing for a range of military contingencies.

At the same time, Taiwan's political system has become increasingly polarized and fragmented. The 2024 elections left no party in control of the legislature, producing gridlock between the ruling Democratic Progressive Party and a combative opposition led by the Kuomintang and the Taiwan People's Party. Contentious parliamentary reforms, judicial pushback, and mass protests have deepened internal divisions, creating openings Beijing may try to exploit.

Meanwhile, the United States has sent mixed signals. Some US officials support stronger defense ties with Taiwan, but President Trump has questioned the island's strategic value, accused it of undermining US industry, and praised Xi Jinping. These comments have raised doubts about American reliability and may further encourage Beijing to test the boundaries of US deterrence.

In this environment, Chinese leaders may calculate that they do not need to rush into war. Instead, they could seek to exploit dysfunction in Taipei and Washington through coercion short of conflict—military signaling, economic pressure, and influence operations—while holding open the possibility of a negotiated deal. For now, the PLA appears to be preparing for multiple scenarios—from blockade to invasion to calibrated intimidation.

Still, the danger remains real. Even if war is not imminent, the scale and pace of China's preparations suggest that military force is no longer a distant contingency. Under the right conditions—or miscalculations—it could become a live option. The current mix of pressure, polarization, and uncertainty may not lead to immediate conflict, but it is placing the region on a far more dangerous footing.

And Taiwan is only the beginning. China's coercive turn extends across the region and beyond. In the South China Sea, it has ramped up aggression—ramming, lasing, and blockading Philippine vessels—while asserting control through militarized outposts and swarms of maritime militia. It has built and fortified seven artificial islands and routinely deploys hundreds of ships to intimidate Southeast Asian claimants. Along the Indian border, China has massed troops and constructed fortified positions since the deadly 2020 clashes. Across Eurasia, it is supplying critical components for Russia's war in Ukraine, deepening military ties with Iran, and conducting joint exercises with authoritarian partners. These efforts are part of a broader strategy to undermine US alliances in East Asia and challenge the foundations of the existing international order.

China's belligerence marks a historical shift. During its high-growth years, Beijing promoted a "peaceful rise," shelved disputes, and used market access to build goodwill. From the 1990s through the mid-2000s, it settled borders, delayed construction of aircraft carriers, and joined major international institutions. In response, the world welcomed China's ascent—fast-tracking WTO membership, returning Hong Kong and Macau, and expanding trade ties. But today, as China's economic leverage fades and its coercive posture hardens, countries are no longer accommodating Beijing—they are moving to contain it. Japan is doubling defense spending and shedding postwar constraints. India has reinforced its Himalayan frontier. The Philippines is rearming and expanding US basing access. Vietnam, Australia, and European powers are sending warships into contested waters. Where Beijing once reshaped the international system through promises of prosperity, it now does so through pressure—and many countries are responding in kind.

America First

Just as China has abandoned its peaceful rise, the United States is shedding its long-standing commitment to liberal hegemony. What is emerging is a rogue superpower: still dominant and globally active, but more unilateral, coercive, and transactional. Like China's slowdown, this transformation is reshaping the international system.

Under its new approach, Washington is no longer trying to uphold a liberal international order. Instead, it is using its military, economic, and technological advantages to pursue narrower strategic objectives while shedding many of the burdens of global leadership. Security commitments have become instruments of leverage rather than lasting guarantees. Alliances are increasingly transactional: frontline partners such as Taiwan, South Korea, and Ukraine still receive US support—but mainly because they help contain key American adversaries. In this logic, they function less as protected allies and more as pawns—potentially expendable in a future deal or positioned to absorb the first blows in a larger conflict.

On the economic front, US strategy has grown more coercive. Rather than promoting multilateral liberalization, Washington is using market access, financial dominance, and technological superiority to discipline allies, punish rivals, and secure domestic advantage. Export controls, tariffs, sanctions, and targeted decoupling are supplanting universal trade rules. Economic agreements are increasingly narrow in scope and designed to extract concessions rather than build shared norms. Key supply chains are being restructured not to integrate the world economy but to reduce US exposure and deny strategic technologies to competitors.

Militarily, the focus has shifted from presence to punishment. The US is moving away from stabilizing regions through permanent deployments and coalition-building, and toward fielding agile, high-tech forces capable of imposing high costs on adversaries. Investments are flowing into long-range strike systems, cyber tools, drones, and space-based assets—all aimed at deterring through the threat of swift and overwhelming retaliation. The objective is not to underwrite regional order but to maintain primacy by dominating the instruments of coercion.

This shift is remaking the global order. As Washington retreats from its postwar role as architect and guarantor of liberal norms, the system built on open markets, collective security, and democratic ideals is giving way to one that is more fragmented, more competitive, and more prone to conflict.

One consequence is the erosion of deterrence and the return of territorial revisionism. With the US less willing to defend international rules for their own sake, aggressors are probing the boundaries. Russia's invasion of Ukraine, Azerbaijan's seizure of Nagorno-Karabakh, China's maritime coercion, and Venezuela's threats against Guyana all reflect a growing belief that borders can be redrawn by force. These are not isolated incidents—they signal a broader breakdown in norms where violations of sovereignty increasingly go unpunished.

As US security guarantees grow less credible, regional instability is mounting. Across Eurasia, militarization is spreading. Japan is executing its largest defense buildup since World War II, driven by China's rise and doubts about American reliability. In South Korea, support for nuclear weapons is growing amid declining faith in US extended deterrence. Gulf Arab states are hedging—expanding arms imports while strengthening ties with China and Russia. In Europe, Germany and Poland have launched major rearmament plans.

Economic fragmentation is accelerating, too. The US has imposed sweeping tariffs, restricted tech exports, and subsidized key industries—moves others are emulating. In the past year alone, more than 1,500 new trade barriers have been introduced worldwide, targeting strategic goods from semiconductors to green tech. Dozens of countries are tightening investment rules, reshoring supply chains, and embracing state-led industrial policy. Meanwhile, the US has kneecapped the WTO by blocking judicial appointments, paralyzing its dispute resolution system.

No doubt Donald Trump has been a historic accelerant of this turn to America First, stamping his unique imprint on a long-simmering trend. A political entrepreneur, he took brewing nationalist instincts and turned them into doctrine—often in cartoonish extremes. He imposed tariffs on allies, slashed foreign aid, abandoned democracy promotion, and openly questioned US alliances. He cast global leadership as a scam and portrayed allies as freeloaders, breaking from elite consensus with a bluntness that resonated with much of the public.

Yet this trend toward "America First" has been building for decades. Without the Cold War's unifying threat, Americans grew skeptical of defending a diffuse liberal order. One election after another reflected this shift. In 1992, Bill Clinton defeated George H. W. Bush—fresh off a military victory—by focusing on the economy. In 2000, George W. Bush ran on a platform of humility in foreign affairs, defeating Al Gore's more ambitious globalism. In 2008, Barack Obama emphasized "nation-building at home" over John McCain's call for a League of Democracies. Again and again, candidates won by promising to pull back from global commitments.

Even when US leaders spoke the language of liberal leadership, their actions often betrayed a more self-interested and selective commitment. In the 1990s, Washington expanded NATO while cutting troop levels in Europe, condemned atrocities in places like the Balkans, Haiti, and Somalia (but pressured others to intervene), and welcomed China into the WTO without demanding real reforms to its mercantilist economy or human rights practices. The US enlarged the liberal order—but on the cheap.

After 9/11 it abandoned major treaties, rejected NATO's role in Afghanistan, and launched a war in Iraq without UN authorization or broad allied support. The costs of those wars, compounded by the 2008 financial crisis, fueled growing pessimism—a sense that the world was ungovernable, the liberal order was a bad deal, and it was time to prioritize American economic interests. Trump didn't invent this disillusionment; he distilled it. His doctrine was not a rupture, but the culmination of long-running trends and a return to an older, more unilateral US foreign policy tradition.

Biden's presidency marked a rhetorical return to liberal internationalism— "America is back"—and his tone, alliances-first posture, and respect for multilateralism clearly differed from Trump's. But the strategic shift away from liberal hegemony continued. Biden kept tariffs on Chinese goods, expanded industrial policy, tightened export controls, and emphasized economic resilience at home. He rallied allies to support Ukraine but also pursued energy diplomacy with Gulf autocracies and eased sanctions on Venezuela to stabilize global oil markets. His administration reengaged with international institutions but steered clear of new binding commitments. In tone and some tactics, Biden diverged from Trump. But in many core policies, the trajectory held. And in 2024, the American public voted to accelerate that shift—returning Trump to office with even broader support than before.

The key point is that liberal hegemony was never the default posture of US foreign policy; it was a Cold War strategy born of necessity. Confronted with the threat of Soviet domination in Eurasia, American leaders built a bloc of capitalist nations and upheld an open, rules-based order to contain communism and prevent a return to great-power war and economic fragmentation. That strategy succeeded—but its very success helped sow the seeds of its unraveling.

By integrating autocratic rivals into the liberal order, the United States enabled them to exploit it from within. China and Russia gained access to global markets and institutions, then used that access to pursue mercantilist policies, spread propaganda, and erode liberal norms. Beijing shields its industries with subsidies and state planning while maintaining open access to Western markets. It has leveraged the liberal order to become the world's manufacturing hub, dominating sectors critical to modern warfare—shipbuilding, drones, batteries, electronics, and precision machinery. State-driven overcapacity has flooded global markets, undercutting Western firms and stalling industrial recovery in the US and its allies. Though still reliant on some foreign inputs, China now has the scale to out-produce its rivals in a prolonged conflict. Moscow, meanwhile, has laundered illicit wealth through global finance, weaponized Europe's energy dependence, and exploited NATO's restraint—even as it invoked the alliance to justify its invasion of Ukraine. Both powers rely on US-secured trade routes while working to redraw Eurasia's map by force. What was once the foundation of US grand strategy—openness—has become a strategic liability.

This shift has also exposed structural weaknesses among US allies. Sheltered under the American security umbrella, many reduced defense spending, expanded welfare programs, and deepened economic ties with China and Russia. Now, they struggle to maintain regional stability, let alone contribute to global order—yet they still rely on the United States to manage emerging crises, stretching American resources thin.

Meanwhile, the liberal order itself has become harder to manage. US-led efforts to promote decolonization, expand global markets, and integrate rising powers once fostered growth and stability. But they also multiplied the number of sovereign states, veto points, and conflicting agendas. Institutions that once served as tools of American power are now gridlocked—or openly opposed to US interests.

At home, globalization created wealth and technological dynamism—but failed to distribute its benefits. While the country as a whole grew richer, industrial regions hollowed out. Offshoring and import competition devastated working-class communities, bred political resentment, and fueled populist backlash. The very regions most harmed by globalization gained leverage in America's political system, driving a shift toward tariffs, border controls, and economic nationalism. Foreign policy is no longer guided by elite consensus around openness but by rising demands for protection, reciprocity, and resilience.

Even as the liberal order has grown more costly and less rewarding, it has also become less essential to the United States. Structural advantages now position Washington to act with greater autonomy. The US remains unmatched in its combination of economic scale and productivity, accounting for 26% of global GDP—nearly twice that of the eurozone and more than the entire Global South. In per capita terms, it outpaces every democratic major power; if Germany or Japan were US states, they would rank as the poorest in average wages.

The United States also retains control over key global systems. The dollar dominates global reserves, cross-border lending, and trade settlement—giving Washington unrivaled financial leverage. US energy production, now the highest in the world, provides cheap domestic fuel and insulation from external coercion. Its consumer market rivals those of China and the EU combined, and its working-age population is the only one among major powers expected to grow this century. This demographic and market strength enhances America's ability to shape global flows and extract concessions.

Technological dominance reinforces this leverage. US firms generate the majority of global high-tech profits and control chokepoints in semiconductor and AI supply chains. Meanwhile, automation and advanced manufacturing are enabling modest but meaningful reshoring. America may not be fully self-sufficient—but in a world trending toward self-reliance, it starts from a position of extraordinary strength.

These shifts are also transforming America's military posture. The Cold War model of forward-deployed forces—meant to reassure and protect allies—is becoming harder to sustain. Precision missiles, drones, and cyberweapons have turned static overseas bases into soft targets. At the same time, advances in surveillance and long-range strike make permanent deployments less necessary. The emerging model emphasizes mobility, reach, and rapid escalation. Forward bases are giving way to flexible strike forces capable of hitting distant targets and withdrawing quickly.

The United States is not retreating from the world, but it is acting with greater autonomy and diminishing concern for preserving global order. Whether this shift will ultimately serve US interests remains uncertain. For now, though, in a more fragmented and self-reliant world, Washington still wields enormous power—and is increasingly focused on extracting narrow, tangible benefits from the system it once built, with national interest now defined largely in terms of money, jobs, and physical security.

The Authoritarian Axis

A defining feature of the emerging international system is the growing alignment among China, Russia, Iran, and North Korea.[8] Though not a formal alliance, these revisionist states are deepening military, technological, and diplomatic ties to weaken US power, erode Western influence, and entrench autocratic rule. Chinese technology supports Russia's war in Ukraine; Iran and North Korea supply Moscow with drones, missiles, and ammunition in exchange for battlefield insights and advanced weapons designs. China and Russia have expanded joint military exercises, and all four coordinate in international forums while amplifying anti-Western narratives. What once appeared as isolated threats are converging into a more coherent and integrated challenge.

This shift is especially consequential because it fills the vacuum left by the United States. As Washington steps back from its role as the guarantor of liberal order, it has grown more transactional, more skeptical of alliances, and more tolerant of spheres of influence. Under the Trump administration, for instance, US officials have floated deals that would trade support for Ukraine in exchange for greater focus on confronting China. This is not an end to great-power rivalry, but a narrowing of its scope—from defending a global system to contesting select regions and interests, defined mostly in terms of money and continental security.

The convergence of these two major trends—the rise of an authoritarian bloc and the erosion of liberal hegemony—is reshaping the strategic landscape. This emerging axis can increasingly stretch US power by acting across multiple theaters, forcing Washington to divide its attention and resources. A war in the Taiwan Strait, for example, could be paired with a Russian offensive in Europe or a

North Korean nuclear provocation—not through formal alliance coordination, but through opportunistic convergence. As these regimes test and refine this model, they further undermine the foundations of deterrence built during the unipolar era.

Yet the bloc's growing coordination also reveals internal strains. China risks entanglement in conflicts it does not control. Russia is draining its resources to sustain its own war and subsidize others. North Korea, though emboldened, is becoming more reliant on Moscow and Beijing. Over time, China may find itself not only the senior partner but also the lender, arms supplier, and guarantor of an increasingly burdensome coalition. That role could force Beijing to balance global ambitions with the liabilities of its fellow autocracies.

What's taking shape is not a return to Cold War–style bipolarity; it is instead a looser, more volatile form of systemic rivalry—marked by a powerful but brittle authoritarian axis and a fragmenting Western alliance. The outcome will depend not just on material power but also on coalition cohesion: how well each side can align partners, share burdens, and coordinate across multiple fronts.

Demographic and Technological Disruption

The US-China rivalry is intensifying just as deeper structural forces are reshaping the global landscape. Demographic decline, technological disruption, and uneven development are transforming the foundations of power and the dynamics of competition. These trends are not background conditions—they are shifting the balance of power, recalibrating incentives for aggression, and destabilizing large swaths of the globe.

For two centuries, great-power rivalry was powered by explosive population growth and industrial expansion. Today, that engine is in reverse. Two-thirds of the world now lives in countries with below-replacement fertility, including nearly all of Europe, East Asia, and North America. The great powers are aging fastest: China, Russia, and nearly all major US allies face severe population decline, with fertility rates collapsing and policy efforts failing to reverse the trend.[9] China's workforce will shrink by over 200 million by 2050; Russia is aging rapidly; and countries like Japan, South Korea, Germany, and Italy face collapsing labor pools and rising dependency burdens. Only the United States stands apart, with modest growth sustained by immigration and higher fertility.

Over time, demographic decline erodes national power by shrinking labor forces, depressing consumption, straining public finances, and reducing both the size and quality of military recruits. But in the near term, it can fuel militarization—especially in autocratic regimes. History offers clear precedents. In the 1970s and 1980s, the Soviet Union doubled military spending even as its population and economy stagnated. More recently, Putin's Russia ramped up defense spending throughout the 2010s despite sanctions and a shrinking workforce, culminating in the full-scale invasion of Ukraine.

China is following a similar path. Its working-age population is already shrinking, and its manpower pool is aging and increasingly unhealthy. Yet Beijing is ramping up military spending, expanding its navy, and modernizing its nuclear arsenal. The Communist Party has framed demographic decline as a national security threat—justifying tighter internal control and sustained defense budgets despite rising welfare costs.

Russia, too, continues to press forward. Its population has dropped by millions since the 1990s and is projected to lose tens of millions more by mid-century. War casualties, emigration, and poor public health are depleting the pool of military-age men. Still, rather than scale back, Moscow has slashed civilian spending, funneled resources into defense, and raised conscription ages to keep its war effort going.

North Korea faces even starker demographic and economic constraints. Yet the regime continues to invest heavily in military capabilities, including nuclear weapons, ballistic missiles, and conventional forces near the DMZ (Demilitarized Zone). The military absorbs a disproportionate share of national resources, even as food insecurity and economic isolation worsen.

What makes this dynamic especially dangerous is that the primary targets of these revisionist regimes—Taiwan, Japan, Ukraine, South Korea, and NATO's eastern flank—are also aging and shrinking. Taiwan's conscription pool is expected to halve in the coming decades. Japan and South Korea are already struggling to meet recruitment goals. In Europe, many governments face fiscal constraints and political resistance to rearmament. As autocracies grow more aggressive, many democracies are finding it harder to build or sustain credible defenses.

Politics sharpens this divide. In aging democracies, older voters tend to prioritize pensions and health care over defense, making rearmament politically difficult. Autocracies, by contrast, securitize demographic decline, treating it as a threat to regime survival. Free from electoral pressure, dictators prioritize coercive strength and preserve patronage networks for the armed forces, even as the broader society weakens—when resources run short, dictators pay the guys with guns first. Across Eurasia, this asymmetry is creating a compressed window of instability, where autocrats respond to demographic decline with militarization and surging nationalism, while democracies are slow to respond. For the United

States and its allies, the challenge is not just preparing for long-term competition but also managing a volatile near term in which demographic pressures could trigger major wars.

While demographic decline steadily erodes the power of Eurasia's great powers, advances in AI and automation are changing how power is projected. These technologies are not yet driving broad-based economic growth: productivity in advanced economies has slowed since the early 2000s; most automation remains confined to narrow tasks; and robots don't buy things, so they can't offset declining demand in aging societies. Even optimistic projections suggest AI may raise growth by only 0.6 to 1.3 percentage points annually—well below the 1.8%–5.5% needed in countries like the US, Germany, or China to offset workforce decline.[10] In short, AI won't save aging economies—but it is shifting the strategic balance.

On the battlefield, automation allows faster decisions, more flexible operations, and greater striking power. AI-assisted targeting, autonomous drones, and precision missiles make it easier to launch bold, high-intensity attacks. For example, China could try to seize Taiwan by overwhelming it early—using drone swarms, missile barrages, and cyberattacks—before the United States has time to respond. In this context, automation makes a quick grab for territory more tempting.

Yet these same tools also complicate efforts to hold territory. Defenders can now deploy loitering munitions, smart mines, and AI-driven surveillance to increase the attacker's exposure and reduce the odds of a clean, rapid victory. In the Taiwan Strait, for example, the US "Replicator" initiative aims to flood the battlefield with autonomous systems—creating what one official called a "hellscape" to delay China's advance and buy time for US reinforcements. But that only works if deployed well before a crisis erupts.

The result is a strategic paradox: automation makes it easier to start a war but harder to end one quickly. It lowers the threshold for conflict while increasing the risk of drawn-out, grinding battles. This dynamic is especially dangerous in a period of demographic decline, when leaders may feel compelled to act before their advantages fade. For China, that could mean striking early. For the United States, it means reinforcing the front lines and deploying systems that can absorb and disrupt an initial attack. In the end, the military impact of AI will depend less on breakthroughs than on who can scale and integrate these technologies fastest—in effect, an arms race.

A final disruption comes from the other end of the demographic spectrum. While Eurasia's great powers age and decline, parts of the developing world—especially sub-Saharan Africa, which is projected to add a billion people by 2050—

are undergoing explosive population growth. Yet the traditional path to prosperity through export-led manufacturing has narrowed. Automation and Chinese industrial overcapacity have squeezed out opportunities for late-industrializing countries. As a result, a growing youth population faces rising unemployment, weak governance, and mounting instability—exacerbated by climate stress and resource scarcity.

These regions may lie outside the core of US-China competition, but they form a volatile backdrop that could disrupt both powers' strategic focus. Demographic surges in fragile states are raising the risk of cascading crises—from pandemics and mass displacement to state collapse and foreign intervention. Most African countries already face debt distress, and nearly a quarter are embroiled in armed conflict.

China is more financially exposed to these risks. It has invested over a trillion dollars in infrastructure and resource extraction across unstable regions to secure long-term access to minerals, farmland, and ports. But many of these projects depend on growth that has failed to materialize. Dozens of Belt and Road countries face mounting debt, and Beijing has limited capacity to absorb defaults or contain the fallout. What was meant to build leverage may instead become a liability.

The United States, with fewer financial entanglements but also fewer tools for peacetime influence, faces two mounting risks. First, it could lose access to critical resources. Africa holds vast reserves essential to clean energy, digital infrastructure, and defense—including two-thirds of global cobalt reserves in Congo and over a third of the world's bauxite in Guinea. As China consolidates control over ports, supply chains, and extraction, Washington risks growing dependence on its rival. Second, the US may be pulled into sudden crises—humanitarian disasters, state collapse, or terrorism—without the presence or influence to shape outcomes early. With few preventive tools, it could face costly, reactive interventions that sap attention from great-power competition. This competition may not be a Cold War–style contest for hearts and minds—but it could become a scramble to contain cascading instability in regions neither power controls yet both may be forced to confront.

Conclusion

The US-China rivalry is entering a new and more unstable phase, driven not just by national decisions but by deeper structural shifts. The liberal international order that once shaped the contours of the relationship has fractured. China is no longer a confident rising power, and the United States is no longer invested in preserving a cooperative global system. Both powers are turning inward, relying more heavily on military and economic coercion while shedding the constraints of multilateralism. A loose but growing alignment among autocracies—China, Russia, Iran, and North Korea—is testing the limits of US influence across multiple theaters. Meanwhile, structural shifts in demography and technology are amplifying the instability: Russia and China, as aging autocratic powers, are militarizing rapidly while aging democratic targets dawdle and fail to respond. At the same time, automation is lowering the threshold for conflict even as it complicates war termination. These trends are not merely background conditions— they are reshaping the very structure in which US-China rivalry plays out. The result is a rivalry unmoored from earlier assumptions—less buffered by shared norms, more vulnerable to miscalculation, and increasingly shaped by mutual suspicion and strategic insecurity.

In this environment, US-China competition becomes less predictable and more dangerous. With no shared vision of order to constrain their actions, both sides are reverting to raw power politics—using economic leverage, military threats, and coalition dynamics to secure advantage. China is no longer waiting patiently for integration to pay off; it is throwing its weight around, especially along what might be called its "borders of defeat." Unlike the Soviet Union, which sought to defend its postwar territorial gains—what Stephen Kotkin has called "borders of victory"—China seeks to overturn borders of defeat and outcomes it views as illegitimate: the continued separation of Taiwan, rival claims in the South and East China Seas, and the disputed Himalayan frontier. Add to this China's historical memory of regional dominance, and the resulting strategy is not defensive but revisionist, animated by the desire to erase perceived humiliations and reclaim lost stature.

The United States, for its part, is no longer operating as a steward of global order. It is pursuing power with fewer constraints and more focus on domestic payoff. Alliances have become transactional; trade policy is now a tool of economic nationalism; and forward deployments are giving way to standoff firepower and preemptive coercion. In such a system, cooperation becomes episodic and conditional, and deterrence depends more on rapid punishment than on shared norms or institutional buy-in. This shift undermines the stabilizing assumptions that once governed US-China relations: that war was unthinkable, that crises could be defused through diplomacy, and that shared prosperity would breed moderation.

This does not mean that conflict is inevitable. China is trying to expand on a crowded Eurasian map, full of developed nation-states and precision-guided munitions. It is, in many ways, a constrained power, with arguably less ability to over-run large swaths of territory than Nazi Germany, Imperial Japan, or the Soviet Union. The United States remains in a position of extraordinary strength, but the rivalry is evolving in ways that make stability harder to achieve and easier to mis-read. Without an overarching system to shape expectations and impose disci-pline, the US-China relationship will increasingly be defined by direct friction—over territory, technology, ideology, and influence. Escalation will become more likely, not necessarily because leaders want war, but because the guardrails that once kept competition bounded are deteriorating.

The task ahead is not to restore the old order but to navigate its absence. The most likely outcome is prolonged competitive entrenchment. Both sides are build-ing rival coalitions, weaponizing economic interdependence, and preparing for confrontation while hoping to avoid it. Taiwan will remain the central flash point—not necessarily because a Chinese invasion is imminent but because the island symbolizes the deeper dynamic at play: a revisionist power racing against time and a status quo power struggling to define what it's defending. In this en-vironment, diplomacy will remain essential, but breakthroughs will be rare. Ne-gotiations will be tactical, not transformational. Conflict may be avoided, but confrontation is likely to become the default condition.

Over the long term, structural forces may favor the United States. Its innova-tion ecosystem, alliance network, and demographic resilience give it strategic depth that Beijing lacks. China, by contrast, may exhaust itself—economically, militarily, and politically—within a decade or two. But for now, the rivalry must be managed, not wished away. There will be no return to the illusions of conver-gence or the certainties of containment. This is a contest without clear rules or boundaries of victory. Success will depend not on achieving dominance but on navigating disruption with discipline, avoiding catastrophic missteps, and shap-ing a balance that is tense but sustainable—until, perhaps one day, it isn't.

NOTES

1. World Bank, "GDP (Current US$)," World Development Indicators, accessed March 29, 2025, https://data.worldbank.org/indicator/NY.GDP.MKTP.CD.

2. Wei Chen, Xilu Chen, Chang-Tai Hsieh, and Zheng Song, "A Forensic Examina-tion of China's National Accounts," NBER Working Paper No. 25754, National Bureau of Economic Research, April 2019, revised December 2019, https://www.nber.org /papers/w25754; "A Study of Lights at Night Suggests Dictators Lie About Economic Growth," *The Economist*, September 29, 2022, https://www.economist.com/graphic

-detail/2022/09/29/a-study-of-lights-at-night-suggests-dictators-lie-about-economic
-growth; Daniel H. Rosen and Logan Wright, "China's Economic Collision Course: As
Growth Slows, Beijing's Moves Are Drawing a Global Backlash," *Foreign Affairs*,
March 27, 2024, https://www.foreignaffairs.com/china/chinas-economic-collision
-course.

3. The Conference Board, Total Economy Database, accessed March 29,
2025, https://www.conference-board.org/data/economydatabase.

4. Bank for International Settlements, "Credit to the Non-Financial Sector,"
accessed March 29, 2025, https://data.bis.org/topics/TOTAL_CREDIT.

5. Jason Douglas and Rebecca Feng, "The Quarter-Trillion-Dollar Rush to Get
Money out of China," *Wall Street Journal*, October 20, 2024, https://www.wsj.com/world
/china/china-economy-capital-flight-2ba6391b.

6. Ilaria Mazzocco and Scott Kennedy, "Is It Me or the Economic System? Changing Evaluations of Inequality in China," Big Data China, Center for Strategic and
International Studies, July 9, 2024, last modified July 12, 2024, https://bigdatachina.csis
.org/is-it-me-or-the-economic-system-changing-evaluations-of-inequality-in-china/.

7. The data and trends discussed in this section are primarily drawn from Michael
Beckley, "The China Hangover Is Here," *The New York Times*, August 19, 2024.

8. Hal Brands, *The Eurasian Century: Hot Wars, Cold Wars, and the Making of the
Modern World* (W. W. Norton, 2025).

9. United Nations, Department of Economic and Social Affairs, Population
Division, *World Population Prospects 2024*, accessed March 29, 2025, https://population
.un.org/wpp/.

10. Daron Acemoglu, "The Simple Macroeconomics of AI," Massachusetts Institute
of Technology, April 2024 (revised May 2024), https://shapingwork.mit.edu/research
/the-simple-macroeconomics-of-ai/; Francesco Filippucci, Peter Gal, Cecilia Jona-
Lasinio, Alvaro Leandro, and Giuseppe Nicoletti, "Artificial Intelligence: Promises and
Perils for Productivity and Broad-Based Economic Growth," *OECD ECOSCOPE* (blog),
April 16, 2024, https://oecdecoscope.blog/2024/04/16/artificial-intelligence-promises
-and-perils-for-productivity-and-broad-based-economic-growth/; Philippe Aghion and
Simon Bunel, *AI and Growth: Where Do We Stand?* (Federal Reserve Bank of San
Francisco, June 2024), https://www.frbsf.org/economic-research/files/AI-and-Growth
-Where-Do-We-Stand.pdf.

Index